PSYCHOLOGY LIBRARY EDITIONS:
COGNITIVE SCIENCE

Volume 8

THE MATCHING LAW

T0393826

THE MATCHING LAW
A Research Review

MICHAEL DAVISON AND DIANNE MCCARTHY

Routledge
Taylor & Francis Group

LONDON AND NEW YORK

First published in 1988 by Lawrence Erlbaum Associates, Inc.

This edition first published in 2017
by Routledge
2 Park Square, Milton Park, Abingdon, Oxon OX14 4RN

and by Routledge
711 Third Avenue, New York, NY 10017

Routledge is an imprint of the Taylor & Francis Group, an informa business

British Library Cataloguing in Publication Data
A catalogue record for this book is available from the British Library

ISBN: 978-1-138-19163-1 (Set)
ISBN: 978-1-315-54401-4 (Set) (ebk)
ISBN: 978-1-138-19427-4 (Volume 8) (hbk)
ISBN: 978-1-138-19431-1 (Volume 8) (pbk)
ISBN: 978-1-315-63891-1 (Volume 8) (ebk)

Publisher's Note
The publisher has gone to great lengths to ensure the quality of this reprint but points out that some imperfections in the original copies may be apparent.

Disclaimer
The publisher has made every effort to trace copyright holders and would welcome correspondence from those they have been unable to trace.

THE MATCHING LAW
A RESEARCH REVIEW

MICHAEL DAVISON
DIANNE McCARTHY

University of Auckland, New Zealand

LEA LAWRENCE ERLBAUM ASSOCIATES, PUBLISHERS
1988   Hillsdale, New Jersey   Hove and London

Lawrence Erlbaum Associates, Inc., Publishers
365 Broadway
Hillsdale, New Jersey 07642

Library of Congress Cataloging in Publication Data

Davison, Michael (Michael C.)
  The matching law.

  Bibliography: p.
  Includes index.
  1. Psychometrics.   2. Matching theory   I. McCarthy,
Dianne. II. Title
 BF39.D324   1987   150.72   87-15544
ISBN 0-90959-923-7

Printed in the United States of America
10 9 8 7 6 5 4 3 2 1

CONTENTS

Preface .... **vii**
Acknowledgments .... **ix**

1. Historical Antecedents **1**
   1.1   Introduction 1
   1.2   Initial quantifications 7
   1.3   Summary 11
   1.4   Some further developments 11
   1.5   Time allocation 12
   1.6   Summary 13
   1.7   Some other independent variables 14

2. The Strict Matching Law **16**
   2.1   Herrnstein's Equations 16
   2.2   Different operants 19
   2.3   Different reinforcers 20
   2.4   Fitting Herrnstein's hyperbola 22
   2.5   Concurrent-schedule equations 24
   2.6   A note on curve fitting and experimental design ... 25
   2.7   Replications 27
   2.8   A discourse on parameter estimates 28

3. Herrnstein's Equations, Multiple Schedules, and Empirical Research **31**
   3.1   Strict matching and multiple-schedule performance ... 31

3.2   The logic of Herrnstein's multiple-schedule equations 32
3.3   Herrnstein's equations: Empirical data 35
3.4   Strict matching and concurrent schedules 38
3.5   Herrnstein's equations and multiple schedules: Contrast 40
3.6   Component duration in multiple schedules 42
3.7   Deprivation in multiple schedules 43
3.8   Overall comments on Herrnstein's model 45

4.   Generalized Matching **48**
4.1   Introduction 48
4.2   Early empirical research on generalized matching 52
4.3   What is the matching law? 55
4.4   The concatenated generalized matching law 58
4.5   Dimensions of experiments 59

5.   Quantitative Methods **63**
5.1   About linear regression 63
5.2   Assumptions of least-squares linear regression 64
5.3   Least-squares regression: Procedure 66
5.4   Interpreting the summary statistics in parametric regression .. 68
5.5   Nonparametric regression 69
5.6   Structural relations 73
5.7   Some other useful statistical procedures 74
5.8   Two related samples, ordinal measurement 74
5.9   Many related samples, at least ordinal measurement 77
5.10   A nonparametric test for trend 78

6.   Concurrent-Schedule Research I: Reinforcer Parameters **80**
6.1   Reinforcer-frequency ratios 80
6.2   Overall reinforcer rates 86
6.3   Reinforcer amount and duration 88
6.4   Quality of reinforcers 92
6.5   Reinforcer delay 96

7.   Concurrent-Schedule Research II: Schedule Types **99**
7.1   Caveat 99
7.2   Concurrent FR FR, VR VR, and FR VR performance 100
7.3   Concurrent FR VI performance 103
7.4   Concurrent FI FI performance 104
7.5   Concurrent FI VI performance 105
7.6   Concurrent VI VR performance 106
7.7   Concurrent FI FR performance 106
7.8   Concurrent DRL DRL performance 107

7.9   Concurrent VI VT performance 108
7.10 More than two concurrently available schedules 109
7.11 Response parameters 113

8.   Concurrent-Schedule Research III: Miscellany **120**
8.1   Transitions and the effects of previous conditions 120
8.2   Continuous concurrent-schedule performance 127
8.3   Punishment 129
8.4   Avoidance 132
8.5   Melioration 135
8.6   Changing over 139
8.7   Stimulus effects 150

9.   Multiple-Schedule Research **152**
9.1   Effects of component reinforcer rates 152
9.2   A note on measurement 159
9.3   Effects of absolute component duration 161
9.4   Deprivation effects 166
9.5   Reinforcer amount 169
9.6   Stimulus effects in multiple schedules 171
9.7   Effects of component-response requirements 173
9.8   Continuous multiple-schedule performance 174
9.9   Theory of multiple-schedule performance 177
9.10 Chain-schedule performance 183
9.11 Summary of multiple-schedule research 184

10.   Concurrent-Chain Performance **185**
10.1   Basic procedure 185
10.2   Measurement in concurrent-chain performances 186
10.3   History and development of concurrent-chain research 188
10.4   Variants of concurrent-chain procedures 191
10.5   Terminal-link effects and generalized-mean analyses 193
10.6   Initial-link effects 198
10.7   Transitivity and functional equivalence 203
10.8   Effects of responding in the terminal links 204
10.9   Choice between chained and tandem schedules 206
10.10 Combinations of independent variables 210
10.11 Generalized matching and concurrent-chain performance 212
10.12 Conclusion 215

11.   Matching Models of Signal Detection **216**
11.1   Introduction 216
11.2   The standard Yes-No detection experiment 217

11.3	Signal detection as matching	219
11.4	Matching models for the standard discrete-trials signal-detection procedure	220
11.5	Stimulus discriminability	225
11.6	Stimulus discriminability and reinforcers for errors	231
11.7	Response bias	233
11.8	The free-operant signal-detection procedure	239
11.9	Stimulus discriminability in free-operant detection	240
11.10	Stimulus and bias functions in free-operant detection	243
11.11	Implications for stimulus-control research	247
12.	**For the future**	**249**
References		**255**
Index		**273**

PREFACE

The purpose of this book is to present a coherent summary of some 30 years' research on the way in which animals and humans distribute their behavior between alternative sources of reinforcement. There are three rasons why this book is needed. First, recent developments in the theory of behavior allocation have often only partly accessed the empirical database that is the subject of these theories. We hope this book will lead to the use of a wider range of empirical results in the developing and testing of theories. Second, both researchers and students need a general source of information from which to gain an understanding of the scope of research on behavior allocation. At present, none is available. Third, a text is needed that describes the techniques of experimental design and data analysis in this area. To this end, we have provided a chapter detailing what we consider to be the most appropriate statistical procedures. In addition, we have interweaved design considerations and research results throughout the book. The general approach taken here is empirical, because the various results at the data level will, by and large, remain stable and unchanging. These data have allowed the formulation of quite general quantitative summaries such as the matching laws. Although such descriptions are discussed in detail here, we have not dealt with the diverse theories that have been offered at a more fundamental level to explain the regularities in the data and in the quantitative summaries—relating all of the theories to all of the data must be the subject of a future work.

Michael Davidson
Dianne McCarthy

Acknowledgments

Numerous people have contributed to this book in many different ways. John A. Nevin has been both a supportive and a critical colleague to us for several years, and many thanks are due to him for maintaining our motivation and for critically reading a version of this book. Particular thanks are due to Douglas Elliffe and Brent Alsop, who critically read and edited this work throughout its preparation.

We also thank, as a group, the students and staff who have worked in our laboratory over the last 15 years. We would particularly like to acknowledge the stimulation of Peter E. Jenkins, who spent over a year with us as a Postdoctoral Fellow, and who contributed greatly to our research with his quick and sure grasp of what we were trying to achieve.

Finally, we thank John Milkins and John Tull, who expertly and lovingly cared for our experimental subjects since 1969, and who have recently retired.

Without these people, and others too numerous to mention, this book could not have been written.

1 HISTORICAL ANTECEDENTS

1.1. INTRODUCTION

Beyond the collection of uniform relationships lies the need for a formal representation of the data reduced to a minimal number of terms. A theoretical construction may yield greater generality than any assemblage of facts. But such a construction will not refer to another dimensional system and will not, therefore, fall within our present definition [of theory]. It will not stand in the way of our search for functional relations because it will arise only after relevant variables have been found and studied. Though it may be difficult to understand, it will not be easily misunderstood....

We do not seem to be ready for a theory in this sense. At the moment we make little effective use of empirical, let alone rational, equations. A few of the present curves could have been fairly closely fitted. But the most elementary preliminary research shows that there are many relevant variables, and until their importance has been experimentally determined, an equation which allows for them will have so many arbitrary constants that a good fit will be a matter of course and cause for very little satisfaction. (Skinner, 1950, pp. 215-216)

Skinner (1956) related how, on a Saturday, he ran short of food pellets for the rats that he was training. To maintain the experiment, he decided to reward the rats once every minute, rather than for each response. Over the weekend, the behavior changed and then stabilized, showing a different but very regular pattern. For any scientist, an orderly pattern of results immediately suggests a fruitful vein of research, and Skinner naturally followed up his finding—discovering the schedules of reinforcement, which were fully described and empirically investigated by Ferster and Skinner (1957). Reinforcers for behavior could be made contingent on either the passage of time (*interval schedules*) or on the numbers of responses emitted (*ratio schedules*). The times, or the number of responses required, could be fixed or variable. Each combination of these variables produced an invariant pattern on a cumulative recorder, each different in some respects from the others. When fixed numbers of responses were required (*Fixed-Ratio*, or FR, schedules), there was a pause in responding after each reinforcer, followed by a sharp transition to a high and constant rate that was maintained until the next reinforcer was obtained—the FR break-and-run pattern. When a fixed time had to elapse before a response could be reinforced (*Fixed-Interval*, or FI, schedules), the pattern was similar, but the transition between pausing and responding was gradual—the FI scallop. When either a variable time had to elapse, or a variable number of responses had to be emitted (*Variable-Interval*, or VI, schedules or *Variable-Ratio*, or VR, schedules), animals responded at a high and relatively constant rate with few periods of pausing. But VR schedules engendered generally higher response rates than did equivalent VI schedules. All these patterns were, by and large, independent of the overall times or numbers of responses required, of the species, of the type of response required, of deprivation level, of the type of reinforcer, and of many other possible variables. Here, then, was a set of invariant patterns with very wide generality. Different patterns were shown even in extinction after training on each of the schedules.

Psychologists immediately understood that the invariant patterns described by Ferster and Skinner (1957) were important to their science. Research turned to the analysis of the relations between parts of the patterns and various independent variables. For instance, it was shown that the pause duration in FR performance was directly related to the number of responses required (Felton & Lyon, 1966), and the pause in FI performance was directly related to the interval length (Schneider, 1969). Using the more developed sciences as their models, researchers began the attempt to write equations for the quantitative relations between independent-variable values and parts of the behavior patterns. Some of these quantifications were quite successful, but few had any great generality over different procedures.

Skinner (1950) noted an interesting quantitative invariance. Skinner trained pigeons to emit two responses on two reinforcer schedules that were available simultaneously (a *concurrent* schedule). Then he simultaneously removed the reinforcers for both responses, and found that, as the behaviors ceased, they continued to be emitted in the same ratio as during reinforced training. The importance of this finding is more than just the invariance itself—it is the discovery that a different sort of measurement (the ratio of two response rates, rather than each rate individually) provided the invariance. It is obvious now, of course, that taking the ratio of two simultaneous measures is most beneficial— it reduces the effects of any concomitant or confounding variables that affect *both* performances. The invariance of the behavior ratio during extinction reported by Skinner, however, seemed to have no immediate or great effect on the behavior of psychologists.

Ferster and Skinner (1957) also reported data on performance on concurrently available schedules, but since they were still concerned mainly with descriptive regularities they discussed the patterns of behavior controlled by these schedules, rather than looking more closely at quantitative measures. Findley (1958) continued the descriptive analysis of concurrent schedules. It was not until 1961 that Herrnstein discovered a quantitative relation between responding and reinforcers in concurrent schedules and effectively began the quantitative analysis of behavior. Suddenly, the science of behavior could move into the sorts of quantitative analyses that, until then, had been the characteristic of only one area of psychology—psychophysics. Herrnstein's report provoked a flurry of research activity that still continues to grow.

In this book, we first trace the development of the strict matching law, culminating in Herrnstein's (1970) statement of the quantitative law of effect. We then summarize the research that discovered and documented deviations from the strict matching law, and its replacement by the generalized matching law (Baum, 1974). We then show how the generalized matching law provides a coherent description of performance on various combinations of concurrent schedules, response parameters, and reinforcer parameters; how it describes performance on successive (multiple) as well as simultaneous (concurrent) schedules; how punishment and avoidance effects may be understood; and how it may help us to account for choice between periods of access to schedules (concurrent chains). Finally, we show how the insights gained from the generalized matching law have been used to incorporate stimulus control into the quantitative law of effect and to account for performance in signal-detection paradigms.

As we have mentioned, the ideas underlying the matching law came initially from studies of performance on concurrent schedules. In such paradigms, two or more reinforcer schedules are simultaneously made available to a subject, and, at least until recently, the two or more operant classes that may be emitted have been clearly differentiated. For instance, two schedules may be arranged on two spatially separated response keys (manipulanda), or they may be made available on a single manipulandum, signaled by two distinctive discriminative stimuli, with access to the two schedules controlled by responses to another spatially separated key. These two procedures are called, respectively, the two-key procedure and the switching-key, or changeover-key, or Findley, procedure. Performance on these two procedures appears to be functionally identical.

1.1a. The Two-Key Concurrent-Schedule Procedure

Two (or more) manipulanda are made available to the subject. Responses on each of these are reinforced according to specified schedules. This procedure is

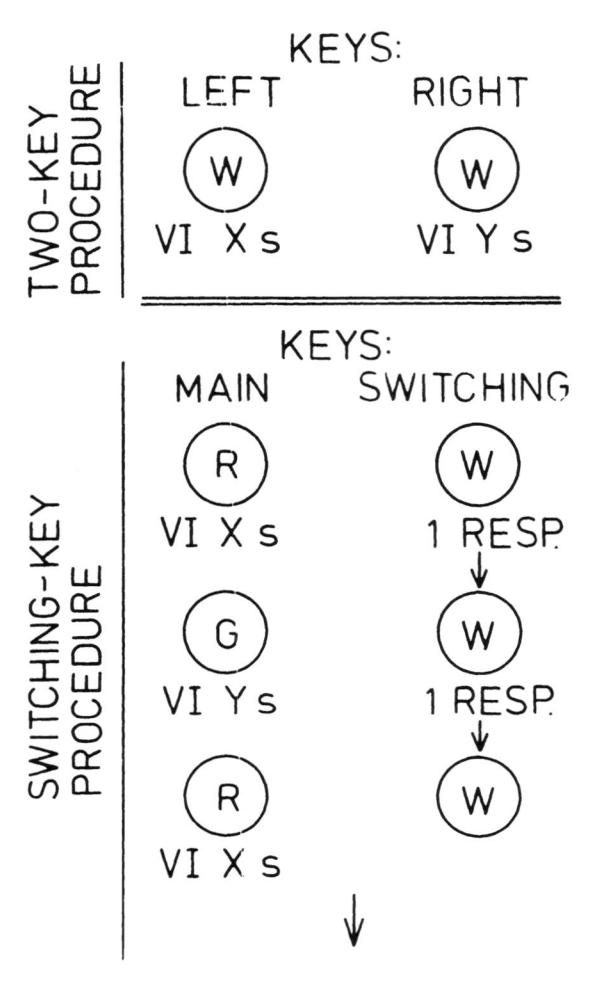

FIG. 1.1. Diagrams of the two-key concurrent-schedule procedure (upper) and the Findley, or changeover-key, concurrent-schedule procedure (lower). The letters within the circles refer to the colors presented on the keys. See text for further explanation.

diagrammed in the upper part of Fig. 1.1. The subject (we will assume a pigeon) is faced with two manipulanda (response keys), which may be illuminated any color but are shown as white in Fig. 1.1. Responding on the left key provides reinforcers on a VI x-s schedule, and responding on the right key provides reinforcers on a VI y-s schedule. During reinforcer delivery, both keys are usually blacked out, and responses on them are ineffective. If the schedules are interval schedules, they continue timing even when the subject is not responding on that manipulandum. If they are ratio schedules, each response on one manipulandum contributes only to the count on the associated schedule. The subject is free to change over between the schedules at any time, but changeovers may be penalized by reinforcers being unavailable immediately after the changeover (the changeover delay, Herrnstein, 1961; see Section 1.2; or the changeover ratio, see Section 1.1b). In the two-key procedure, the changeover delay normally starts from the first response on a manipulandum after responses have been emitted on the other manipulandum. All responses are counted as being part of the performance on the schedules (that is, responses that are changeovers are not deducted from the schedules' totals). When time allocation is measured, the allocation to one schedule's total normally starts with the first response on a manipulandum and ends with the first response on the other manipulandum.

1.1b. The Changeover-Key or Findley Concurrent-Schedule Procedure

This procedure (Findley, 1958) is shown in the lower part of Fig. 1.1. Two manipulanda are available to the subject—the switching manipulandum and the main manipulandum. Each switching response changes the discriminative stimulus (red or green key in Fig. 1.1) and its associated schedule arranged on the main manipulandum (VI x s and VI y s in Fig. 1.1). All reinforcers are obtained for responding on the main manipulandum. Usually, a switching response (on the right, white key in Fig. 1.1) also starts a changeover delay during which time reinforcers are unavailable. Effective switches may, or may not, be allowed during the changeover delay, and switches emitted during the changeover delay may reset the delay duration. Sometimes a number of switching responses, rather than a single response, is required before the schedules and discriminative stimuli change. This constitutes a changeover ratio. Responses on the main manipulandum may, or may not, be allowed during the changeover ratio. Switching responses do not contribute to the measured allocation of responses on the schedules. Time allocation on the two schedules is normally measured from one effective switch to the subsequent effective switch. But the time during the changeover performance often does not contribute to the times spent on the schedules if a changeover-ratio procedure is used. If interval schedules are arranged, they time even when the discriminative stimulus associated with that schedule is not presented. With ratio schedules, only responses emitted during the presentation of the discriminative stimulus contribute to the correlated schedule requirement.

1.1c. Scheduling of Reinforcers

Another major procedural dimension is concerned with whether there is any dependency between the delivery of reinforcers from the available sources. With *independent* scheduling, the arranging of a reinforcer, by the equipment, for one response does not affect the availability of a reinforcer for another response. When the schedule on one key sets up a reinforcer, the schedule on the other key or keys continues timing, and may set up a reinforcer for that key or those keys also. It is therefore possible that both keys (or all keys, if there are more than two responses available) may have a reinforcer available at any one time. When one of these reinforcers is collected, only the schedule associated with that reinforcer is restarted, and the other reinforcer(s) remain available. Contrasted with this procedure is the *dependent* (also termed *nonindependent, interdependent,* or *forced-choice*) procedure. In this, when one schedule arranges a reinforcer, the other schedule(s) stop timing until that reinforcer is collected. At this point, the schedule from which the reinforcer was obtained is restarted, and the timing of the intervals on the other schedule(s) continues. The dependent-scheduling procedure ensures that the subject obtains the same distribution of reinforcers between manipulanda as that arranged by the experimenter. Clearly, if one response is never emitted because choice is extreme, the subject will obtain no more reinforcers once a reinforcer is arranged for that response. The independent-scheduling procedure does not ensure any particular distribution of reinforcers. If choice is extreme, the subject may not take any of the nonpreferred reinforcers. Dependent- versus independent-scheduling procedures normally apply only to concurrent interval schedules, since a dependency on concurrent ratio schedules will change the number of responses required for a reinforcer to be delivered.

It is not particularly easy to capture the essence of concurrent schedules because of the many different nuances of procedure that have been used. For example, our description has largely focused on two-schedule concurrents, but any number of schedules may be concurrently arranged (see Section 7.10). Most procedural differences have not been shown to cause differential effects. However, some, like changeover delays and changeover ratios, clearly cause performance differences. We deal with these differences in Section 8.6. Procedures even different from those described above exist which have also been termed "concurrent schedules." We stress that the *name* of a procedure generally provides insufficient information for an experimental analysis. Further, a name is certainly a very poor independent variable to manipulate in an experiment or to use to explain an experimental result.

1.1d. Introduction Continued

As we have mentioned, initial demonstrations of concurrent-schedule performances were nonquantitative. For instance, Ferster and Skinner (1957) investigated concurrent VI VI, concurrent FR FI, and concurrent VI FI schedule performances using a two-key procedure. Cumulative records showed that the patterns of responding on each key (and thus, on each schedule) were typical of the schedules when they were arranged nonconcurrently, except in the case of concurrent VI FI. In the latter, typical scalloping failed to develop on the key associated with the FI schedule (but see Catania, 1962). Ferster and Skinner also introduced the notion of the "one-key concurrent schedule," a procedure in which two or more schedules are simultaneously arranged on a single key. They used concurrent FI avoidance schedules. Research on one-key concurrent schedules has not subsequently been common, but they are logically of interest. For instance, a one-key concurrent VI 60-s VI 60-s schedule is nominally a VI 30-s schedule. But, if different nominal schedules are arranged on a single key, the results may not be verbally classifiable. However, the feedback function (see Section 7.1) may be mathematically specifiable.

Findley (1958) provided more parametric data on concurrent VI VI schedule performance by keeping one schedule constant and varying the rate of reinforcers provided by the other. He noted that the response rate on each key was both increased by higher reinforcer rates on the correlated schedule and decreased by higher reinforcer rates on the alternate schedule. He also reported that the time spent responding on a schedule was similarly affected by the two reinforcer rates. Findley's major contribution was the specification of, at that time, a novel method of arranging concurrent schedules—the changeover-key, or switching-key, procedure, in which a response on a switching key changed the schedules and associated stimuli on the main key (see Section 1.1b).

1.2. INITIAL QUANTIFICATIONS

Herrnstein (1961) reported an experiment in which responses on two keys were reinforced on a number of different concurrent VI VI schedules keeping the arranged overall reinforcer rate at 1.5 reinforcers per minute. In most of his experimental conditions, he penalized changeovers between the keys by arranging that a reinforcer on one key could not be obtained, even if arranged by the schedule, until 1.5 s had elapsed from the first peck on that key (after pecking the other key). He termed this procedure, which requires at least two responses to be emitted on a key if a reinforcer is to be gained, a *changeover delay* or COD. Under these conditions, Herrnstein noted that the percentage of responses emitted on one key approximately equaled the percentage of reinforcers obtained from that key—that is, the subjects *matched* relative frequency of responding to relative obtained frequencies of reinforcers. Algebraically, this relation is:

$$\frac{B_1}{B_1 + B_2} = \frac{R_1}{R_1 + R_2}. \tag{1.1}$$

where B refers to the behavior frequency and R refers to the obtained reinforcer frequency. The subscripts refer to the two choices (e.g., responses on the two keys). Equation 1.1 was thus termed the *matching equation*, but in order to

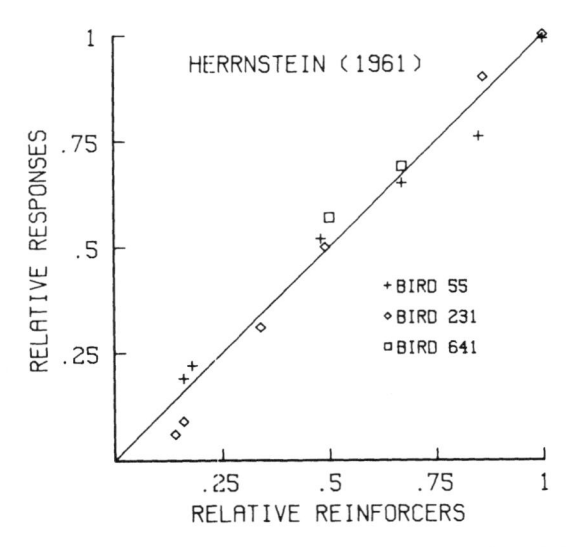

FIG. 1.2.   Relative response rates emitted on two keys as a function of the relative rate of reinforcers obtained from the two keys. The data are from Herrnstein (1961).

differentiate it here from other similar equations we shall call it the *strict matching equation*.

Herrnstein's (1961) results are shown in Fig. 1.2. The data from all three birds fell close to the major diagonal which describes the equality in Equation 1.1. Herrnstein discussed the possibility that the matching relation was a result of the rate of behavior being a linear function of the rate of reinforcers, i.e.,

$$B_i = kR_i ,$$

which, when applied to the behavior on each key, produces Equation 1.1. However, data from performance on single schedules, and from Findley's (1958) experiment, did not support that notion. Thus, Herrnstein concluded that the relation between a rate of behavior and its rate of reinforcement was more likely to be concave downward (or negatively accelerated). We return to this issue in Chapter 2.

Herrnstein (1961) also compared performance on concurrent VI VI schedules using a changeover delay with that produced when no changeover delay was in effect. He reported that the changeover delay substantially decreased the frequency of switching between the two keys. He also noted that it might play a role in the production of strict matching. A comparison of the matching performance with and without a changeover delay for two birds on a concurrent VI 135-s VI 270-s schedule (i.e., a relative reinforcer frequency of about 0.66) showed that relative response measures were closer to 0.5 when no changeover delay was arranged. These were somewhat limited data, but a later and more extensive set from Catania and Cutts (1963), using humans, validated the use of the changeover delay in concurrent-schedule research. This procedure subsequently became standard.

Research reported by Catania (1963a) supported Herrnstein's (1961) finding of strict matching on concurrent VI VI schedules. Catania used a switching-key, rather than a two-key, concurrent-schedule arrangement. He also compared performance with, and without, a 2-s changeover delay. Like Herrnstein, he reported some extreme deviations from strict matching if no changeover delay was in effect. Catania's data also showed that the response rate on one key was not a linear function of the reinforcer rate on that key. He offered a hyperbolic equation to describe absolute response rates. In this equation, the response rate on one key is increased by higher reinforcer rates on that key but is decreased by higher reinforcer rates on the alternate key:

$$B_1 = \frac{kR_1}{(R_1 + R_2)^{0.83}} . \tag{1.2}$$

The fact that response rates on one key are a joint function of the reinforcer rates obtained for those responses and for alternate responses has not subsequently been doubted, but the form of the equation has been varied. Note particularly that Equation 1.2 has no upper asymptote—as reinforcer rates increase, the response rate continues to increase without bound. Both the constant k and the power modifying the denominator are fitted constants. Neither seem to have any particular psychological significance. Equation 1.2 describes strict matching because when relative response rates are predicted, both the constant k and the denominator cancel out:

$$\frac{B_1}{B_1 + B_2} = \frac{kR_1}{(R_1 + R_2)^{0.83}} \cdot \frac{(R_1 + R_2)^{0.83}}{k(R_1 + R_2)} = \frac{R_1}{R_1 + R_2} .$$

Catania (1963a) was the first to propose a *total output* equation, that is, an equation that describes the total rate of all measured behavior. This was:

$$B_1 + B_2 = \Sigma B = k(R_1 + R_2)^{0.17} . \tag{1.3}$$

Equation 1.3 can easily be fitted to data by plotting the logarithm of the total response rate against the logarithm of the total reinforcer rate and fitting a straight line. The slope of the resulting line is the value of the power in Equation 1.3 (and is also the complement of the power on the denominator in Equation 1.2). It is evident from Catania's plot of this relation that, for all subjects except Findley's (1958) Bird 5, the slopes of the lines were close to 0.17, and all the data were well fitted by straight lines.

Another important aspect of Catania's (1963a) paper was his interpretation of the effects of a changeover delay. He stated that this "prevented one schedule of reinforcement exerting accidental control over the changeover-key pecking and the pecks maintained by the other schedule" (p. 255). This interpretation was supported by Catania and Cutts (1963), and has remained one of the standard interpretations of the procedural effects of changeover delays.

It has become evident from the experiments discussed so far that varying reinforcer rates on single schedules have rather small effects on response rates (Catania, 1963a, Equation 1.2), but the effects are much greater on concurrently arranged schedules (Equation 1.1). In other words, concurrent VI VI schedule performance is more sensitive to the variation of one of the reinforcer rates than is single VI-schedule performance. This increased sensitivity led to the extensive use of concurrent VI VI schedules, simply because of the better properties of the measurement. For instance, Catania (1963b) showed that variations in reinforcer duration had little effect on the response rate on a single VI 120-s schedule, but had a substantial effect on the response rate on one key of a concurrent VI 120-s VI 120-s schedule. Because the total duration of food reinforcers was constant, Catania's (1963b) result can be taken as an example of the strict matching of relative response rates to relative reinforcer durations:

$$\frac{B_1}{B_1 + B_2} = \frac{M_1}{M_1 + M_2} \, , \tag{1.4}$$

where M is the duration of the food presentation. Catania's results are shown in Fig. 1.3. The generality of the strict matching law thus, at this time, extended across both reinforcer-rate and reinforcer-duration variations.

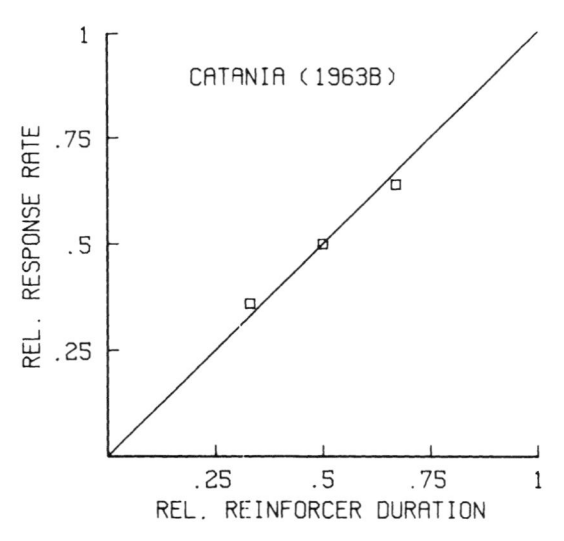

FIG. 1.3.   Relative response rate as a function of relative reinforcer duration. The data, from Catania (1963b), have been averaged across subjects.

1.3. SUMMARY

By 1963, the empirical fact that relative response rates closely matched relative reinforcer rates was well substantiated and replicated. No systematic deviations from strict matching had been reported, and the empirical matching law gained more support from a related area—concurrent-chain schedules (see also Section 6.5 and Chapter 10). These schedules arrange concurrent VI VI schedules, but the reinforcers are not the immediate delivery of food. Rather, completion of each concurrent schedule produces a stimulus change that is itself associated with a schedule of food reinforcement. These latter schedules, known as the *terminal links*, or *outcome phase*, occur as single schedules—that is, only one terminal link is in effect at a time, and the concurrent VI VI *initial links* are unavailable during the terminal links. Autor (1960) and Herrnstein (1964a) reported strict matching between relative initial-link response rates and relative *terminal-link* reinforcer rates. Reynolds (1963a) also reported strict matching on a concurrent-chain schedule. These data sets initially seemed to support the notion of strict matching in quite different procedures, and hence to provide increased generality. In the light of subsequent research (Chapter 10), however, they should not be taken as supporting strict matching. Indeed, Herrnstein (1964b) failed to find strict matching when the terminal links were FI versus VI schedules.

1.4. SOME FURTHER DEVELOPMENTS

Shull and Pliskoff (1967) used switching-key concurrent VI VI schedules to extend Herrnstein's (1961) report that changeover delays helped produce strict matching of relative response rates to relative reinforcer rates. Using two different (one unequal and one equal) concurrent VI VI schedule pairs, they varied the changeover delay from 0 to 20 s. It is worth noting that with a switching-key procedure, a 0-s changeover delay specifies a minimum of one changeover response and one main-key response for reinforcement, whereas the two-key procedure with a 0-s changeover delay requires a minimum of two successive pecks to a key. The difference is not so much in the behavior of the subject, but in the data that are collected. In the switching-key procedure, the switching response does not add to the response totals used to assess matching. In the two-key procedure, the switching response is counted. It is also worth noting that no changeover delay and a 0-s changeover delay are one and the same contingency for a switching-key procedure. They are, however, different contingencies for a two-key procedure—no changeover delay allows the response that constitutes the changeover to be reinforced, whereas a 0-s changeover delay requires two successive responses to a key before a reinforcer may be gained. Shull and Pliskoff reported that, as the changeover delay was increased, relative response rates, relative time spent responding, and relative obtained reinforcers all became more extreme on the (unequal) concurrent VI 60-s VI 180-s schedules. For the (equal) concurrent VI 90-s VI 90-s performance, these measures showed no consistent trend. Given that strict matching is an equality between relative response and relative reinforcer rates, it is evident from their data that strict matching was more likely to result with longer changeover delays. When the changeover delays were short, relative response rates were less extreme than relative obtained reinforcer rates. Herrnstein's (1961) and Catania's (1963a) findings were thus systematically replicated and supported.

A caveat is in order here. As we see in Section 9.3, the design of this experiment cannot discriminate between two different ways in which an equality between relative response rates and relative reinforcer rates can occur. Shull and Pliskoff's (1967) results were taken as indicating that a changeover delay of sufficient length must be provided if strict matching is to be obtained. As a result, most subsequent studies rather unquestioningly used changeover-delay values of, usually, between 2 and 5 s, despite the fact that even 5 s was not long enough to produce an equality between relative response rates and relative reinforcer rates in Shull and Pliskoff's study. On the other hand, changeover delays of 1.5 s and 2 s, respectively, were sufficient to obtain the equality in Herrnstein's (1961) and Catania's (1963a) studies.

Shull and Pliskoff's (1967) study is notable for being the first to measure time allocation on a concurrent schedule. They noted that relative response and relative time measures were isomorphic and suggested that this showed that the *local response rates* (i.e., the number of responses divided by the time allocated to that schedule) were equal between the two keys. This further suggests that subjects respond at a particular constant overall rate but distribute these responses between the two keys via time allocation.

1.5. TIME ALLOCATION

Time-allocation measures were given major prominence in a study of concurrent variable-time variable-time (VT VT) schedule performance by Brownstein and Pliskoff (1968). A VT schedule simply delivers reinforcers after varying periods of time without any response being necessary. Brownstein and Pliskoff used switching-key concurrent schedules, allowing the subject to alternate between the two VT schedules. They also determined an individual changeover-delay value for each subject that was of a value sufficient to produce equality of relative time spent responding and relative obtained reinforcer rate on a concurrent VT 60-s VT 180-s schedule. Varying the VT schedules, they found strict time-allocation matching for all schedule combinations. Their data are replotted in Fig. 1.4. Brownstein and Pliskoff suggested that time allocation must be a basic process and that response allocation might be a by-product, because no superstitious responding was noted while the animals were in the experiment.

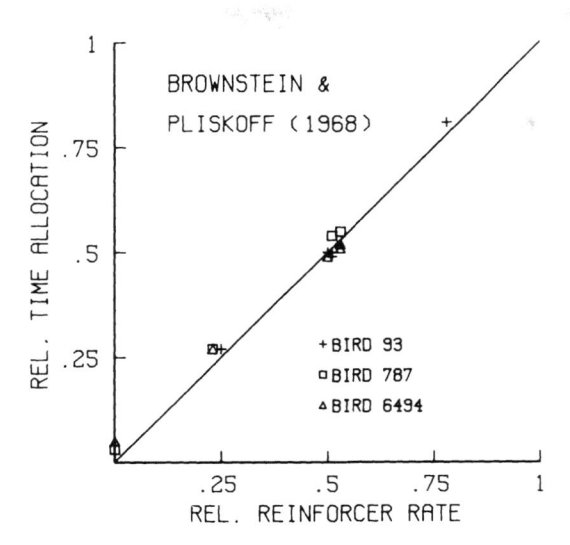

FIG. 1.4.   Relative time spent responding as a function of relative reinforcer rate reported by Brownstein and Pliskoff (1968). A different changeover-delay duration was arranged for each bird: 2 s for Bird 93; 7.5 s for Bird 787; and 5 s for Bird 6494.

Time-allocation matching was also the major subject of an experiment reported by Baum and Rachlin (1969). Unlike Brownstein and Pliskoff (1968), Baum and Rachlin used an analogue of the two-key concurrent-scheduling procedure. A long experimental chamber with the floor divided into two halves, each resting on microswitches, was used. Feeders situated at both ends of the chamber operated on VT schedules when the subject was at the appropriate end of the chamber and when a 4.25-s changeover delay had elapsed. The time-allocation data did not include the time during which both floors were depressed, the time during reinforcer delivery, nor the time in the changeover delay. The exclusion of changeover-delay time is unusual in time-allocation studies of concurrent-schedule performance. It would be expected to increase measured time-allocation differentials between unequal schedules, as it is akin to subtracting a constant from both of the time totals (see Section 8.6). Baum and Rachlin varied the VT schedules over a wide range, and obtained a close approximation to strict matching. They also argued that time allocation "may be more widely applicable to behavior than laws of response distribution" (p. 869).

1.6. SUMMARY

By 1969, two measures (relative response rate and relative time allocated) had been shown to equal or match relative obtained reinforcer rates. These two measures had usually been obtained from different experiments, but Catania (1966) showed that both isomorphic measures could be obtained from standard concurrent VI VI schedule experiments. The procedure of collecting both measures from single experiments became common from this time, allowing ultimately a more detailed comparison of the two measures.

Generality, at this time, also extended across the two procedures for arranging concurrent schedules, across species to a limited extent (pigeons, rats, and humans had been used), and across reinforcers (both grain and brain stimulation had been used). Another area of generality was also evident, but by default rather than by explicit experimentation. The absolute reinforcer rate provided by the schedules had *not* been shown to affect the degree of matching. Again, by default, the type of response required appeared not to affect the degree of matching, though only situations in which the same response was required on the two concurrently available schedules had been investigated.

1.7. SOME OTHER INDEPENDENT VARIABLES

At this period in the development of the matching law, some other experiments had been reported that also supported forms of strict matching. First, Neuringer (1967) extensively replicated Catania's (1963b) report of matching between relative response rates and the relative size of reinforcers. The size of reinforcers is often designated as reinforcer amount, A, or magnitude, M, though the procedure most often used is to vary the duration of presentation of reinforcers. Neuringer's result can be written as:

$$\frac{B_1}{B_1 + B_2} = \frac{M_1}{M_1 + M_2}.$$

In the same year, Chung and Herrnstein (1967) studied the effects of delay of reinforcers on concurrent VI VI schedule performance. Reinforcers for each of the concurrent-schedule responses were delayed by fixed times in blackout, with the concurrent schedules unavailable during the delay. They reported that relative response rates matched relative delays (D) to reinforcers according to the following matching relation:

$$\frac{B_1}{B_1 + B_2} = \frac{D_2}{D_1 + D_2}.$$

The reciprocal form of matching arises because, unlike reinforcer rate or duration, the longer the delay the less frequently the response is emitted. Defining the reciprocal of the delay to reinforcers as the immediacy of the reinforcers ($I = 1/D$) leads to the more usual matching form:

$$\frac{B_1}{B_1 + B_2} = \frac{I_1}{I_1 + I_2}.$$

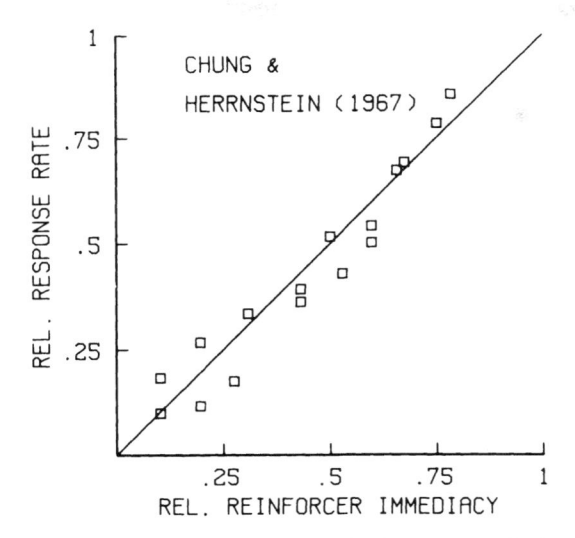

FIG. 1.5   Relative response rates as a function of relative immediacies of reinforcers. These data were obtained using concurrent VI 60-s VI 60-s schedules. The delays were varied between 1 and 30 s, but the 1-s delay was taken as effectively a 1.6-s delay because the subjects took about this time to start eating from the food hopper (see Chung & Herrnstein, 1967).

Chung and Herrnstein's data are shown in Fig. 1.5 as a function of the relative immediacy of reinforcers. The immediacy form of the equation asserts the matching of relative response rates to the *relative reinforcer rates in the delay periods*. It is thus the same result as Herrnstein (1964a) obtained with concurrent-chain schedules. Indeed, Chung and Herrnstein's procedure is a concurrent-chain schedule.

Thus, the generality of strict matching had been asserted across reinforcer delay and magnitude variation and even into the concurrent-chain procedure with either fixed-delay or variable-interval terminal links. However, we must again issue a caveat: Chung and Herrnstein's (1967) experiment has been replicated and reanalyzed (Williams & Fantino, 1978). This further work shows that Chung and Herrnstein's data were not consistent with strict matching (see Section 6.5). Also, subsequent concurrent-chain results have consistently failed to find strict matching to terminal-link relative reinforcer rates (Chapter 10).

The results summarized above, all of which supported strict matching (when the changeover delay was of sufficient length), culminated in a paper by Herrnstein (1970). Herrnstein's approach to matching and behavior allocation is the subject of Chapter 2.

2

THE STRICT
MATCHING LAW

2.1. HERRNSTEIN'S EQUATIONS

Research on matching in concurrent schedules culminated in two papers by Herrnstein (1970, 1974) in which he proposed a coordinated and logically consistent approach to both matching and absolute response rates. He suggested that all behavior was choice behavior—that animals always have the option of emitting responses other than the operant that we, as experimenters, have defined and measured. Thus, if keypecking is the defined operant class, other responses such as scratching and foraging around the experimental chamber could also be emitted, and could be reinforced. The other responses we shall designate as B_e (the literature also uses P_o and P_e), and the reinforcer rate for these responses as R_e (R_o is also used in the literature).

Apart from these organizing principles, Herrnstein made two specific quantitative assumptions. The first was that the overall rate of emission of all responses taken together, and measured in common units, is a constant. This constant is designated k, and is measured in responses (of whatever sort) per unit time. The second assumption was that this total output is allocated to simultaneously available alternatives in proportion to the rate of reinforcers (again measured in common units) obtained from each alternative. This second assumption is, of course, an assumption of strict matching. If p_i is the proportion of reinforcers obtained from Alternative i, then:

$$p_i \cdot k = B_i ,$$

or, to expand the equation,

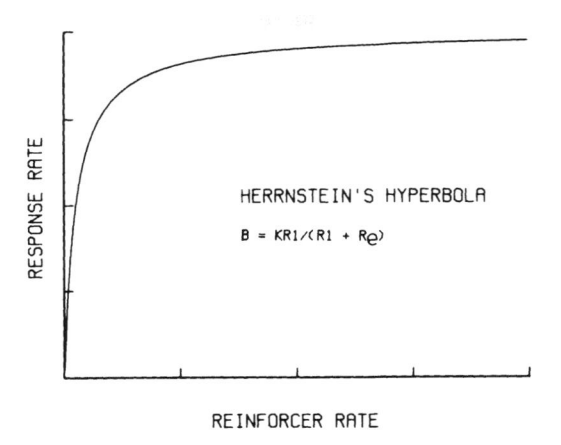

FIG. 2.1. Response rate as a function of reinforcer rate on a single schedule as predicted by Equation 2.1 (Herrnstein, 1970).

$$B_i = \frac{kR_i}{R_i + R_j + R_k \ldots} = \frac{kR_i}{\sum R}. \qquad (2.1)$$

For a single VI schedule, this equation can be written:

$$B_1 = \frac{kR_1}{R_1 + R_e}, \qquad (2.2)$$

where R_e is the rate of reinforcers from sources extraneous to those arranged by the experimenter. It is thus termed the "extraneous reinforcer rate." The expression (in its general form, Equation 2.1, or in one of its specific forms, e.g., Equation 2.2) has been called *Herrnstein's equation* or Herrnstein's hyperbola. As written in Equation 2.2, this expression describes the response rate under a specific set of conditions—particular values of R_1, of R_e, and of k. We can generalize this equation by assuming that k is constant for a particular subject and for a particular response type. We can also generalize it further if, like Herrnstein, we assume that R_e remains constant for all values of R_i. Given these assumptions, Equation 2.1 describes the function relating B_1 to R_1 as a rectangular hyperbolic function with two constant terms. Fig. 2.1 shows an example of this function.

It is important to understand Equation 2.1, and related general equations, fully to appreciate Herrnstein's (1970) model. We stated that this equation described matching, but it does not look like the matching equations written in Chapter 1. Remember, though, that the constant k is the total rate of output, that is, it equals $(B_1 + B_e)$ in Equation 2.2, where B_e is the rate of responding associated with extraneous reinforcers, *measured in the same units as B_1 and B_2*. Thus, rewriting Equation 2.2 gives:

$$B_1 = \frac{(B_1 + B_e) \cdot R_1}{R_1 + R_e},$$

and, consequently:

$$\frac{B_1}{B_1 + B_e} = \frac{R_1}{R_1 + R_e}.$$

This last equation looks like a matching equation (cf. Equation 1.1). It states that the rate of responses emitted on one key, relative to the rate of all responses emitted, equals the rate of reinforcers obtained for pecking one key, relative to the rate of all reinforcers obtained. Herrnstein's equation for response rates in single schedules is thus a strict matching equation with the added assumption that the total rate of output is constant.

The form of the general equation for the response rate on one schedule of a two-schedule concurrent procedure is:

$$B_1 = \frac{kR_1}{R_1 + R_2 + R_e}. \tag{2.3}$$

with a similar equation for the response rate on the other schedule. We may even write an equation for the rate of unmeasured responses:

$$B_e = \frac{kR_e}{R_1 + R_2 + R_e}. \tag{2.4}$$

Although Equation 2.4 is of very little use, it is instructive to look more closely at what it asserts. In Equations 2.3 and 2.4, k is the total rate of behavior output *measured in terms of keypecks*. This is defined by our definition of the operant class (keypecking) that we have measured. Equally, R_e is the rate of extraneous reinforcers *measured in terms of the number of experimenter-defined reinforcers (e.g., 3-s grain presentations) per unit time*. Thus, Equation 2.4 could, for example, relate extraneous responses measured as keypecks per time to the rate of extraneous reinforcers measured as 3-s accesses to grain per time. The responses measured, and the reinforcers delivered, define the modulus in which k and B_e, and R_e, are to be measured. There is no way of measuring these quantities except in relation to the defined operant and its reinforcer.

The constants k and R_e have a straightforward interpretation when one response and one reinforcer are used on all arranged schedules. The situation becomes complex, however, when different operants are concurrently reinforced, or when different reinforcers are arranged for concurrent identical operants, or when both of these circumstances apply.

2.2. DIFFERENT OPERANTS

Let us consider first the case of different operants. If we define keypecking as our operant and reinforce it on a series of VI schedules differing in reinforcer rate, we obtain a function like that in Fig. 2.1. The asymptote of this function is k, and the rate at which the function reaches the asymptote is related to the size of R_e. The larger is R_e, the slower the function increases to the asymptote. Two sets of functions with different R_e values, but with the same asymptote k, are shown in Fig. 2.2. If, however, we were to define our operant as lever pressing (in the pigeon; see Davison & Ferguson, 1978), the functions would look quite different. With keypecking, the asymptote would be expected to be between 60 and 120 pecks per minute. With lever pressing, it might only be 25 presses per minute. The two different k values for the same subject and the same series of VI schedules arise because k is measured in different units in the two cases.

Now let us arrange concurrent keypeck and lever-press schedules. For the keypeck schedule:

$$B_p = \frac{k_p R_p}{R_p + R_\ell + R_e} , \qquad (2.5)$$

where the subscripts p and ℓ refer to pecking and lever pressing, respectively.

We could write an equivalent equation for B_e, which would give us a measure of B_e as pecks per time for any value of R_p and R_ℓ. For the lever-press schedule,

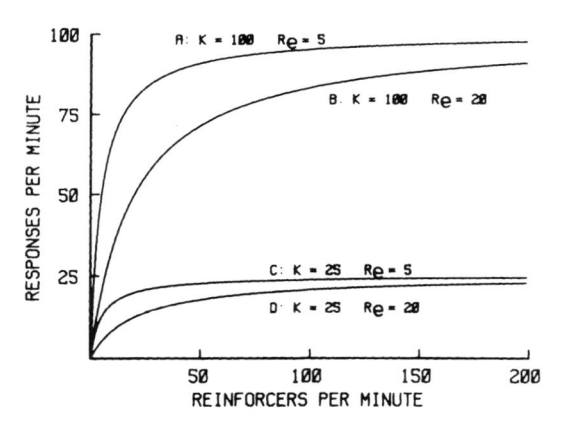

FIG. 2.2. Response rate as a function of reinforcer rate as predicted by Herrnstein's (1970) hyperbola. For two of the curves, $k = 100$, a value appropriate for k measured as keypecks per minute. For the other two curves, $k = 25$, a value appropriate for k measured as lever presses per minute in pigeons. For each value of k, two values of R_e (measured as reinforcers per minute) are shown.

the following equation would apply:

$$B_\ell = \frac{k_\ell R_\ell}{R_p + R_\ell + R_e} .$$ (2.6)

This equation describes the rate of lever pressing, measured as lever presses per time, as a function of the reinforcer rates. Again, an equation for B_e can be written, but for a particular pair of schedules, B_e obtained using Equation 2.5 would be a quite different value from that obtained using Equation 2.6. The reason is, of course, that they are measured on different scales. This result is not, as some have thought, an indicator of an internal inconsistency in the model—rather, it is the reverse, an indicator of consistency.

Thus, in concurrent keypeck and lever-press schedules, if we simply measure the rates of the two responses, we will find a form of matching. Dividing B_p (Equation 2.5) by B_ℓ (Equation 2.6), and converting to relative measures, gives:

$$\frac{B_p}{B_p + B_\ell} = \frac{k_p R_p}{k_p R_p + k_\ell R_\ell} .$$

If we now divide the numerator and denominator of the right side of this equation by k_ℓ, and set $k_p/k_\ell = k'$, we get:

$$\frac{B_p}{B_p + B_\ell} = \frac{k' R_p}{k' R_p + R_\ell} .$$ (2.7)

Now, k' is the ratio of the two asymptotes (k_p/k_ℓ), and thus is a scaling factor that relates the measurement of keypecks to the measurement of lever presses. It is likely to have a value of, perhaps, 5, meaning that five keypecks equal one lever press. Thus, obtaining this scaling factor subsequently allows keypecks and lever presses to be measured on the same common scale—for instance, a count of 50 lever presses in a session can be taken as equivalent to 250 keypecks. If this is done, then strict matching will be obtained between the relative scaled response rates and the relative obtained reinforcer rates.

2.3. DIFFERENT REINFORCERS

The scaling of different responses, discussed above, leads naturally to the appropriate method for dealing with different reinforcers. If we define a scaling factor s, which converts one of the reinforcer (R_2) magnitudes or durations or even qualities onto the scale of R_1, we can write an equation entirely in the modulus of R_1:

$$B_1 = \frac{k R_1}{R_1 + s R_2 + R_e} ,$$

and:

$$B_2 = \frac{ksR_2}{R_1 + sR_2 + R_e} .$$

Thus, we can form a matching equation:

$$\frac{B_1}{B_1 + B_2} = \frac{R_1}{R_1 + sR_2} . \tag{2.8}$$

The scaling factor, s, is the ratio M_2/M_1 (for reinforcer magnitude differences), or perhaps A_2/A_1 for reinforcer amounts. Thus, expanding Equation 2.8 gives:

$$\frac{B_1}{B_1 + B_2} = \frac{M_1 R_1}{M_1 R_1 + M_2 R_2} . \tag{2.9}$$

Equation 2.9 asserts that relative response rates strictly match the relative product sums of reinforcer rates and magnitudes. Thus, if the reinforcer rates in an experiment were constant and equal, and the reinforcer magnitudes were varied, these measures would cancel, giving strict matching to relative reinforcer magnitudes:

$$\frac{B_1}{B_1 + B_2} = \frac{M_1}{M_1 + M_2} .$$

Strict matching to relative reinforcer magnitudes would not occur, however, if the reinforcer rates R_1 and R_2 were constant but not equal. For instance, if R_1 occurred at one-half the rate of R_2 ($R_1 = 2R_2$), then the following equation would be correct:

$$\frac{B_1}{B_1 + B_2} = \frac{M_1}{M_1 + 2M_2} .$$

Of course, if the experimenter was unsure of the relation between the two magnitudes of reinforcers (a common occurrence—perhaps they are different types of reinforcers, for instance, food and brain stimulation), Equation 2.9 would have to be fit to the data. This is most conveniently done by fitting the simplified version, Equation 2.8, with only one free parameter, s. This would provide the information needed on the relation between the two reinforcers—that is, it would allow one to be measured in terms of the other. This relation is, in fact, the best information that can be obtained, for there is no way in which the *absolute* value of reinforcers can be measured.

2.4. FITTING HERRNSTEIN'S HYPERBOLA

Various methods, some better than others, are available for fitting Herrnstein's equation (Equation 2.2) to obtain estimates of k and R_e. The first procedures offered (Cohen, 1973) used methods from enzyme kinetics that usually linearized the equations in some way. An example is the reciprocal method: Given

$$B_1 = \frac{kR_1}{R_1 + R_e},$$

then, by some algebra:

$$\frac{1}{B_1} = \frac{1}{k} + \frac{R_e}{kR_1}. \qquad (2.10)$$

Equation 2.10 has the form of a straight line, $Y = c + mX$. If $1/B_1$ is plotted as a function of $1/R_1$, the data plot should be a straight line with intercept $1/k$ and slope R_e/k. While mathematically appealing, statistically there are problems. If we were to assume that B_1 was distributed normally with equal error variance at all values of R_1 (i.e, the measure is homoscedastic), consider what happens when the measure is reciprocated. The assumptions are shown in Fig. 2.3(A), and the results of reciprocating both the independent and the dependent variables are shown in Fig. 2.3(B).

After transformation, the measures $(1/B_1)$ are no longer normally distributed. Neither are the variances the same at all values of the independent variable. As a result, least-squares linear regression (Section 5.2) may not be used to fit the data as two assumptions of linear regression (normal distributions and equal variances at all values of the independent variable) are violated. In more practical terms, the large variance of higher values of $1/B_1$ will lead to the slope of the relation being unduly influenced by large values of $1/B_1$ (low response rates). As a result, this procedure is likely to give unreliable, and often ludicrous, parameter estimates.

Other methods of linearizing Equation 2.2 have also been used (Dowd & Riggs, 1965), and all violate the assumptions of least-squares regression in one way or another.

Wetherington and Lucas (1980) provided a method for fitting Herrnstein's hyperbola using a nonlinear least-squares procedure. This requires an iterative fit to reduce successively the partial derivatives to zero. From our experiences, the method does not guarantee a solution, at least not without extensive modifications to initial-step sizes within the computer program. Its other drawback is that the program presented by Wetherington and Lucas provides only an estimate of the total variance accounted for by the fit (that is, the total variance in the data minus the error variance, divided by the total variance—this is also the square of the product-moment correlation). This measure of goodness

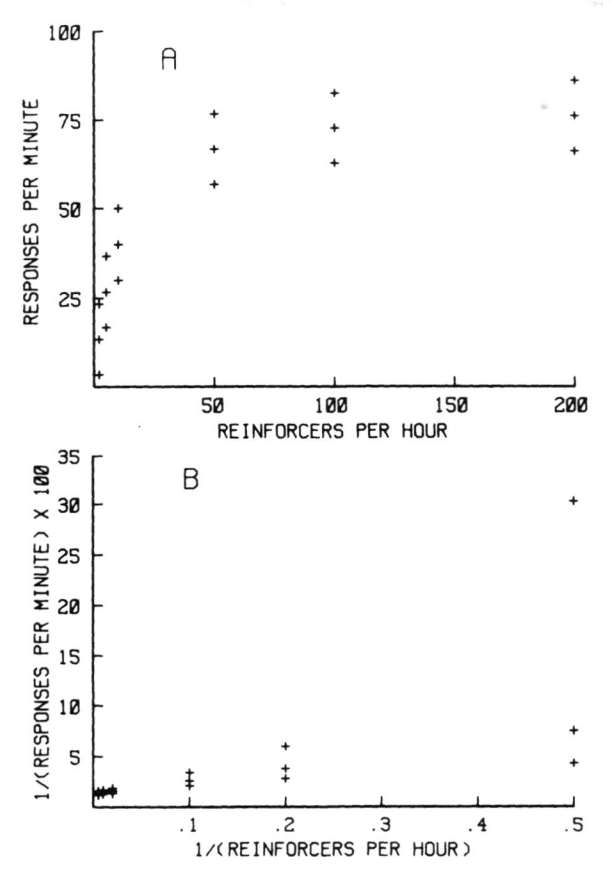

FIG. 2.3.   In Panel A, response rates are shown as a function of a series of reinforcer rates. The variation of the data around the mean is the same for each reinforcer rate. In Panel B, both axes have been reciprocated, and the data replotted.

of fit is notoriously poor (e.g., Anderson, 1978). It gives low values of variance accounted for (VAC) with excellent fits to data with little systematic variance, and spuriously high VAC values for poor fits to data with extreme total variance.

Wetherington and Lucas (1980) failed to mention another method of fitting Herrnstein's equation. This method is due to Wilkinson (1961) and has seen useful service in the research of Bradshaw and his colleagues (e.g., Bradshaw, Szabadi, & Bevan, 1976). The method was reemphasized by McDowell (1981) in response to the Wetherington-Lucas article. The Wilkinson procedure first estimates k and R_e using a weighted least-squares fit to the reciprocals of the independent and dependent variables, and then revises these estimates. This second step may be repeated to refine further the estimates, but that is seldom necessary. The benefits of this procedure are, first, that it can be done on a hand calculator and, second, that the standard errors of the parameter estimates can easily be calculated. These latter measures are, as McDowell pointed out, important when the precision of the estimates or their constancy over experimental conditions is at issue. They are also much better measures of the adequacy of a curve fit than is VAC.

A third, rather more general, method is available. This uses an iterative parametric nonlinear curve-fitting procedure (Ruckdeschel, 1981). This procedure has not been used in the literature to obtain the parameters of Herrnstein's equation. The program is able to fit highly nonlinear models in one dimension (i.e., one independent variable) with a large number of free parameters. We refer to it again elsewhere.

In summary, three major and effective methods exist for fitting Herrnstein's equation. All of them require some hard work. At the present time, we favor Wilkinson's (1961) method over all others.

2.5. CONCURRENT-SCHEDULE EQUATIONS

By default, we concentrated in the last section on fitting Herrnstein's equation for absolute response rates on a single schedule. Fitting the equations for the case in which more than one response is reinforced is more difficult:

$$B_1 = \frac{kR_1}{R_1 + R_2 + R_e} . \tag{2.11}$$

The problem is this: If R_1 and R_2 are both varied, the equation is two-dimensional, and methods for fitting such equations are not well known.

The problem can be overcome by experimental design. For instance, if sufficient conditions have been arranged with R_2 held constant (that is, empirically constant), we can set $(R_2 + R_e) = g$ and solve the rectangular hyperbola

$$B_1 = \frac{kR_1}{R_1 + g}$$

using one of the standard procedures for fitting Herrnstein's equation. Subtracting the constant reinforcer rate R_2 from the estimate of g gives the estimate of R_e. But remember that the standard deviation of R_e will be affected by the variability in R_2 over conditions.

Finally, if R_2 alone was varied, and R_1 was empirically constant (equal to c), then:

$$B_1 = \frac{kc}{c + R_2 + R_e} = \frac{c'}{c'' + R_2} .$$

The simplest way to fit this equation is using the parametric curve-fitting routine (Ruckdeschel, 1981) to obtain c' ($= 2kR_1$) and c'' ($= R_1 + R_e$). Then, knowing the value of R_1, one can obtain the values of k and R_e.

2.6. A NOTE ON CURVE FITTING AND EXPERIMENTAL DESIGN

When a curve is to be fitted to data, the most important point to bear in mind is that we shall need to interpret the meaning of the obtained parameters. A function can be fitted successfully to almost any set of data—that is, the fitting program will provide an answer. We are more concerned, though, with the validity of the answer, rather than with the fact that an answer has been obtained. We believe, therefore, that the following points should be considered when designing an experiment in order to obtain the parameters of an equation:

1. A graph of the relation should be updated after each experimental condition has been completed to help answer some of the following questions.

2. The data collected should, normally, be stable data—that is, some reasonable stability criterion should be set and adhered to. A number of stability criteria have been specified in the literature (see Killeen, 1978), and these are useful in some cases. However, while the specification of a stability criterion is straightforward in many cases, in others it is not. Let us·take two examples. First, consider performance on concurrent VI VI schedules. A criterion that we frequently use (e.g., Trevett, Davison, & Williams, 1972) calculates the relative numbers of responses in each session, takes the medians of these measures over five sessions, and compares successive 5-day medians. When these have been less than 0.05 apart on five, not necessarily consecutive, occasions for each of the subjects, the performance is deemed stable and the experimental conditions are changed. This is a relatively strict criterion, and on concurrent VI VI schedules it usually leads to stability after about 20 sessions on average. The second example might be concurrent FR VI performance. This is quite different from concurrent VI VI performance. On concurrent VI VI schedules, variations in response rates on the keys do not usually lead to noticeable changes in the rates, or relative rates, of reinforcers. On concurrent FR VI schedules, changes in the response rate on the FR schedule do change the rate, and the relative rate, of FR reinforcers. Because of the nature of the matching law, there is likely to be a positive feedback relation between the relative response rate and the relative reinforcer rate on the FR key. Thus, there will be considerably more variation in relative response rates on concurrent FR VI schedules than on concurrent VI VI schedules, and the same stability criterion may not be reasonable for both. The specific criterion used for concurrent FR VI schedules might depend on what

aspect of that performance was being investigated, but it must in any case take into account the correlation between the response and reinforcer rates. (This section is, in a formal sense, concerned with *feedback functions*, which are discussed in more detail in Section 7.1.)

3. The minimum number of experimental conditions arranged must be at the very least as many as the number of free parameters (unknown constants) in the equation under study. This minimum is almost always unsatisfactory. Generally, the experimenter should try to arrange many more conditions than there are free parameters. Note here that we are *not* speaking of the number of data sets taken from each stable condition. One stable condition from which data are taken five times in no way substitutes for five different conditions.

4. Again, the number of experimental conditions is of considerably less importance than where they lie in relation to, at the start of the experiment, the expected function and, during the experiment, the currently estimated function. In order to attain maximum generality, it is clearly important to cover the widest possible range of values of the independent variable. In fitting Herrnstein's hyperbola, for example, we would want to arrange one very low reinforcer rate (possibly even Extinction, though the hyperbola is constrained to pass through 0,0), and one very high reinforcer rate, perhaps VI 15 s. Some data to exemplify the design process are shown in Fig. 2.4.

Now, in order to obtain the parameters of Herrnstein's equation accurately, the rest of the experimental conditions will be spread between these extreme points in a particular sort of way. Clearly, if a set of high reinforcer rates is arranged, k may be estimated precisely, but R_e may not be (all the points will fall close to the asymptote). If a set of low reinforcer rates is arranged, R_e may be well estimated but k may not be. The problem is, of course, that the effect of the data points on the accuracy of the parameter estimates is not known because, at this point, the values of the parameters are unknown. In Fig. 2.4B, two more data points have been added, and it is now becoming evident that the range of the independent variable is quite satisfactory for Bird 22, but the data for Bird 21 indicate that R_e is small (three of the four data points still fall close to the asymptote). There may also be a problem with Bird 23, which seems to have a large value of k, and we can no longer be certain that the highest reinforcer rate arranged is, in fact, on the asymptote. Thus, on the basis of the data collected, two more experimental conditions are arranged, one with a very high reinforcer rate and the other with a moderately low reinforcer rate. After this (Fig. 2.4C), the functions for all the subjects are reasonably complete, and we can have some confidence in the parameters estimated from the curve fit.

We note here that the problems we have graphically illustrated in Fig. 2.4B may also be seen in the curve fits carried out at this point in the experiment. For Bird 21, the standard error of R_e might be high, and for Bird 23, the standard error of k might also be large. But a statistical analysis is no substitute for a graphical

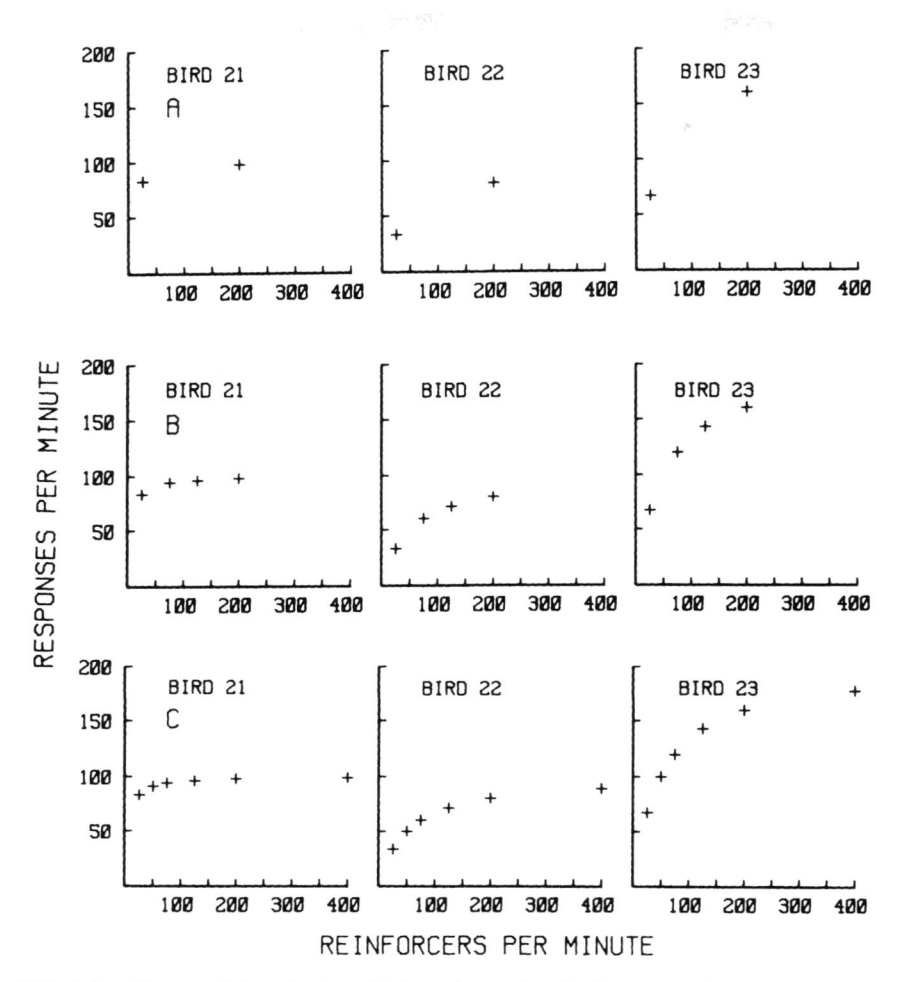

FIG. 2.4.. Theoretical data for three birds at three points in the course of an experiment to determine k and R_e in Herrnstein's (1970) hyperbola for single VI-schedule performance.

analysis, for these unacceptably large standard errors could equally have been caused by one aberrant data point due to some extraneous event (a broken beak, or even data collection or data analysis errors). The graphical display allows the experimenter to check and, if necessary, to reanalyze and/or replicate that condition.

2.7. REPLICATIONS

The replication of data points that appear to be aberrant is an essential part of any experimental design. It may lead to the discarding of the original data or, if the replication is precise, the further replication of other possibly aberrant data points. Replication also has another function; it is to guard against the possibility that the behavioral measures are being affected by the passage of time or by exposure to successive experimental conditions. A successful replication of the first experimental condition as the last condition of an experiment gives a reader considerable confidence that the behavior under study is indeed controlled by the manipulated independent variable. Despite this, replications to control for order effects may be relevant only if the order of experimental conditions has not been randomized. Given that all the independent-variable values lie on the same dimension, that the order has been randomized, and that the resulting function is continuous, there is a strong sense in which each data point contributes to the internal replication of all other data points. Thus, given that the results are relatively clear, and that the parameters are estimated precisely, replications to control for order effects or for time are unnecessary.

One further aspect of replication must be discussed. In Section 2.6, we mentioned that stability might be difficult to attain with some types of scheduling arrangements because the dependent and independent variables were correlated via the function under investigation (another phrase used is that the independent variable is *reactive*). Replication under these conditions may be impossible, or, if it is successful, it may be more by chance than by the process under investigation. So, in the assessment of a function between an independent and a dependent variable, when the value of the independent variable is replicated, a successful replication is not one that necessarily provides the same dependent-variable values. Rather, it is one for which the data fall on the same function. We might call this *functional replication*.

Note here that the problem is one of semantics. In replicating the FR-20 condition in a concurrent FR x VI 60-s schedule, we are referring to the *nominal* schedule value—FR 20. But this is *not*, most likely, the independent variable under study, which is probably the reinforcer rate provided by the FR-20 schedule. Since the independent variable (but not its name!) is reactive, replicating the name will probably not replicate the independent variable.

2.8. A DISCOURSE ON PARAMETER ESTIMATES

When a parameter and its standard deviation have been estimated for a group of subjects, a number of questions can be asked about those estimates. These questions, and their answers, have often been confused in the literature, and we shall try to clarify the difficulties here.

First, we can ask questions about the accuracy of the absolute parameter estimates. For example, if we have estimated k as 110 responses per minute (SD 5.5 responses per min) and R_e as 0.6 reinforcers per min (SD 0.03 reinforcers per min), are these accurate estimates? The question is difficult to answer for two reasons: There is no accepted absolute standard, and we need to answer the question, For what purpose? But both the standard deviations of the estimates are one-twentieth of the estimates themselves, and that, by the rather lax standards of scientific psychology, is very good. By other standards (e.g., those of physics), it is rather mediocre. So while we have proposed (Davison, 1987) the rule of thumb that, at least in matching research, a precise parameter estimate has a standard deviation that is less than one-tenth the parameter estimate, this suggestion must be subject to evolution and refinement—we should set the relation between the standard deviation and the parameter as small as we reasonably can at each step as psychology progresses. Thus, the question concerning the accuracy of the parameter estimates may be asked of the parameter values of each subject individually, and answered according to the *zeitgeist*.

The second question that may be asked is, Is the estimate different from another estimate? This is subdivisible into a question about two or more estimates from an individual subject, and a question about two or more estimates from a set of subjects, over a manipulation of some third variable. The individual-subject question is not always easily answered, though if we were satisfied that the parameter estimates were normally distributed (and we might not be sure for estimates of k and R_e), we could carry out a standard t test. The second question asks, in effect, whether it is generally the case that the manipulation of the third variable affects the parameter estimates for all subjects in the same way. The ability to answer this question in the affirmative brings with it generality over subjects as well as generality over the third-variable change for single subjects. It is thus a more useful question to answer. Given sufficient data, we can again use a t test if we assume normally distributed estimates. Alternatively, depending on the level of measurement we believe we have attained, we could use a Sign test, a Wilcoxon Matched-Pairs Signed-Ranks test (see Section 5.8), or, if more than two third-variable levels are being considered, a Friedman analysis of variance (Section 5.9). Notice that we are assuming here that the same subjects completed all experimental conditions.

A third question that can be asked is about the relation between a parameter estimate and some normative value. This question has recently come to be important in aspects of matching research (Baum, 1979, 1983). It is worthwhile discussing here the whole question of normative values. Almost by default, researchers working with Herrnstein's equation have assumed that the values of k and R_e are not estimates of some normative value. Rather, they are estimates of *individual-subject* parameters—that is, each subject would naturally be expected to show different values. This is quite reasonable because, for instance, pigeons with larger heads might be expected to peck more slowly (lower k), and some of the subjects could be more infested with mites than others (high R_e).

The idea of normative parameter values seems to come more from the physical sciences. For instance, the power in the inverse-square law is -2, and black-body radiation is described by Stephan's law, which contains a power of 5. Most physical constants are either whole numbers or reciprocals of whole numbers, when they are powers, but they can be any number when they are additive or multiplicative. The question that arises is, Is this estimate an approximation to a normative constant? Baum (1983) suggested that this question could be answered in the affirmative if the parameter estimate was close to the normative value, even though (1) it was statistically significantly different from the normative value; and (2) the population distribution of estimates was strongly skewed to one side of the normative value. This is a reasonable point of view if it is the case that failures of technique, or just plain error variance, will by the nature of the function always push the parameter estimate in one direction away from the assumed normative value. It is, however, an empirical matter to *demonstrate* that this will be the case.

However, an experimenter who, for one reason or another, does not wish to view a set of data through the "normative" spectacles may reasonably ask, Are these parameter estimates (statistically) different from the normative ideal? Again, for example, Sign tests and Wilcoxon Matched-Pairs Signed-Ranks tests are available to answer this population question. Such an experimenter may feel that the parameter being estimated is an individual parameter (to the subject and/or to the procedure), rather than a parameter fixed for the species (or for all species). The normative- and the individual-parameter experimenters may have quite opposing opinions about which way research should progress. The normative approach may suggest that the experimental procedures be tightened so that a more pure estimate (i.e., one closer to the normative value) can be obtained. The individual approach might be more concerned with discovering whether the assumed individual parameters can be modified by other independent variables and procedures. By and large, we feel that the latter approach is the more useful, but the theoretical significance of the normative-value approach will always be extremely important if it can be sustained.

3 HERRNSTEIN'S EQUATIONS, MULTIPLE SCHEDULES, AND EMPIRICAL RESEARCH

3.1. STRICT MATCHING AND MULTIPLE-SCHEDULE PERFORMANCE

Herrnstein (1970) extended his strict matching model to account for performance on multiple schedules. In these schedules, two or more simple schedules are arranged successively in time, with a distinctive stimulus associated with each. The discriminatively signaled periods are termed "components" of the multiple schedule. Herrnstein made the same basic assumptions as those for his theoretical approach to single schedules and concurrent schedules (strict matching, constant rate of total output, the presence of other reinforcers and responses), but added one more parameter. This parameter is m, which describes the degree of interaction between multiple-schedule components. Its value lies between 0 (no interaction between the components) and 1 (maximal interaction). The equation that Herrnstein suggested for the response rate in one component of a two-component multiple schedule was:

$$B_1 = \frac{kR_1}{R_1 + mR_2 + R_e} . \tag{3.1}$$

A similar equation applies to the response rate in the alternate component:

$$B_2 = \frac{kR_2}{R_2 + mR_1 + R_e} .$$

A comparison of these equations with those for concurrent schedules shows that the denominators differ. For concurrent schedules (Equation 2.11), reinforcers on one schedule occur in the *context* of all other reinforcers, equally weighted. To put this another way, when all reinforcers are concurrently available, the interaction due to reinforcers from other sources is maximal (m for concurrent schedules is 1.0). In multiple schedules (Equation 3.1), the influence of the reinforcer rate in the alternate component is less than maximal ($m < 1$) because those reinforcers are occurring at other, presumably discriminable, times. Of course, if the alternate component is very distant (temporally) from the component in question, m might be zero, and the response rate in that component would be just like that in a single schedule (Equation 2.2).

It is implicit in the development above that Herrnstein (1970) assumed that the value of R_e is the same in both components. This, as Herrnstein pointed out, is a simplifying assumption, and could well be untrue. Indeed, the validity of this assumption rests very largely on the nature of the *feedback function* for the extraneous reinforcers—put simply, if the rate of these is response dependent (e.g., ratio scheduled), R_e will be different in the two components if R_1 does not equal R_2. If the extraneous reinforcers are not response dependent (e.g., interval scheduled), R_e could be the same in the two components independent of R_1 and R_2. But the assumption that Herrnstein made (and indeed *any* assumption that could be made) is valid given that it is explicitly specified and not hidden. A more correct equation could be written, one which also takes into account the possibility of interaction between different R_e rates in the two components:

$$B_1 = \frac{kR_1}{R_1 + mR_2 + R_{e1} + mR_{e2}}. \qquad (3.2)$$

Equation 3.2 is extremely difficult to assess. While there are now only two free constant parameters (k and m), there are four independent variables (R_1, R_2, R_{e1}, and R_{e2}), and the last two of these cannot be directly measured (though they could be varied in analog fashion). We will therefore mainly use Equation 3.1 to display some of the implications of Herrnstein's approach to multiple-schedule performance.

3.2. THE LOGIC OF HERRNSTEIN'S MULTIPLE-SCHEDULE EQUATIONS

Sometimes a logical analysis of a system of equations can provide important and surprising results. With more recent developments, it may be thought unnecessary to spend a great deal of time on Herrnstein's (1970) theory. We believe it to be useful for two reasons. First, there is an historical reason. It is from these equations, and their undoubted inadequacies, that more recent formulations evolved. Second, there are lessons to be learned from a logical analysis of these equations that might, we trust, help us to avoid similar traps in future. The situation is this: There are so many empirical data available now in the area of matching that any new theoretical formulation must address a very wide area, or else fail immediately on the grounds of incompleteness. Much of Herrnstein's theory has fallen to the onslaught of data, and only subsequently have the logical inconsistencies been discussed. Perhaps the development should have proceeded the other way.

Equation 3.2 is an assertion of the way in which the constant total output is allocated between responding on the schedules and emitting other behaviors in a component of a multiple schedule. This division is on the basis of the delivered reinforcers in that component divided by the context, weighted by the interaction parameter m, in which these reinforcers occur. The equation has the correct connotations in that it reduces to Herrnstein's (1970) single-schedule equation (Equation 2.2) when component interactions are minimal. But let us investigate the total output of behavior in a component by writing an equation for the rate at which B_{e1} is emitted in Component 1 (in an equivalent measure to that of B_1, for example, pecks per minute). We can presumably write:

$$B_{e1} = \frac{kR_{e1}}{R_1 + mR_2 + R_{e1} + mR_{e2}} \quad . \tag{3.3}$$

Notice that Equations 3.2 and 3.3 imply strict matching between the concurrently available responses in each component—this is consistent with the concurrent-schedule analysis given above. But if we *add* Equations 3.2 and 3.3, we gain an expression for the total output (in responses per minute) in a component:

$$B_1 + B_{e1} = \frac{k(R_1 + R_{e1})}{R_1 + mR_2 + R_{e1} + mR_{e2}} \quad .$$

This equation shows that the total output in a component is *not* constant, that is, it does not sum to k. Now, because Herrnstein assumed that the components of a multiple schedule interact less than maximally, this result should not necessarily concern us immediately. For instance, it may be that in such a successive schedule, instead of the total output in a component summing to k, because of the interactions, the total output across the two components should sum either to k, or possibly to $2k$. Let us investigate this possibility by forming the equation for the total output in Component 2. By the same logic as that used previously:

$$B_2 + B_{e2} = \frac{k(R_2 + R_{e2})}{R_2 + mR_1 + R_{e2} + mR_{e1}} \quad .$$

It should be quite evident, without going any further, that if the two-component total-output equations are summed, neither k nor $2k$ is the answer. Rather, total output is somewhat less than $2k$. (Of course, when $m = 1$, which is the appropriate value for a concurrent schedule, the total output does equal k.) Thus, the total output from a multiple schedule (with $m < 1$) does not sum to the originally assumed constant value of k. It is equally evident that the original assumption that k was a constant has been seriously compromized by the assumption made about the way of dealing with interactions, that is, by the invention of the constant m. The system of equations becomes internally inconsistent when it is extended to multiple schedules.

A cursory glance at the above equations shows quite clearly where the problem is: the parameter m does not appear in the numerator, and thus it can never cancel with the denominator. A very simple way around this problem, that retains the m parameter, would be to make the assumption that the generalization to multiple-schedule performance must suggest that the response rate in a component is a function of two independent variables—the reinforcer rate in that component and, via an interaction, the reinforcer rate for the same response in the alternate component. Thus:

$$B_1 = \frac{k(R_1 + mR_2)}{R_1 + mR_2 + R_{e1} + mR_{e2}}. \tag{3.4}$$

Equation 3.4 is consistent with the original assumptions. Equation 3.4 may be used to describe single-schedule performance either by setting the interaction parameter $m = 0$, or by noting that in a single schedule, $R_1 = R_2$ and $R_{e1} = R_{e2}$. Either way, Equation 3.4 simplifies to Equation 2.2. We can make exactly the same simplifying assumptions in order to describe concurrent schedules of B_1 and B_{e1} responses, giving:

$$\frac{B_1}{B_1 + B_e} = \frac{R_1}{R_1 + R_e},$$

which is the equation for strict matching. But also note that if the interaction was submaximal, and there were periods of different reinforcer rates, relative response rates would be less extreme than relative reinforcer rates.

If the component response-rate equations based on Equation 3.4 are summed, we obtain:

$$B_1 + B_e = \frac{k(R_1 + mR_2) + k(R_{e1} + mR_{e2})}{R_1 + mR_2 + R_{e1} + mR_{e2}} = k.$$

and the original assumptions are preserved. Equation 3.4 has not been suggested in the literature, but it is obviously logically preferable to Herrnstein's (1970) version. In addition, once a logical system of equations is constructed, by a process similar to that described above, the question must be asked whether the equations are empirically viable. We believe that Equation 3.4 may be, but it is not the place to investigate it. We hope that the above dissection of an equation, and its subsequent reformulation, displays to the theoretically novice reader the sorts of processes that are followed in quantitative theory analysis and construction. By the way, the next step in the analysis of such an equation is to ask the simple question, Are the limits of the equation appropriate?

Many other alternatives to Herrnstein's (1970) equation have been proposed, both on logical and on empirical grounds. We first discuss the empirical research.

3.3. HERRNSTEIN'S EQUATIONS: EMPIRICAL DATA

Empirical research on Herrnstein's (1970) system of equations has focussed on three main areas: response rates on single VI schedules, relative response rates on concurrent schedules, and behavior on multiple schedules as a function of component duration and of deprivation.

There is no doubt that Herrnstein's (1970) equation for response rates on single VI schedules (Equation 2.2) fits the available data excellently. Early data were summarized by de Villiers and Herrnstein (1976) and de Villiers (1977). de Villiers and Herrnstein, for example, investigated 40 experiments in which a variety of independent variables was manipulated (reinforcer rate; immediacy, magnitude, or type of reinforcer; and avoidance procedures) with a variety of dependent measures (response rate; running speed; and latency) using a variety of subjects. Over 90 percent of the data variance was accounted for in the majority of experiments, for both group and individual data. The parameter estimates of k and R_e were reasonable values in most cases. All estimated k and R_e values were positive, though the iterative curve-fitting procedure used, which was not described, may have precluded negative R_e values. Davison and Hunter (1976) found a number of negative R_e values in their analysis of performance on single VI schedules within concurrent schedules. However, Davison and Hunter used the reciprocal method for fitting Equation 2.2, which may have given erroneous parameter estimates. Better curve-fitting procedures (Section 2.4) do give negative R_e values, but much less frequently. A negative value of R_e indicates that response rates tend to fall from an asymptotic level as reinforcer rates increase. Such negative estimates will, of course, occur rather frequently if no data on low response and reinforcer rates have been collected.

In a number of reports, Bradshaw and his colleagues (e.g., Bradshaw, Szabadi, & Bevan, 1976, 1977, 1978, 1979) have reported fits to Equation 2.2 using data obtained from humans. These have been done using the Wilkinson (1961) procedure (Section 2.4), and they again show excellent proportions of data variance accounted for.

A feature of Herrnstein's (1970) approach is that k and R_e are assumed to be constant. More specifically, k should not change with variations in reinforcer parameters, but should change with variations in response parameters. R_e should vary with changes in reinforcer parameters, but not with changes in response parameters. Because the parameters are affected by different manipulations, they should be independent of one another. Indeed, one of the most important goals in a science is that of parameter independence. If parameters are related, then the wrong algebraic equation has most likely been assumed. de Villiers and Herrnstein (1976) did find some examples of inconstancies in k under conditions of reinforcer-parameter variation, but in only one case was the discrepancy major.

Herrnstein's single-schedule equation (Equation 2.2) has fared less well in subsequent tests. For instance, Snyderman (1984) varied food-reinforcer rates on single VI schedules at 70 percent and 90 percent of free-feeding body weights in rats. He used six schedules (ranging from VI 10 s to VI 320 s) at each weight, and fitted Equation 2.2 using the Wilkinson (1961) procedure. All subjects showed lower k values when they were less deprived, and, for four of the five subjects, R_e was larger when they were less deprived. The change in R_e would be expected from Equation 2.2 if the food reinforcers were less valuable under lower deprivation conditions, thus changing the modulus for measuring R_e. But deprivation should not have affected k. Snyderman's result is similar to one reported by McSweeney (1975a). She used concurrent VI VI schedules at three body weights using pigeons and analyzed these data as if they were a single schedule performance:

$$B_1 + B_2 = \frac{k(R_1 + R_2)}{R_1 + R_2 + R_e} .$$

McSweeney fitted her data using the reciprocal method (Section 2.4) and reported that k fell with decreasing deprivation for all three subjects. The estimates of R_e changed substantially with deprivation, though in no particular direction, and three of the six estimates were negative. These results may, of course, have been seriously affected by the parameter-estimation technique used. It is, therefore, instructive here to compare the reciprocal method with both the Wilkinson (1961) and the Wetherington-Lucas (1980) procedures. These results are shown in Table 3.1.

The estimates of k are quite consistent across the three procedures, with only one clear difference (the reciprocal procedure for Bird 394 at 105 percent body weight). Irrespective of the way in which the data were analyzed, the conclusion that k fell with decreased deprivation would be sustained. However, the standard errors of the parameter estimates obtained with the Wilkinson (1961) method compromised the conclusion, for these were very large in many cases. For one subject (Bird 5, 80 percent body weight), the estimate was not significantly different from zero. With this possible degree of error, many more subjects would need to be run in this procedure before a strong conclusion with any across-subject generality could be sustained. Alternatively, we should note that

TABLE 3.1

A Comparison of Three Methods of Fitting Herrnstein's (1970) Hyperbola to the Data Reported by McSweeney (1975a)

Bird	80% body weight		105% Body Weight	
	k	R_2	k	R_e
K and R_e Estimated by the Reciprocal Method:				
394	69.4	0.9	16.0	-28.6
259	101.0	57.4	36.9	-5.0
5	66.2	-2.4	42.4	3.9
k and R_2 (and standard errors) Estimated by the Wilkinson (1961) Method:				
394	69.3(8)	0.30(6)	47.0(27)	1.1(33)
259	109.3(45)	63.5(50)	37.8(8)	$-4.6(11)$
5	56.8(58)	$-49.1(91)$	42.9(13)	$-4.4(12)$
k and R_e Estimated by the Wetherington-Lucas (1980) Method:				
394	69.3	0.26	46.3	0.43
259	109.5	64.1	38.2	-3.7
5	74.2	1.2	42.9	-4.4

there were only four data points per fit (really insufficient) and that the arranged overall reinforcer rates were varied only from 0.625/min to 2.5/min (VI 96 s to VI 24 s). This range is unlikely to contain any low response-rate data, and indeed did not. The situation is very like that for Bird 21 in Fig. 2.4B. The standard errors of R_e are, to put it mildly, huge. The Wetherington-Lucas (1980) estimates of R_e (and indeed the reciprocal-method estimates) do fall within two standard errors of the Wilkinson estimates. Further, the Wetherington-Lucas and the Wilkinson estimates do generally tend to agree quite well. Clearly, deprivation did not consistently affect the value of R_e estimated by any of the three procedures, but the standard errors do not allow any, even weak, assertion of a constancy of R_e. In fairness to McSweeney (1975a), though, it is doubtful whether the overall-output analysis was a concern when the experiment was carried out.

An experiment specifically designed to test the independence of the parameters of Herrnstein's (1970) single-schedule equation was reported by McDowell and Wood (1984). They used humans responding on five different VI schedules with reinforcer magnitudes ranging from one quarter of a cent to 35 cents. The mean intervals of the VI schedules were 17, 25, 51, 157 and 720 s. Equation 2.2 was fit, using Wilkinson's (1961) method, for each of the reinforcer-magnitude levels and for each subject, giving 34 fits in all. In by far the majority of fits, the standard error of the estimates of k was less than one-tenth the parameter estimates, indicating a set of excellent fits. The evidence was very strong that k

increased with reinforcer magnitude. This finding was replicated and extended to response-force variation by McDowell and Wood (1985).

In summary, then, analyses of response rates on single VI schedules have suggested that the k and R_e parameters of Equation 2.2 are not independent, hence implying that the theoretical model is incorrect. It is instructive to note, though, that excellent fits to Herrnstein's hyperbola are, almost without exception, obtained in empirical research when measured in variance-accounted-for terms. Thus, it must always be borne in mind that a large amount of data variance accounted for by an equation guarantees neither that the equation is correct nor that the parameters of the equation are precisely estimated. The interpretation of the parameter values is important. For instance, Equation 2.2 may fit nicely, but with a negative (although precise) value of R_e—which is not easily interpreted within Herrnstein's (1970) system of equations. Simply fitting an equation is generally a much poorer and weaker test of a model than is manipulating variables that are assumed to have effects on only one of the parameters, or even that are assumed to affect neither of the parameters. Indeed, the implications of Herrnstein's approach when two schedules are arranged concurrently is the subject of the next section.

3.4. STRICT MATCHING AND CONCURRENT SCHEDULES

Herrnstein's (1970) equations predict—in fact assume—strict matching on concurrent VI VI schedules. That strict matching reliably occurs has been doubted in a great many empirical reports. Lobb and Davison (1975) noted that a number of studies had reported a deviation from strict matching when response allocation was the dependent variable, though they found no consistent deviation from strict matching when time-allocation measures were used. The type of deviation commonly found was nicely demonstrated in an analysis reported by Myers and Myers (1977). Using orthogonal-polynomial analyses, they showed that both a linear component (that is, $Y = mX$; strict matching) and a cubic component ($Y = mX^3$) were necessary to describe the relation between relative response and relative reinforcer rates. The cubic deviation from strict relative matching is shown in Fig. 3.1, along with both linear and quadratic ($Y = mX^2$) components. Like Lobb and Davison, Myers and Myers reported that relative time measures more closely matched relative reinforcers than did relative responses. Since Myers and Myers' paper was published, the quadratic and cubic deviations from strict matching shown in Fig. 3.1 have frequently been reported, both singly and in combination. We return to consider them in Section 4.1.

McSweeney, Melville, Buck, and Whipple (1983) approached the problem of whether strict matching was the norm for concurrent schedules in another way. They investigated *local* response and reinforcer rates in reports of concurrent-

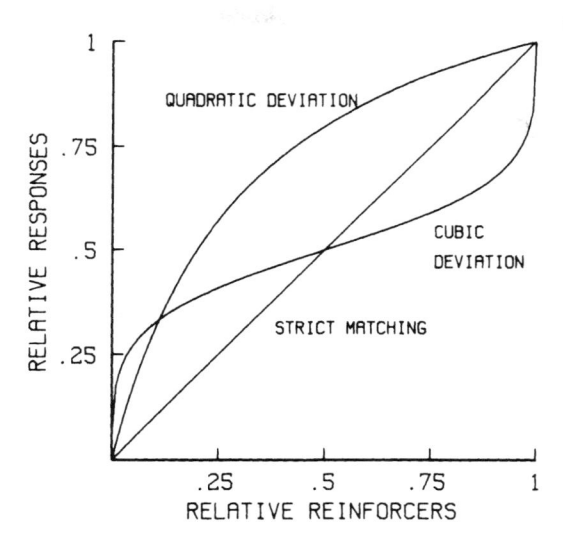

FIG. 3.1.   Quadratic and cubic deviations from strict matching.

schedule performance. A terminological note is useful here. We shall use the following terms throughout this text:

Overall rate is the number of (response or reinforcer) events divided by the total session time.

Local rates are the numbers of events divided by the time spent switched into that schedule.

Component rates (in multiple schedules) are the numbers of events in a component divided by the time spent in that component.

The difference between the last two measures is important—the timebase for local rates results from the subject's behavior, whereas the timebase for component rates derives from the procedure arranged by the experimenter. These latter measures have often been rather badly confused in the literature, with the two terms—local rate and component rate—frequently being used interchangeably.

Strict matching implies the following relations:

$$\frac{B_1}{B_1 + B_2} = \frac{R_1}{R_1 + R_2} \tag{3.5a}$$

$$\rightarrow \quad \frac{B_1}{R_1} = \frac{B_2}{R_2}, \tag{3.5b}$$

where B denotes the number of responses emitted per session. Equation 3.5b is obtained by cross multiplying Equation 3.5a and eliminating terms that occur on both sides of the equality in the subsequent equation. The implication is that the numbers of responses emitted per reinforcer obtained on concurrent schedules are the same on both keys whatever the schedules. This relation was first noted by Revusky (1963). Equally true, under strict matching, is:

$$\frac{T_1}{T_1 + T_2} = \frac{R_1}{R_1 + R_2} \rightarrow \frac{T_1}{R_1} = \frac{T_2}{R_2} \rightarrow \frac{R_1}{T_1} = \frac{R_2}{T_2}. \tag{3.6}$$

Equation 3.6 implies that the local rates of reinforcers obtained on two concurrent schedules are equal. Finally, it follows that:

$$\frac{B_1}{B_1 + B_2} = \frac{T_1}{T_1 + T_2} \rightarrow \frac{B_1}{T_1} = \frac{B_2}{T_2}, \tag{3.7}$$

and thus, the local rates of responding on two concurrent schedules are the same for all schedule values. Using analyses of variance, McSweeney et al. (1983) found that Equation 3.6 was generally supported except when the concurrently arranged schedules were of different types. Thus, relative time allocation generally matched the relative number of reinforcers obtained. McSweeney et al. (1983) also reported that local response rates were frequently the same between two concurrently available schedules (Equation 3.7), implying that relative response and time measures were similar. But while it was true that relative responses equaled relative times, which matched relative reinforcers, McSweeney et al. still concluded that Herrnstein's (1970) concurrent-schedule equation (Equation 1.1) was generally violated because the above equalities and matching relations most frequently did not all occur together in a data set. The total situation is thus confusing. McSweeney et al., by the way, did not assess Equation 3.5b to determine whether the numbers of responses emitted per reinforcer obtained on the two schedules were similar, and this remains only an implication from two findings of no significant difference. We must note the usual problem with statistical analyses here: Result A may not be statistically different from Result B, and Result B may not be significantly different from Result C. But this set of results does *not* imply that A does not differ from C.

3.5. HERRNSTEIN'S EQUATIONS AND MULTIPLE SCHEDULES: CONTRAST

We shall now investigate the way in which Herrnstein's (1970) equations deal with *contrast* in multiple schedules. Contrast describes the situation in which, when one component reinforcer rate on a multiple schedule is decreased, the response rate in the alternative component (with its reinforcer rate unchanged) increases. The increase in the response rate in the unchanged component above the equal-schedules baseline is technically called *positive behavioral contrast*. How does Herrnstein's multiple-schedule equation deal with this? The equation for the response rate in one component prior to discrimination training is given by:

$$B_r = \frac{kR_r}{R_r + mR_g + R_e},$$ (3.8)

where the Subscripts r and g denote components signaled by red and green stimuli, respectively. Initially, let us assume that $R_r = R_g = 0.5$ reinforcers per minute. If R_g is then changed to Extinction, the equation says that B_r will increase as mR_g is now zero. The only situation in which this contrast will not be predicted is when m is itself zero. This prediction appears straightforward, and consistent with the available data. However, Equation 3.8 also has an implication about the *magnitude* of contrast. The implication was derived by Spealman and Gollub (1974). It is that contrast produced by a transition from multiple VI VI to multiple VI Extinction schedules should increase with increasing overall reinforcer rates. This prediction can readily be shown by choosing some reasonable values of k, m and R_e, and calculating the predicted response-rate changes. Spealman and Gollub discovered that, contrary to prediction, contrast was generally greater in the transition from multiple VI 180 s VI 180 s to multiple VI 180 s Extinction than it was in the transition from multiple VI 30 s VI 30 s to multiple VI 30 s Extinction. These empirical findings were also consistent with Reynolds' (1963b) report that contrast decreased with increasing reinforcer rates.

Now we ask, What will Herrnstein's multiple-schedule equation predict if initial training is carried out on a single schedule in the presence of red; and then the green, Extinction, component is introduced? Prior to the discrimination training:

$$B_r = \frac{kR_r}{R_r + R_e},$$ (3.9)

but after discrimination training, Equation 3.8 will apply. Whatever the value of m, mR_g will be zero, so no response-rate increase in the red component will be predicted. However, contrastlike effects do reliably occur under such a manipulation.

A third problem is this. If the subject is trained on a VI schedule in the presence of red, and then the conditions are changed to a multiple VI VI schedule with the same reinforcer rates as were arranged in red alone, Equation 3.9 applies to the red-alone condition, and Equation 3.8 applies to the multiple VI VI condition. If $m > 0$, mR_g will be greater than zero, and so the response rate in the red component of the multiple VI VI schedule will be less than the response rate in the red component arranged alone. Herrnstein (1970) suggested that this might indeed occur, but subsequent research (McSweeney, 1980; McSweeney & DeRicco, 1976; Spealman & Gollub, 1974) provided contrary evidence. For example, Spealman and Gollub, in their Experiment 2, found no response-rate differences between VI 30 s and multiple VI 30 s VI 30 s, nor between VI 180 s and multiple VI 180 s VI 180 s. Such problems have been researched empirically (see also McSweeney & DeRicco, 1976), and have been summarized by Williams (1983) and by McLean and White (1983). The problems obviously arise because of the failure of logical consistency, in relation to k in the multiple-schedule model, caused by the introduction of the interaction parameter, m.

3.6. COMPONENT DURATION IN MULTIPLE SCHEDULES

The research discussed above was directly concerned with Herrnstein's (1970) multiple-schedule equations, but more indirect research has also brought the equations into question. One implication of the interaction parameter m is that its value might be affected by the frequency of component alternation. Initial research on multiple schedules tended to use long components (2 or 3 minutes), and Herrnstein suggested an m of 0.3 to 0.5 was appropriate. Shimp and Wheatley (1971) and Todorov (1972) argued that if Herrnstein's multiple-schedule equation was correct, shorter components would increase m and thus move relative response rates toward relative reinforcer rates—a movement toward strict matching in multiple-schedule performance. Their results showed exactly this effect, and the measures matched at component durations of 5 to 10 s (see also Section 9.3). These results were taken as providing quite strong indirect support for the multiple-schedule equation. However, Edmon (1978) noted that Herrnstein's equation predicted that decreasing component durations, and hence increasing m values, should decrease the response rates within both multiple-schedule components. His reanalysis of Shimp and Wheatley's and Todorov's data showed, however, that the response rates in the higher reinforcer-rate components *increased* as component durations were shortened (again, see Section 9.3). Charman and Davison (1982) and McSweeney (1982) found the same effect. These findings are a good example of how one aspect of a data set (in this case, the matching relation) can support a quantitative model, but other analyses of the same data (absolute response rates) can refute the same model.

The so-called *short-component effect*, which is supportive of Herrnstein's (1970) multiple-schedule equations, was taken as a robust effect for a long time. Its interpretation as a movement toward strict matching under short component durations was not doubted until a report by Charman and Davison (1982) (see also Section 9.3). Strict matching implies that relative response rates equal relative reinforcer rates *for all relative reinforcer rates*. A finding of a simple equality between relative response and reinforcer rates for a particular schedule combination does not necessarily entitle us to assert strict matching. Charman and Davison assessed this interpretation by varying the component schedules at 6-s component durations. They found the same relation between relative response and reinforcer rates at this component duration as they did at considerably longer component durations, and even under unequal component durations (which were varied from 600:120 s to 25:5 s). They did obtain the short-component effect, but only when they kept the component schedules constant, and unequal, and varied the component durations. They showed that any movement toward an equality of relative response rates and relative reinforcer rates under short components could be eliminated completely by a change in the component schedules. They therefore termed the short-component effect a "fragile" effect, which had resulted from previous studies using largely (Shimp & Wheatley, 1971) or only (Todorov, 1972) one pair of component reinforcer rates. Charman and Davison concluded that the interpretation of "matching" under short-component multiple schedules was in error. Their data can thus be used to support the suggestion originally made by Lobb and Davison (1977) that neither absolute nor relative component durations affect the relation between relative response rates and relative reinforcer rates on multiple schedules.

3.7. DEPRIVATION IN MULTIPLE SCHEDULES

Herrnstein and Loveland (1974) pointed out that the deprivation of the subject should affect performance on multiple VI VI schedules (see also Section 9.4). When the subject is made less deprived of the defined reinforcer, the value of the defined reinforcer (for example, 3-s access to grain) will decrease. This will result in a change in the modulus for measuring reinforcers. Thus, the apparent value of R_e (which is the value of R_e relative to R_1) will increase. Think of it this way: Under high food deprivation, 15 scratches might equal 3-s access to food. But under low deprivation, one scratch might equal 3-s access to grain. In Equation 3.1, if R_e increases relative to the defined reinforcers R_1 and R_2, B_1 will clearly fall. Ultimately, when R_e is very large relative to R_1 and R_2, Equation 3.1 tends toward:

$$B_1 = \frac{kR_1}{R_e} ,$$

and thus:

$$\frac{B_1}{B_1 + B_2} = \frac{R_1}{R_1 + R_2} ,$$

the strict matching equation. Herrnstein and Loveland (1974) varied the deprivation of their pigeons under unequal-component multiple VI VI schedules,

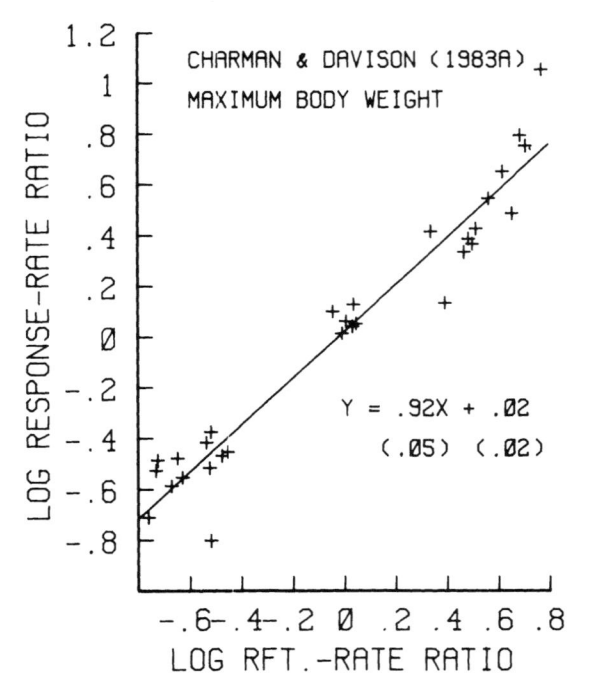

FIG. 3.2.   Data reported by Charman and Davison (1983a, Part 2, Conditions 6 to 10). The log of the red/green component response-rate ratio is plotted as a function of the log of the obtained component reinforcer-rate ratio. The data are means taken over the last five sessions of each condition for all six birds.

and found that relative response rates did equal relative reinforcer rates when deprivation was minimal. But note that, like the short-component effect, asserting *matching* in multiple VI VI schedules under minimal deprivation on the basis of such results goes well beyond the data collected. After finding the "fragile" short-component effect (see Fig. 9.8, Section 9.3), Charman and Davison (1983a) reinvestigated the multiple-schedule deprivation effect to determine whether this too was "fragile." It was not, as Fig. 3.2 shows. Varying the schedules at 100 percent or more of the pigeons' free-feeding body weights did produce a close approximation to strict matching. Thus far, it would appear that deprivation data do support Herrnstein's (1970) multiple-schedule equation.

But Charman and Davison (1983a) carried out further analyses of their data (see also Section 9.4), and these did not support Herrnstein's (1970) model. In the first part of their experiment, they increased their subjects' body weights from 80 percent to 100 percent, in steps of 5 percent, on a multiple VI 90-s VI 30-s schedule. In the second part, they decreased the body weights from 100 percent to 80 percent, in steps of 5 percent, on a multiple VI 27-s VI 135-s schedule. These procedures gave two data points at each of five body weights.

For the ascending series (Subscript a), applying Equation 3.1 to each component gave this equation:

$$\frac{B_{1a}}{B_{2a}} = \frac{R_{1a}}{R_{2a}} \cdot \frac{R_{2a} + mR_{1a} + R_e}{R_{1a} + mR_{2a} + R_e},$$

and for the descending (d) series:

$$\frac{B_{1d}}{B_{2d}} = \frac{R_{1d}}{R_{2d}} \cdot \frac{R_{2d} + mR_{1d} + R_e}{R_{1d} + mR_{2d} + R_e}.$$

There are only two unknowns in these equations, m and R_e, and thus the values of these constants may be algebraically obtained by simple substitution. But notice the assumptions that are being made here: (1) a value of R_e is assumed that is the same in each component (compare with Equation 3.2) at each body weight, but this value is not assumed to be constant across body weights; and (2) m is also assumed to be constant at a particular body weight, but not across body weights.

From this analysis, Charman and Davison (1983a) found no trend in either m or in R_e across deprivation levels. This result is illustrated in Fig. 3.3. Under Herrnstein's (1970) interpretation, a trend in R_e would be expected. Thus, here again, the matching data are consistent with Herrnstein's equations, but other ways of analyzing the same data make it clear that the data are in fact inconsistent with these equations. Charman and Davison pointed to m as the problem, and showed that their data were consistent with an alternative model (McLean & White, 1983) that assumes no explicit interaction parameter like m. Charman and Davison concluded that Herrnstein and Loveland's (1974) interpretation of the effects of deprivation change (varying the value of R_e relative to R_1 and R_2) was, in fact, correct—but that the model in which they realized these effects was in error. It is interesting here to see how an interpretation can be correct, but can provide incorrect predictions when used in conjunction with the wrong model. Further details are given in Chapter 9.

3.8. OVERALL COMMENTS ON HERRNSTEIN'S MODEL

Herrnstein's (1970) simple model has received extensive disconfirmation since it was proposed. Thus, it cannot be sustained in its original form. However, a quantitative model is no more than the sum of its assumptions, and these assumptions are (or should be) the simplest and most parsimonious for the situation. If data do not fit a quantitative model, then the assumptions must be revised. We believe that, except under the most extreme conditions, the model per se should not be rejected in favor of a radically different model. Many of Herrnstein's (1970) proposals remain, in almost all cases, reasonable. R_e as the

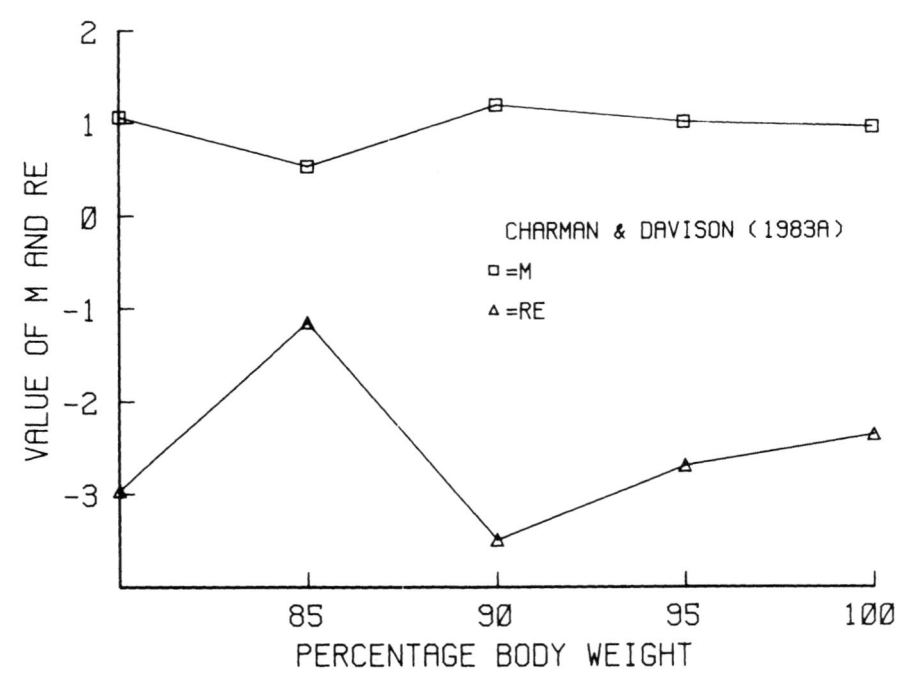

FIG. 3.3.   Median estimates of m and R_e for the group data reported by Charman and Davison (1983a; Fig. 6) as a function of percentage ad lib body weight.

rate of alternative, unmeasured, reinforcers measured in R_1 equivalents, and B_e as the rate of unmeasured responses in B_1 equivalents, are entirely reasonable and logical conceptions. There is, currently, no good reason for changing them. k, as the constant total rate of output, is perhaps more questionable on intuitive grounds, and some empirical considerations must be taken into account. For instance, response rates on FR schedules can be consistently higher than the rate on the highest reinforcer-rate VI schedules. But, this could be caused by a redefinition of the operant as a fixed-number unit for FR performance. However, at the time of writing, it may be worthwhile to maintain k in its original form.

The interaction parameter m is clearly badly conceived and the effects that it attempts to describe will have to be dealt with in some other way. It was the most parsimonious way of dealing with component interactions at the time the model was proposed. An alternative method for dealing with interactions was proposed by McLean and White (1983; see Chapter 9), and this looks promising.

The assumptions we have discussed above might be called *functional* assumptions. A quantitative model also requires *structural* assumptions—the form of the equation, or how the functional assumptions are convolved to produce a prediction. Herrnstein's (1970) basic structural assumption is strict matching, and empirical research has shown that this may be questionable. Strict relative-response relative-reinforcer matching does not always occur in concurrent VI VI schedule performance (Taylor & Davison, 1983), and a power-function alternative may be preferable (e.g., Davison & Hunter, 1976; McDowell, 1986):

$$B_1 = \frac{kR_1{}^a}{R_1{}^a + R_2{}^a + R_e{}^a} .$$

This equation retains the logical consistency of summing to k over the three alternatives. Its superiority over Equation 3.1 is, empirically, extremely difficult to show, as the above equation has three free parameters (a, R_e, and k) and thus is bound to fit better. One benefit is, though, that it implies generalized, rather than strict, matching in concurrent schedules. A second benefit is that it is consistent with the multiple-schedule model proposed by McLean and White (1983).

A final point needs to be made to clarify the relation between theories and equations. Herrnstein's (1970) theory of single- and concurrent-schedule performance is more than just a set of equations. In addition, there are assumptions about the constancy of k and R_e. As we noted in Section 3.3, Herrnstein's single-response equation (Equation 2.2) fits the available data very well, but the assumptions of constancy have not been found to be correct. McDowell (1986) pointed out that the equation (which we termed a structural assumption, but which McDowell calls the *formal model*) can be assessed and tested with no functional assumptions (McDowell's *quasi-formal* model) at all. McDowell pointed out that McDowell and Wood's (1984, 1985) research did not dispute the adequacy of the hyperbolic relation between response and reinforcer rate, but it did disprove the assumption that k was a constant under reinforcer-magnitude variation. If the structural assumptions appear correct, but the functional assumptions are incorrect, then we revert to a position in which the generality of the constant-k model is constrained, but the generality of the variable-k model is less constrained. It then becomes an important task to quantify the dependency between k and (for instance) reinforcer magnitude. Such a dependency indeed exists in McDowell and Kessel's (1979) linear systems theory, which may therefore have more generality as a description of behavior than does Herrnstein's account.

4 GENERALIZED MATCHING

4.1. INTRODUCTION

The generalized matching law was developed so that data that clearly did not conform to strict matching could be described in the same terms as strict matching data. It is a generalization of the strict matching law in the sense that the strict matching law is a special case of the generalized law (see Allen, 1981; Prelec, 1984). Notice that, in its simplest form, the strict matching relation for concurrent schedules has no free parameters:

$$\frac{B_1}{B_1 + B_2} = \frac{R_1}{R_1 + R_2},$$

where the Subscripts *1* and *2* denote the two alternatives. In this equation, both the two responses and the two reinforcers are identical. Recall, though, that when the asymptotic rates of two concurrent operants were different (Equation 2.7), or when the reinforcers for these were different (Equation 2.8), a free parameter is appropriate to scale the response or reinforcer rates. Equation 2.7 was:

$$\frac{B_p}{B_p + B_\ell} = \frac{k'R_p}{k'R_p + R_\ell},$$

where p and ℓ denote pecks and lever presses respectively. If this equation is cross multiplied and the common terms are subtracted from each side of the equality, we obtain, after some manipulation:

$$\frac{B_\text{p}}{B_\ell} = \frac{k'R_\text{p}}{R_\ell} \, , \tag{4.1}$$

where $k' = k_\text{p}/k_\ell$ (see Section 2.2). Thus, the strict matching law already has built into it one generalized feature—the ability to deal with *bias*. A bias is a constant proportional preference for one response over another for all levels of the independent variable. In Equation 4.1, whatever the values of R_p and R_ℓ, B_p/B_ℓ (the response ratio) is related to R_p/R_ℓ (the reinforcer-frequency ratio) via a multiplicative constant. In other words, the relation between the behavior ratio and the reinforcer ratio is a straight-line function of slope k' (Fig. 4.1E). Notice that this relation, when plotted on *relative* coordinates (Fig. 4.1B), describes the quadratic deviation from strict matching exemplified in Fig. 3.1.

Strict matching states that relative response measures equal relative reinforcer measures. Algebraically, this translates to an equality of response ratios and reinforcer ratios (Fig. 4.1D). Clearly, a biased matching line is much easier to fit on ratio coordinates (Fig. 4.1E) than it is on relative coordinates (Fig. 4.1B). On the latter, a bias produces a curve. There continues to be some terminological disparity between researchers as to whether a biased matching relation should be termed "matching" (unmodified by any adjective). Here we shall follow Baum (1974a) who identified "bias" as a deviation from "matching," and thus we shall use the term "biased matching." Such terminological differences underline the scientific imperative that, in describing the results of another's experiment, you should always consider the data from that report, rather than what the researcher *said* about those data.

Bias has routinely been accepted as a real deviation from matching. More discussion has centered on the existence of the cubic deviation (Fig. 3.1) reported by Myers and Myers (1977). This type of deviation, in combination with a bias, is shown in Fig. 4.1C on relative coordinates. Such a deviation, either alone or in combination with a bias, does not transform to a linear function on ratio coordinates (Fig. 4.1F). However, such data are linear when both axes of the plot are transformed logarithmically (to any base, though we shall use base 10). Figure 4.1I shows the relative ogival plot on log-ratio coordinates. Indeed, such a transformation also shows strict matching and biased matching as linear (Figs. 4.1G and H, respectively). The form of the equation implied by the linearity of the logarithmic transform is:

$$\log\!\left(\frac{B_\text{p}}{B_\ell}\right) = a \, \log\!\left(\frac{R_\text{p}}{R_\ell}\right) + \log c \, , \tag{4.2}$$

which is a straight line relating the dependent variable (Y, $\log B_\text{p}/B_\ell$) to the independent variable (X, $\log R_\text{p}/R_\ell$) with a slope a and an intercept of $\log c$. Equation 4.2 is the *generalized matching law*. In nonlogarithmic form, it describes a power function:

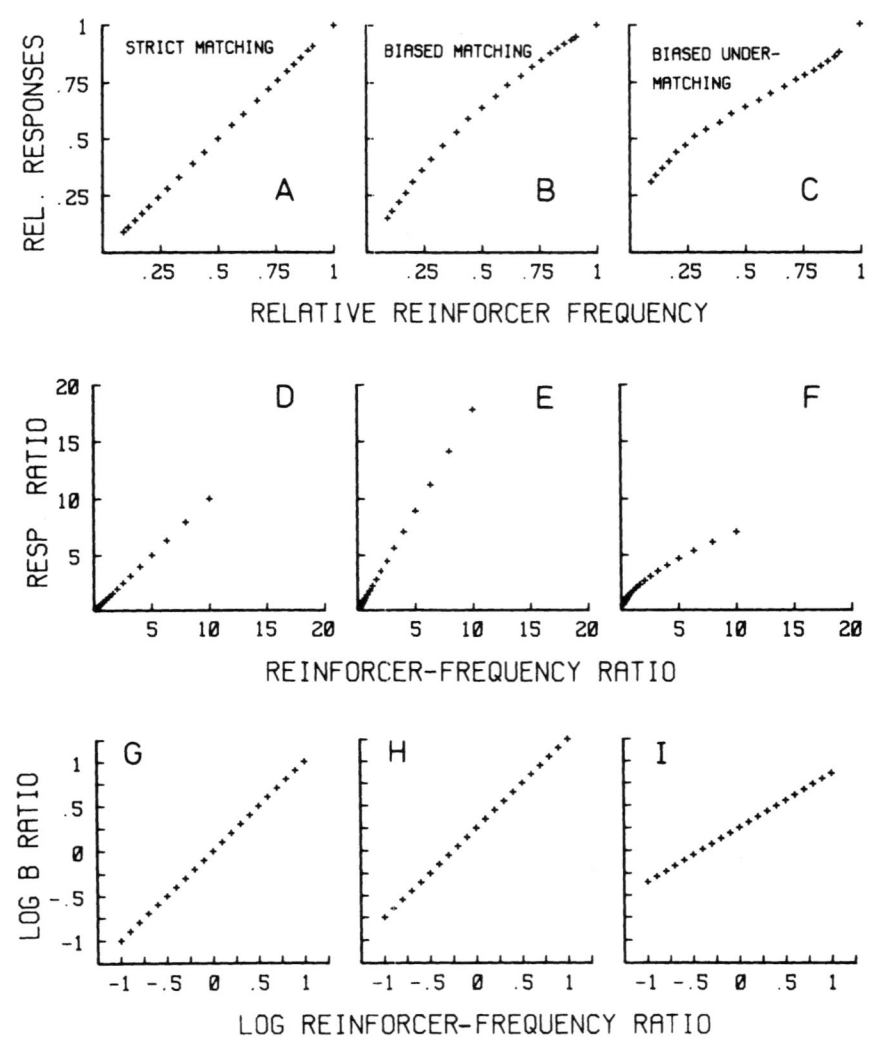

FIG. 4.1.   Strict matching, biased matching, and biased undermatching data plotted on relative coordinates (top panel), on ratio coordinates (middle panel) and on log-ratio coordinates (lower panel). The same (theoretical) data are used in each column.

$$\frac{B_p}{B_\ell} = c\left(\frac{R_p}{R_\ell}\right)^a , \qquad (4.3)$$

that is also known as the generalized matching law. We shall discriminate the two by referring to Equation 4.2 as the logarithmic generalized matching law and to Equation 4.3 as the power generalized matching law, when necessary.

Otherwise, we shall use the term generalized matching law to refer to either interchangeably.

Log c (Equation 4.2) is called *bias*, and the constant multiplicative relation in ratios (Equation 4.3) is an additive constant in the logarithmic form (Equation 4.2) of the equation. A terminological note is in order here. Both c and log c may be termed bias, since the latter is a mathematical transformation of the former. When discussing values of bias, we shall be referring to log c values. When necessary, we will term c values *ratio bias* values. As our discussion has indicated, bias (log c) describes differences between response requirements or reinforcer parameters. These differences remain constant through an experiment as, in Equation 4.2, the reinforcer-frequency ratio is varied. In one sense, it is a catchall constant that even can act as an individual parameter, describing a preference on the part of the subject to respond on the left alternative, or to respond on the red key, and so on. Equally, it may describe the fact that one manipulandum, by chance, requires a more forceful response, or perhaps a longer response, or that the timer controlling the reinforcer for one of the two responses gives a slightly different reinforcer duration than that for the other response. In these cases, the *source* of a bias is unknown (but in principle it can be uncovered). In other cases, an experimenter may arrange a biaser (say, different response forces) that is constant over one set of conditions in which a variable (say, the reinforcer-frequency ratio) is manipulated, and that is again constant, but different, under a second set of reinforcer-frequency manipulations. In this example, differences in bias between the two sets of conditions measure the effects caused by different forces between the keys.

Baum (1974a) introduced the term ''undermatching'' to describe values of a less than the strict matching value of 1.0. Undermatching implies that the behavior ratio has a less-than-unit sensitivity to the reinforcer ratio when the latter is varied. He also used the term ''overmatching'' to describe a values greater than unity. We shall try to avoid this dichotomy (or trichotomy, if ''matching'' categorizes an a value of, or close to, 1.0). Rather, we shall endeavor to use the term ''sensitivity to reinforcer frequency (or amount, or immediacy)'' as the name for any a value. Baum's motivation for his categorization was probably related to his theoretical position that $a = 1$ is the norm (Baum, 1979), and that a values differing from 1 represent a deviation that may be caused by some failure in procedure (see also de Villiers, 1977).

Figures 4.1C, F and I show a biased nonunit sensitivity performance. This relation, of course, is described by a straight line on log-ratio coordinates. It has a nonunit slope (a does not equal 1) and a substantial bias (log c does not equal 0). The major point to make about Figs. 4.1C, F and I is that it is *impossible* to determine, from a single point on the graph, whether the performance has a bias, a nonunit sensitivity, or both. It is also very difficult to determine whether a set of data is showing bias or nonunit sensitivity, or both, from a plot of those data on relative coordinates (Baum, 1974a). We recommend therefore, that such an interpretation should not be attempted without considerable experience with both relative and log-ratio plots. One can find some annoying reports in the literature, in which points falling above the major diagonal on relative plots are interpreted as, or perhaps called, overmatching points. Rather, from Fig. 4.1 it is evident that these could well be biased data points.

Before continuing with the development of the generalized matching law, we will consider some of the early results that used the law.

4.2. EARLY EMPIRICAL RESEARCH ON GENERALIZED MATCHING

The generalized matching relation was discussed and suggested in a number of papers before the relation was formally introduced by Baum (1974a).

Chronologically, the first use of the generalized matching law was in a paper by Lander and Irwin (1968). They investigated the relation between response rates and reinforcer rates on multiple VI VI schedules. The components were both of 180-s duration. So, in this case, the ratios of component response and reinforcer rates, which are the natural measures of performance on successively arranged schedules, are the same as the ratios of response numbers (N_1/N_2) and reinforcer numbers (n_1/n_2). The equation that Lander and Irwin wrote was:

$$\frac{N_1}{N_2} = \left(\frac{n_1}{n_2}\right)^a .$$

They reported that a was about 0.33 for multiple VI VI performance, and interpreted it as representing the "sensitivity of the distribution of responses between components to the distribution of reinforcers between the components" [p. 523]. They also pointed out that $a = 0$ would indicate no discrimination between components, and that $a = 1$ described matching. Finally, they also noted that $a = \infty$ could "in certain instances" be interpreted as maximizing. It is unclear what they mean here. If maximizing is to mean exclusive responding in one component or on one choice when the obtained reinforcer ratio is not infinite (an impossible situation, anyway), they are in error. Exclusive responding in one component will, in their experiment, produce an infinite or zero reinforcer ratio. This is an example of tautologous *strict matching*, rather than an example of maximizing. Remember that the matching law applies to obtained reiniforcers, rather than to arranged or programmed reinforcers.

Lander and Irwin (1968) did not suggest the full generalized matching relation—they had no bias parameter. Indeed, bias would not be expected in their experiment unless strong stimulus preferences for the stimuli signaling the components (dynamism) were present.

Staddon (1968) reported a parametric investigation of concurrent differential-reinforcement-of-low-rates (DRL) schedule performance. One DRL schedule provided reinforcers each time its contingencies were met, and the other provided reinforcers on a VI schedule. Technically, this is a concurrent second-order schedule, concurrent FR 1 (DRL 10 s LH 1 s) VI (DRL 2 s LH 1 s), where LH is limited hold. LH 1 s indicates that the reinforcer may be delivered only for a response emitted within 1 s after the DRL time requirement has been completed. Staddon varied the VI schedule, and thus the obtained reinforcer ratio between the two interresponse times (IRTs), and found a power-function relation:

$$\frac{B_1}{B_2} = .24\left(\frac{R_1}{R_2}\right)^{.66}$$

where Subscript 1 denotes the longer IRT. Staddon thus obtained both a bias toward the shorter IRT ($c < 1$, or log $c < 0$) and clear nonunit sensitivity ($a = 0.66$). He demonstrated the relation on double-logarithmic coordinates, which, as he pointed out, are a natural form of representation for ratios. He thus became the first experimenter to describe the full generalized matching relation, and he suggested it as a more general version of the strict matching law.

In their study of time allocation on concurrent VT VT schedules, Baum and Rachlin (1969) plotted log time-allocation ratios as a function of log reinforcer ratios for six birds. They found some large, but individual, biases ranging from -0.49 to -0.06, and averaging -0.22. They also reported sensitivities to reinforcer frequency (slopes) ranging from 0.63 to 1.29. But, as the average across birds was 1.02, they concluded that "within the limits of variation," the ratio of times was directly proportional to the ratio of reinforcers—that is, biased matching, rather than generalized matching. They did not calculate whether the individual slopes differed significantly from 1.0, though their Fig. 2 suggests that at least two subjects probably showed a slope significantly less than 1.0.

However, the major importance of Baum and Rachlin's (1969) paper is their suggestion about how different choice-affecting independent variables *combine* to affect behavior. They proposed that the product sum of the ratios of independent variables was the appropriate combination rule:

$$\frac{T_1}{T_2} = \frac{R_1}{R_2} \cdot \frac{M_1}{M_2} \cdot \frac{I_1}{I_2} \, .$$

As written, this is a strict matching relation (bias is absent, and the sensitivities to each of the independent variables are 1.0), though their discussion makes it clear that a bias parameter would be acceptable to them. We shall discuss this type of product-sum rule under the heading of the "Concatenated Generalized Matching Law" in Section 4.4.

As researchers commenced plotting their concurrent-schedule data on log-ratio coordinates, the generalized matching law was, by default, in use as an effective descriptor. However, the full generalized law (i.e., with an a value different from 1.0) could be asserted only if it could be shown that accurate prediction of behavior *required* a nonunit a value. As we have noted already, Lander and Irwin (1968) found a clear nonunit a value for multiple VI VI performance, and Staddon (1968) reported a values consistently less than 1 for concurrent DRL DRL performance. Lander and Irwin's result had little effect on concurrent-schedule thinking, as the data were from multiple schedules. Staddon's results were seen (for example by Baum and Rachlin, 1969) as a rather distant limit to the generality of the strict or biased-strict, matching relation. Baum and Rachlin's finding that overall a was 1.0 fitted nicely with the large number of reports supporting strict matching that we have already mentioned. As a result, the increasing number of nonunit sensitivity results (principally, $a < 1$) reported over the succeeding years were treated as orphans that had somehow failed to make the grade of unit sensitivity. Often the reasons suggested by the experimenters, or by reviewers of the area, were procedural (e.g., Baum, 1974a; de Villiers, 1977). An example of this is a paper by Hollard and Davison (1971), who used a generalization of the strict matching product-sum rule proposed by Baum and Rachlin (1969) to measure preference for food over brain stimulation (see also Section 6.4). Responding on one key of a two-key concurrent schedule was reinforced by 3-s access to wheat, while responding on the other key was reinforced by a 15-s train of brain stimulation. They varied the VI schedule for food over a wide range. The quantitative relation they used was:

$$\frac{B_1}{B_2} = \frac{R_1}{R_2} \cdot \frac{Q_1}{Q_2} .$$

where Q represents the qualities of the two reinforcers and Subscript 1 indicates the food performance. Since the ratio Q_1/Q_2 remained constant over the schedule variation, a plot of $\log B_1/B_2$ should be linearly related, with a slope of 1.0, to $\log R_1/R_2$ and should have an intercept of $\log Q_1/Q_2$. Hollard and Davison's results are shown in Fig. 4.2 (Note that we have re-fitted their data, and have obtained slightly different parameter estimates from those reported by Hollard and Davison. This probably resulted from the data being taken to different numbers of significant figures.) For time-allocation measures, the slope of the relation ranged from 1.01 to 1.13 (mean 1.08), with all three birds showing a strong positive bias (mean 0.71) toward the food-reinforced alternative. The antilog of 0.71 is 5.13, so this result indicated that the food reinforcer was five times more effective than the brain stimulation. These results, therefore, fitted well with Baum and Rachlin's results and with many other studies that reported strict matching. But when the behavioral measure was responses, while strong positive biases were again found (mean 0.65), all three birds showed sensitivities that were less than 1.0 (range 0.65 to 0.88, mean 0.78). The difference between the response- and time-allocation sensitivities themselves, and between the obtained response-allocation sensitivities and previous strict matching results, was not confronted in their paper. It is interesting to note,

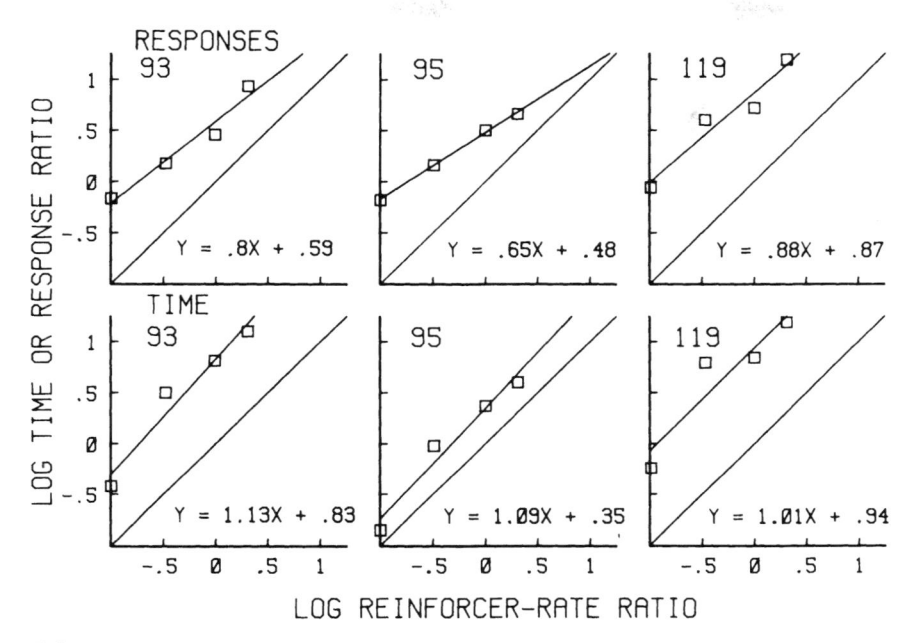

FIG. 4.2.   Log response ratios (upper panels) and log time-allocation ratios (lower panels) as a function of log obtained reinforcer-frequency ratios when the reinforcer for Key 1 was 3-s food and that for Key 2 was 15-s brain stimulation (Hollard & Davison, 1971). The diagonal line shows the locus of strict matching. The equations are those of the best-fitting straight lines obtained by the method of least squares.

however, that Hollard and Davison did arrange two concurrent VI Extinction schedules (that cannot be analyzed in the log-ratio form of the matching law). These conditions showed that their use of 2-s changeover delays was highly effective in preventing concurrent superstitions. Thus, it is not likely that the changeover delay was insufficiently long to produce unit sensitivity.

Trevett, Davison and Williams (1972) investigated concurrent FI VI schedule performance. They obtained sensitivities consistently less than 1.0 for response-allocation measures for both concurrent FI VI performance and for their concurrent VI VI baseline performances. Their response to these results was much the same as the response of Hollard and Davison (1971). They stated, "The reason for this [$a < 1.0$] is not clear, and speculation on this finding is probably unprofitable" [p. 373].

4.3. WHAT IS THE MATCHING LAW?

Rachlin (1971) suggested that the matching relation was not an empirical law, but a restatement of assumptions made prior to empirical testing. Rachlin was speaking specifically of the relation:

$$\frac{T_1}{T_2} = \frac{R_1}{R_2} \cdot \frac{A_1}{A_2} \cdot \frac{I_1}{I_2} \cdot \frac{X_1}{X_2} = \frac{V_1}{V_2} \ , \tag{4.4}$$

where R is the rate of reinforcers, A is the amount of reinforcement, I is the immediacy of reinforcers, and X comprises unknown choice-affecting independent variables (that is, $X_1/X_2 = c$ in Equation 4.3). V_1/V_2 is the ratio of the *values* of the outcomes. This measure summarizes the product sum of all choice-affecting independent variables specified in the equation. Equation 4.4 *assumes* that time ratios equal value ratios, and the product-sum part of the equation *defines* the summary variable, value. This definition is, of course, not subject to empirical test.

Killeen (1972a) pointed out that Equation 4.4 actually consists of three equations:

$$\frac{T_1}{T_2} = \frac{R_1}{R_2} \cdot \frac{A_1}{A_2} \cdot \frac{I_1}{I_2} \cdot \frac{X_1}{X_2} \ , \tag{4.5}$$

$$\frac{T_1}{T_2} = \frac{V_1}{V_2} \ , \tag{4.6}$$

and

$$\frac{V_1}{V_2} = \frac{R_1}{R_2} \cdot \frac{A_1}{A_2} \cdot \frac{I_1}{I_2} \cdot \frac{X_1}{X_2} \ . \tag{4.7}$$

Rachlin (1971) had allowed that some transformation of the physical variables (R, A, I, and X) might be necessary in Equation 4.4, so Killeen suggested that these transformations should be formally represented in Equation 4.5:

$$\frac{T_1}{T_2} = \frac{f_1 R_1}{f_2 R_2} \cdot \frac{f_3 A_1}{f_4 A_2} \cdot \frac{f_5 I_1}{f_6 I_2} \cdot \frac{f_7 X_1}{f_8 X_2} \ , \tag{4.8}$$

where f_1 to f_8 are unspecified functions. Hence, for Equation 4.6 to be true, Equation 4.7 would need modifying by the eight functions also. So, as Killeen pointed out, Equation 4.4 serves only to define a redundant intervening variable, *value*. However, if Equation 4.8 is taken as the "matching law" (it is, of course, the generalized matching law when f_1 to f_8 are power functions and $f_1 = f_2, f_3 = f_4$, and so on), the equation is falsifiable if, and only if, constraints are placed on the functions. Such constraints might arise from theory, and might require one of the following (in a rough order of the strength of the constraint): (1) all functions are identical; (2) all functions are of the same form; (3) all functions are independent of other parameter values; (4) both functions for a particular independent variable are identical; (5) both functions for a particular independent variable are of the same form; (6) each function should remain the same across equivalent procedures; and (7) each function should be constant over time. The falsification of one or more of these constraints is of major interest if theory testing is our business. But there is a radical alternative to such an approach: Equation 4.5 can be asserted simply as a formal equation with no constraints, and the constraints that do operate can be experimentally investigated to discover the level and generality of empirical invariances. It seems to be a matter of personal preference which of these approaches is taken. We favor the latter approach, and this book is concerned almost exclusively with this approach. Thus, our criterion of an effective model is not that it has defied falsification, but that a wide generality of empirical invariance has been obtained. Our starting point is the *formal* (McDowell, 1986), or *empirical*, matching law.

The generalized matching law is a generalized relation between physical measures of behavior and physical inputs to the animal, possibly transformed in some way. Such transformations of physical events are common in all sciences. We should avoid calling these transformations "subjective," for a falling body is not usually said to transform subjective gravity and subjective time into velocity. The transformations are scaling parameters. It does not seem likely that, for instance, the way we habitually measure reinforcer rate (number of reinforcers divided by total time) should be the same measure that the organismic system responds to. A subject may not mensurate this variable as the arithmetic mean, but as some other average (e.g., the harmonic mean, Killeen, 1968a). Also, if the subject is sensitive to short-term (seconds) changes in the frequency of reinforcers (which is likely), the appropriate average may be only approximately specifiable at the *molar* (minutes, hours) level. But, until the local processes are understood (see Commons, Herrnstein, & Rachlin, 1982), a molar approximation may suffice to describe and predict behavior. Indeed, the molar approximation may well continue to be more practically useful on a much longer term. For instance, Ohm's law is of considerably more use than particle physics in mending electric heaters.

Psychophysics is the study of the relation between measured stimulus input and measured behavioral output. The study of the empirical matching law (Equation 4.8) is no more and no less than this. At the present, the functions working for us are power functions, and the approach is similar to that taken by S.S. Stevens in psychophysics. One difference must be noted, though. In psychophysics, the relation under investigation is often seen as the relation between the physical stimulus S and the sensation s:

$$s = qS^a .$$

Sensation, though, is *measured* behavior, so we can assert:

$$B = s = qS^a .$$

It is evident that s, the sensation, is here a redundant intervening variable as is *value* in the generalized matching law (Equation 4.6).

One last point. We have stressed above the transforming of the physical input to predict behavior. Perhaps, though, it is not that we cannot measure the physical input in organismic terms, but that we cannot adequately yet measure the *behavior*. Maybe:

$$\frac{1}{c} \cdot \left(\frac{B_1}{B_2}\right)^{(1/a)} = \frac{R_1}{R_2} ,$$

and maybe strict matching would always occur if we measured behavior properly. This possibility should not be neglected (Staddon, 1977), and may become important if we discover that the functions in Equation 4.8 are all idiosyncratically different. A closer look at the behavior emitted could show that a simple count of responses fails to describe the fact that, say, 1000 responses can be emitted in a very large number of different ways. A different behavior measure might give strict matching to ratios of independent variables.

4.4. THE CONCATENATED GENERALIZED MATCHING LAW

We have already stated the generalized matching law in its most general form (Equation 4.8) with time allocation as the dependent variable. It may be stated in a similar way with response allocation as the dependent variable. In Equation 4.8, the way in which the independent variables combine to predict behavior is defined as the product sum—that is, all ratios multiply together, and even unknown choice-affecting variables combine in the same way. This product-sum structure was suggested by Baum and Rachlin (1969), but not in a generalized form. They suggested that:

$$\frac{T_1}{T_2} = \frac{R_1}{R_2} \cdot \frac{A_1}{A_2} \cdot \frac{I_1}{I_2} . \tag{4.9}$$

First, they specified time-allocation measurement, but the relation should also apply to response allocation, which usually follows time allocation closely when both are measured. Second, no power-function transforms of the independent variables were specified, as such transforms were not thought necessary at the time they were writing. Third, there is no bias or unknown independent-variable term, though they discuss such a term. Thus, generalizing Baum and Rachlin's ideas gives us the *concatenated* generalized matching law. The most general form of this would be Equation 4.8 (with time or response allocation as the dependent variable). This equation has, potentially, a different transform for both the numerator and denominator of each independent-variable ratio. It has generally been found, however, that the same power transform is appropriate for both constituents of each ratio (but see Davison, 1982), so we can assert:

$$\frac{B_1}{B_2} = c \left(\frac{R_1}{R_2}\right)^a \cdot \left(\frac{A_1}{A_2}\right)^b \cdot \left(\frac{I_1}{I_2}\right)^d , \tag{4.10}$$

which is the common form of the concatenated generalized matching law. The bias multiplier, c, accounts for any unknown ratios of independent variables *that remain constant for variations in the three defined ratios*. We will discuss later some other variables that have been found to affect behavior allocation. In logarithmic form, Equation 4.10 becomes:

$$\log\left(\frac{B_1}{B_2}\right) = a \log\left(\frac{R_1}{R_2}\right) + b \log\left(\frac{A_1}{A_2}\right) + d \log\left(\frac{I_1}{I_2}\right) + \log c . \tag{4.11}$$

Equation 4.11 is an equation that is linear in three dimensions, and is therefore extremely difficult to conceptualize. It also specifies that there are no *interactions* between independent variables in their effects on behavior. For instance, different values of $\log A_1/A_2$ will not affect the relation between $\log B_1/B_2$ and $\log R_1/R_2$—it is not the case that a, sensitivity to reinforcer frequency, is any different when the reinforcer amounts, A, are very small versus when they are very large, or even when one amount is very small and the other is very large. But note that this is a theoretical assertion, and that it requires empirical confirmation. This confirmation for only two independent variables in concurrent schedules was not attempted until recently (Hunter & Davison, 1982), and we should note here that the independence of independent-variable effects is not a feature of concurrent-chain performance (Chapter 10). Some examples of the theoretical operation of Equation 4.11, in relation to reinforcer qualities, are shown in Fig. 4.2.

4.5. DIMENSIONS OF EXPERIMENTS

Experiments can be designed as one-dimensional, two-dimensional, or multidimensional. In a one-dimensional experiment, one choice-affecting independent variable is systematically manipulated while all the others are kept constant. For instance, the ratio of reinforcer rates may be varied while the reinforcer durations and immediacies are kept constant (e.g., Herrnstein, 1961). Or, the reinforcer-rate ratio and the immediacy ratio can be held constant, and the ratio of reinforcer magnitudes can be varied (Catania, 1963b). Alternatively, the reinforcer-rate and amount ratios can be held constant while the immediacy ratio is varied (Chung & Herrnstein, 1967). In all the experiments referenced here, the constant ratios were not only constant, but also *equal*. If they were held constant and unequal, then those variables would have been seen in the data analysis as a *bias*—a constant proportional preference for one alternative over the other. Let us assume, for instance, that $a = 1$, $b = 1$, $A_1 = 4$ s, $A_2 = 2$ s, and that there were no other sources of bias. Then, if we vary the reinforcer-rate ratio over a wide range, collect the data, and fit a straight line to the relation between $\log B_1/B_2$ and $\log R_1/R_2$, we would obtain a slope (a) of 1.0, and a bias ($\log c$) of:

$$b \log(A_1/A_2) = 1 \log(4/2) = .30 .$$

This bias toward Alternative 1, shown by a positive logarithmic value, is the result of the unequal reinforcer amounts that remained constant through the whole experiment. Alternatively, if we did not know the value of b, and a bias value ($\log c$) of 0.2 had been obtained, we could calculate the value of b, the sensitivity to reinforcer amount:

$$\log c = b \log(A_1/A_2)$$
$$.2 = b \log(4/2) = .30b$$
$$b = .2/.3 = .67.$$

But, this latter calculation may *not* be done if there are other sources of bias present in the performance (for instance, if the immediacies of the two reinforcers were slightly different). When other sources of bias are present, the value of b obtained would not be independent of these other sources of bias.

Figure 4.3 shows the theoretical results obtained when some of the reinforcer-rate, amount, and immediacy ratios are varied and other ratios are kept constant.

A two-dimensional experiment systematically varies two independent-variable ratios. Given that at least five experimental conditions are necessary for a reasonable straight-line fit, a two-dimensional experiment formally requires at least 25 experimental conditions (and with 15 to 20 sessions per condition—a very long experiment). However, it is possible to reduce this number somewhat without fatally weakening the results by, say, arranging conditions from the perimeter of the 5 x 5 matrix of conditions shown in Table 4.1.

If, in Table 4.1, Conditions 1, 2, 3, 4, 5, 6, 10, 11, 15, 16, 20, and 21 to 25 were arranged (in an irregular order), two complete curve fits can be carried out for

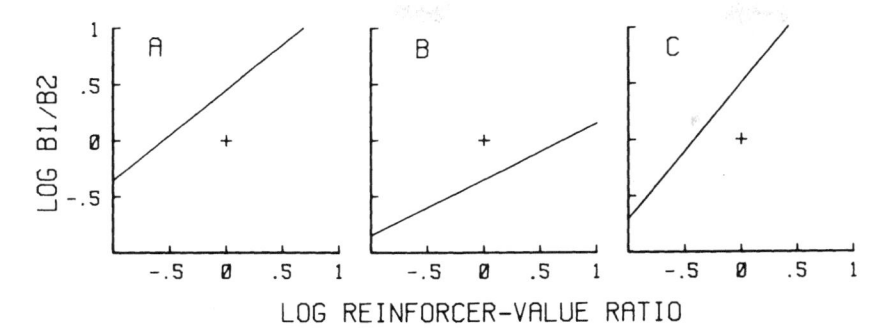

FIG. 4.3.   Effects of combinations of reinforcer rates, amounts, and immediacies. The (theoretical) data for each function are plotted against the log ratio of the varied independent variable. In Panel A, the sensitivity to the varied reinforcer-rate ratio was 0.8, $b \log A_1/A_2 = 0.6$ and $d \log I_1/I_2 = -0.25$. In Panel B, sensitivity to the varied reinforcer-amount ratio was 0.5, $a \log R_1/R_2 = -0.2$, and $d \log I_1/I_2 = -0.25$. In Panel C, sensitivity to the varied reinforcer-immediacy ratio was 1.2, $a \log R_1/R_2 = -0.2$ and $b \log A_1/A_2 = 0.6$. Log c was $+0.1$ in all three panels. The origin of each graph (0,0) is indicated by a cross.

TABLE 4.1

Example of a Two-Dimensional Experimental Design[a]

			Log Reinforcer Ratios:				
			−1.0	−0.5	0	0.5	1.0
	A	R	1.0 │ 1	2	3	4	5
L	m	a	0.5 │ 6	7	8	9	10
o	o	t	0.0 │ 11	12	13	14	15
g	u	i					
	n	o	−0.5 │ 16	17	18	19	20
	t	s	−1.0 │ 21	22	23	24	25

[a]The numbers within the matrix refer to notional condition numbers.

reinforcer-ratio variations (Conditions 1, 2, 3, 4, 5, and Conditions 21, 22, 23, 24, 25), and two for amount-ratio variations (Conditions 1, 6, 11, 16, 21, and Conditions 5, 10, 15, 20, and 25). Then, algebraic estimates of slopes and intercepts can be obtained for three other pairs of data points for both reinforcer-ratio variations (Conditions 6 and 10, 11 and 15, 16 and 20) and reinforcer-amount ratios (Conditions 2 and 22, 3 and 23, 4 and 24). Given the data were relatively free from noise, this should suffice to convince a reader of the viability of the concatenation and of the sensitivities to each of the ratios of independent variables.

Two-dimensional designs are uncommon, but are extremely powerful and informative (Anderson, 1978). We very strongly recommend them. More common is a design part-way between one and two dimensions, with a systematic variation of one independent-variable ratio at just two values of another independent-variable ratio. Even more common, sadly, is what we call the fly-swatting approach, in which points on two, and frequently more, dimensions appear to be chosen capriciously and with no forethought, so that a quantitative analysis is impossible. There is a sense in which psychology is almost characterized by this approach!

Finally, systematic three-dimensional experiments are as rare as hens' teeth. While they appear to require at least 125 conditions, the approach taken above can be used to reduce this total considerably. The design is obviously very powerful indeed, but the power is seriously compromised when each of the three dimensions is completed by a different experimenter in a different laboratory with different subjects—which, of course, is the common way of generalizing a relation across dimensions (for instance, the separate experiments of Herrnstein, 1961, Catania, 1963b, and Chung & Herrnstein, 1967).

5 QUANTITATIVE METHODS

5.1. ABOUT LINEAR REGRESSION

Linear regression is the name of the technique commonly used to fit a straight line to a set of data points. The equation of the straight line is:

$$Y = sX + c ,$$

where Y is the dependent variable and X is the independent variable. Both s and c are *constants*, s being the slope of the relation and c being the intercept. Thus, Y is related to X via one multiplicative and one additive constant. The sizes of both the slope and the intercept depend on the units of measurement of the two variables. If both are measured in the same units (e.g., centimeters), the slope has *no* dimensions (i.e., it is a dimension-free number), and the intercept, in this case, has the dimensions of length (L). This can be shown by a *dimensional analysis*. The dimensions of this example are:

$$L = sL + c .$$

Since the dimensions on both sides of an equality in an equation must be the same, then, in the above equation, s must have no dimensions (i.e., must be simply in units). Only expressions with the same dimensions may be added together (one cannot add grams to centimeters), so c must be in centimeters also.

On the other hand, if Y was measured as a length (L) and X was measured as time (T), say, then the dimensions of the equation would be:

$$L = sT + c \, .$$

Now, the units on the right-hand side of this equality must also be length, so the dimension of s must be L/T (velocity) in order that sT should have the dimension of length. The additive constant c must again have the dimensions of length by the rule given above.

When any quantitative relation is being suggested, the dimensions of equations must be carefully considered to ensure that the equation is dimensionally correct. Further, the units of both variables and constants should always be stated unambiguously. Matching equations, of course, have no dimensions as both the independent and the dependent variables are ratios or proportions of rates. However, equations like Herrnstein's (1970) equation for response rates on single schedules have the dimensions of $1/T$ (response rates and reinforcer rates).

A simple form of quantitative relation is a straight-line relation between a dependent variable (the Y variable) and an independent variable (the X variable). Much of the quantitative approach to behavior consists of estimating the parameters of such straight-line relations. The technique known as *least-squares linear regression* is one method of achieving this. It is a statistical procedure that fits a straight line to data in a particular sort of way and that has, underlying it, a particular set of assumptions. Effectively, this procedure minimizes the sum of the squares of the deviations of the data from the straight line, and the deviations are measured in terms of the Y variable. This procedure is diagramed in Fig. 5.1. The reason that the Y variance is minimized (and not the X variance, or the variance of the data point from the closest point on the fitted line) is given in Assumption 1 below. Techniques that minimize variance in other ways are available, and one is discussed in Section 5.6. For now, though, we stress that it is most important that the procedures and assumptions of any statistical procedure are always borne in mind when that procedure is used.

5.2. ASSUMPTIONS OF LEAST-SQUARES LINEAR REGRESSION

Assumption 1. The independent variables (X_i) are fixed and have no variance. This states that there is no measurement error in the values of X. For instance, if something is placed on the pan of a weighing machine and the scale is read, there may be some error in the reading of the scale (the Y variable), but there is none in the effect of the material placed on the pan. This has a constant effect. If we remove it from the pan, and then replace it, our reading might be different (measurement error), but the material has exactly the same effect on the machine. Thus, we can state that Substance A weighs x grams, give or take a small measurement error.

Is the same true in research on matching? In one sense, yes. If response rate

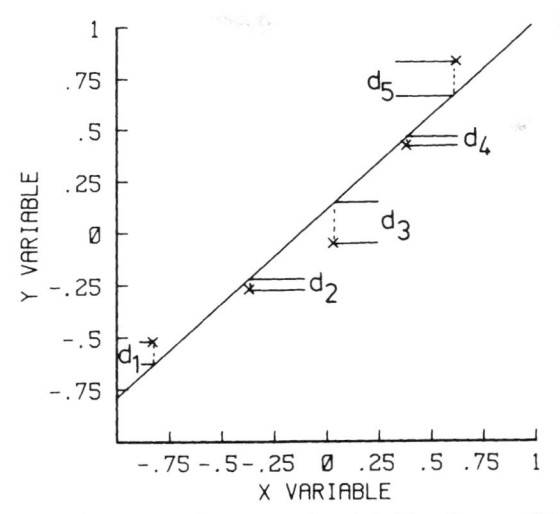

FIG. 5.1. Least-squares linear regression operates by minimizing the sum of the squares of the deviations of the obtained data from the best-fitting straight line in terms of the Y variable. The deviations are shown as d_1 to d_5, which correspond to the difference between the data point and the predicted data point $(Y_i - Y'_i)$ in the text.

is related to, say, *nominal* VI-schedule value, the nominal value has no variance. But as soon as we try to relate response rate to, say, arranged reinforcer rate, variance creeps in, for nominal "VI 60-s schedules" may all differ slightly. When we try to relate response rate to the obtained reinforcer rate, we are relating two *measures* both of which have measurement error, and thus clearly fail to meet Assumption 1. (Note also that the sequence of VI intervals that the animal is exposed to does depend on the behavior that the animal emits—if it fails to respond for a while, the rate falls.)

This discussion shows that Assumption 1 of linear regression is very often not met. So we must now ask, what is the effect of violating this assumption? It is to decrease the estimate of the slope of the relation (Isaac, 1970; Kendall, & Stuart, 1977). However, traditionally, least-squares linear regression has been used in matching research with rather little thought, and some of the alternative techniques are neither well known nor well developed. This state of affairs is unsatisfactory (Davison & McCarthy, 1981), and we believe that strong statements about slopes in relation to normative slopes should be avoided until more appropriate techniques are developed.

Assumption 2. The data (Y values) are normally distributed for each value of X. Is this assumption generally met in matching research? The answer to this depends on the measures that are related. For instance, Tustin and Davison (1978) showed that log-response ratios were normally distributed for five different values of log-reinforcer ratios. But we do not know whether we can generalize from this result to assert that all log response-ratio measures are normally distributed. On the other hand, relative response rates $[B_1/(B_1 + B_2)]$ *cannot* be normally distributed over the range 0 to 1. Obviously, close to the extremes, the distribution will be truncated by the upper and lower limits of the relative measure, and the effect of this will again be to decrease the estimated slope.

Assumption 3. The data have equal variance for all X values. Again, Tustin and Davison (1978) showed this was true for log response-ratio measures under log reinforcer-ratio variations. But, again, the assumption cannot be met (for the reason above) by relative measures.

5.3. LEAST-SQUARES REGRESSION: PROCEDURE

N is the number of (X_i, Y_i) pairs, and summations are always over N. Y'_i is the value of Y predicted from the best-fitting line for X_i. X_m and Y_m are mean values of X and Y.

1. Slope, s:

$$s = \frac{\Sigma(X_iY_i) - NX_mY_m}{\Sigma(X_i^2) - NX_m^2} = \frac{N\Sigma(X_iY_i) - \Sigma X_i\Sigma Y_i}{N\Sigma(X_i^2) - (\Sigma X_i)^2} \, .$$

2. Intercept, c:

$$c = Y_m - sX_m \, .$$

3. Variance accounted for, VAC:

$$VAC = \frac{\Sigma(Y'_i - Y_m)^2}{\Sigma(Y_i - Y_m)^2} = \frac{\Sigma(Y_i - Y_m)^2 - \Sigma(Y_i - Y'_i)^2}{\Sigma(Y_i - Y_m)^2} = r^2 \, ,$$

where r is the product-moment correlation. In words, the proportion of variance accounted for is the Y variance accounted for by the fitted line divided by the total Y variance. If it is negative, it indicates that more variance in the data is accounted for by the mean (that is, $Y = c$) than by the fitted line.

4. The standard error of the estimate, σ:

$$\sigma_{y \cdot x} = \sqrt{\left(\frac{\Sigma(Y_i - Y_m)^2}{N - 2} \right)} \, .$$

5. Mean square error, MSE:

$$MSE = \frac{\Sigma(Y_i - Y'_i)^2}{N} \, .$$

6. Standard deviation of the slope, σ_s:

$$\sigma_s = \frac{\sigma_{y \cdot x}}{\sqrt{\Sigma(X_i - X_m)^2}} \, .$$

7. t test against a defined slope, s_o:

$$t = \frac{s - s_o}{\sigma_s} \, , \quad \text{d.f.} = (N - 2) \, .$$

8. Standard deviation of the intercept, σ_c:

$$\sigma_c = \frac{\sigma_{y \cdot x} \sqrt{\Sigma(X_i)^2}}{\sqrt{N \, \Sigma(X_i - X_m)^2}} \, .$$

9. t test against a defined intercept, c_o:

$$t = \frac{(c - c_o)}{\sigma_c} \, , \quad \text{d.f.} = (N - 2) \, .$$

10. t test for a slope difference between two fitted lines, s_1 and s_2:

$$\sigma^2_{(1,2)y \cdot x} = \frac{\Sigma(Y_{1i} - Y'_{1i})^2 + \Sigma(Y_{2i} - Y'_{2i})^2}{N_1 + N_2 - 4} \, ,$$

$$\sigma_{s1-s2} = \sqrt{\left[\sigma^2_{(1,2)y \cdot x} \left(\frac{1}{\Sigma(X_{1i} - X_{m1})^2} + \frac{1}{\Sigma(X_{2i} - X_{m2})^2} \right) \right]} \, .$$

If the theoretical slope difference to be tested is $s_{o1} - s_{o2}$:

$$t = \frac{(s_1 - s_2) - (s_{o1} - s_{o2})}{\sigma_{s1-s2}} \, , \quad \text{d.f.} = (N_1 + N_2 - 4) \, .$$

5.4. INTERPRETING THE SUMMARY STATISTICS IN PARAMETRIC REGRESSION

The obtained slope, s, and intercept, c, are estimates of the true relation between the Y and X variables, given the assumptions are met. Unless the straight line fits the data perfectly, these parameters will be estimated with a certain degree of error. This error is measured by the standard deviations of the slope and intercept. (Of course, a standard deviation is a reasonable measure only if the estimates are normally distributed.) Clearly, the poorer the line fits, the larger are the standard deviations. There will be a point at which the parameter estimates are not statistically significantly different from a zero estimate (or from another, theoretically predicted, estimate). This situation can be tested by the t tests given in Section 5.3, Parts 7 and 9, if normally distributed estimates can be assumed. It is our contention that these standard deviations are the best indices of the goodness of fit of the straight line—small standard deviations indicate that the parameters have been precisely estimated. No absolute criterion can be given, but Davison (1987) suggested that an acceptable standard deviation of slope was less than one tenth the slope estimate. This may be reasonable for a slope around 1.0, but this criterion cannot be generally asserted. For instance, a slope of 0 with a standard deviation of 0.01 is an excellent fit and an excellent parameter estimate. From such arguments, perhaps an absolute criterion of, say, 0.1 would prove more satisfactory. But two other points should be borne in mind. First, the importance of a data set usually derives from a number of subjects, rather than a single subject, and a range of slope and intercept standard deviations is to be expected. All contribute to the final interpretation of the data. Second, a developing science should expect criteria such as these to tighten progressively as we learn better to control experimental confounds.

The standard error of the estimate is an estimate of the standard deviation of the data from the fitted line. Again, this should be small, though no numerical criterion can be given. Mostly, though, we shall be interested in parameter estimates rather than the general accuracy of prediction. The mean-square error measures a similar quantity. Being related to the square of the standard error of the estimate, which in matching research is usually less than 1.0, it is a smaller quantity than the standard error. Hence, it must be confessed, it looks rather better than the standard error! Another quantity of the same sort is the mean error, which is the mean of the unsigned Y deviations from the fitted line. These measures all have very reasonable *relative* significance, indicating a better or a worse fit, but they are difficult to interpret absolutely. Between fits on different coordinates (e.g., relative plots versus log-ratio plots), they even have no relative significance.

The most common measure of goodness of fit reported in the literature is the variance accounted for, either as a proportion or as a percentage. To gain this measure, the error sum of squares, $[\sum (Y_i - Y'_i)^2]$ is subtracted from the total sum of squares, $[\sum (Y_i\text{-}Y_m)^2]$, and divided by the total sum of squares. This measure appears to have superb face validity, but it has fatal drawbacks. The first of these is that the measure is directly correlated with the slope. Given the same absolute error variance, if the slope tends to zero, then the VAC tends to zero, because all the variance is error variance. As the slope tends to infinity, so the VAC tends to 1.0. A second problem is that a straight line can fit a perfect curve with a very high VAC—but the standard deviations of the slope and intercept would be substantial. Of course, there is absolutely no substitute for plotting the data, at which point a systematic deviation from the straight line would become obvious, at least to a trained observer. Skills of this sort are, however, difficult to train because they are not verifiable on any fixed criteria. Rather, they are based on a consensus across researchers. A more formal way of determining the presence of systematic deviations from straight lines is to plot the deviations of the data from the predictions $(Y_i - Y'_i)$ as a function of the independent variable for each subject, and to test these deviations using, say, a Friedman analysis of variance (Section 5.9).

Notice that the original linear-regression assumption that the Y data be equally and normally distributed for the regression to provide unbiased estimates of the slope and intercept is replaced, in the t tests, by an assumption that the slope and intercept estimates are themselves normally distributed. If a researcher is unwilling to make this assumption, nonparametric methods may be used to test slopes and intercepts (Section 5.5) estimated by least-squares regression. Remember always, though, that a nonsignificant finding does *not* entitle us to assert an identity—only that a significant difference has not been obtained. But viewing the suitably plotted data may allow us to assert an identity, though we may not be able to assert it with much generality. Statistical analyses, we have found, can even irretrievably muddy a set of data that shows clear effects visually. The interocular trauma test (does the relation hit you between the eyes?) is often the best, most convincing, test.

5.5. NONPARAMETRIC REGRESSION

Because least-squares linear regression assumes that the data are distributed normally with equal variance for each value of the X variable, that procedure is called a *parametric* procedure. Nonparametric regression makes fewer assumptions about the data than does parametric regression. In particular, the data do not have to be normally distributed, nor do they have to be homoscedastic (distributed with the same variance at each X value). The requirements are:

1. The X values have no variance.
2. The errors are mutually independent.
3. Each error comes from the same continuous population.

The method is due to Theil, and is well described by Hollander and Wolfe (1973). The procedure is quite simple, but is rather tedious even with a computer. The slope of the line between every different combination of data points (X_i,Y_i and X_j,Y_j), and the intercept that this slope implies, are calculated. Thus, for five data points, there will be $4 + 3 + 2 + 1 = 10$ slopes and intercepts. The nonparametric estimates of the slope and intercept of the relation are the medians of the obtained sets of slopes and intercepts.

Computation

The slope between each pair of data points $(X_i,Y_i),(X_j,Y_j)$ is given by:

$$s = \frac{Y_i - Y_j}{X_i - X_j},$$

and the intercept, c, by:

$$c = Y_i - sX_i = Y_i - X_i\left(\frac{Y_i - Y_j}{X_i - X_j}\right).$$

Example

The data shown in Table 5.1 were obtained by Beautrais and Davison (1977) in an experiment on concurrent second-order schedules. We have calculated the slope between each pair (i, j) of data points. The median slope is 0.840, and the median intercept is -0.023. Thus, the best-fitting straight line is:

$$Y = .84X - .02 .$$

This equation is rather similar to the results of a parametric least-squares regression, which gives:

$$Y = .86X - .05 .$$

One possible measure of the goodness of fit of a nonparametric regression is the proportion of Y variance accounted for by the fit, but problems with that measure have already been noted. A measure of the accuracy of the estimates of the slope and intercept measures can be obtained by finding the interquartile range (IQR) of the distribution of estimates. For the slope, the sixth-ranked slope is 0.684, and the sixteenth is 1.012. For the intercept, the IQR is -0.077 to + 0.058.

Such summary statistics can be supplemented by inferential statistics. For instance, a test of whether the obtained slope is different from a defined slope, s_o, is available (Hollander & Wolfe, 1973). This is known as the Theil test. It asks whether a set of data systematically trend away from a theoretical slope.

TABLE 5.1

Data Obtained by Beautrais and Davision (1977) From Pigeons Responding on
Concurrent Second-Order Schedules[a]

Condition	X	Y	Pair	Slope	Intercept
1	0	−0.077	1,2	1.485	−0.077
2	0.301	0.370	1,3	−0.04	−0.077
3	−0.125	−0.072	1,4	0.860	−0.077
4	−0.477	−0.487	1,5	0.820	−0.077
5	0.477	0.314	1,6	0.903	−0.077
6	−0.776	−0.778	1,7	0.767	−0.077
7	0.778	0.520	2,3	1.038	0.058
			2,4	1.012	0.065
			2,5	−0.318	0.466
			2,6	1.066	0.049
			2,7	0.315	0.275
			3,4	1.179	0.075
			3,5	0.641	0.008
			3,6	1.084	0.064
			3,7	0.656	0.010
			4,5	0.840	−0.086
			4,6	0.973	−0.023
			4,7	0.802	−0.104
			5,6	0.872	−0.102
			5,7	0.684	−0.012
			6,7	0.835	−0.130

[a] X, the independent variable, is the log obtained reinforcer-frequency ratio, and Y, the dependent variable, is the log ratio of the numbers of completions of first-order FR-5 components.

Theil Test: Method

First, order the X and Y values in increasing size of X, then construct a column labeled P, which is the expected value of Y given the theoretical slope s_o (that is, $P_i = s_o X_i$). A further column, D, is then constructed, which is the difference between Y_i and P_i. It should be evident that the values of D_i, the obtained-predicted difference, which are ordered according to the value of X_i, will show a trend if the data differ in slope from the theoretical slope. To test this trend, we use a nonparametric trend test (e.g., Ferguson, 1965; see Section 5.10). This is most simply done by counting instances of increases and decreases between each D_i and subsequent D_is (there are thus 21 combinations). Increases are counted as $+1$, and decreases as -1, and then the total is summed to give the statistic, K. The significance of this statistic is then assessed from Tables (e.g., Table A.21 in Hollander & Wolfe, 1973, or Table XI in Bradley, 1968).

Example

The following example is shown in tabular form using the data from Beautrais and Davison (1977) previously given.

X	Y	P (s_oX)	D $(Y - P)$
-0.776	-0.778	-0.078	-0.700
-0.477	-0.487	-0.048	-0.439
-0.125	-0.072	-0.013	-0.059
0	-0.077	0	-0.077
0.301	0.370	0.030	0.340
0.477	0.314	0.048	0.266
0.778	0.520	0.078	0.442

We will assess whether the slope is significantly greater than 0.1. The rank-ordered X values and their associated Y values are given in the first two columns in the above table. All subsequent D_is are greater than D_1, so count $+6$. All are also greater than D_2, so count $+5$. For D_3, one is less and three are greater, so count $+2$. For D_4, all are greater ($+3$), for D_5, one is greater and one is smaller ($+0$), and for D_6, one is greater ($+1$). Thus, $K = 17$. With $\alpha = 0.05$, the critical value of K for $N = 7$ is 13, on a one-tailed test. We conclude that the estimated slope was significantly greater than 0.1.

Notice that because a trend test was used here, the intercept value is irrelevant. Thus, all the D_is might be negative (or positive) in the above example if the intercept was very different from zero, but the trend will be the same.

Testing the Intercept

Given that a difference from a theoretical intercept was to be tested, the numbers of intercept estimates in the nonparametric regression below, and above, the theoretical intercept could be counted, and a Binomial test (e.g., Siegel, 1956) used to assess the significance of the distribution. A similar procedure could be used to test slope estimates.

A Nonparametric Test for Parallel Lines

The test of whether $s_1 = s_2$ is given by Hollander and Wolfe (1973). There are no further assumptions beyond those for nonparametric regression.

The procedure is first to compute the slopes between all pairs of points as in nonparametric regression, for both data sets. Then, each slope for Line 1 is *randomly* paired with a slope for Line 2 (if there are unequal numbers of slopes, that is, unequal numbers of data points for the two fits, slope estimates from the larger set are randomly discarded to equalize the numbers). The differences between each pair of estimates are then calculated, and a Wilcoxon Matched-Pairs Signed-Ranks test is carried out (Section 5.8). This requires (e.g., Marascuilo & McSweeney, 1977) ranking the differences, attaching the sign of the difference to the rank, and summing the positive (or the negative) ranks. If the lines differ in slope, then clearly there will be more positive (or negative) ranks than expected by chance. This is assessed by consulting, for example, Table A.21 in Marascuilo and McSweeney.

5.6. STRUCTURAL RELATIONS

The requirements of both the regression models discussed so far have included the assumption that the X variables are fixed and have no variance. These procedures, therefore, do not allow two dependent measures to be regressed one on the other. The structural-relations procedure (Kendall & Stuart, 1977) is a *parametric* procedure that assumes that the X variable does have variance. As a parametric procedure, it does require that both the X and Y variables are normally distributed and that the variances of the distributions are the same *within*, but not between, the variables. Procedures for various cases are given by Kendall and Stuart, but here we describe only the most useful in this area.

The most common problem occurs when we attempt to regress one dependent variable on another. For the procedure we outline, we need to know only the ratio of the variances of the distributions. For instance, if we were regressing one dependent variable on another with properties that we can assume identical (for instance, a log response-rate ratio on another such measure), we could assume that the ratio of variances was 1.0.

The standard least-squares regression procedure minimizes the square of the deviations of the Y measure from the predicted Y', that is, in a vertical direction on the plot. This is known as regression of Y on X. Regression of X on Y would minimize the X variance, that is, horizontally on the plot. The structural-relations procedure minimizes variance measured between these two extremes depending on the ratio of the Y and X variances, that is, at an angle between 90° and 180°. When the ratio of Y to X variances is infinite, standard least-squares regression (Y on X) results. When the ratio is zero, the regression is X on Y as all the variance is in the X measure.

Computation

The parameter λ is the ratio of the Y to X data variances. The slope estimate, s, is given by:

$$s = \frac{V(Y) - \lambda V(X) + \sqrt{[(V(Y) - \lambda V(X))^2 + 4\lambda C(XY)^2]}}{2C(XY)} \, ,$$

where

$$V(Y) = \Sigma(Y_i - Y_m)^2 \, ,$$
$$V(X) = \Sigma(X_i - X_m)^2 \, ,$$

and

$$C(XY) = \Sigma(X_i - X_m)(Y_i - Y_m) \ .$$

The intercept is, as usual:

$$c = Y_m - sX_m \ .$$

Confidence limits for structural relations fits are given by Kendall and Stuart (1977).

Using a standard least-squares linear regression with data that do have X variance will lead to an underestimate of the slope of the relation between the variables (Isaac, 1970). It has been argued (Davison & McCarthy, 1981) that data collected for matching law analyses do have X variance (as the log obtained reinforcer ratio varies both from time to time and from session to session). Thus, the standard linear-regression analysis may underestimate sensitivity to reinforcer frequency.

5.7. SOME OTHER USEFUL STATISTICAL PROCEDURES

Here, we shall assume that we are dealing with data from a small number of subjects (up to six or eight) and, in the spirit of the experimental analysis of behavior, that each subject is exposed to all conditions. Under such conditions, we shall naturally use nonparametric procedures to assess significance. The choice of a particular test depends on the level of measurement we believe we have achieved in an experiment. Generally, in this area, we should attain at least *ordinal* measurement—that is, each data point meaningfully asserts a greater than, or less than, relation with any other data point. Often, we may want to assume that our measures reach at least an *interval* scale, in which the distances between two points are meaningful, but in which the scale and the zero point are arbitrary. Siegel (1956) gives an extensive discussion of measurement scales.

In selecting an appropriate test, we also need to take into account the design of the experiment, for instance, whether there are only two samples (two levels of the independent variable), or whether there are more. We stress again that we are assuming that the samples are from the same subjects across all levels of the independent variable.

5.8. TWO RELATED SAMPLES, ORDINAL MEASUREMENT

We may wish to discover whether slope (sensitivity to reinforcer frequency) values obtained from six subjects working on multiple VI VI schedules are different at two different levels of deprivation. The following algebraic estimates of a values (each from two experimental conditions) were obtained by Charman and Davison (1983a) at 80 percent and 90 percent body weights.

Data

	a Value at:	
Bird	80%	90%
151	0.44	0.48
152	0.55	0.64
153	0.21	0.31
154	0.21	0.16
155	0.40	0.43
156	0.25	0.62

On the basis of previous research (Herrnstein & Loveland, 1974) we expect that the a values will be greater for 90 percent body weights, implying a one-tailed test. (Note that Charman & Davison did not report such an analysis.)

Two tests may be used to assess the significance of the difference in a values:

Sign Test

This test is very rapid with a small number of subjects (small N). All that is required is to count how many of the matched pairs of data differ in the same direction. Five of the pairs show a positive difference, and one a negative difference (that is, favoring H_o). A table of binomial probabilities (e.g., Table D in Siegel, 1956) shows that the probability of this result on a one-tailed hypothesis is 0.11. With a rejection criterion of $\alpha = 0.05$, the obtained differences were nonsignificant.

Wilcoxon Matched-Pairs Signed-Ranks Test

This more powerful test can be carried out if we can assume that both the difference between measures within subjects and the differences between measures across subjects are at least ordinal. For this test, we calculate the differences between each a value at the two deprivation levels, rank the *absolute* (unsigned) differences, and attach the sign of the difference to the ranks. This procedure is shown in the table on page 76.

One set of like-signed ranks is now summed, giving $\bar{T} = 3$, and a table of critical values of $\bar{T}$ is consulted (e.g., Table A.21 in Marascuilo and McSweeney (1977). [The table given by Siegel, 1956, does not give a critical value of $\bar{T}$ for a one-tailed test at $\alpha = 0.05$.] Table A.21 gives a probability of 0.078, and thus

Bird	a Value at:		Diff.	Signed Rank
	80%	90%		
151	0.44	0.48	0.04	+2
152	0.55	0.64	0.09	+4
153	0.21	0.31	0.10	+5
154	0.21	0.16	0.05	−3
155	0.40	0.43	0.03	+1
156	0.25	0.62	0.37	+6

again the difference is nonsignificant. Indeed, the table shows that significance could only be attained if either there were no negative differences, or only the smallest difference was negative.

Thus, neither the Sign test nor the Wilcoxon Matched-Pairs Signed-Ranks test allowed us to assert that there were statistically significant differences between the estimates of a at the two deprivation levels. Generally, the Wilcoxon test is to be favored as it is the more powerful of the two.

If we were to claim that our measures of a reached an interval scale, and if the conditions of an experiment were carried out in a random order, an even more powerful test is available: the Randomization test for matched pairs.

The Randomization Test for Matched Pairs

The Randomization test assumes that the signs of the differences that we observed between the two deprivation levels come from a distribution of differences with different signs that might have occurred if, for example, we had conducted the two conditions in reverse order. The differences we obtained were:

0.04   0.09   0.10   −0.05   0.03   0.37

From this data set, the sum of the differences, ΣD_i, was 0.58. But if the sign of the differences was random, there would be 2^{64} such ΣD_is. With $\alpha = 0.05$, there would be 0.05 x 64 = 3.19 of these in the extreme regions of rejection. Rounding this to three cases, and dividing these into upper and lower rejection regions, on such a two-tailed test only the most extreme results would have a probability of occurrence of less than 0.025. The most extreme ΣD_is in the above set occur when either all the differences are positive, or when they are all negative ($\Sigma D_i = \pm 0.68$). For a one-tailed test, all three cases of rejection will occur at only one end of the distribution of ΣD_is. With the directional hypothesis that the higher deprivation condition will give larger a values, they will all be positive. The most extreme positive ΣD_is are:

+0.04   +0.09   +0.10   +0.05   +0.03   +0.37 $\Sigma D_i = 0.68$
+0.04   +0.09   +0.10   +0.05   −0.03   +0.37 $\Sigma D_i = 0.62$
−0.04   +0.09   +0.10   +0.05   +0.03   +0.37 $\Sigma D_i = 0.60$

The obtained ΣD_i was smaller than these three most extreme ΣD_i values, and so again the null hypothesis cannot be rejected at $\alpha = 0.05$.

All three tests on the present data agreed that the observed differences were nonsignificant. However, such an agreement will not always occur as the three tests are differentially powerful in rejecting the null hypothesis. The Randomization test is the most powerful of the three.

5.9 MANY RELATED SAMPLES, AT LEAST ORDINAL MEASUREMENT

For this situation, the Friedman analysis of variance is useful. The data used here are from k conditions over N subjects (if $k = 2$, the Friedman test is a Sign test). To demonstrate this test, we extend the data used in the above examples (Charman & Davison, 1983a) by including two more body weights (85 percent and 100 percent). Thus we have $k = 4$ conditions and $N = 6$ subjects. The slopes obtained for each of these conditions are shown in the following chart:

	Percent Body Weight			
Bird	80	85	90	100
151	0.44	0.41	0.48	0.94
152	0.55	0.57	0.64	0.59
153	0.21	0.17	0.31	1.57
154	0.21	0.18	0.16	0.53
155	0.40	0.48	0.43	1.04
156	0.25	0.47	0.62	0.61

The test commences by ranking the a values within birds across conditions. The rank matrix is:

	Percent Body Weight			
Bird	80	85	90	100
151	2	1	3	4
152	1	2	4	3
153	2	1	3	4
154	3	2	1	4
155	1	3	2	4
156	1	2	4	3
$R_j =$ 10 11 17 22				
$R_j^2 =$ 100 121 289 484				

The sum of the ranks, R_j, and the squares of these sums, are shown in the lower section of the chart. If all conditions had given essentially the same value of a, the sums of the ranks would all be about equal. The squares of the sums are themselves summed over the $k = 4$ conditions, to give $\Sigma R_j^2 = 994$. The Friedman statistic, χ_r^2 is then obtained from the equation:

$$\chi_r^2 = \frac{12\Sigma R_j^2}{N \cdot k \cdot (k+1)} - 3 \cdot N \cdot (k+1) \, .$$

The value for the above data set is $\chi_r^2 = 9.4$, and this value is checked for significance against the χ^2 distribution (e.g., Siegel, 1956, Table C) with $(k-1) = 3$ degres of freedom. For $\alpha = .05$, the criterion is $\chi_r^2 = 7.82$, and thus the null hypothesis of no difference can be rejected. Post hoc tests (Marascuilo & McSweeney, 1977) can be used to determine just which of the differences is or are significant.

Note, however, that the Friedman test was not optimal for this example. Since the condition (body-weight percentages) fall on an ordinal scale, rather than just being nominal, further tests may be carried out. For example, orthogonal polynomial analyses can be carried out to assess the presence of a linear, or nonlinear, trend (see the Page test, Marascuilo & McSweeney, 1977, p. 374). Such a test is particularly useful when a series of conditions is arranged, and the measures are expected to be ranked over conditions in some particular way. Note, however, that any orthogonal polynomial test for trend is a test directly on the ordering of the ranks, not of the data themselves. Remember, also, that any orthogonal polynomial analysis is a test for a linear (or whatever) *component*, and that many curves do have, for example, strong linear components. Thus, such a test for linearity, say, does not tell us whether the relation is linear or nonlinear.

The Friedman test can, however, be used directly as a nonparametric test for departures from linearity. This would be done by fitting a straight line to a data set, and then testing the *residual* $(Y_i - Y'_i)$ values for the set of conditions with a Friedman test. A significant result indicates a significant departure from linearity.

5.10. A NONPARAMETRIC TEST FOR TREND

A useful test for trend is that given by Ferguson (1965). It can be applied to single subjects, or equally to a group of subjects exposed to the same set of conditions.

To demonstrate the use of this test, we shall use the same data that we used with the Friedman analysis of variance (Charman & Davison, 1983a). The data are reproduced as follows:

| Bird | Percent Body Weight | | | | S |
	80	85	90	100	
151	0.44	0.41	0.48	0.94	4
152	0.55	0.57	0.64	0.59	4
153	0.21	0.17	0.31	1.57	4
154	0.21	0.18	0.16	0.53	0
155	0.40	0.48	0.43	1.04	4
156	0.25	0.47	0.62	0.61	4

Note that the experimental conditions (percentage body weights) are ordered from small to large. The statistic, S, is calculated for each bird by taking the measure in each successive column, and counting $+1$ for each measure to the right of it that is larger and -1 for each that is smaller. For example, the first sensitivity value for Bird 151 is 0.44. At 85 percent body weight, the sensitivity was 0.41 (count -1), at 90 percent it was 0.48 (count $+1$), and at 100 percent it was 0.94 ($+1$). The second sensitivity was 0.41 (at 85 percent), at 90 percent it was larger ($+1$), and at 100 percent it was larger ($+1$). At 90 percent, the measure was 0.48, and it was larger at 100 percent ($+1$). Thus, the total for Bird 151 was $+4$. The same summation procedure is carried out for all the subjects, and the values of S are summed over birds to give a statistic called ΣS, which is 20 in this case. The significance of ΣS is assessed against the normal deviate thus:

$$z = \frac{\mid \Sigma S \mid - 1}{\sqrt{[Nk(k - 1)(2k + 5)/18]}}$$

For a two-tailed test, significance at $\alpha = 0.05$ is attained if $z > 1.96$, and significance at $\alpha = 0.01$ if $z > 2.58$. The corresponding values for a directional test are 1.64 and 2.33. For the present data, $N = 6$ subjects and $k = 4$ conditions, and $z = 2.64$. Thus, on a directional test (based on previous research), we can conclude that the value of a increased significantly with increasing body weight for these data.

Note that this trend test is for a monotonic trend only. The nature of the trend (linear, curvilinear) is not assessed. Also note that it is easy, from the formula above, to construct a table of critical values for ΣS for commonly used Ns and ks. Care must be taken, however, with small values of N and/or k for which the normal-deviate (z) method given above is inaccurate. As a very rough rule of thumb, if $N.k$ is less than about 12, the exact tables given by Ferguson (1965) should be consulted.

In the above formula, when $N = 1$, the test for trend is for a single subject over k conditions. For $N = 1$ and k less than 10, the table given by Ferguson (1965) must be consulted. Because of the effect of small k values on the sampling distribution of ΣS, significance cannot be attained at $\alpha = 0.05$ with fewer than 4 conditions (directional test) or 5 conditions (nondirectional test). At $\alpha = 0.01$, at least 5 conditions (directional) or 6 conditions (nondirectional) are required for significance to be possible. These limitations, and those generally for small N and/or k values, must be taken into account in experimental design.

6 CONCURRENT-SCHEDULE RESEARCH I: REINFORCER PARAMETERS

This chapter and the two following chapters deal with the effects of several independent variables on performance on concurrent schedules. Initially, we focus on concurrent VI VI schedules, the schedule pair for which the matching and generalized matching relations were developed. In this chapter, we consider the effects on behavior allocation of reinforcer rate, reinforcer duration (or amount), reinforcer quality, and reinforcer delay in isolation. We also look at the interactions between some of these variables.

6.1. REINFORCER-FREQUENCY RATIOS

In Chapter 4, we discussed the initial results obtained by varying reinforcer frequencies on concurrent VI VI schedules. In particular, we showed how some systematic deviations from the equality of response and reinforcer ratios led researchers in the early 1970s to use a generalized version of the matching law. This approach was summarized by Baum (1974a). Baum, with support from Myers and Myers (1977), reported that sensitivity values in the generalized matching law (Equation 4.2) often fell below 1.0. He took the view that this probably represented the effects of error variance (uncontrolled fluctuations in other independent variables that control choice) in combination with a true sensitivity of 1.0. In trying to understand the sources of error, Baum mentioned three factors: poor discrimination between the alternatives, changeover delay, and deprivation.

1. *Poor Discrimination Between the Alternatives.* By this, Baum (1974a) clearly meant the discrimination of the stimuli signaling the two alternatives

(e.g., key colors in the switching-key procedure, or left versus right in the two-key procedure). The effects of discriminability on sensitivity to reinforcer frequency have been shown by Miller, Saunders, and Bourland (1980, see Section 8.7). They investigated changeover-key concurrent performance with the two components signaled by different line orientations displayed on the main key. Sensitivity to reinforcer frequency decreased with decreasing orientation differences. However, it seems unlikely that a lack of stimulus differentiation is a major source of undermatching in concurrent schedules. Research in our own laboratory (Charman & Davison, 1983b, see Chapter 9) has shown that red versus green keylight stimuli, which are commonly used to signal concurrent-schedule alternatives, are perfectly discriminable to pigeons even in multiple VI VI schedules, in which discrimination might be expected to be worse. Left versus right keys are also highly discriminable to pigeons, as a considerable amount of research on detection performance has shown (Chapter 11).

A second source of discrimination failure, not mentioned by Baum (1974a), but which appears much more likely, is the failure to discriminate perfectly the different reinforcer rates obtained from two keys or in the presence of two stimuli. This possibility has not been directly investigated, so far as we know, but it would be surprising if a pigeon mensurated a VI 30-s schedule as twice the reinforcer rate of a VI 60-s schedule. This possibility has been discussed by Wearden (1980), who related Stevens' Law for time estimation (a power of about 0.8) to the oft-reported sensitivity to reinforcer-ratio values in concurrent VI VI schedule performance.

Yet another possibility is that the subjects may "misallocate" reinforcer deliveries to either incorrect responses or incorrect reinforcer sources. Indeed, some unpublished research in our laboratory by Peter E. Jenkins showed that pigeons were very poor at reporting, after a reinforcer, which response produced that reinforcer. This finding is consistent with research reported by Killeen and Smith (1984) that showed that reinforcer deliveries may "erase" control by events occurring before them (a sort of retroactive interference). A working model for this effect can quite easily be constructed, and has been formally described by Davison and Jenkins (1985; see also Section 8.7). For instance, if d_r was the discriminability of the reinforcer sources,

$$\frac{B_1}{B_2} = c\left(\frac{d_r R_1 + R_2}{d_r R_2 + R_1}\right). \tag{6.1}$$

If discrimination is perfect, $d_r \to \infty$, and strict matching results. If discrimination is absent, $d_r = 1$, and the behavior ratio does not change with variations in R_1 and R_2. Equation 6.1 mimics the generalized matching law rather well, though it is slightly nonlinear on log response ratio versus log reinforcer-frequency ratio coordinates. Equation 6.1 fits Miller, Saunders, and Bourland's (1980) data well with d_r values for 0°, 15° and 30° separations of, respectively, 1.5, 2.5 and 39. The parameter d_r is, clearly, related to the parameter d in Davison and Tustin's (1978) signal detection model (Chapter 11). d_r should, of course, take a value of 1.0 when the orientation differences were zero. But the subjects in Miller, Saunders, and Bourland's experiment were probably discriminating, to some extent, on the basis of reinforcer frequency (i.e., "staying" following a reinforcer delivery). This finding is discussed more fully by Davison and Jenkins (1985).

2. *Changeover Delay.* The second variable that Baum (1974a) implicated in the production of undermatching ($a < 1$) was the changeover delay (see Section 8.6). At present, the best *published* data on the effects of changeover-delay duration come from Shull and Pliskoff (1967). Using independent concurrent VI 60-s VI 180-s schedules in a switching-key procedure, Shull and Pliskoff increased the changeover delay from 0 to 20 s, and then reduced it again. Because the procedure used independent schedules, the obtained reinforcer ratio did covary with the changeover-delay duration. Figure 6.1 shows point estimates of the value of a in the generalized matching law as a function of changeover-delay value. (Note that such point estimates are obtained by assuming zero bias, log $c = 0$, and therefore the absolute values of a cannot be unambiguously interpreted. The trends are, however, interpretable if bias is simply assumed constant.) Figure 6.1 rather clearly shows that while a values did increase with changeover delay in the ascending series, they did not decrease when the changeover delay was reduced. Thus, Baum's (1974a) conclusion that "with no changeover delay or too short a changeover delay preferences tend to . . . (remain) too near indifference" (p. 232) does not accurately represent the reported data. After exposure to longer changeover delays, performance tends to remain sensitive to reinforcer-frequency variation, though the time course of this maintenance is unknown (Shull and Pliskoff generally conducted only five sessions per condition). Similarly, while Shull and Pliskoff reported no trends within conditions, it remains questionable whether extended exposure to a short changeover delay might increase the value of a. But, contrary to this suggestion, recent evidence (Todorov, Castro, Hanna, Bittencourt de Sa, & Barreto, 1983) suggests that a may fall with an extended exposure to a 3-s changeover delay.

In a much more extensive investigation of the effects of changeover-delay value on concurrent VI VI performance, Scown (1983) found essentially no change in a values for changeover delays of 2 to 15 s, though she did report that a was lower when *no* changeover delay was arranged. (Since she used a two-key concurrent schedule, "no changeover delay" indicates that a reinforcer could be delivered for the first response on the alternate key. A 0-s changeover delay in this procedure would require at least one response on the alternate key before a response could be reinforced as the changeover delay normally commences with the first response on the alternate key. For a switching-key concurrent schedule,

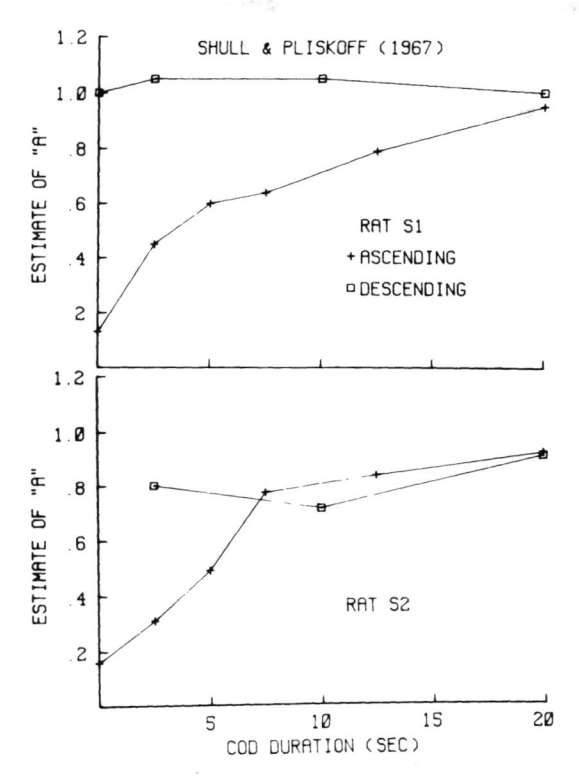

FIG. 6.1.   Effects of increasing and decreasing the changeover-delay interval on point estimates of sensitivity to reinforcer frequency. The data are from Shull and Pliskoff (1967).

in which the changeover delay is timed from the switching response, "no changeover delay" and "0-s" changeover delay are identical.)

   Overall, then, research does not strongly suggest that changeover-delay value systematically affects the value of *a* except, possibly, in the sense of a history of exposure to different changeover-delay values. More work clearly needs to be done, and Baum's (1974a) conclusion may require modification.

   3. *Deprivation.* The third parameter that Baum (1974a) suggested affected *a* was deprivation. Here, Baum referred to research on multiple VI VI schedule performance (Herrnstein & Loveland, 1974) which showed that *a* tended to 1.0 when deprivation was decreased. (Generally, reviewers of this area have been wary of using multiple-schedule data to support arguments about concurrent-schedule performance. The average *a* value for multiple VI VI performance is about 0.45 [Charman & Davison, 1982; McSweeney, Farmer, Dougan, & Whipple, 1986], but these values have not been taken as part of the population of *a* estimates for concurrent schedules.) Deprivation, however, does not affect concurrent VI VI schedule performance (McSweeney, 1975a).

Baum (1979) again suggested three factors that may promote a values less than 1.0. One of these (changeover delay) was the same as in his 1974a paper, and we dealt with this effect previously. The second was asymmetric pausing. To extend his argument, as did Taylor and Davison (1983), if a subject paused for a time (T_p) after responding on a schedule as a simple proportion of the time it spent responding on that schedule (T_b), that is,

$$T_{p1} = kT_{b1}, \text{ and } T_{p2} = kT_{b2} ,$$

then the ratio of the usual measures of time allocation (T_1/T_2) would be perfect estimates of the ratio of times actually spent responding:

$$\frac{T_1}{T_2} = \frac{T_{p1} + T_{b1}}{T_{p2} + T_{b2}} = \frac{kT_{b1} + T_{b1}}{kT_{b2} + T_{b2}} = \frac{T_{b1}}{T_{b2}} .$$

But, if the subject paused proportionally longer on the lower reinforcer-rate schedule, then:

$$\frac{k_1 T_{b1} + T_{b1}}{k_2 T_{b2} + T_{b2}} ,$$

will be more extreme than T_1/T_2, and thus $a < 1$ will be found for conventional time-allocation measures. If the subject paused more on the higher reinforcer-rate schedule, then T_1/T_2 would *overestimate* the relation between time-allocation ratios and reinforcer ratios. There are no published data on this question, but data collected in our laboratory have almost always favored the second alternative. This suggests that the finding that a for time measures is greater than a for response measures (and is closer to 1.0 for time measures) should be interpreted as an overestimation of the time a value, rather than an underestimation of the response a value.

The third reason for undermatching given by Baum (1979) is what he called "inconstancy of preference." By this, he means that schedules such as FI schedules may contain periods in them in which the reinforcer rate is effectively zero—that is, that an FI schedule may approximate a Tandem Extinction VI schedule (see Schneider, 1969). As a result, there may be periods within concurrent VI FI performance when the reinforcer ratio is infinite (concurrent VI Extinction) and other periods when it is not (concurrent VI VI). Averaging across these periods could give underestimates of a values. Baum extended the argument to VI schedules by noting that the smallest interval comprising the VI may define a period of Extinction. It has been common for some researchers employing arithmetic VI schedules to use a smallest interval that is a linear function of the average interval. By contrast, those who use exponential (constant probabilty or geometric, see Catania & Reynolds, 1968) schedules generally have kept a constant shortest interval. A similar suggestion was made by Taylor and Davison (1983).

Under the same heading of inconstancy of preference, Baum (1979) also suggested that differential satiation for two different reinforcers may affect the slope of the matching relation.

Like Baum (1974a, 1979), de Villiers (1977) also argued that the normative value of a was 1.0 for concurrent VI VI schedules, but that uncontrolled variation of aspects of procedure (like changeover delay) tended always to decrease the value of a. We are not convinced, though. If it were the case that Equation 6.1 is a correct description, it is evident that any suboptimal differentiation of either the stimuli signaling the reinforcer sources, or the alternative rates of reinforcers themselves, would tend to produce a shift toward $a < 1$. A changeover delay would help these differentiations and shift the value toward 1.0. But a values would still have an error of estimation. If these errors were normally distributed, a values greater than 1.0 (not allowed by Equation 6.1) would occasionally be reported. Indeed, exactly this type of distribution of a, skewed toward lower values of a, with a mode less than 1.0, has been clearly documented by Baum (1979), Wearden and Burgess (1982), Mullins, Agunwamba, and Donahoe (1982), Taylor and Davison (1983) and Baum (1983). The question disputed in these papers is whether the obtained values of a from empirical research indicate that a is significantly, or consistently, less than 1.0. However, the assumption that there is an a value that characterizes concurrent VI VI schedule performance may be wrong. As soon as we admit that the value of a can be affected by independent variables (like changeover-delay duration, or even situations in which the time allocated to the concurrent schedules is constrained [Tustin & Davison, 1978]), we can perhaps only assert a maximum a value of 1.0 and a range of values depending on the values of other dependent variables and on statistical sampling.

Many researchers (see Baum, 1979, and Wearden & Burgess, 1982) have found that modal values of a for time allocation do not depart reliably from 1.0. We have already suggested above that time-allocation sensitivities may be overestimated for other reasons (Taylor & Davison, 1983). Taylor and Davison also found higher response-allocation a values for concurrent exponential-VI schedules than for concurrent arithmetic-VI schedules, which might indicate generally better differentiation of the former. There is even some indication from the data of Heyman (1979) that relatively high a values may be obtained from concurrent exponential schedules when no changeover delay is arranged.

In summary, then, it seems that a range of sensitivities to reinforcer-frequency ratios has been obtained and that these values may be affected by changeover delays (perhaps irreversibly), by schedule types (e.g., exponential versus arithmetic, or FI versus VI, see Chapter 7), by the discriminability of stimuli signaling the responses, and by temporal constraints placed on the performances. In Chapter 11 we discuss sensitivity to reinforcer frequency measured in signal-detection procedures and show that those values, like concurrent-schedule values, typically are less than 1.

6.2. OVERALL REINFORCER RATES

Only one experiment has explicitly investigated the effects of overall reinforcer rates on the relation between response ratios and obtained reinforcer ratios (Fantino, Squires, Delbrück & Peterson, 1972). Using a two-key procedure, with independently arranged concurrent VI schedules and a changeover delay of 1.5 s, they studied performance on concurrent VI 6-s VI 12-s, VI 60-s VI 120-s, and VI 600-s VI 1200-s schedules. The first of these schedule pairs gave exclusive choice, and thus an infinite reinforcer ratio, for six of the seven subjects. This necessitated replicating this condition with a dependent-scheduling procedure. Fantino et al. reported that strict matching occurred for all overall reinforcer rates, but this assessment was done, according to the *zeitgeist*, on relative response and reinforcer measures. Table 6.1 shows point estimates of a values calculated from Fantino et al.'s data. Again, we note that a point estimate of a assumes zero bias, and that the data of prime interest are the trends in a, rather than their absolute values.

TABLE 6.1
Point Estimates of a From Fantino, Squires, Delbrück, and Peterson (1972)[a]

Subject	VI 600–1200	VI 60–120	VI 6–12 (I)	VI 6–12 (D)
1	0.48	0.61	—	—
2	0.88	1.16	—	—
3	0.47	0.75	—	—
4	1.19	0.62	0.98	0.93
5	0.47	0.78	—	0.90
6	0.58	0.72	—	0.91
7	0.39	1.07	—	−0.36
Mean	0.64	0.82		

[a] I and D refer to independent- and dependent-scheduling procedures respectively. VI-schedule values are in seconds.

Table 6.1 shows some interesting effects. First, six of the seven birds showed an increase in a between VI 600 s VI 1200 s and VI 60 s VI 120 s. Of the four birds that were exposed to both concurrent VI 60 s VI 120 s and dependent concurrent VI 6 s VI 12 s, three showed an increase in a (the other, Bird 7, showed a substantial decrease). Thus, there were no statistically significant trends in a. While this result is consistent with Fantino et al.'s finding, the conclusion is weak, and the failure to reject the null hypothesis is largely due to a lack of data. There are, in fact, indications that the conclusion could be wrong. It seems important to replicate this experiment extensively, at least varying reinforcer ratios over five values at three different overall reinforcer rates. According to the generalized matching law, three identical functions should be found. A strong parametric test for parallelism of the functions could determine whether this was the case.

If the data in Table 6.1 were taken as reasonable estimates of absolute values of a (the mean data, for instance, should be relatively free from bias unless there were systematic differences between the key forces or the reinforcer durations), Fantino et al.'s (1972) conclusion that the data showed strict matching is not supported. The mean a values are all below 1.0, and only three of the 19 individual values were above 1.0.

Despite the small amount of explicit research done on the effects of variations in overall reinforcer rates in concurrent schedules, there is a strong laboratory lore that a is independent of overall reinforcer rates. Much of this lore is due to experiments that have varied reinforcer ratios by keeping one schedule constant and varying the other—thus concomitantly varying the overall reinforcer rate. Many such experiments, especially early in concurrent-schedule research, reported strict matching, thus supporting the independence of a from overall reinforcer rate. In later research of this type, using generalized matching analyses, any effect of overall reinforcer rate could be hidden by the sensitivity parameter itself, because a progressive decrease in a as the schedules are made more disparate would simply result in an overall lower estimate of a. Consider the following data set:

Schedules	a	$log\ B_1/B_2$	$log\ R_1/R_2$
Conc VI 20 s VI 60 s	1.0	.477	.477
Conc VI 30 s VI 60 s	0.9	.271	.301
Conc VI 60 s VI 60 s	0.8	0	0
Conc VI 120 s VI 60 s	0.7	−0.211	−0.301
Conc VI 180 s VI 60 s	0.6	−0.286	−0.477
Conc VI 240 s VI 60 s	0.5	−0.421	−0.602

A curve fit to these data gives $a = 0.79$ (SD = 0.05) and $log\ c = 0.05$ (SD = 0.02) with 99 percent of the variance accounted for. From this example, it is clear that if a did decrease with overall reinforcer rate, the resulting data would not be discriminable from published populations of a values (e.g., Baum, 1979), nor from general expectations about values of $log\ c$. This discussion suggests that one of the suppressed requirements of the generalized matching law—that a be independent of overall reinforcer rate—has not been adequately tested (Anderson, 1978). Lab lore is no substitute for explicit experimental analyses.

6.3. REINFORCER AMOUNT AND DURATION

We have already discussed early research on reinforcer duration (Catania, 1963b; Neuringer, 1967) in Sections 1.2 and 1.7. These reports of strict matching to reinforcer-duration ratios were confirmed by Brownstein (1971), who showed that time-allocation ratios also strictly matched reinforcer-duration ratios. However, Fantino, Squires, Delbrück and Peterson (1972) investigated response allocation on concurrent equal-VI schedules (VI 600 s VI 600 s, VI 60 s VI 60 s, and VI 10 s VI 10 s) with a 6-s reinforcer duration on one schedule and a 1.5-s duration on the other. A changeover delay of 1.5 s was used. As the schedules were independent, response allocation tended toward exclusivity for the concurrent VI 10-s VI 10-s conditions. Because of this result, it is possible to analyze the data on the relation between response ratios and obtained reinforcer-frequency ratios to give a slope estimate (sensitivity to reinforcer frequency) and an intercept (bias toward the 6-s reinforcer duration over the 1.5-s duration). Taking the data from all six birds and three conditions together, a was 0.88 (SD 0.06) and the intercept value was 0.32 (SD 0.04) with 92 percent of the data variance accounted for. The intercept is an estimate of:
Assuming that log c is statistically zero, and given $M_1 = 6$ s and $M_2 = 1.5$ s, the estimate of b, sensitivity to reinforcer duration, is 0.53. Fantino et al.

$$b \log(M_1/M_2) + \log c .$$

reported that behavior ratios failed to equal (strictly match) the frequency-times-duration ratios, that is:
and the sensitivities to reinforcer-frequency ratios and reinforcer-duration ratios that we calculated above support their conclusion. The reanalysis allows us to

$$\frac{R_1 \cdot M_1}{R_2 \cdot M_2} ,$$

discriminate between reinforcer-frequency and reinforcer-duration effects. It allows us to assert mild undermatching to reinforcer-frequency ratios, and strong undermatching to reinforcer-duration ratios. Again, research on discrete-trial signal-detection procedures supports this assertion (Chapter 11).

The results of this reanalysis are supported by two further experiments. Todorov (1973) reported data from pigeons exposed to three pairs of concurrent schedules, signaled by different key colors, within each session. A blackout of between 0 and 1 s followed each changeover. It is unclear whether the schedules were dependent or independent. In this somewhat unusual procedure, Todorov varied both the reinforcer durations and the reinforcer frequencies on the keys. Using a generalized matching analysis (though the fitting procedure is unspecified—presumably multiple linear regression), he reported a mean sensitivity to reinforcer duration of 0.27 (range 0.2 to 0.4), and a mean sensitivity to reinforcer rate of 0.9 (range 0.5 to 1.2). Time-allocation sensitivities tended to be lower than response-allocation sensitivities for both reinforcer duration (0.17) and reinforcer frequency (0.5).

The second experiment that found lower sensitivities to reinforcer amounts than to reinforcer frequencies was reported by Schneider (1973). He used dependent concurrent VI VI schedules, a changeover delay of 1.5 s, and varied both reinforcer frequencies and the number of pellets delivered to pigeons per reinforcer. From a multiple linear-regression analysis, he reported a sensitivity to reinforcer frequency of 0.6 and a sensitivity to the ratio of the number of pellets of 0.34. These three results are, therefore, quite convincing and consistent— behavior is less sensitive to changes in reinforcer durations or amounts than to changes in reinforcer frequencies.

However, some problems remain. First, the amount eaten is likely not to be a linear function of reinforcer duration. In other words, except in the Schneider (1973) report, the obtained food amounts are not the independent variable in the fits as required by the generalized matching law and by the logic that behavior should be related to input, not potential input. Epstein (1981) has shown that the amount eaten from a standard pigeon magazine is a negatively accelerated function of the duration of the magazine cycle. This implies that if the ratio of magazine times was kept constant and the mean duration increased, the ratio of amounts eaten will progressively move toward 1.0. If amount eaten was the controlling variable, this would suggest that the relation between log response ratios and log duration ratios, given, say, one duration constant at 3 s, would be nonlinear and concave downward.

Sufficient data to test this possibility were not reported by Fantino et al. (1972), by Schneider (1973), nor by Todorov (1973). They were, however, provided by Davison and Hogsden (1984). Their experiment was concerned primarily with trying to quantify the effects of arranging mixed reinforcer durations on one key of a two-key concurrent VI VI schedule with a 3-s changeover delay. Two different reinforcer durations (M) were arranged on the left key, and these are designated M_{L1} and M_{L2}, respectively. The obtained numbers of reinforcers of each duration per session are designated N_{L1} and N_{L2}. A single reinforcer duration (M_R) was arranged on the right key, and N_R of these reinforcers were obtained per session. Any quantitative model of such performance must reduce to the generalized matching law when $M_{L1} = M_{L2}$. The specific model investigated was:

$$\frac{B_L}{B_R} = c \cdot \frac{(N_{L1}M_{L1}{}^d + N_{L2}M_{L2}{}^d)^a}{N_R{}^a M_R{}^{ad}} , \qquad (6.2)$$

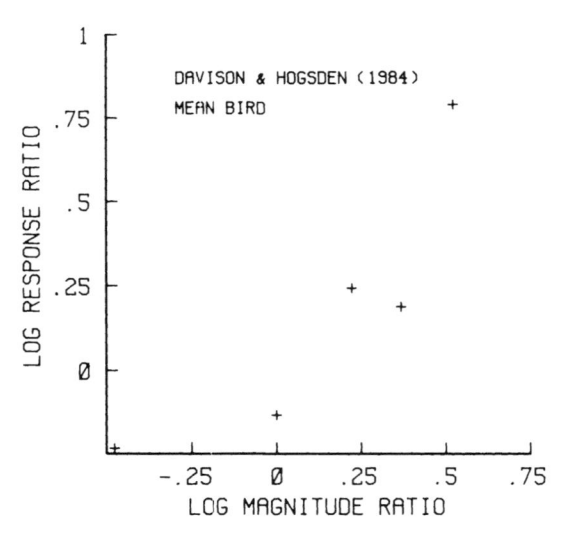

FIG. 6.2. Log response ratio as a function of log reinforcer-magnitude (duration) ratio. The data were averaged from Davison and Hogsden (1984).

which, when $M_{L1} = M_{L2}$, reduces to

$$\frac{B_L}{B_R} = c \cdot \frac{M_{L1}^{ad}}{M_R^{ad}} \cdot \frac{(N_{L1} + N_{L2})^a}{N_R^a} \ .$$

The power ad on the reinforcer-duration terms means that overall reinforcer-duration sensitivity will depend on reinforcer-frequency sensitivity, and that any variable that affects the latter will affect the former.

In Part 1 of Davison and Hogsden's (1984) experiment, M_{L1} was 1 s, M_{L2} was 7 s, M_R was 3 s, the schedules were both VI 120 s, and the probability with which the 1-s reinforcer occurred on the left key was varied. Part 3 was the same as Part 1 except that M_{L1} was 3 s and M_{L2} was 10 s. In Part 2, M_{L1} was 3 s, M_R was 3 s, the schedules were concurrent VI 60 s (left) VI 120 s (right), the probability of the left-state 1 reinforcer was 0.5, and the reinforcer duration in left-state 2 was varied from 0 to 10 s. The quantitative model proposed by Davison and Hogsden (Equation 6.2) described the data rather poorly. As a result, Davison and Hogsden were led, in Part 4 of their experiment, to arrange a baseline series of concurrent VI VI schedules with 3-s reinforcers on both keys. This produced an entirely standard set of a values ranging from 0.72 to 1.05 (mean 0.87). Finally, in Part 5, they arranged VI 120-s schedules on both keys, 3-s reinforcers on the right key, and varied the reinforcer duration on the left key from 1 to 10 s. The results, averaged over the six birds, are shown in Fig. 6.2. The data were clearly nonlinear on log-log coordinates, and hence could not be fitted with a constant value of b.

Davison and Hogsden's (1984) result is surprising in the light of previous research. But, as they pointed out, the generalized matching law for reinforcer duration had been accepted on the basis of a rather sparse data set. Notice that the data shown in Fig. 6.2 cannot be explained by assuming that the relation between the amount eaten and the reinforcer duration was nonlinear in the manner described by Epstein (1981). His results would predict a concave-downward function. Neither can they be explained by assuming that the subjects took a constant time to move from the key to the food hopper, thus decreasing all reinforcer magnitudes by a constant amount. If this constant time was 0.5 s, say, the reinforcer-duration ratio of 1/3 would become a ratio of 0.5/2.5 (a log ratio of -0.7). With reinforcer durations of 10 and 3 s, the corresponding ratio would be 9.5/2.5, a logarithmic value of 0.58. It is evident from Fig. 6.2 that assuming a constant latency of eating would do little, if anything, to linearize the data.

A second, and quite different, potential problem comes from the research reported by Keller and Gollub (1977). They used independent concurrent VI VI schedules arranged on two keys with a 2-s changeover delay. In Experiment 1, they varied both reinforcer frequencies (keeping a total of 60 per hour) and reinforcer durations (keeping the sum at 6 s) over seven experimental conditions. Seven conditions in a study with two independent variables is rather too few from which to make strong conclusions. However, they reported that relative response rates were generally less extreme than relative frequency-times-duration measures (that is, less extreme than strict matching to the combined independent variables would predict). Thus, the data were generally consistent with the three experiments discussed above. The data presented by Keller and Gollub can be used in multiple linear regression analyses to assess the parameters of the concatenated generalized matching law. The results of this analysis are shown in Table 6.2. Using all three subjects' data, sensitivity to arranged reinforcer-duration ratios (0.5) was less than sensitivity to reinforcer-frequency ratios (0.62). This confirmed the reports of Schneider (1973) and of Todorov (1973). However, the overall estimate of sensitivity to reinforcer frequency (which of course contains some between-subjects variability) had quite a large standard deviation, indicating some nonlinearity or other error variance. Individually, the subjects showed a range of sensitivity values. Neither frequency nor duration sensitivity was consistently the greater, but sensitivity to reinforcer frequency always had the larger standard deviation.

In a second experiment, Keller and Gollub (1977) investigated whether the source of ''undermatching'' was the prolonged exposure to a variety of experimental conditions in Experiment 1. This latter experiment used (presumably) independent concurrent VI VI schedules, but the VI schedules were constant-probability schedules, rather than arithmetic schedules as used in Experiment 1. There is no statement that a changeover delay was used in Experiment 2, but the implication of the procedure is that it was the same as for Experiment 1. Each of seven pigeons was initially trained on concurrent VI 120-s

TABLE 6.2

The Results of Multiple Linear Regression Analyses of the Data Reported by Keller and Gollub (1977: Experiment 1)[a]

Bird	b(SD)	a(SD)	%VAC
P108	0.25(0.16)	0.87(0.22)	88
P128	0.57(0.10)	0.23(0.12)	93
P129	0.59(0.08)	0.72(0.11)	97
All data	0.50(0.09)	0.62(0.12)	84

[a]*a* is sensitivity to reinforcer frequency, and *b* is sensitivity to reinforcer amount.

(3-s reinforcer) VI 120-s (3-s reinforcer) schedules. They were then exposed to one other condition in which either the reinforcer-frequency ratio or the reinforcer-duration ratio, or both, was varied. Reinforcer rates again summed to 60 per hour, and reinforcer durations to 6 s. The relative response rates in the second condition closely matched the relative obtained reinforcer frequency-times-arranged-duration ratios. The results therefore seem to suggest that continued exposure to experimental conditions depresses sensitivity values (see also Todorov et al., 1983), but this conclusion is not unequivocal. First, the change in Experiment 2 to constant-probability (exponential) schedules would be expected to increase sensitivity to reinforcer frequency (Taylor & Davison, 1983). This is, in retrospect, a major confound. Second, the data from Conditions 1 (equal schedules and reinforcer durations) and 2 (either unequal schedules or unequal reinforcer durations or both) can be used to provide point estimates of sensitivity to the frequency-times-duration ratios. This sensitivity averaged 1.12, in line with Keller and Gollub's conclusions. But there were large variations in the sensitivities for the individual birds (range 0.78 to 1.69, with two estimates greater than 1.5). Naturally, point estimates of sensitivities will have a large error of estimation, but this reanalysis again shows that the experimental results do not strongly support the conclusions.

Another way to approach Keller and Gollub's (1977) Experiment 2 data is to carry out a multiple linear regression across the two conditions and seven birds. This gives estimates of 1.06 for both sensitivities (reinforcer frequency and duration), but the standard deviation of the duration sensitivity is 0.2, giving a ± 2 SD range of 0.66 to 1.46. The frequency sensitivity is rather better estimated (SD 0.11). Keller and Gollub's conclusions require further empirical support.

6.4. QUALITY OF REINFORCERS

This aspect of matching research is an example of the normative use of the generalized matching law—that is, using the relation as a measuring stick to obtain other, not directly accessible, measures. First, though, why do we use the term "quality"? Quality is a property of reinforcers that does not lie on a single, clearly defined dimension, for example, a hamburger and a piece of candy. We probably cannot predict which will be the more effective reinforcer even in particular situations. But we can adequately name the events, and thus the scale of quality is nominal.

The generalized matching law (Equation 4.2) bias term allows the *quantitative* measurement of the relative effectiveness of two reinforcers. We can assert:

$$\log\left(\frac{B_1}{B_1}\right) = a \log\left(\frac{R_1}{R_2}\right) + q \log\left(\frac{Q_1}{Q_2}\right) + \log c ,$$

where Q is a measure of quality. The simplest use of this equation is to measure preference with equal reinforcer rates ($R_1 = R_2$) such that:

$$\log\left(\frac{B_1}{B_2}\right) = q \log\left(\frac{Q_1}{Q_2}\right) + \log c . \tag{6.3}$$

If $\log c$ was zero, then the log behavior ratio equals q times the log quality ratio. However, such point estimates, as we have mentioned, have a large error of estimation. Also, for an individual subject, the assumption that $\log c = 0$ is unreasonable.

We can overcome both these problems to some extent if, in a second condition, the qualities are reversed between the keys (two-key procedure) or key colors (switching-key procedure). In the second condition,

$$\log\left(\frac{B_3}{B_4}\right) = q \log\left(\frac{Q_2}{Q_1}\right) + \log c , \tag{6.4}$$

and subtracting Equation 6.4 from Equation 6.3 we obtain:

$$\log\left(\frac{B_1}{B_2}\right) - \log\left(\frac{B_3}{B_4}\right) = q \log\left(\frac{Q_1}{Q_2}\right) - q \log\left(\frac{Q_2}{Q_1}\right) , \text{ or}$$

$$.5 \log\left(\frac{B_1 \cdot B_4}{B_2 \cdot B_3}\right) = q \log\left(\frac{Q_1}{Q_2}\right) , \tag{6.5}$$

which is a point estimate of the effects of the quality ratio that is not confounded by the inherent bias. Equally, an estimate of the bias can be obtained by adding Equations 6.3 and 6.4:

$$.5 \log\left(\frac{B_1 \cdot B_3}{B_2 \cdot B_4}\right) = \log c .$$

The behavioral measure specified by Equation 6.5 measures the quality sensitivity (q) times the log quality ratio (log Q_1/Q_2), and is a useful measure of the relative reinforcing effects of the two qualities. It remains, however, a point estimate, derived from a minimum number of conditions. It is not a least-squares estimate. We might note here, by the way, that q and the quality ratio (Q_1/Q_2) cannot be separated without varying Q_1/Q_2 *quantitatively*—which cannot, by definition, be done. Second, note that the effectiveness of reinforcers as measured is entirely relative and cannot be absolute. Unless a standard reinforcer is prescribed, the assessment of quality differences must always be pairwise, and cannot be related to a nonoverlapping set of qualities. In an early version of the first paper on this topic (Hollard & Davison, 1971), the authors suggested setting up an International Standard Reinforcer (750ml of a well-loved New Zealand beer) in Paris, along with the other international standards. Reviewers of the paper did not find this suggestion humorous, nor did they take it seriously.

We might note here that Equation 6.5, which is an algebraic combination of the data from two conditions of an experiment, can be obtained in quite a different way. The reversal of the keys that provided Q_1 and Q_2 could be arranged within sessions, rather than across conditions, using conditional discriminations. Two highly discriminable stimuli would be used, which we will call S_1 and S_2. When S_1 is presented, Q_1 is obtained for left-key responses, and Q_2 for right-key responses. In the presence of S_2, the outcomes are reversed between the keys. Left-and right-key responses in the presence of S_1 (B_1 and B_2) and in the presence of S_2 (B_3 and B_4) are measured. Such a procedure has not, we believe, been used in conventional concurrent-schedule research, but it is always used in the matching approach to signal detection (Chapter 11) in order to measure stimulus discriminability and response bias.

A more accurate way of measuring the quantitative effects of different qualities is to estimate the measure from a least-squares curve fit. Thus, Hollard and Davison (1971; see Section 4.2) used a dependent concurrent VI VI procedure with a changeover delay of 2 s. They varied the reinforcer rates on the VI schedules over four conditions (in two other conditions, Extinction was arranged on one key, but such data cannot be used in a generalized matching fit). On one key the reinforcer was 3-s access to wheat, and on the other it was 15 s of brain stimulation. The brain stimulation was aimed at the ectostriatum, but was actually delivered in the paleostriatum (Hollard & Davison, 1978). The brain-stimulation intensity was between 200 and 300 μA for the three subjects. As Fig. 4.2 shows, mean sensitivity to reinforcer frequency was 0.78 (responses) and 1.08 (time allocation), and the intercepts to the fitted lines were 0.65 (responses) and 0.71 (time). Thus, for response measures, assuming that log c was zero, $q \log(Q_1/Q_2) = 0.65$. The antilog of this value is 4.5, suggesting that 3-s access to wheat is 4.5 times more reinforcing than 15 s of paleostriatal brain stimulation. However, such a bold conclusion must be tempered with statements concerning the intensity, location, and duration of the brain stimulation, the type of wheat, the deprivation level, and so on. Also, the assumption that $\log c = 0$ is not warranted. A much better experimental practice would be to conduct a set of control manipulations in which the relative frequencies of two identical wheat reinforcers on the two schedules were parametrically varied to assess properly the individual values of $\log c$. The effects of the quality differences would then be measured by the difference in intercepts of the two fitted lines. A problem would arise, however, if the *slopes* of the two fitted lines were significantly different.

The Hollard and Davison (1971) technique, despite some methodological defects, remains a good demonstration of how the generalized matching law can be used normatively. Subsequently, the technique was used by Miller (1976) to construct hedonic scales for three types of grain (buckwheat, hemp and wheat) for pigeons. Miller used a switching-key concurrent VI VI schedule with a 6-s changeover delay. The schedules were independent. Miller arranged five different reinforcer-frequency ratios for each of the three pairwise combinations of grains, and hence obtained a least-squares estimate of the intercept ($q \log Q_i/Q_j + \log c$) for each combination. Taking the data averaged across four subjects, the slopes of the relations were very close to 1.0. The log intercept for buckwheat versus hemp was 0.043, for wheat versus buckwheat it was 0.145, and for hemp versus wheat it was -0.15. We may now write three equations:

$$b \log Q_b - b \log Q_h + \log c = .043$$

$$b \log Q_w - b \log Q_b + \log c = .145$$

$$b \log Q_h - b \log Q_w + \log c = -.15,$$

where the Subscripts b, h and w denote buckwheat, hemp, and wheat, respectively. Adding these equations gives:

$$3 \log c = .038 ,$$

and thus $\log c = 0.013$. Therefore, bias (between the key colors) was effectively zero. We shall take it as zero in subsequent calculations. The hedonic scale is constructed by assigning an arbitrary value of 1 to $b \log Q_b$. Thus:

$$1 - b \log Q_h = .043$$

$$b \log Q_w - 1 = .145$$

Thus, $b \log Q_h = 0.957$ and $b \log Q_w = 1.145$. Taking antilogarithms, if buckwheat has a scale value of 10, hemp has a scale value of about 9, and wheat has a value of about 14. Time-allocation data gave a similar ordering of the grains, but slightly different absolute values.

A second experiment using the Hollard and Davison (1971) technique was reported by Matthews and Temple (1979), who measured preferences between hay and dairy meal in cows. The cows worked on concurrent VI VI schedules for these two reinforcers. The schedules were dependently arranged, and the changeover delay was 2 s. The value of log c was obtained from a single experimental condition in which hay was delivered for both responses on concurrent VI 60-s VI 60-s schedules. When this bias was removed from the data obtained from five reinforcer-frequency variations, two subjects showed preferences for hay, while the other four showed preferences for dairy meal. Time-allocation measures gave similar results. A feature of these results is the very low sensitivity to reinforcer ratios shown by the cows—for responses, $a = 0.41$ and for time allocation, $a = 0.63$. These low a values may be related to the amount of "other" or extraneous behavior (B_e, Section 3.2) shown by cows, who spend a great deal of the session time chewing the cud and licking around the food hoppers. Drs. Temple and Foster, at Ruakura Animal Research Station, Hamilton, New Zealand, have done a great deal more work on food, food-additive, and lick-block preferences in cows, and have extended their research to questions of agricultural feed preferences in sheep, goats, and chickens as well. We believe that a similar technique is being used with dog feeds. Given that such measures are relatively stable, this normative use of the generalized matching law clearly has economic and commercial value, as well as the potential to answer some important questions about physiological and pharmacological effects.

6.5. REINFORCER DELAY

Chung (1965a) and Chung and Herrnstein (1967; see Section 1.7) were the first researchers to explore the effects of delay of reinforcers on concurrent VI VI schedule performance. Chung and Herrnstein used independent concurrent VI 60-s VI 60-s schedules with a changeover delay of 1 s. For four subjects, left-key responses were reinforced after an 8-s delay (with both keys blacked out and, presumably, the VI timers stopped), while the delay in blackout on the right key was varied from 1 to 30 s. For the other subjects, the left-key delay was 16 s, and the right-key delay was varied from 1 to 30 s. Chung and Herrnstein reported strict matching to inverse-delay (D) ratios, or direct matching to immediacy (I) ratios, where immediacy is the reciprocal of delay. That is, in ratio terms:

$$\frac{B_1}{B_2} = \frac{D_2}{D_1} = \frac{I_1}{I_2}.$$

The data appeared clearly to support strict matching, when plotted on relative coordinates. However, some other results did not lend support to strict matching to relative reinforcer immediacy. Neuringer (1969) and Shimp (1969b) showed

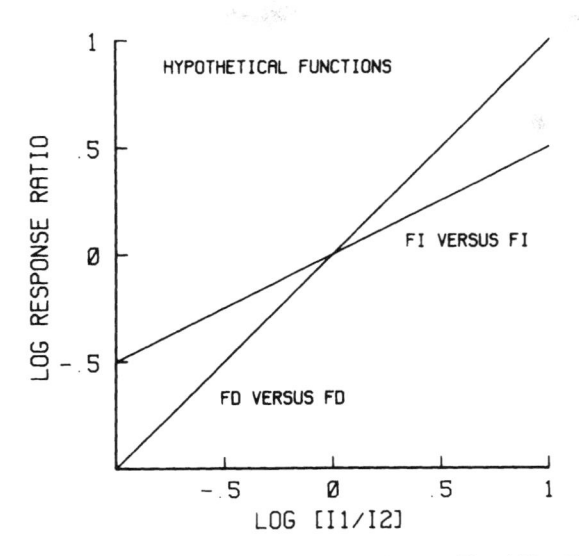

FIG. 6.3.   Two hypothetical generalized matching relations between FI and FI and between FD and FD that could result if subjects were indifferent between FI and FD schedules when they were the same interval to reinforcers. The two functions could, however, have different sensitivities to unequal delays or unequal intervals, as shown in the figure.

that pigeons were indifferent between (showed equal choice for) delays to reinforcement in blackout and FI schedules of reinforcement of the same time value. The latter procedure is usually thought of as a *concurrent-chain schedule*, as mentioned in Section 1.3 and discussed more fully in Chapter 10. Given Neuringer's and Shimp's results, all the studies that have varied FI terminal links in concurrent-chain schedules (e.g., Davison & Temple, 1973, 1974; Duncan & Fantino, 1970) become relevant data for the delay of reinforcement question. None of these found strict matching to immediacy ratios. Thus, some problem exists in this apparently logical train of evidence, and there are three possibilities.

First, the Neuringer (1969) and Shimp (1969) findings might not have generality. For instance, these studies were done with only one value of the equal initial-link VI schedules, and indifference might not, say, be found for shorter concurrent VI VI initial links. Second, while the indifference point between FI and fixed-delay (FD) schedules might indeed occur when the delays and intervals are equal, the functions relating preference to immediacy ratios for FD and for FI schedules might be different. This means that, for example, preference between FD 10 s versus FD 60 s will not be the same as between FI 10 s and FI 60 s. Such a situation is diagrammed in Fig. 6.3. Third, Chung and Herrnstein's (1967) conclusion could be wrong. These problems were faced by Williams and Fantino (1978), who showed that Chung and Herrnstein's data were indeed misconstrued. Substantial differences existed between data obtained when the varied delay was less than, versus more than, 16 s. As a result, we can probably assert that fixed delays and fixed intervals to reinforcement do control concurrent-schedule performance in the same way, and that neither generally produces strict matching. The situation is much more complex than originally envisioned, and is described in more detail in Chapter 10. To anticipate our later conclusion, the generalized matching law with constant parameters does not apply to delays and to fixed intervals to reinforcers. Rather, the sensitivity parameters are (currently) variables that are controlled by the values of experimental parameters.

We would be foolish to focus only on the third possibility mentioned above. Without explicit research, we cannot reject by default the possibility that Neuringer's (1969) and Shimp's (1969) results lack generality or that FD and FI schedules affect preference differently.

7
CONCURRENT-SCHEDULE RESEARCH II: SCHEDULE TYPES

7.1. CAVEAT

This chapter must begin with a caveat. The name of a schedule is not, when research becomes relatively advanced, a useful "independent variable." That is, it is often uninformative, and occasionally totally misleading, to compare, for example, FI and VI schedules. The defining feature of a VI schedule is that the intervals between reinforcers are not constant. Yet, there is clearly a difference between a VI schedule comprising 12 intervals and one comprising three intervals. A VI schedule that comprises two intervals is called a mixed-interval (MI) schedule, and one with a single interval is called an FI schedule. Thus, one extreme of the continuum "number of intervals" is a VI, and the other is an FI. Again, as the mean interval of a VI (or an FI) schedule is decreased, the contingency becomes more and more like an FR 1 schedule. Many other dimensions are probably important to a schedule's effect on behavior, and these, too, may not be adequately reflected in a schedule's name.

Research in the experimental analysis of behavior did, of course, commence with the schedule name as the qualitative independent variable (Ferster & Skinner, 1957). This approach has continued, though the nominal aspect of the schedule has become less important (e.g., Killeen, 1968). There are two roads from nominalism to quantification. The first is to conduct empirical research that determines what dimensions of schedules (e.g., mean interval, number of intervals, variance in intervals, etc.) affect behavior. Rather little of this has been done. The second, and more radical, is to rid ourselves of the schedule names provided by Ferster and Skinner, and, in the absence of such a framework, to provide measures of the supposedly important aspects of the relation between behavior and reinforcers. One of these approaches is exemplified by the *feedback function*, which quantitatively describes the way that the environment changes (e.g., changes in the rate of reinforcers) when an animal's behavior changes (e.g., changes in the rate of responding).

In the long term, the more profitable approach is to eschew the names of schedules altogether and to design experiments that use mathematically defined absolute feedback functions (AFFs) or relative feedback functions (RFFs) to investigate behavioral effects. (An RFF defines a distribution of reinforcers between two behaviors or between a defined behavior and other, undefined, behaviors. An AFF defines the overall rate of reinforcers for various rates of one or more responses.) An elegant example of this approach was reported by Vaughan (1981; see Section 8.5). These considerations are, however, more for the future than for the present.

7.2. CONCURRENT FR FR, VR VR, and FR VR PERFORMANCE

Because there is a fixed molar relation between response rate and reinforcer rate in concurrent-ratio schedules, a sensitivity of 1.0 always occurs trivially in generalized matching analyses of performance on these schedules. This can easily be shown from the *feedback function* for these schedules:

$$R_1 = \frac{B_1}{c_1} ,$$

where B is the response rate, R is the reinforcer rate (on the same timebase), and c is the average number of responses per reinforcer. Thus, for two concurrent-ratio schedules,

$$B_1 = c_1 \cdot R_1$$

and

$$B_2 = c_2 \cdot R_2 ,$$

and hence:

$$\log\left(\frac{B_1}{B_2}\right) = \log\left(\frac{R_1}{R_2}\right) + \log\left(\frac{c_1}{c_2}\right) .$$

The size of the bias ($\log c_1/c_2$) is the ratio of the average response requirements. Hence, the data obtained from a particular pair of concurrent-ratio schedules will have a sensitivity to reinforcer frequency of 1.0, but with a bias that is idiosyncratic to that schedule pair. The data from a different pair of schedules will not lie on the same generalized matching function. The relation between response and reinforcer ratios is therefore empirically uninteresting. The point on the function at which behavior on a pair of schedules stabilizes is, though, unpredictable by the generalized matching function and could be of some interest. In fact, research on concurrent FR FR schedules (Herrnstein, 1958) and on concurrent VR VR schedules (Herrnstein & Loveland, 1975) has shown that this aspect of preference is also rather uninteresting. Generally, subjects respond exclusively on the schedule with the fewer responses required, thus minimizing the number of responses emitted per reinforcer obtained and also maximizing the overall reinforcer rate. One should be careful in interpreting such data as demonstrating the "law of least effort," though. The relation between response allocation and reinforcer deliveries on the two choices has a strong positive feedback relation—that the more responses emitted on a key, the more reinforcers obtained from that key. In other words, the relative feedback function for concurrent-ratio schedules has a slope of 1.0 and is not flat over part of its range as is the RFF for concurrent VI VI schedules (see Fig. 7.1). A unit-slope RFF produces a trivial sensitivity of 1.0. Thus, the exclusive responding that characterizes concurrent FR FR and concurrent VR VR schedule performance is not necessarily controlled by differences in the response requirements, but is probably also controlled by the change in the reinforcer ratio consequent on any change in the response ratio (via positive feedback). If the reinforcer-frequency ratio is maintained at 1.0 while the FR response requirements are varied (e.g., via a second-order concurrent VI [FR:S] VI [FR:S] schedule; Beautrais & Davison, 1977), preference is not exclusive, but is controlled directly by the requirement ratio. Thus, in the interpretation of results, it is important to bear in mind any dependently changing choice-controlling variables that are confounded with the independent variable under study. The same point has been made extensively by McCarthy and Davison (e.g., 1981a) in their research on signal-detection performance (Chapter 11).

A somewhat different set of results is obtained when concurrent FR VR schedule performance is investigated. Rider (1979), using rats, investigated concurrent FR x VR 50 schedules. No changeover delay was arranged, and a forced-choice procedure supervened whenever nine consecutive reinforcers had been obtained from one schedule. This procedure was used in order to keep the subjects in contact with the experimental contingencies. Whether exclusive preference would have developed without the forced-choice procedure is unclear. As we mentioned earlier, trivial, biased, response matching occurs on such a procedure. However, Rider also reported time-allocation data, which would not be trivially related to the reinforcer ratios unless response rates were constant on the two schedules. The time-allocation data for the four birds, excluding the forced-choice trials, are shown in Fig. 7.2. All sensitivities were less than 1.0, and all biases were toward the VR schedule. The values of the bias estimates were small, but the result should be reliable because Rider changed the

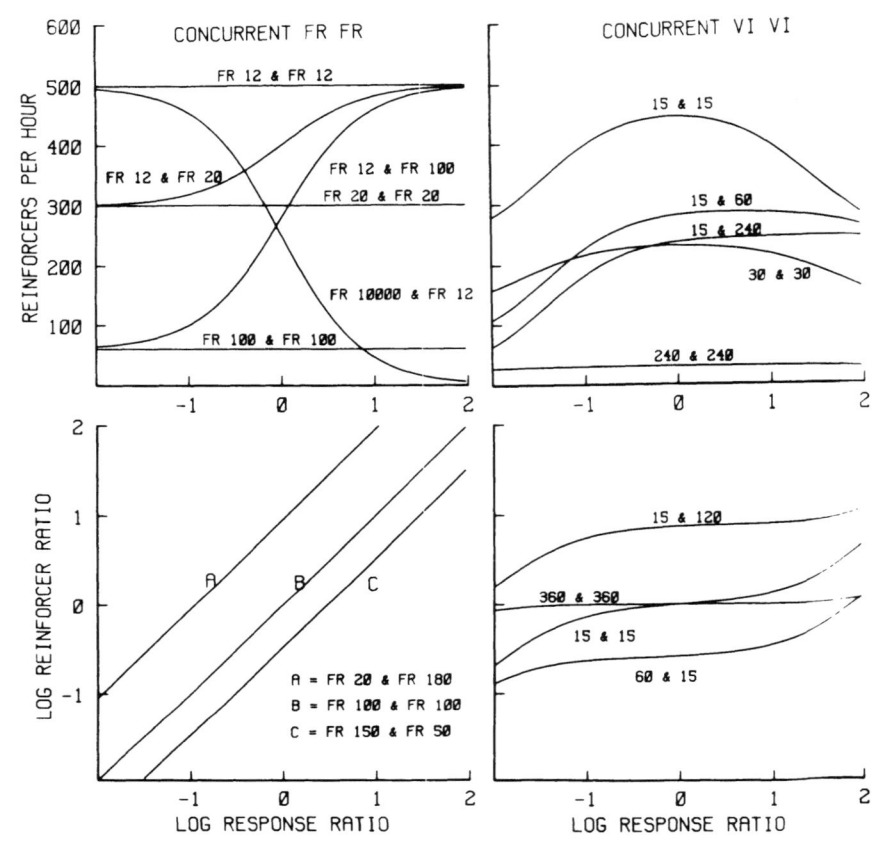

FIG. 7.1.   Representative feedback functions for concurrent FR FR schedule performance (left panels) and *independent* concurrent VI VI schedule performance (right panels) when the subject emits 100 responses per minute. The top panels show the total number of reinforcers per hour obtained on particular schedule pairs (the parameters shown on the graphs) when the subject allocates its behavior between the alternatives in various ways (the X axis). These are absolute feedback functions. For example, on a concurrent FR 12 FR 12 schedule at 100 responses per minute, 500 reinforcers per hour are obtained whatever the behavior allocation, whereas on a concurrent VI 15-s VI 15-s schedule, the greatest overall reinforcer rate is obtained when behavior is equally allocated to the two alternatives. The lower panels show how the distribution of behavior between alternatives affects the distribution of reinforcers between alternatives (relative feedback functions). The slope of all concurrent FR FR (or VR VR) functions is 1.0, indicating that any change in the distribution of behavior is matched by an equal change in the reinforcer distribution. Different ratio requirements arranged concurrently cause this relation to become biased toward the lower-requirement schedule. On concurrent VI VI schedules, the reinforcer distribution is much less affected by changing response distributions, but higher reinforcer rates (e.g., concurrent VI 15 s VI 15 s) are more reactive to changes in response distributions than are lower reinforcer rates. [Note that the graphs shown in Fig. 7.1 are *theoretical*. They were obtained using the feedback functions suggested by Staddon and Motheral (1978) (see also Nevin & Baum, 1980) assuming that the subject emitted 100 responses per minute. A different assumed response rate would change the absolute feedback function for concurrent FR FR performance, and both feedback functions for concurrent VI VI performance. Note also that the relative feedback function for *dependent* concurrent VI VI schedule performance is always a horizontal line and that the associated absolute feedback function would not be the same as for independent schedules.]

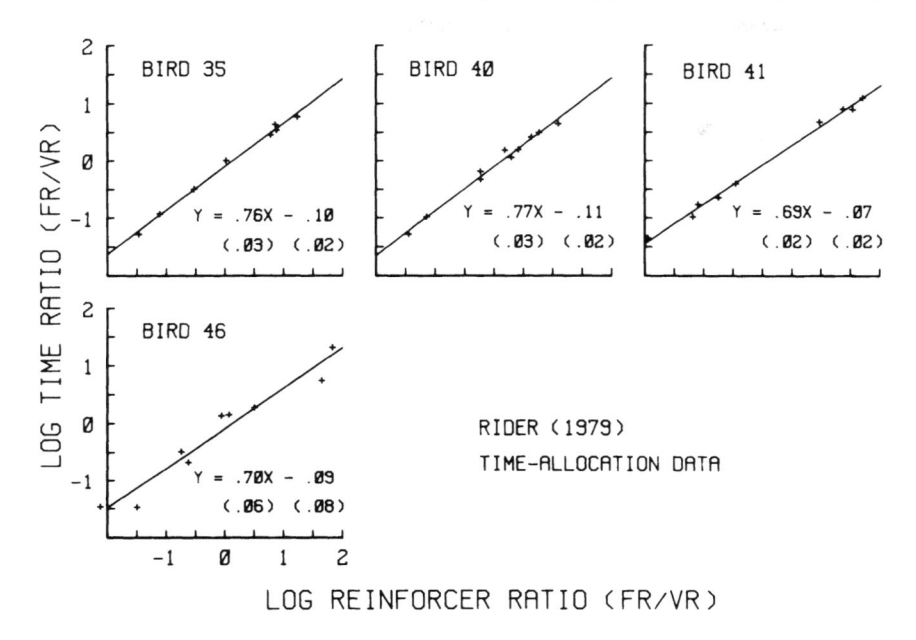

FIG. 7.2. Log time-allocation ratios as a function of log obtained reinforcer-frequency ratios for performance on concurrent FR VR schedules. The data are from Rider (1979).

FR and VR schedules between the keys, thus making a concurrent VI VI baseline to control for position bias unnecessary—though a stimulus bias (FR, continuous light; VR, flashing light) cannot be ruled out.

Rider (1979) also provided data on concurrent mixed-ratio (two-valued) FR schedule performance.

7.3. CONCURRENT FR VI PERFORMANCE

Two studies (Bacotti, 1977; Davison, 1982) have looked in detail at preference on concurrent FR VI schedules. Bacotti kept one schedule at VI 240 s, and varied the FR schedule between 25 and 100 responses per reinforcer. He found a mean response sensitivity of 1.12 and a mean time sensitivity of 1.04. In addition, all three time sensitivities were less than the corresponding response sensitivities. Bacotti also found a strong bias (mean 0.39 for responses, 0.80 for time, with all time measures larger than response measures) toward the VI schedule. The duration of the changeover delay (0, 1.5, or 5 s) had no demonstrable effect on sensitivity or bias.

Bacotti's (1977) results were systematically replicated by Davison (1982), who showed that the situation was more complex than Bacotti's data had indicated. Davison used both concurrent VI FR and concurrent VI FR VI schedules. He showed that sensitivities were close to 1.0 when the FR schedule was varied, but were lower (about 0.59 for response allocation and 0.87 for time allocation, on average) when the VI schedule was varied. He also showed that the degree of bias toward the VI versus the FR schedule depended on the VI reinforcer rate—at lower VI reinforcer rates, subjects were *more* biased to the VI schedule. Davison suggested that the data could be described by a dual-sensitivity generalized matching relation:

$$\log\left(\frac{B_{VI}}{B_{FR}}\right) = m \log(R_{VI}) - n \log(R_{FR}) + \log c , \qquad (7.1)$$

where m and n are the VI and FR sensitivities respectively. This extension of the generalized matching relation accounts also for the varying biases to the VI schedule as the VI reinforcer rate is changed. By the way, if the relation is to be independent of session length, R_{VI} and R_{FR} must be measured as reinforcer *rates* because of the different power values. In the standard generalized matching relation, both reinforcer measures are raised to the same power, and so can be taken as either reinforcer numbers or rates. Equation 7.1, consequently, has some dimensional difficulties (Davison, 1982).

7.4. CONCURRENT FI FI PERFORMANCE

Two experiments have reported data on concurrent FI FI schedules. First, Shimp (1971) used a two-key procedure with dependent scheduling, and reinforced only interresponse times (IRTs) greater than 1 s (which also provided a 1-s changeover delay). He reported strict matching. The second report was by White and Davison (1973) who used a changeover-key procedure and a changeover delay of 3 s. Eleven of the 12 experimental conditions used independent scheduling, the other being a replication but using dependent schedules. An unusual, and fortuitous, feature of the experiment was that cumulative records of the performances on the keys were taken. Two examples of generalized matching were found that were dependent on the type of performances shown on the cumulative records. First, as expected, the bias was zero. The sensitivity of the response ratios to the reinforcer-frequency ratios was about 1.0 when similar types of performance were evident on the cumulative records. That is, if both performances showed typical FI scalloping (Ferster & Skinner, 1957), or if both showed typical VI-type performances (an approximately constant response rate between reinforcers on both keys), sensitivity was about 1.0. But when the patterns of behavior were different on the two keys, sensitivity was evidently below 1.0. This latter aspect of the results related to the low sensitivity estimates obtained from concurrent FI VI schedules (Lobb & Davison, 1975; Trevett, Davison, & Williams, 1972; see Section 7.5).

7.5. CONCURRENT FI VI PERFORMANCE

In a study using concurrent FI VI schedules, Nevin (1971) reported a sensitivity of 0.5, on average, with two pigeons showing a bias to the VI schedule and one to the FI schedule. He used independent schedules in a two-key arrangement with a 2-s changeover delay.

Trevett, Davison, and Williams (1972) also used a two-key procedure and independent schedules, and a changeover delay of 3 s. They conducted a set of conditions using concurrent FI VI schedules in which the reinforcer rates on both keys were varied, and a comparison (baseline) set with concurrent VI VI schedules. The average sensitivities are shown in Table 7.1.

TABLE 7.1
Data From Trevett, Davison and
Williams (1972) Averaged Across Four
Subjects

	Responses		Time	
	a	log c	a	log c
Conc VI VI	0.69	−0.10	0.83	−0.08
Conc FI VI	0.62	−0.25	0.66	−0.36

Sensitivity to reinforcer frequency (a) appeared similar for both schedule combinations, at least for response measures. All bias measures showed a shift from baseline toward the VI on the concurrent FI VI schedule. Since Nevin (1971) did not report any baseline data, it is possible that the bias to the FI schedule found for one bird in his study was due to an inherent bias toward a key or key color that was larger than the probable bias to the VI schedule.

However, not all aspects of the results reported by Trevett et al. (1972) withstood replication by Lobb and Davison (1975). In a more extensive study, using a switching-key procedure, independent schedules, and a changeover delay of 3 s, Lobb and Davison also investigated concurrent FI VI performance in comparison with concurrent VI VI performance. They replicated Trevett et al.'s finding of a bias toward the VI schedule when compared to the concurrent VI VI baseline. However, they also found a significant difference (that is, the same directional difference in all five birds) between concurrent VI VI sensitivities (responses, 0.80; time, 1.07) and concurrent FI VI sensitivities (responses, 0.68; time, 0.72). Lobb and Davison were not able to reconcile the two findings. However, Davison (1982) suggested that the dual-sensitivity model (Equation 7.1) could account for their findings with a sensitivity of 0.41 to FI reinforcer-rate variation, and a sensitivity of 0.78 to VI reinforcer-rate variation. This suggestion does clarify the reason for the replication failure and, as Davison

(1982) pointed out, also helps explicate some other hitherto unexplained slope differences that have been reported.

7.6. CONCURRENT VI VR PERFORMANCE

Herrnstein and Heyman (1979) varied both schedules of concurrent VI VR over five experimental conditions and one replication. The VI schedules were varied from VI 15 s to VI 40 s, and the VR schedules from VR 30 to VR 60. A switching-key concurrent schedule, with a changeover delay of 1.5 s, was used. Note that a dependent-scheduling procedure cannot be used with ratio schedules without upsetting the contingencies. Also, a changeover delay with a ratio schedule will, to some extent, increase the average number of responses per reinforcer. The mean sensitivity to the reinforcer-frequency ratio was 1.0 (responses) and 0.86 (time), but these did not differ in a consistent direction across the subjects. Bias was -0.12 (i.e., to the ratio schedule) for response measures, and 0.20 (i.e., to the interval schedule) for time measures, demonstrating, as in the single-schedule case, a higher *total* response rate on VR compared with VI schedules.

Herrnstein and Heyman (1979) used these data to test a theory, proposed by Rachlin, Green, Kagel, and Battalio (1976). This theory, known as *molar maximizing*, suggests that matching arises from subjects responding so as to maximize the total obtained reinforcer rates obtained over substantial periods of time. From feedback functions for VI and VR schedules (Section 7.2), Herrnstein and Heyman calculated the distribution of time required to maximize total reinforcer rates when these schedules were arranged concurrently and showed that time allocation should be biased toward the VR schedule, not toward the VI schedule as obtained. Herrnstein and Heyman took this finding as strong evidence against molar-maximizing theory, but Ziriax and Silberberg (1984) argued against this conclusion. They showed that, because of the feedback function in concurrent VI VR schedules, obtained reinforcer ratios tended to match behavior ratios, rather than vice versa. As a result, the matching process could be an *environmental*, rather than a *behavioral* process in that procedure. Hence, Herrnstein and Heyman's evidence against molar maximizing was weak at best. The question of the process underlying empirical matching—matching as process versus molar maximizing, versus molecular maximizing, versus melioration (Section 8.5)—has recently been the subject of considerable argument and counter argument (see, for example, Commons, Herrnstein, & Rachlin, 1982).

7.7. CONCURRENT FI FR PERFORMANCE

Performance on concurrent FI FR schedules was studied by LaBounty and Reynolds (1973) using independent schedules in a two-key procedure with a changeover delay of 2.5 s, which could, of course, occasionally have lengthened the FR requirement. The interval schedule was always FI 240 s. Their data, originally interpreted from relative response-rate graphs, were reanalyzed by Baum (1974a) using the generalized matching relation. Averaged over the five birds from which satisfactory data were obtained, response sensitivity was 0.83, response bias was 0.03 to the FI schedule, time sensitivity was 0.85, and time bias was 0.28 to the FI schedule. While the response and time sensitivities did not differ in a consistent direction across subjects, time biases were more extreme for all five birds and, as in concurrent VI VR performance (Section 7.6), time biases again favored the interval schedule when compared to response biases. The fact that *only* the FR schedule was varied in this experiment could conceivably have affected the obtained sensitivity and bias estimates (Davison, 1982).

7.8. CONCURRENT DRL DRL PERFORMANCE

Staddon (1968) trained pigeons on concurrent DRL LH schedules in which interresponse times (IRTs) between 2 s and 3 s were reinforced on a VI schedule (varied over conditions) and IRTs between 10 s and 11 s were always reinforced. Staddon carried out a generalized matching analysis on 15 such experimental conditions—the first such analysis reported in the literature—and he concluded that a power-law relation between ratios (the relation that was to become known as the generalized matching law) might be a more general law of choice than the equality of relative frequencies (the strict matching law). Averaging across birds, Staddon obtained a sensitivity to the reinforcer-frequency ratio of 0.66, with a strong and consistent bias (log c = 0.62) toward responding in the lower IRT band, that is, between 2 s and 3 s.

A similar set of results may be obtained from a reanalysis of data reported by Shimp (1968). In this experiment, Shimp reinforced the behavior of pigeons in two IRT bands, 1.5 s to 2.5 s, and 3.5 s to 4.5 s. Over a series of experimental conditions, he varied both the relative frequency and relative duration of reinforcers for responses in the two bands. Shimp measured the frequency of IRTs falling into 0.5-s bands, and found clear bimodal distributions of IRTs corresponding to the reinforced bands. Taking the frequencies of IRTs between 1 s and 2.5 s, and between 3 s and 4.5 s, as measures of the two operants, we may carry out a generalized matching analysis using both reinforcer frequency and reinforcer duration as the independent variables. (Dependent schedules were used, so in this analysis arranged reinforcer-frequency ratios were used.) The results of the reanalysis are shown in Table 7.2. This reanalysis shows, as did Staddon's (1968) data, that preference between IRTs is characterized by undermatching to reinforcer-frequency (and reinforcer-duration) ratios, with a strong bias toward the shorter IRT response.

TABLE 7.2
Reanalysis of Data Reported by Shimp (1968)[a]

Bird	Frequency Data		Duration Data	
	Slope(SD)	Intercept(SD)	Slope(SD)	Intercept(SD)
1	0.42(0.11)	0.18(0.05)	0.45(0.05)	0.44(0.02)
2	0.67(0.07)	0.37(0.03)	0.48(0.09)	0.45(0.05)
3	0.95(0.24)	0.68(0.11)	0.48(0.19)	0.59(0.09)

[a]The data are the ratios of shorter- to longer-IRT bands. Separate analyses were carried out for reinforcer-frequency and reinforcer-duration conditions.

7.9. CONCURRENT VI VT PERFORMANCE

Bauman, Shull, and Brownstein (1975) conducted an experiment in which various concurrent VI VT schedules were arranged in a switching-key procedure using a 2-s changeover delay. The schedules were arranged dependently, and performance on a set of concurrent VI VI schedules was also investigated in control conditions. They found it rather difficult to eliminate responding during the VT schedule, though turning off all lights in the chamber, apart from the changeover-key light, was effective. The appropriate measure of behavior in such an experiment is obviously time allocation. They plotted the data as log ratios but did not attempt to fit the generalized matching relation, presumably because the maximum number of data points was only four. Bauman et al. reported a certain degree of undermatching for Birds R3 and R4 only, but suggested that the functions were the same for concurrent VI VI and concurrent VI VT performance. They did not mention any bias toward either schedule, which is interesting in view of the rather clear effects of varying response requirements on concurrent VI VI schedules (Section 7.11). The lack of bias may, however, be a result of time measurement when both schedules are time based. Does the reanalysis shown in Table 7.3 support their conclusions?

TABLE 7.3
Reanalysis of Data Reported by Bauman, Shull, and Brownstein (1975) for
Concurrent VI VI and Concurrent VI VT Schedule Performance[a]

Bird	Concurrent VI VI			Concurrent VI VT		
	N	Slope(SD)	Intercept(SD)	N	Slope(SD)	Intercept(SD)
R1	4	0.68(0.07)	0.01(0.02)	3	0.71(0.10)	0.04(0.03)
B3	3	1.06(0.02)	0.03(0.01)	3	0.78(0.11)	0.02(0.03)
R3	—	—	—	4	0.68(0.03)	0.10(0.02)
R4	—	—	—	4	0.73(0.10)	0.28(0.07)

[a]The number of data (N) for each least-squares fit is also shown. For the concurrent VI VT analysis, only the data from the conditions in which no responses were emitted during the VT component are shown.

Table 7.3 makes the conclusions of Bauman et al.'s (1975) experiment less clear. All four birds, rather than just R3 and R4, showed sensitivities to reinforcer frequencies that were less than 1.0. For Subjects R1 and B3, for which adequate baseline concurrent VI VI data are available, neither the sensitivity to reinforcement nor the bias show any consistent differences between the two schedule arrangements. However, Birds R3 and R4 showed strong biases toward the VI schedules over the VT schedules. A decision as to whether these biases were caused by the schedules, or were "key" or "color" biases is difficult to make without baseline data from concurrent VI VI schedules. But even if these data were available, the interpretation would still be difficult, as different stimulus conditions signaled the VI schedule (amber) and the VT schedule (blackout, save for the changeover key). Overall, five of the six sensitivity estimates showed undermatching quite typical of concurrent VI VI schedule performance.

7.10. MORE THAN TWO CONCURRENTLY AVAILABLE SCHEDULES

Data on the performance of pigeons on an independent five-key concurrent VI 60-s VI 120-s VI 180-s VI 240-s VI 300-s schedule were reported by Miller and Loveland (1974). They arranged a 2-s changeover delay between all keys. The five keys were transilluminated different colors, and responses emitted, time spent responding, changeovers, and obtained reinforcers were all measured. Miller and Loveland interpreted their data as supporting strict matching because the data points fell near the diagonal (on relative coordiantes) described by:

$$\frac{B_i}{\sum B} = \frac{R_i}{\sum R},$$

and by a similar equation for time allocation. This conclusion can be investigated with more precision by calculating log response, time, and reinforcer ratios for all pairwise combinations of keys and fitting a straight line. The results of this reanalysis are shown in Table 7.4

TABLE 7.4
Log-Ratio Reanalysis of the Data Obtained by Miller and Loveland (1974)[a]

	Responses		Time	
Bird	Slope(SD)	Intercept(SD)	Slope(SD)	Intercept(SD)
258	0.98(0.09)	0.02(0.04)	0.81(0.24)	0.05(0.09)
348	0.27(0.30)	0.17(0.13)	0.66(0.19)	−0.10(0.08)
261	0.92(0.26)	0.14(0.12)	1.40(0.12)	−0.01(0.05)
299	1.22(0.20)	−0.06(0.09)	1.56(0.16)	−0.10(0.07)

[a]The number of data was 10 except for Bird 348, for which it was 6.

The fits, especially for Bird 348, are not strikingly good, but overall this reanalysis supports Miller and Loveland's (1974) contention that the data did not consistently deviate from strict matching. Note, however, that there is a major problem with bias in this experiment. The bias between each pairwise grouping of the five keys was not measured and could have been substantial. Such a bias could have been assessed by an equal-schedules condition, but this is not really recommended as in an independent-schedules procedure, the frequencies of reinforcers obtained from the keys could differ. Alternatively, the schedules could be varied across the keys in a number of experimental conditions. In a procedure such as that used by Miller and Loveland, a bias toward or away from one of the keys could easily change the apparent sensitivity to reinforcer frequency. Notice also that the intercept in the present fit to Miller and Loveland's data has no meaning—it is not a bias, because it is aggregated across all the pairwise combinations of keys.

Miller and Loveland's (1974) research is interesting in that it shows how an assessment of the relation between, say, response ratios and reinforcer ratios could in principle be carried out in a single experimental condition, rather than in a series of conditions as conventionally done.

An experiment reported by Pliskoff and Brown (1976) can be used to address some of the concerns about Miller and Loveland's (1974) results. Pliskoff and Brown used a switching-key concurrent procedure with three VI schedules and associated stimuli on the main key. They varied the schedules associated with the discriminative stimuli over nine experimental conditions, but some schedules were Extinction and so cannot be used in a generalized matching reanalysis. The changeover delay was 1.5 s. The data are reanalyzed in Table 7.5 as log ratios, taking each bird and each pair of discriminative stimuli separately.

Pliskoff and Brown (1976) reported that their data, on relative coordinates, were distributed about the major diagonal (strict matching), but they noted some undermatching (e.g., Bird 7, response data, Bird 9, time data, and to a lesser degree, Bird 7, time data). They calculated mean-squared deviations of the data from strict matching and concluded that the time data showed a close correspondence to strict matching. Our reanalysis is not consistent with such a conclusion. First, eight of the nine sensitivity estimates for both response and time allocation showed undermatching ($a < 1$). On average, response sensitivity was greater than time sensitivity, but this difference was not individually consistent. Pliskoff and Brown's mean-squared-deviation analysis was compromised by the greater response undermatching than time undermatching shown by Bird 7, and by the large bias toward the green key shown by Bird 9's response data. Both these effects increased the mean-squared deviation for the response data. It is interesting to note that the bias in response allocation shown by Bird 9 was not reflected in its time-allocation data. It is evident from this and other research that response and time biases are frequently quite different.

This reanalysis suggests, therefore, that performance on a trio of concurrent

TABLE 7.5
Log-Ratio Reanalysis of the Data Reported by Pliskoff and Brown (1976)[a]

		Responses		Times	
Bird	Pair	Slope(SD)	Intercept(SD)	Slope(SD)	Intercept(SD)
7	Y/G	0.75(0.03)	−0.01(0.02)	0.69(0.06)	−0.02(0.04)
7	G/R	0.66(0.05)	−0.05(0.02)	0.91(0.06)	0.04(0.02)
7	Y/R	0.65(0.05)	−0.09(0.03)	0.75(0.05)	0.04(0.03)
9	Y/G	0.68(0.20)	−0.29(0.12)	0.64(0.09)	−0.01(0.05)
9	G/R	0.69(0.30)	0.28(0.11)	0.69(0.14)	0.10(0.05)
9	Y/R	0.85(0.09)	0.04(0.05)	0.65(0.04)	0.09(0.02)
11	Y/G	0.89(0.05)	−0.05(0.03)	0.76(0.12)	−0.01(0.07)
11	G/R	1.14(0.09)	0.11(0.04)	1.06(0.08)	0.13(0.03)
11	Y/R	0.99(0.06)	0.08(0.03)	0.77(0.05)	0.12(0.03)
Mean		0.81		0.77	

[a]The schedules were arranged in the presence of three discriminative stimuli, Red (R), Yellow (Y), and Green (G). The analysis was done separately for each stimulus pair, each bird, and response and time measures.

VI schedules is the same as on a duo of such schedules, though we would normally expect time-allocation sensitivity to be greater than response-allocation sensitivity (Section 6.1). Bird 9's performance also highlights the potential problems caused by bias in Miller and Loveland's (1974) results, and suggests that it is not possible to conduct a complete matching-law analysis from a single experimental condition with multiple operants. Such data are not necessarily equivalent to the data obtained from a two-choice procedure over a number of experimental conditions.

The conclusions we have drawn from Pliskoff and Brown's (1976) study are supported by the results of an experiment investigating performance on VI schedules arranged on one, or concurrently on two, or three keys by Davison and Hunter (1976). A changeover delay of 1.5 s was also used in this experiment. In a series of conditions, they: (1) kept two of the schedules constant at VI 60 s and VI 120 s and varied the third schedule; (2) kept two of the schedules constant at VI 120 s Extinction and varied the third; and (3) kept two of the schedules constant at Extinction and Extinction and varied the third. Across six generalized matching analyses with six birds, Davison and Hunter obtained a mean response sensitivity of 0.73 and a mean time sensitivity of 0.74. There were no sensitivity differences that could be ascribed to arranging two versus three schedules or to any pairwise combination of keys. Analyzing the individual performances, both response and time sensitivities were significantly less than unity, and response sensitivities were significantly less than time sensitivities (using Sign tests, Section 5.8). The only difference between these results and those of Pliskoff and Brown (as reanalyzed here) was the finding of response- and time-allocation sensitivity differences by Davison and Hunter. Both experiments used arithmetic VI schedules (Taylor and Davison, 1983).

Davison and Hunter (1976) interpreted their data as supporting the *principle of indifference from irrelevant alternatives* (Luce, 1959). This principle describes the state of affairs when the preference shown between two alternatives is unaffected by the addition or subtraction (hence, variation generally) of a third alternative. Davison and Hunter's data supported this principle in that response allocation between VI 60 s and VI 120 s was unaffected by the variation in the third schedule. This principle would *not* be expected to hold, of course, if variations in the third schedule caused a change in the *obtained* reinforcer-rate ratio on the concurrent VI 60-s VI 120-s schedules—if it did, then that preference would change. A more general statement of the indifference principle would be that variations in the third (or nth) schedule would not affect the *relation* between log response or time ratios and log reinforcer ratios shown on the first two schedules. In other words, a and c in the generalized matching analysis of the two-key performance would not be affected by the reinforcer rate on the third (or nth) key. Davison and Hunter's data supported this suggestion also. It may be thought that the simple finding that a choice between two schedules was unaffected by variations in a third schedule would support the more general principle, but this is not necessarily so. A fortuitous choice of reinforcer rates on the first two schedules could find the indifference principle supported for that particular choice, but it could break down for other pairs of schedules. It is important that the more general principle (which adds "for all schedule pairs") is experimentally assessed. There are a number of cases in the literature (for instance, the effects of short multiple-schedule components; Section 9.3) in which the assertion of "for all variations in an independent variable" has been made without experimental investigation and has subsequently turned out to be untrue.

The preceding discussion also relates to research reported by Prelec and Herrnstein (1978). They arranged concurrent VI VI VR schedules with a 1-s changeover delay between the interval schedules. When one of the VI-schedule keys was covered, leaving a concurrent VI VR schedule, responding increased on the VR schedule but not on the remaining VI schedule. This was taken by Prelec and Herrnstein as a violation of the indifference principle ("the constant ratio rule," as they term it), but it is not necessarily so. Increases in the VR response rate naturally increase the VR reinforcer rate, and hence change the VR/VI obtained reinforcer-rate ratio. It is likely, therefore, that the generalized matching *relation* for concurrent VI VR performance was not affected by the removal of one VI alternative. Unfortunately, Prelec and Herrnstein presented no data on reinforcer rates, and so we cannot check this possibility. Evidence supporting this reinterpretation comes from Davison (1982), who showed that the concurrent VI FR generalized matching *relation* was unaffected by the variation of a third VI schedule, though such variations did affect the FR reinforcer frequency.

7.11. RESPONSE PARAMETERS

Response effects on concurrent-schedule performance have been investigated in three ways: (1) by quantitative variation of the required force of responses (Chung, 1965b; Hunter & Davison, 1982); (2) by investigating performance with qualitatively different responses (Davison & Ferguson, 1978; McSweeney, 1975b); and (3) by the use of second-order schedules in which first-order operant definitions are quantitatively varied (Beautrais & Davison, 1977; Cohen, 1975).

7.11a. Response Force

The major experimental report of the effects of (static) response force on performance on concurrent VI VI schedules was by Hunter and Davison (1982). Hunter and Davison used arithmetic VI schedules and a 2-s changeover delay. They varied the force required for a response to be counted by changing lead weights in pans attached to the keys. In 43 experimental conditions, they varied both relative and absolute required forces from 13 to 49 g, and both relative and absolute reinforcer rates in the range VI 15 s to VI 480 s. The empirical results of this experiment may be summarized thus: Neither relative nor absolute force requirements affected the sensitivity to the reinforcer-frequency ratio; neither relative nor absolute reinforcer rate affected sensitivity to force ratios. These conclusions strongly support the method of concatenating independent variables suggested by Baum and Rachlin (1969; Section 4.4). It was necessary, however, to raise the independent-variable ratios to powers:

$$\log\left(\frac{B_1}{B_2}\right) = a \log\left(\frac{R_1}{R_2}\right) + d \log\left(\frac{F_2}{F_1}\right) + \log c \ . \tag{7.2}$$

Equation 7.2 asserts that there is no interaction between log force ratios and log reinforcer-frequency ratios in their effects on choice. This equation was compared by Hunter and Davison with a series of equations that predict interactions. The most extreme of these was:

$$\log\left(\frac{B_1}{B_2}\right) = a \log\left(\frac{R_1}{R_2}\right) + d \log\left(\frac{F_2}{F_1}\right) + e \log(\Sigma F) + f \log(\Sigma R) \ . \tag{7.3}$$

Given that Equations 7.2 and 7.3 have different numbers of free parameters, their relative abilities to predict the data are difficult to compare. For instance, if Equation 7.3, with four free parameters, accounted for 2 percent more of the data variance than did Equation 7.2, with two free parameters, which equation should be chosen as the best predictor? Hunter and Davison used the Akaike criterion (Akaike, 1969, 1974) to compare the equations as this criterion takes into account the number of free parameters in the models. The equation for the criterion is:

$$Q = (N\text{–}k) \log_e\left[\frac{\sum(Y_i - Y'_i)^2}{N + 2}\right] + (k+1) \log_e(N + 2),$$

where N is the number of data, k is the number of free parameters, and Y_i and Y'_i are the data and the predictions, respectively. The most efficient model is the one that yields the lowest value of Q. This was given by Equation 7.2, the power-transformed Baum-Rachlin concatenation, for all five birds for response data, and for four of the five birds for time data.

For response measures, mean sensitivity to reinforcer-rate variation was 0.88 and to force-ratio variation was 0.71. Four of the five individual-subject sensitivities to reinforcer-ratio variation were less than 1.0, and the two sets of sensitivities were not reliably different. Different results were obtained for time-allocation measures: Mean time-allocation sensitivity to reinforcer-rate variation was 0.98 (not significantly different from 1 on a Sign test), but time-allocation sensitivity to force ratios was 0.41. This latter value was significantly less than 1, and was significantly less than the sensitivity to the reinforcer-rate ratio. Comparing these sensitivities in the alternate way, for log reinforcer-rate variation, time-allocation sensitivity was significantly greater than response-allocation sensitivity; but for force-ratio variations, time-allocation sensitivity was significantly smaller than response-allocation sensitivity.

While Hunter and Davison (1982) found that force-ratio variations were well described by the generalized matching law, another aspect of these results is also of interest. This concerns the change in response rate on one component schedule that is often obtained when the reinforcer rate on a concurrently available schedule is varied. Under some conditions, such an interaction between schedule performances can be termed *behavioral contrast* (Section 3.5). This result can be described by Herrnstein's (1970) equation for absolute response rate (Section 3.1), though two recent papers (McLean & White, 1983; Williams, 1983) have discussed some major problems for that equation in describing contrast. Equivalently, it would be expected that an increase in the force required on one of the concurrent-schedule manipulanda would increase the response rate on the other schedule, but this was not found either by Chung (1965b) or by Hunter and Davison. Equation 7.4 is the force analogue to Herrnstein's response-rate equation (Equation 2.3):

$$B_1 = \frac{kF_2}{F_2 + F_1}, \tag{7.4}$$

which predicts that B_1 will increase if F_2 is increased. Hunter and Davison offered Equation 7.5 to describe their obtained data:

$$B_1 = k'\left(\frac{F_m - F_1}{F_m}\right) \cdot \left(\frac{R_1}{R_1 + R_2 + R_e}\right), \qquad (7.5)$$

where k' is a constant and F_m is the maximum force that the subject will emit. In Equation 7.5, F_2 does not occur, and changing a required force affects only the response rate on that manipulandum. If we generalize the reinforcer-rate aspect of Equation 7.5, Equation 7.6 should describe concurrent VI VI schedule response allocation when both reinforcer rates and forces are varied.

$$\frac{B_1}{B_2} = c\left(\frac{R_1}{R_2}\right)^a \cdot \frac{F_m - F_1}{F_m - F_2}. \qquad (7.6)$$

Equation 7.6 fitted the preference data slightly better than did Equation 7.2 (the concatenated generalized matching law) with F_m values of between 57 and 98 g. Because Equation 7.6 has the same number of free parameters as Equation 7.2 (F_m replacing d), it is preferable on the Akaike criterion. Further, as Hunter and Davison suggested, F_m has a more straightforward interpetation than does d.

The fact that response-force variation does not produce changes in the response rates of concurrently available operants has some interesting implications. First, it may suggest that there are two basic aspects to the generalized matching relation, one reinforcer (or input) aspect, and one response (or output) aspect. Moreover, the two aspects of control may operate differently. For instance, the effects of reinforcer parameters may be essentially unbounded—that is, absolute reinforcer rates over the range 0 to ∞ may affect behavior in the same way. However, response-parameter effects may be bounded or have an upper threshold such as F_m in Equations 7.5 and 7.6. The second implication from the finding that force variation does not produce interactive effects on other operants is that increases in force requirements cannot be likened to punishment effects, because the addition of punishment in one component of a multiple schedule does produce "contrast" in the other (Brethower & Reynolds, 1962). Punishment, under the present suggestion, must therefore be seen as decrementing reinforcer parameters. Indeed, this is the very process suggested in recent versions of the matching law for punishment (de Villiers, 1980; Farley, 1980; Farley & Fantino, 1978; see Section 8.3). The sort of question that arises from the above discussion is whether the other variables known to affect choice do so via response effects (thus, with no interactive effects or "contrast") or via reinforcer effects (thus with interactive effects). We can ask this question of reinforcer delays and even of reinforcer qualities. If, for example, a change to another reinforcer type changed preference, this could result from a change in the time needed to assimilate that reinforcer (handling time), rather than from a change in reinforcer magnitude *per se*.

The discrimination between response effects (k) and reinforcer effects (for example, R_1, R_2, etc.) is already embodied in Herrnstein's (1970) theoretical approach. In such a theory, one would ask whether a particular manipulation affected k or R_e. There is a sense, therefore, in which, if a reinforcer manipulation affected k, as theoretically it should not do, then we might suggest that the effect was one of handling time rather than of reinforcer value. Such an interpretation *could* be made for McDowell and Wood's (1984, 1985) finding that k varied with reinforcer amount with humans—but this seems so unlikely that further speculation is unprofitable.

7.11b. Second-Order Schedules

In a second-order schedule, a schedule performance is defined as the operant, and is itself reinforced on the basis of another schedule. Thus, keypecking might be the first-order operant class, and completing an FR 5 requirement of pecks might be the second-order operant. Completion of the second-order operant is signaled to the subject, usually by a brief stimulus presentation, and is indicated by ":S" in the schedule shorthand. This second-order operant might then be reinforced on, say, a VI 60-s schedule. The total schedule designation is thus, in this example, VI 60 s (FR 5:S). (The tandem control to a second-order schedule has no brief stimulus presentation.) One feature of second-order schedules is that the response patterns are normally typical of the schedule on which the operant is reinforced. Thus, on a VI 60-s (FR 5:S) schedule, keypecking will show a normal FR pattern (perhaps with a pause after each FR completion that is longer than for a food-reinforced FR 5 performance). The second-order operant, FR 5 completions, will show a typical VI pattern.

The first experiment on concurrent second-order schedules was reported by Cohen (1975). He used concurrent VI 480-s (FI 8:S) VI 160-s (FI x:S) schedules with three subjects, and concurrent VI 240-s (FI 8:S) VI 240-s (FI x:S) schedules with three other subjects. The value of x was varied from 0 s to 32 s over six conditions. Appropriate concurrent VI VI control conditions (that is, both FI schedules 0 s) were also conducted, as were some tandem controls. It is, however, difficult to provide a meaningful generalized matching analysis of the results because: (1) only two reinforcer ratios were arranged, and these were for different birds; (2) within subjects, while there was a range of obtained reinforcer ratios, the range was generally small; (3) the data reported were keypecks, rather than second-order operant completions; and (4) the second-order operants were not unitary, because a changeover emitted during an FI component caused the recommencement of the FI schedule. Thus, for our purposes, Cohen's data are not useful.

Beautrais and Davison (1977) collected a set of concurrent second-order schedule data specifically for the purpose of a generalized matching analysis of the effects of response requirement. They used concurrent VI w-s (FR x:S) VI y-s (FR z:S) schedules and varied w, x, y, and z. The VI schedules were arranged dependently with a 2-s changeover delay. The first keypeck of each FR second-order operant, which could be emitted on either key, removed the availability of the alternative second-order response (and thus of a changeover) until the current second-order response had been completed. Thus, the second-order responses were unitary. Three series of conditions were arranged. First, both FR requirements were 5 pecks (x = z = 5), and both VI schedules were varied. Second, the FR requirements were 5 and 10, and the VI schedules were again varied. Last, the VI schedules were kept constant at VI 30 s and VI 180 s, and both FR (x & z) requirements were varied. The data collected and analyzed were the numbers of completions of the second-order operants (the FR components) and the times spent emitting them, measured from the first *peck* to the last in the second-order responses. Beautrais and Davison's results are shown in Table 7.6.

TABLE 7.6
Generalized Matching Results Obtained by Beautrais and Davison (1977) for
Performance on Concurrent VI (FR:S) VI (FR:S) Schedules

	FR Completions		Time Allocation	
Bird	*Slope*	*Intercept*	*Slope*	*Intercept*
1. FR 5 versus FR 5, varied VI schedules				
181	0.57	−0.23	0.66	−0.03
182	1.00	−0.04	0.90	−0.04
183	0.88	0.17	0.80	0.09
184	0.78	0.01	0.72	−0.04
185	0.83	−0.02	0.74	−0.10
186	0.79	−0.12	0.65	−0.07
Mean	0.81	−0.04	0.75	−0.03
2. FR 5 versus FR 10, varied VI schedules				
181	0.37	0.01	0.48	0.01
182	0.57	0.34	0.50	−0.06
183	0.68	0.44	0.73	0.10
184	0.74	0.46	0.70	0.10
185	0.77	0.33	0.67	−0.27
186	0.71	0.27	0.70	−0.14
Mean	0.64	0.31	0.63	−0.04
3. VI 30 s VI 180 s, varied FR requirements[a]				
181	0.90	0.18	−0.33	0.57
182	0.98	0.58	−0.14	0.51
183	0.94	0.76	−0.20	0.74
184	0.91	0.55	−0.22	0.47
185	0.49	0.77	−0.48	0.35
186	0.89	0.57	−0.65	0.56
Mean	0.85	0.57	−0.34	0.53

[a]Note that the parameters for the FR variation were obtained from fits to the inverse FR requirement (FR_b/FR_a).

There are a large number of comparisons possible with these data, and a full analysis is rewarding. First, when the FR components were both 5 pecks, performance was similar to standard concurrent VI VI performance except that time-allocation sensitivities were not significantly different (Sign test) from response-allocation sensitivities. There was no consistent bias. However, when the FR components were 5 and 10 responses, response sensitivity to the reinforcer ratio fell by an average 0.17, and time-allocation sensitivity fell, on average, by 0.12. All response-allocation biases increased (by an average 0.35), but time-allocation biases remained the same. If response force and FR requirements had similar effects, we would expect *no* sensitivity change between the two pairs of FR requirements according to the concatenated generalized matching relation. This relation predicts no interaction between the effects of concatenated independent variables. The fact that sensitivity changed might suggest that these variables interact, but other analyses (see following discussion) are possible. A bias change would be expected when the requirements were made unequal. Such a shift was found for the completion measures, but not for the time-allocation measures. The fact that time-allocation measures showed no bias shift (and perhaps no sensitivity shift either) is interesting. These results could indicate that the fundamental process of matching is time allocation (as suggested by Baum & Rachlin, 1969), and that the frequency of completing the second-order operants might decrease or increase simply because less or more time was allocated to them. (We note here, however, that the results of the third part of the experiment, discussed below, seem to rule out this explanation.) Another way of viewing the above results is to note that the change in FR requirements from 5 and 5, to 5 and 10, is purely a response-requirement change, and thus it may affect only response-type (completion) measures. Here again, this cannot be the whole story, because an FR 10 requirement will take longer to complete than an FR 5, so a duration-of-operant change has also occurred.

The results of the variation of FR requirements (Table 7.6, Part 3) show clearly that when the FR requirement was shortened, more completions occurred. Completion ratios undermatched FR requirement ratios—halving the FR requirement on one key did not double the completions on that key. More interesting are the effects of FR-requirement variation on time allocation. These sensitivities were all negative, averaging -0.34, indicating that decreasing the FR requirement led to less time allocated to completing that requirement, even though more completions were emitted. What do such results say about the measurement of choice? When, for example, the FR requirements were FR 2 and FR 8, the subject completed more FR 2 than FR 8 components, but spent more time completing FR 8 than FR 2 components. Naive notions of choice and preference would indeed suggest that if both second-order operants were equally frequently reinforced, then the smaller requirement would be preferred. We would expect our experimental measures of preference to reflect this notion.

Thus, in these conditions, response allocation is a more natural measure of preference than is time allocation (contra Baum & Rachlin, 1969).

Notice that the difference between Beautrais and Davison's (1977) and Hunter and Davison's (1982) experiments is that, in the former, the operants had varied temporal extent, whereas in the latter the variations (of force) were instantaneous. The evident difference in results must be at least partly concerned with the temporal extent of the operant and its effect both on behavior allocation and the measurement of choice.

7.11c. Different Responses

In matching research, it is convenient to use keypeck responses with pigeons, lever-press responses with rats, and typically morse-key, lever-pressing, or button-pressing responses with humans (but see Schroeder & Holland, 1969, who used eye movements with humans). What are the effects on matching if more unusual (perhaps unnatural) responses are used? McSweeney (1975b) investigated concurrent VI VI treadle-pressing performance with pigeons. The data she presented were not extensive (four conditions without a changeover delay, and one with a changeover delay), but the results indicated an approximation to strict matching, especially when a changeover delay was arranged.

A set of data on concurrent VI (lever-press) VI (keypeck) performance in pigeons was provided, as a control experiment, by Davison and Ferguson (1978). A changeover delay of 2 s was used, and both response- and time-allocation measures were taken. Both the response- and time-allocation sensitivities averaged 0.87, and neither mean was consistently different from 1.0. Lever/key bias was -0.65 for response measures, and -0.32 for time measures. These results agree, qualitatively at least, with those of Beautrais and Davison (1977) in that a response-requirement differential produced a more extreme bias in response than in time measures. Thus, again, preferences measured by response and time allocation do not agree. Informal observation of the experiment suggested that the lever-press response was difficult for the pigeons to emit, and that the business of getting into an appropriate position to press the lever took time. Hence, as in Beautrais and Davison's experiment, the two operants may have taken different times to execute. It is evident that response-duration effects should be investigated parametrically to determine their effects on both response and time allocation on concurrent schedules. To our knowledge, this has not been done.

8

CONCURRENT-SCHEDULE RESEARCH III: MISCELLANY

The purpose of this chapter is to complete our summary of concurrent-schedule research by touching on a number of areas that have either received, as yet, only passing attention, or that are adjuncts to the research we have discussed so far. We expect that many of these areas will undergo considerable development over the next few years.

8.1. TRANSITIONS AND THE EFFECTS OF PREVIOUS CONDITIONS

The matching law and the generalized matching law have been rather exclusively concerned with the description and understanding of stable-state performance. Data are typically taken when stability criteria have been met—usually necessitating some 15 to 30 sessions of training. The generalized matching law serves to specify quite accurately both the beginning and end points of transitions between concurrent schedules. Given such effective anchoring, can the performance between these end points be described using the generalized matching law extended in some way? If we accept the Baum-Rachlin (1969) concatenation of ratios, and subscript reinforcer rates with numerals representing the number of sessions prior to the current session (subscripted 0), with L and R representing the two choice alternatives, then we might suppose that:

$$\log\left(\frac{B_{0L}}{B_{0R}}\right) = a_0 \log\left(\frac{R_{0L}}{R_{0R}}\right) + a_1 \log\left(\frac{R_{1L}}{R_{1R}}\right) + a_2 \log\left(\frac{R_{2L}}{R_{2R}}\right) \ldots$$
$$\ldots + \log c . \quad (8.1)$$

Equation 8.1 states that performance in the current session is a joint function of the reinforcer ratios in the current session and in previous sessions (with the addition of bias). When the inputs are stable, that is, all reinforcer ratios in Equation 8.1 are the same, then Equation 8.1 becomes:

$$\log\left(\frac{B_{OL}}{B_{OR}}\right) = (\textstyle\sum a_i) \log\left(\frac{R_L}{R_R}\right), \qquad (8.2)$$

and we know that the overall power value ($\sum a_i$) is, for arithmetic schedules (Taylor & Davison, 1983), about 0.8. The question is: What constitutes the value of $\sum a_i$? We would expect a_i to fall, presumably to zero, as i increases—that is, long-distant sessions' inputs will have little effect on current-session performance. But how do these powers fall with time? In order to investigate such effects, it is clearly necessary to change inputs (log reinforcer ratios) sufficiently frequently to demonstrate the change in a values, or to analyze, session by session, a substantial number of transitions between stable states of behavior.

The latter procedure was arranged by Davison and Hunter (1979) using concurrent arithmetic VI VI schedules with a changeover delay of 3 s. They commenced with a concurrent Extinction VI 60-s condition and progressively increased the reinforcer ratio over a further six conditions, ending with a concurrent VI 60-s Extinction condition. The step size was 0.3 of a log reinforcer-ratio unit except when the transitions were to, or from, conditions in which one schedule was Extinction. This series was then reversed to give a descending sequence, and then both the ascending and descending sequences were repeated. Finally, a series of conditions was arranged in which the schedule pairs comprising the ascending and descending sequences were arranged in an irregular order. Conditions in which an Extinction schedule was arranged were run to stability, but all other conditions were in effect for only six sessions.

Davison and Hunter (1979) carried out generalized matching analyses of performances in the first, third, and sixth (last) sessions of the ascending and descending series of conditions using the current session's (i.e., today's) obtained reinforcer ratio as the independent variable. (Extinction conditions were not part of these analyses.) It is evident from Equation 8.1 that in the ascending sequences, because previous-sessions' log reinforcer ratios will be smaller than current-session log reinforcer ratios, a generalized matching analysis will estimate a negative bias to the extent that previous-conditions' log reinforcer ratios affect current-session performance. By the same reasoning, the bias in the descending sequence will be positive because previous reinforcer ratios will be larger. In the irregular sequence, on the other hand, we might expect to find lowered a values for the current session because previous log reinforcer ratios might either be smaller or larger. Indeed, if previous-sessions' inputs have a substantial effect, log response ratios may appear to be randomly scattered. The results from this experiment are summarized in Table 8.1.

Consider first the data from the sixth session after a transition (the session immediately prior to the next transition). There were no significant differences (Sign test on individual subjects) between the ascending or descending slopes or intercepts. Both these data and those from the irregular sequence appeared to be standard concurrent VI VI data. Thus, by the sixth session of training no effects of the previous experimental condition were discernible. The analysis of the third-session data also showed no significant sensitivity differences between the ascending and descending data, but the intercepts for the ascending sequence were significantly smaller (that is, less positive) than those from the descending sequence. The difference between the ascending and descending intercepts was $+0.22$ on average. This difference suggests that exposure to the previous experimental condition did affect performance during the third session of training after a transition. However, the data from the irregular sequence did not show any sensitivity decrease when compared with the sixth session, and appeared to be typical concurrent VI VI data.

TABLE 8.1

Generalized Matching Analyses of Performances in the First, Third, and Sixth Sessions After a Change in Reinforcer Ratios (Davison & Hunter, 1979)[a]

Session	Slope	Intercept
Ascending		
Session 1	0.53	−0.13
Session 3	0.68	−0.05
Session 6	0.73	0.05
Descending		
Session 1	0.59	0.29
Session 3	0.59	0.17
Session 6	0.67	0.13
Irregular		
Session 1	0.00	−0.14
Session 3	0.71	0.04
Session 6	0.65	0.01

[a]The data are averaged across two ascending sequences of reinforcer ratios, two descending sequences, and one irregular sequence, and across the four birds completing all parts of the experiment.

In the first session after a transition, the ascending and descending sensitivities were again similar and, in value, typical of concurrent VI VI schedule performances. But, the difference between the ascending and descending intercepts was 0.42 (ascending -0.13, descending 0.29). As expected, the data from the irregular sequence showed a zero slope and extremely poor fits. Thus, the previous experimental condition had a large effect on performance in the first session after a transition.

The decreasing intercept differences from the first through the sixth sessions showed that previous reinforcer ratios did exert an effect on current-session performance. Also, such effects could be described by the generalized matching law in the form prescribed by Equation 8.1. The data indicated that there was still some measurable effect of previous conditions after three sessions of training but that this effect disappeared in fewer than six sessions. This latter finding corresponds to Shull and Pliskoff's (1967) report that performance on concurrent VI VI schedules stabilized within seven sessions.

Given that Equation 8.1 is correct, and that it describes response allocation in each of a series of sessions, then it follows that the effects of the reinforcer ratio in the sessions prior to the current session can be summarized by the *response ratio* in the session immediately prior to the current session. Thus:

$$\log\left(\frac{B_{0L}}{B_{0R}}\right) = a_0 \log\left(\frac{R_{0L}}{R_{0R}}\right) + a_{1B} \log\left(\frac{B_{1L}}{B_{1R}}\right) + \log c . \tag{8.3}$$

Davison and Hunter (1979) assessed Equation 8.3 and found: (1) the mean current-session sensitivity to reinforcement (a_0) was 0.48, and (2) the mean sensitivity to the response ratio in the previous session (a_{1B}) was 0.28. If a particular reinforcer ratio was in effect until performance stabilized, then the overall sensitivity to reinforcement would equal ($a_0 + a_{1B}$), which is, in this case, 0.76, well within the usual range.

Note, however, one problem with Equation 8.1. Reinforcer ratios in sessions in which one schedule was Extinction cannot be used in generalized matching analyses, as the reinforcer ratio is infinite. Such sessions' data were therefore not used in fitting Equation 8.1. The incorporation of such conditions must await further research. Also note that since performances in the sixth sessions were similar to those obtained under explicit stable-state experiments, concurrent-schedule undermatching cannot result from the *order* in which experimental conditions were arranged (as was suggested by de Villiers, 1977).

In the simplest sense, *learning* is the way in which behavior changes from one stable state to another. It appears that the generalized matching law does a good job of describing these changes when they are conceptualized as a bias from previous conditions that dissipates over time. We now need some clear description of how the value of bias changes with time. For this, we need to know how sensitivity to previous-sessions' log reinforcer ratios falls with time. For instance, we might ask whether the value of a_i in Equation 8.1 decreases hyperbolically with time as does the effect of delayed reinforcers (Mazur, 1984, 1986) and the effect of delayed choice on discriminability in detection paradigms (Harnett, McCarthy, & Davison, 1984).

Answers to some of these questions may be obtained from research recently reported by Hunter and Davison (1985). They used two experimental conditions, a concurrent VI 60-s VI 240-s schedule and a concurrent VI 240-s VI 60-s

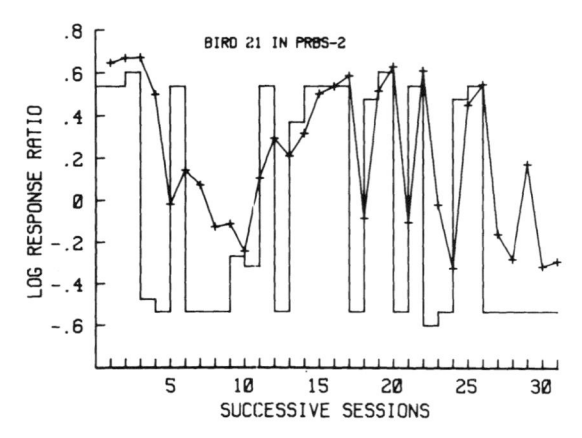

FIG. 8.1.   Obtained log reinforcer ratios and log response ratios during a 31-step pseudorandom binary sequence of concurrent VI 240-s VI 60-s schedules and concurrent VI 60-s VI 240-s schedules. The data are from Bird 21 in PRBS-2. Data points (+) show the subject's log response ratio, while the step function shows the obtained log reinforcer ratio in each session.

schedule. Which of the two conditions was in effect in each session was determined by a pseudorandom binary sequence (PRBS)—a sequence that is "white" in the sense that it has no sequential dependencies and thus cannot be predicted by the subject. The sequence, and hence the experiment, lasted 31 sessions, but the whole sequence was replicated for all six birds. A changeover delay of 1.5 s was used. Hunter and Davison carried out a systems identification on their data. This is a procedure, derived from engineering, that allows a description of the dynamic (as distinct from stable-state) behavior of a system. Because this book is concerned with matching, rather than being a primer of systems identification, we here provide an alternative analysis of Hunter and Davison's data in generalized matching terms.

As the reader may imagine, the behavior of the subjects over the 31 sessions appeared largely random, though certain general effects could be seen. For instance, the more sessions that were spent on one reinforcer ratio, the more the response ratio moved toward that reinforcer ratio. An example of one bird's performance in response to the pseudorandom binary input is shown in Fig. 8.1.

We will analyze Hunter and Davison's (1985) data, averaged over six birds in two PRBS sequences according to Equation 8.1. Notice first that the mean input (log reinforcer ratio) is approximately zero, and that the two *arranged* log reinforcer ratios are equidistant from this zero point. Most birds also showed no significant trend in the response ratios over the 31 sessions. First, we use linear regression to fit today's data against today's *obtained* reinforcer ratios. This gives an N of 31, and an estimate of the a_i value for $i = 0$ (no lag). The mean value averaged over all birds and replications was 0.293. We then subtract the predictions of this fit from the data to produce the residuals. These residuals are

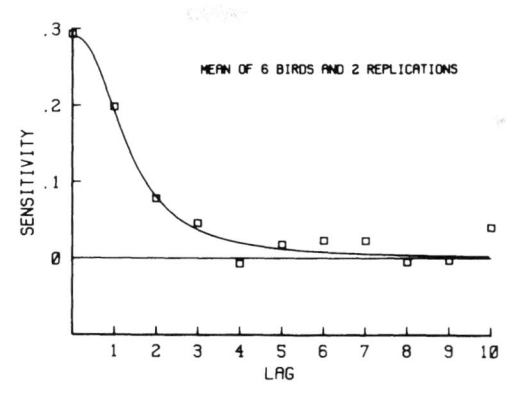

FIG. 8.2. Estimates of a_i values as a function of lag (i). The data shown are means across birds and replications. The smooth curve shows the best-fitting power hyperbola.

then regressed against the log reinforcer ratio from the previous session (lag = 1). Again, the residuals are obtained, and these are regressed against the inputs from two days prior to the current data. Each time we increase the lag, we decrease the N in the linear regression simply because the input data from sessions before the first in the PRBS are not available. In Fig. 8.2 we show the values of a_i as a function of i, the lag. From the analyses of individual subjects and replications, we find that the a_i values were significantly positive up until a lag of 3 (Binomial test), at which point the mean Σa_i ($i = 0$ to 3) across subjects was 0.615. This agrees with Davison and Hunter's (1979) finding that performance in the third session after a transition was still affected by the transition. If the number of sessions' lag is increased to 10, Σa_i increased to 0.704, indicating that there are possibly longer lasting effects of previous conditions than were discovered by Davison and Hunter. The average variance accounted for by the individual-subject fits was 89 percent (range 74 to 98).

In Fig. 8.2 we have shown one function that describes the change in a_i values as a function of lag with high accuracy. It is a power hyperbola of the form:

$$a_i = \frac{a_o}{1 + b\,i^j} = \frac{.29}{1 + .51i^{2.36}} \, ,$$

where i is the lag and b is a constant. Hence the log response ratio in a session may be predicted quite accurately from the equation:

$$\frac{B_{1i}}{B_{2i}} = \sum_{i=0}^{N} \left[\frac{.29}{1 + .51i^{2.36}} \log\left(\frac{R_{1i}}{R_{2i}}\right) \right] + \log c \, .$$

Of course, this specific equation does not have great generality, as individual animals' performances varied quite widely. It perhaps serves best as a suggestion of the general form of a transition equation.

The estimates of Σa_i found here were somewhat low for estimates of the stable-state a value. Hunter and Davison (1985) obtained even lower estimates from their analyses. The reason for this is, interestingly, probably due to prediction. Sometimes we tend to get prediction mixed up with teleological explanations of behavior, and to discard both. But prediction is not control by the future—it is control by a possible future *because* of the past. In a consistently varying environment, current discriminative stimuli can and do predict future environmental conditions. In the standard multiple schedule, for instance, the trained subject does not have to relearn the reinforcer rate (via the function in Fig. 8.2) each time a component is entered. Rather, the discriminative stimuli signal the start of the component, and behavior changes immediately. When an unpredictable series of inputs is arranged (a PRB sequence), prediction cannot occur. In stable-state experimentation, prediction can, and doubtless does, occur. To make this discussion concrete, in a stable-state experiment, the subject at stability will start the session with an appropriate response ratio. This cannot occur on a PRBS schedule. If we were, however, to collect data from only the last quarter of each session on a PRBS schedule, the a_i values in Fig. 8.2 would have been considerably higher, at least for a lag of zero, giving a higher total Σa_i. This procedure would be precisely analogous to the usual policy of analyzing data only when performance had stabilized.

One final point. The function used to describe the a_i values in Fig. 8.2 cannot be entirely correct for more frequent changes in input. The analysis of within-session changes deserves to be done. There is bound to be a certain amount of hysteresis before a change in input affects behavior, and so a_i values for very short lags will be zero. A better theoretical function would start at zero at the commencement of Session zero rather than at some substantial value at the end of Session zero as shown. Since the data are unavailable, we have not attempted to do this.

Similar effects of prior experimental exposure have been reported by Mitchell and White (1977). They investigated phenomena known as "freeloading" and "contrafreeloading." The question asked here is: Do animals prefer to work for food when food is freely available? The interest in the area stems from frequent reports that, when tested, animals prefer to work. Mitchell and White saw the problem as one of prior-training effects. They showed that more training to respond for food *biased* the results of a work versus free-food test toward work. However, more training to eat free food biased the test toward eating free food. Equal amounts of training gave intermediate results, but a bias toward free food was still evident. In a second experiment, White and Mitchell (1977) showed, as did Bauman, Shull and Brownstein (1975), that there was no bias toward either schedule in concurrent VI VT performance. Of course, under such *stable-state* conditions, no bias would be expected.

We should note here that Herrnstein (1979) has proposed a quantitative model for the acquisition of single responses that is consonant with his strict matching law. It is essentially a "new learning" model, but it could presumably be applied to both transitions for single responses and to response allocation during transitions between concurrent schedules.

8.2. CONTINUOUS CONCURRENT-SCHEDULE PERFORMANCE

In conventional experimentation, we arrange sessions of about one hour per day. Supplementary feeding, or postfeeding, follows each session in order to maintain a percentage body weight of between 75 percent and 85 percent. A number of researchers have wondered whether the same quantitative relations would be found if subjects were given 24 hours-per-day access to the same schedules. Hursh (1980) has discussed a number of large differences in performance on single schedules between short sessions at around 80 percent body weight, with postfeeding, and continuous performances in which the subject is provided with no postfeed. For instance, on a continuously available single VI schedule, response rates *fall* with increasing reinforcer rates, rather than increase as in conventional experiments.

There are a number of procedural differences between conventional and continuous experiments. It is important to specify at least the obvious differences before trying to identify which dimension may be responsible for a particular experimental effect. The differences are:

1. The level of deprivation may be different between short-session and continuous experiments. We can, of course, arrange continuous performances at standard deprivation levels, but only by decreasing either the reinforcer rate or the reinforcer amount.

2. As in 1, obtained and/or arranged reinforcer rates may be different.

3. Reinforcer amounts may be different.

4. An absence of postfeed in continuous procedures may have an effect. In Economic terms, the absence of postfeed defines a ''closed economy'' for food, whereas the provision of postfeed defines an ''open economy'' for food (see Hursh, 1980). Short-session experiments typically use an open food economy, and continuous experiments have typically used a closed economy for food, though these are by no means necessary relations. However, the descriptive terms ''open'' and ''closed'' economy are in many ways not very useful for two reasons: First, the description depends on the time span within which one is working—while a single one-hour session may be an open economy, presumably the food economy is theoretically closed over longer time spans. Second, the description may hide a series of different independent variables, some of which are mentioned above. It is, perhaps, bad practice to replace known and measurable independent variables (including amount of postfeed, and the relation between postfeed amount and body weight) with a qualitative designation. Despite this, the open-closed dichotomy (more properly, dimension) has

served to draw our attention to some potentially important independent variables and aspects of conventional procedures which may limit the generality of our results.

In regard to the first difference, we ask: Do continuous performances on concurrent schedules give rise to a different matching relation from that obtained in short sessions? This question must be answered in the negative if laboratory research on concurrent-schedule performance is to have any direct relevance to real-life situations. The answer does appear to be negative. Baum (1972) kept a single pigeon in a two-key experimental chamber for seven months. He exposed the subject to a variety of concurrent VI VI schedules that provided, overall, between 15 and 23 reinforcers per hour. The changeover delay was 1.8 s. Response allocation was very close to strict matching (a sensitivity of 1.0), though some hysteresis was evident as reinforcer ratios were first increased, then decreased, then increased again. The pigeon's body weight stabilized at about 92 percent of its free-feeding weight. This single experiment appears to allow us to make the generalization that neither session duration nor closed economies affect concurrent VI VI response allocation. Two further points should be noted: (1) Baum did not report time-allocation data; conventional measures of time allocation (from first response to first response) would probably not have produced time-allocation matching simply because the long pauses (for instance, overnight) that probably occurred would confound such data; and (2) Baum noted that the obtained reinforcer ratios were somewhat more extreme than the arranged reinforcer ratios. Since strict matching to the obtained ratios occurred, this finding supports the notion that matching is to obtained, rather than arranged, reinforcer ratios. Had the data been plotted as a function of the arranged ratios, substantial overmatching would have been found. While this experiment used only one subject, and thus has little generality, Davison (unreported) systematically replicated Baum's experiment and obtained the same strict matching result.

In a related experiment, Baum (1974b) allowed a flock of free-ranging pigeons access to concurrent VI VI schedules in the attic of a house. Only one bird could gain access to the two manipulanda at any one time, and no changeover delay was arranged. The data clearly indicated that at least 10, and probably 20, pigeons participated, yet the overall performance was again very close to strict matching. The birds were presumably operating under continuous sessions (though the presence of a bird already in the chamber would constrain this) and were in, so far as the experiment was concerned, an open economy. The birds were also, presumably, at their normal body weights, though the normal body weight of a free-ranging pigeon might be rather different from the stable weight in the laboratory under ad libitum feeding.

In summary, concurrent VI VI performance seems to be independent of deprivation (see also McSweeney, 1975a), type of economy, and session duration. We do not know, as yet, whether this independence extends to other concurrent-schedule types, to variations of reinforcer amounts or delays, and so forth.

Some further data on the effects of economy and deprivation (on multiple VI VI schedule performance) are discussed in Section 9.8. The invariance of response-allocation sensitivity with respect to these variables does not extend to multiple VI VI schedule performance.

8.3. PUNISHMENT

The definition of punishment (the process) is something of a vexed question because, like reinforcement, most definitions (example: "Punishment decreases the probability of responses that it follows") are circular when used to define what a punisher is ("a contingent stimulus that decreases the probability of a response"). We strongly favor a relativistic (Premack, 1971) definition of reinforcement and punishment. Such a definition suggests that a response is decreased in probability if it is followed by another response of lower probability, and increased if it is followed by another response of higher probability. This approach brings with it the notions (1) that reinforcers and punishers lie on the same dimension; (2) that no response, except in the limit, can be defined a priori as a reinforcer or a punisher—rather, its action depends on the context in which it occurs; and (3) that the probability of a response, and hence its action in a particular situation, can be changed in various ways, for instance, by deprivation or by training. Premack's Indifference Principle states that the reason for the current response probability is irrelevant to the reinforcement relation (taking "reinforcement" now as generic to include both response-increasing and response-decreasing contingencies).

Holz (1968) was the first to examine the effects of the prototypical punisher—electric shock—on concurrent VI VI performance. He arranged concurrent VI 114-s VI 450-s schedules with a changeover delay of 0.65 s. He varied punishment intensity for every response from 0, through 3, 6, 7.5, to 9 mA for one bird, and up to 7.5 mA for another. Absolute response rates fell more with increasing shock intensity on the higher than on the lower reinforcer-rate key. However, when this rate decrease was expressed as a percentage of the no-punishment baseline response rates, the proportional changes on both keys were identical. In other words, the distribution of responses between components obtained under no-shock conditions was maintained across all shock intensities.

Notice that in Holz's (1968) experiment, since each response was punished, the punishment frequency equaled the response rate on each key. The data provided by Holz can be used to calculate point estimates of sensitivity to reinforcer frequency (assuming no bias). The mean values for the two birds were 0.75 and 0.87, and there was no significant trend with shock intensity. This result suggests—weakly at least—that if every response is punished, subjects will simply (under)match to the obtained reinforcer ratio.

Holz's (1968) initial work was extended by Deluty (1976) in a study that allowed the relative shock frequency for concurrent VI VI behavior to be varied independently. Equal exponential VI 90-s food schedules were arranged. The shock frequency on Lever 1 was 10 per hour, and that on Lever 2 was varied from 0 to 20 per hour over five conditions and a number of replications. The changeover delay was 2 s, the shock duration was 0.5 s, and the shock intensity was set at different levels for the three rats. Deluty found that as the punishment frequency on Lever 2 was increased, the response rate on that lever fell, and the response rate on Lever 1 increased—an example of the punishment contrast effect (Brethower & Reynolds, 1962; see Section 7.11a). Deluty suggested a strict matching model to account for his data. With S denoting shock frequency,

$$\frac{B_1}{B_2} = \frac{R_1 + S_2}{R_2 + S_1}.$$ (8.4)

This equation, in relative form, accounted for 88 percent of the data variance. A strict matching reinforcer-frequency-only model accounted for 81 percent of the data variance, presumably because obtained reinforcer ratios deviated rather widely from the arranged ratios at some punishment frequencies. Notice that Equation 8.4 does not deal well with the implication of Holz's study. If $S_1 = B_1$ and $S_2 = B_2$, then increasing the *values* of S_1 and S_2 (increasing shock intensity) will produce a decreasing sensitivity to R_1/R_2—unless, of course, the behavior ratio changes, which in Holz's study it did not do.

de Villiers (1977, 1980) suggested an alternative quantitative approach that had originally been mentioned by Estes (1969) in qualitative form. The assumption is that punishers decrease the values of positive reinforcement. Thus:

$$\frac{B_1}{B_2} = \frac{R_1 - \alpha S_1}{R_2 - \alpha S_2},$$ (8.5)

where the parameter α scales the effects of a constant-intensity punisher to the effects of a constant-value positive reinforcer. To take an example, if $\alpha = 5$, then five punishers are equal to one food reinforcer—though, of course, opposite in sign as indicated in Equation 8.5. Logically, Deluty's (1976) Equation 8.4 must also have such a scaling factor in it.

de Villiers (1980) pointed out that if the rates of shock were the same for the two concurrent schedules, and $R_1 > R_2$, then increasing shock intensities are predicted, by Equations 8.4 and 8.5, to change response allocation in different ways. Deluty's (1976) equation suggests a decreased response ratio (toward undermatching), and de Villiers' equation predicts an increased response ratio (toward overmatching). In two experiments, one using independent schedules and one using dependent schedules to arrange both food and shock, de Villiers found a clear trend toward overmatching. This finding supports the subtractive model (Equation 8.5). The data that de Villiers obtained were also inconsistent with a finding by Bradshaw, Szabadi, and Bevan (1978). They investigated the effects of punishment (points loss with humans) of single VI schedule performance on the values of k and R_e in Herrnstein's (1970) equation (Equation 2.2). Punishment increased R_e and reduced k. If this was the only effect of punishment, then increasing punishment intensities should produce no change in concurrent-schedule response allocation (see Section 2.1).

Farley and Fantino (1978) also suggested the subtractive model of punishment (Equation 8.5) in a study of the effects of punishment in the terminal links of concurrent-chain schedules. Following this work, Farley (1980) provided strong support for the subtractive model of punishment in concurrent VI VI schedules. His first experiment was similar to that reported by de Villiers (1980). Farley found the same movement toward overmatching when equally frequent punishers were introduced for both alternative responses reinforced at different rates. In his second experiment, Farley investigated the effects of shock-frequency changes on absolute response rates when both the reinforcer frequencies and the shock frequencies were equal on the two alternatives. Following Herrnstein (1970) (Section 2.1), absolute response rates under punishment may be described by Equation 8.6 for the subtractive model:

$$B_1 = \frac{k(R_1 - \alpha S_1)}{(R_1 - \alpha S_1) + (R_2 - \alpha S_2) + R_e}, \qquad (8.6)$$

and, for the additive model, by Equation 8.7:

$$B_1 = \frac{k(R_1 + \alpha S_2)}{(R_1 + \alpha S_2) + (R_2 + \alpha S_1) + R_e}. \qquad (8.7)$$

If the values of S_1 and S_2 are incremented by a constant amount, with $S_1 = S_2$, Equation 8.6 predicts that absolute response rates will fall, while Equation 8.7 predicts that they will rise. The two equations make the same opposing predictions when $R_1 < R_2$ and $S_1 < S_2$. Farley found that absolute response rates fell strongly when shock frequencies were increased.

The third experiment reported by Farley (1980) investigated the effects of keeping both R_1/R_2 and S_1/S_2 constant, and increasing the absolute values of R_1 and R_2. When $R_1 > S_1$, the subtractive model predicts a decrease in preference, whereas the additive model predicts an increase in preference. A decrease was obtained.

Overall, Farley's (1980) three experiments give very strong support to the subtractive model, which he takes as being a quantitative statement of the negative law of effect "devoid of irrelevant speculation about the weakening of

S-R connections (Thorndike, 1913)'' (p. 324). Farley characterized the additive model as being a quantification of previous (verbal) competing-response models in which adding punishment to one response increases the value of alternative responses.

de Villiers (1982) has summarized quantitative research on punishment and the support for the subtractive model. But he notes that some results are not entirely consistent with this model. One difficulty comes from concurrent VI VI research with humans (Bradshaw, Szabadi, & Bevan, 1979) On these schedules, without punishment, subjects showed a mean response sensitivity of 1.31 (all three estimates were greater than 1). When the performance on one key was punished (loss of monetary reinforcers) on a VR 34 schedule, response-allocation sensitivity to the VI reinforcer ratio fell to an average of 0.09. Mean bias also increased from 0.18 (no punishment) to 1.27 toward the unpunished schedule. Similar effects occurred for the time-allocation data, but all time sensitivities were *lower* than the corresponding response sensitivities. As de Villiers notes, the procedure used by Bradshaw et al. has not been employed with animals. In particular, punishment was arranged only for the constant VI 51-s reinforcer schedule while the alternate schedules were changed in the range VI 8 s to VI 720 s every 10 minutes.

A second problem with the subtractive model is that it would appear that the ratio can become negative if shock effects are greater than reinforcer effects on a schedule. This, however, is unlikely because as shock effects become great, both shock frequencies and reinforcer frequencies will decrease until no responses are emitted and no shocks and reinforcers are obtained. At this point, the ratio becomes infinite and exclusive responding occurs. As a stable-state model, this is probably not a difficulty for the subtractive model.

Finally, the subtractive model also does not seem to be able to account for Holz's (1968) results, except perhaps as a serendipitous special case.

8.4. AVOIDANCE

The move toward an acceptance of the negative law of effect for punishment has been paralleled in the literature by a similar trend in the explanation of avoidance behavior. In a prototypical experiment, Baum (1973) gave pigeons 7-mA shocks every second, and reinforcers consisted of 2-min timeout from shocks. Access to these timeout periods was controlled by two concurrent exponential VI schedules, and the periods were produced by the pigeons standing on one side or the other of a tilt box. A changeover delay, which allowed no timeouts to be produced until the subject had been standing on one side for more than 1 s, was used. Changeover delays and periods during which the pigeons were standing on both sides were signaled by a white light. Time allocated to the two sides of the chamber, excluding white-light time, was the main behavioral measure. The VI schedules were varied over nine conditions from concurrent VI 30 s VI 480 s to concurrent VI 480 s VI 30 s. The behavior took a substantial time (up to four weeks) to stabilize. But, when log time-allocation ratios were plotted against the log ratio of the numbers of timeouts produced, the data were generally quite well fitted by straight lines of slope varying from 0.38 to 1.5, with various biases. Over the four birds, the slopes averaged 1.01, and the biases -0.12. As a result, Baum suggested that the reduction in the rate of shock plays the same role in avoidance as does the rate of reinforcement in appetitive behavior, and that both types of performance fit within the matching law.

Conceptually, however, the situation is a little less clear. Both Baum and Rachlin (1969) and Brownstein and Pliskoff (1968) investigated time allocation on concurrent VT VT schedules, and both found an approximation to matching. The procedure they used was standard in that both VT schedules ran continuously, stopping only when a reinforcer was arranged. The schedules did not stop when the animal was in the other component. When this procedure is used in an avoidance situation, an approximation to matching does *not* result (Deluty & Church, 1978, Experiment 2). Rather, the subject remains exclusively on the alternative with the lower shock rate. Deluty and Church used a 2-s changeover delay, which, in their experiment, was a time during which shocks could not be delivered. Deluty and Church's result is not surprising because the probability of a shock following a changeover is an increasing function of the time spent before the changeover. In shock-frequency reduction terms, the subject is emitting the response that provides the greater decrease in shock frequency. Responding on both alternatives would lead to a higher shock rate. Thus, for example, on a concurrent VI 30-s shock VI 60-s shock schedule, emitting only Response 1 gives 2 shocks per minute, emitting Response 2 will give 1 shock per minute, and responding on both schedules will give up to 3 shocks per minute. The question that remains, however, is this: In shock-frequency reduction terms, *from* what baseline level is the subject reducing the shock frequency?

In their Experiment 1, Deluty and Church (1978) arranged that the VI shock schedules *stopped* when the subject was on the alternate schedule. Since shocks were delivered with a fixed probability every 0.1 s, the expected time to a shock is quite independent of the amount of time spent on the alternate schedule before a switch. Under these conditions, a matching relation was obtained. To a first approximation:

$$\frac{T_1}{T_2} = \frac{S_2}{S_1},$$

where S is the number of shocks obtained by the subject. This result accords very well indeed with Deluty's (1976) additive model for punishment (Equation 8.4) when $R_1 = R_2 = 0$. It does *not* seem derivable from the Farley (1980), Farley and Fantino (1978), and de Villiers (1980) subtractive models (Section 8.3).

Response allocation in concurrent VI VI avoidance schedules was investigated by Logue and de Villiers (1978). Using rats, they arranged shock deliveries when each VI schedule timed an interval. A single response in each VI interval canceled the next shock arranged by that schedule, and a COD of 1 s ensured that shocks were not canceled until the rats had been responding on a lever for more than 1 s. Logue and de Villiers arranged eight concurrent VI VI schedule pairs for the two rats. They found a straightforward relation between log response-allocation or time-allocation ratios and the log ratio of the numbers of shocks avoided by responding on the two levers. Response-allocation sensitivities were 0.82 and 0.92, and time-allocation sensitivities were, as often found, greater at 1.22 and 1.32. One rat showed a positive response bias and a negative time bias, while the other showed exactly the opposite result. Logue and de Villiers also showed that the log ratio of shocks *received* as the independent variable was not convincingly related to log response or time allocation. Thus, the results were consistent with subtractive, rather than with additive, models.

Taking a shock-frequency reduction approach, but using a different procedure, de Villiers (1972) investigated performance on multiple random-interval (RI) schedules. Shocks were delivered at two different frequencies in the two components, and the rats could eliminate the next shock by emitting at least one lever press after a scheduled shock. De Villiers fitted Herrnstein's (1970) equation for absolute response rates on multiple schedules (Section 3.1) using two possible reinforcer variables: Shock-frequency obtained, and shock-frequency reduction (that is, the arranged minus the obtained shock frequencies). Reasonable parameter values of k, m and R_e were obtained for both fits in his Experiment 1. Then the obtained k and R_e values were used to predict absolute response rates on single RI-avoidance schedules in Experiment 2. The shock-frequency reduction model predicted more accurately than the obtained shock-frequency model. This finding was supported by a further experiment.

The above procedure was also used by de Villiers (1974) in a parametric study of single- and multiple-schedule avoidance. In Experiment 1, using single VI-avoidance schedules, he varied the VI schedules from 15 s to 75 s and showed that Herrnstein's (1970) equation for single-schedule performance (Equation 2.2, Section 2.1), with shock-frequency reduction as the reinforcer, described the performance accurately. In Experiment 2, he used four multiple VI VI avoidance schedules with component durations varying from 13.3 s to 900 s. Again, using shock-frequency reduction as the putative reinforcer generally produced a close approximation to strict matching. At 40-s component durations, the mean deviations from strict relative matching given by the shock-frequency reduction account (with those given by the obtained shock-frequency account in parentheses) were 0.033 (0.066), 0.021 (0.048) and 0.032 (0.072) for the three birds. The assumption here is this: Since relatively short component durations produce matching on multiple VI food schedules, the finding of matching on multiple VI avoidance schedules supports the generality of the matching to shock-frequency reduction account. Unfortunately, strict matching on short-component VI food schedules under conditions similar to those investigated by de Villiers may not be a robust effect (see Section 9.3).

Overall, it is evident that shock-frequency reduction provides an adequate qualitative description of avoidance performance, and often a quantitative shock-frequency reduction model fits well. It is also evident, however, that we have not quite understood all the quantitative possibilities here. The outstanding problems are:

1. How does the subject compute the frequency of shock that is the baseline for shock-frequency reduction in the light of the fact that it is very seldom exposed to that frequency?

2. What is the appropriate measure of shock-frequency reduction in the concurrent VT avoidance situation used by Deluty and Church (1978)?

It is generally evident that *molar* shock-frequency reduction (that is, the overall average rate by which shock frequency is decreased) is an inappropriate measure anyway. Either more molecular measures have to be considered, or shock frequency and shock-frequency reduction may not be measured as shocks per unit time. For instance, "avoidance" performance can be maintained when a response either does not decrease, or even increases, the overall shock frequency (Hineline, 1970; Lewis, Gardner, & Hutton, 1976). This occurs in situations in which the higher frequencies of shocks overall have a smaller average immediacy (are more distant in time from the start of the shock period). Such results exactly parallel the same situation with positive reinforcement in which, given equal reinforcer rates, animals prefer the option that gives them the reinforcers sooner (Davison, 1968; Killeen, 1968; Chapter 10). There is some merit, then, in the suggestion of Deluty and Church (1978) that, in avoidance, behavior allocation is an inverse function of the expected times to shock—and equivalently, in appetitive behavior, it is a direct function of the expected time to reinforcement. This explains the exclusive responding on concurrent VI VI food schedules when only the currently-accessed schedule runs.

8.5. MELIORATION

Various mechanisms have been proposed to account for, or to underlie, matching. It appears that many researchers are not satisfied with a molar matching process. Rather, they prefer to see it as resulting from some more fundamental process such as maximizing the probability of reinforcement for each response or maximizing the total reinforcer rate. Many of these suggestions are reviewed, and their links with other sciences drawn, in Commons, Herrnstein, and Rachlin (1982). One such suggestion is discussed here because it has generated some potentially interesting experimental procedures. The topic is *melioration* (Herrnstein & Vaughan, 1980). Melioration is a dynamic process in which a difference between local rates of reinforcers leads to a continuous change in the distribution of behavior in the direction of an equality of local reinforcer rates. Thus, if T_1 and T_2 are the times allocated to the two responses, the local difference in reinforcer rates, R_d, is:

$$R_d = \frac{R_1}{T_1} - \frac{R_2}{T_2} .$$

The change in behavior leads to changing time allocation (or perhaps time allocation is directly changed by the existence of the inequality of local reinforcer rates), and the system stabilizes when $R_d = 0$. Melioration will sometimes predict that a subject will choose in such a way as to maximize the overall rate of reinforcers. Sometimes, however, it will predict that a subject will accept a lower reinforcer rate than the maximum available in that situation. Vaughan (1981) specifically tested melioration against molar maximization. The procedure was complex in that various reinforcer rates and ratios were available for different time allocations, which were assessed every 4 min.

The contingencies arranged by Vaughan (1981) are shown in Table 8.2, and are displayed as feedback functions in Fig. 8.3. There were two parts to the experiment, labeled A and B. Each schedule ran only when the birds were switched into that alternative. As a result, the *local* reinforcer rates were controlled. Panels A1 and B1 in Fig. 8.3 show the arranged relation between relative reinforcer frequency for the two responses and the relative time allocated to the two responses. There were two regions, shown by heavy lines, in which relative time allocation could equal (or match) relative reinforcer frequencies, and these regions were the same in the two parts of the experiment. In Panels A2 and B2 the overall reinforcer-rate feedback functions are shown as a function of relative time allocation. The time-allocation regions producing maximum reinforcer rates are shown by heavy lines, and these regions were again the same in the two parts of the experiment. Finally, Panels A3 and B3 of Fig. 8.3 show relative local reinforcer rate feedback functions as a function of relative time allocation. Stable-state melioration implies relative local reinforcer rates of 0.5, and there were two such regions in each part of the experiment. However, the dynamics of melioration require that when the relative local reinforcer rate is above 0.5, relative time allocation to the first key will increase. Equally, when the relative local reinforcer rate is below 0.5, relative time allocation will decrease. The direction of these dynamic effects is shown by arrows. In the light of these effects, the predicted time-allocation regions in which performance should stabilize are shown by heavy lines, and the regions are different between the two parts of the experiment.

The results of the experiment were quite clear. In Part A, the relative time allocation for the three birds was 0.2, 0.16, and 0.15, well within the maximizing region, and also consistent with matching. However, in Part B, the

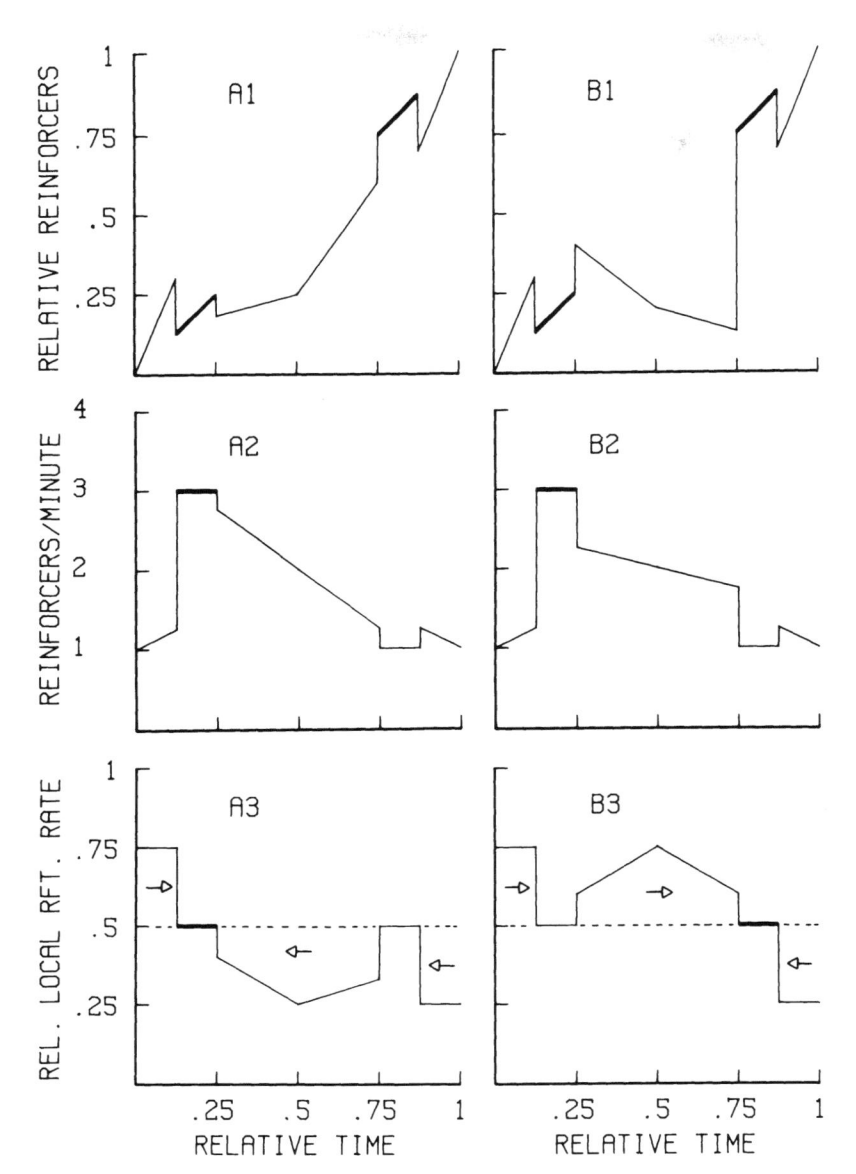

FIG. 8.3.   A diagram of the feedback functions arranged by Vaughan (1981). The two parts of the experiment are designated A and B. For each part, the top panels show relative reinforcer frequency as a function of relative time allocation; the center panels show total reinforcers per minute as a function of relative time allocation; and the bottom graphs show relative *local* reinforcer rates as a function of relative time allocation. Note that, for each procedure, the three feedback functions are simply different ways of describing that procedure. Heavy lines show the regions in which a subject's time allocation should fall according to matching (top panels), molar maximizing (center panels), and melioration (bottom panels). Arrows show the direction in which dynamic melioration will change time allocation.

final time-allocation proportions were 0.79, 0.77, and 0.78, with an overall reinforcer rate of about 1 per minute rather than the 3 per minute available for time-allocation proportions of 0.125 to 0.25. This result is also consistent with matching. The subjects clearly did not maximize overall reinforcer rates, leaving two possibilities: matching, or melioration. Vaughan argued that for the subjects to move from the obtained Part A performance to the Part B performance, their behavior had to move through very considerable deviations from matching (Fig. 8.3, Panel B1). The fact that behavior did move through these deviations suggests, as Vaughan notes, that the dynamic process is *not* one of minimizing deviations from matching.

TABLE 8.2
The Procedure Used by Vaughan (1981)[a]

Rel. Time Alloc. to Right	A: Schedules		B: Schedules	
	Right	Left	Right	Left
0–0.125	20	60	20	60
0.125–0.25	20	20	20	20
0.25–0.5	30–60	20	20	30–60
0.5–0.75	60	20–30	20–30	60
0.75–0.875	60	60	60	60
0.875–1.0	60	20	60	20

[a]All schedules were VI schedules and their values are shown in seconds. Where two values are shown (e.g., 30–60), the schedule values changed progressively with relative time allocation.

It is a little too early to assess the impact of melioration. There are some obvious, though maybe minor, problems. If time allocation undermatches obtained reinforcer ratios, the model has to be more complicated than the strict matching model presently suggested. Second, as Herrnstein (1982) points out, it is not obvious how to apply melioration theory to performance on multiple schedules. To develop this point further, if melioration is to be a competitor for molar generalized matching, melioration theory will have to be extended to account for most of the phenomena discussed in this book. It must also be subject to assessment at the molecular level to determine the rules by which time allocation changes dynamically in response to an inequality of local reinforcer rates.

On the other hand, the value of melioration theory may be in the technique that Vaughan (1981) developed to test the theory, rather than in the theory itself. As we have suggested in Section 7.1, the move away from schedule naming and toward the specification of experimental procedures in terms of absolute feedback functions (AFFs, which determine the overall reinforcer rate) and relative feedback functions (RFFs) must occur. Vaughan has shown how this can be done and how useful the technique is.

8.6. CHANGING OVER

Changing over between schedules has been investigated both as a measurable aspect of behavior (a dependent variable) and as a procedural contingency that affects matching performance. We deal with both aspects here, though we have dealt with the effects of changeover-delay length on sensitivity to reinforcer frequency in Section 6.1.

8.6a. Changeover Contingencies and Changeover Performance

Changeover performance on concurrent schedules (both two-key and switching-key procedures) has frequently been reported, but rather less frequently have such data been subjected to any quantitative analysis. The first basic, descriptive, finding is that changeover rates (numbers of changeovers per total session time) are maximal when schedules are equal and decrease with increasing inequality (Baum, 1974a; Catania, 1963a; Herrnstein, 1961; Stubbs & Pliskoff, 1969). The second is that changeover rates decrease as the changeover delay is increased (Stubbs, Pliskoff, & Reid, 1977). The third is that main-key (food-key) response rates are higher during the changeover delay than after it (Dreyfus, Dorman, Fetterman, & Stubbs, 1982; Menlove, 1975; Pliskoff, 1971; Pliskoff, Cicerone, & Nelson, 1978). The fourth is that response rates during the changeover delay on the lower reinforcer-rate key are higher than those on the higher reinforcer-rate key (Dreyfus et al., 1982; Silberberg & Fantino, 1970). Indeed, Silberberg and Fantino's data can be analyzed to show that the sensitivity of the behavior ratio during the changeover delay to the reinforcer-rate ratio is overall *negative*, whereas response ratios after the changeover delay show very strong overmatching (*a* values around 1.5). Attempts have been made so far to quantify only some of the above effects.

Stubbs, Pliskoff, & Reid (1977) analyzed a large number of experimental reports on the effects of changeover delay on performance. They suggested that there was in general a power-function relation between average interchangeover time (ICT) and the value of the changeover delay or changeover ratio. (The latter is a procedure in which a fixed number of responses on the switching key is required to produce a change in schedules.) If *ICT* denotes interchangeover time, and T_c denotes changeover-delay duration, then:

$$ICT_i = c \, (T_{ci})^{.85} \left(\frac{R_i}{R_j} \right)^m , \qquad (8.8)$$

where i and j are two alternatives. For later purposes, we will rewrite Equation 8.8 in terms of the local changeover rate, c_{ij}, that is, the number of changeovers per time spent on the schedule:

$$c_{ij} = \frac{1}{c(T_{ci})^{.85}} \cdot \left(\frac{R_j}{R_i}\right)^{2m} , \qquad (8.9)$$

where c_{ij} is the rate of changing from i to j. The ratio c_{ji}/c_{ij} is, of course, the time-allocation ratio T_i/T_j, so Equation 8.9 implies:

$$\frac{T_i}{T_j} = \left(\frac{T_{ci}}{T_{cj}}\right)^{.85} \cdot \left(\frac{R_i}{R_j}\right)^{2m} . \qquad (8.10)$$

It is difficult to estimate the value of m from the plots shown by Stubbs et al., but the slopes for Equation 8.8 would appear to be about half that for the generalized matching law. Hence, the power $2m$ in Equation 8.10 equals about 1.0, and is indeed quite consonant with the generalized matching law. The relation in Equation 8.10 predicts (1) matching to changeover-delay ratios, and (2) biased matching to reinforcer ratios when changeover delays are unequal. It deserves to be more fully investigated.

Other quantitative models of changeover performance have been given, usually verbally, by Herrnstein (1961), Miller and Loveland (1974), and Baum (1974c). These accounts were quantitatively interpreted by Hunter & Davison (1978). Herrnstein (1961) suggested that overall changeover rate is an unspecified inverse function (f) of the absolute difference in the proportions of the reinforcers provided by the two schedules. If C_{ij} refers to overall changeover frequency (changeovers per session), then:

$$C_{ij} = f\left[\frac{R_i - R_j}{R_i + R_j}\right] .$$

Given that f is an inverse function, this equation reaches a maximum when $R_i = R_j$ and a minimum when R_i or $R_j = 0$. Hence, it can, in principle, describe the fact that changeover rates are maximal when the schedules are equal. However, the equation suggests that changeover rates on, for example, concurrent VI 6-s VI 6-s schedules would be the same as on concurrent VI 6000-s VI 6000-s schedules, which seems unlikely.

Miller and Loveland (1974) suggested:

$$\frac{C_{ij}}{\Sigma C} = \frac{R_j}{\Sigma R} ,$$

for their five-key concurrent VI VI data. The problem, as pointed out by Hunter and Davison (1978), is that this equation cannot account for changeovers in two-alternative concurrent schedules in which C_{ij}/C_{ji} has an expected value of 1.0 for any combination of schedules.

Baum (1974c, 1976) plotted total changeover rates as a function of reinforcer-, response-, and time-allocation ratios but did not specify a function relating the dependent variable to the various independent variables. As Hunter and Davison (1978) pointed out, it is unclear how such equations could account for performance when the number of alternatives is greater than two.

Hunter and Davison (1978) also attempted to model changeover performance. They suggested three equations:

$$C_{ij} = m_1 \frac{B_i \cdot B_j}{\Sigma B} , \qquad (8.11)$$

$$C_{ij} = m_2 \frac{T_i \cdot T_j}{(\Sigma T)^2} , \qquad (8.12)$$

$$\text{and} \quad C_{ij} = m_3 \frac{R_i \cdot R_j}{(\Sigma R)^2} . \qquad (8.13)$$

Equations 8.11 to 8.13 fit Hunter and Davison's (1978) multi-key concurrent VI data quite well, with a mean of 86 percent, 88 percent, and 83 percent of the data variance accounted for, respectively, across 6 birds and 63 data points. Equations 8.11 and 8.12 are obviously more powerful than Equation 8.13 in the sense that they can deal directly with a biased performance without modification. (Presumably, for a biased performance, the maximal changeover rate for a constant overall reinforcer rate occurs when the behavior, or the time, allocations are equal, rather than when the reinforcer rates are equal.) However, Equation 8.13 is able to predict changeover rates from *independent* variables, and would do so if it was extended to take into account other choice-affecting variables according to the Baum and Rachlin (1969) concatenation (Section 4.4). Equations 8.11 and 8.12 are relations between *dependent* variables. Hunter and Davison extended Equations 8.11 to 8.13 to deal with the effect of changeover-delay durations (which changes the slope *m* of the equations) and of unequal changeover delays. These extended equations accounted for substantial proportions of the data variance in a wide variety of experiments.

Equation 8.13 has one essential feature. It predicts maximal changeover rates when the schedules are equal. However, like Stubbs, Pliskoff, & Reid's (1977) equation (Equation 8.8), it predicts that changeover rates are independent of overall reinforcer rates. If it is the case that both time- and response-allocation ratios are independent of overall reinforcer rates on concurrent schedules, Hunter and Davison's (1978) Equations 8.11 and 8.12 also imply independence from overall reinforcer rates. Additionally, Hunter and Davison's equations predict that overall changeover rates are always equal on two-alternative concurrent schedules. This is tautologously true for standard concurrent-schedule arrangements, but it is not true of all possible concurrent VI VI procedures, as we now demonstrate.

Research reported by Tustin and Davison (1979) discriminated between two aspects of changeover delays. These are: (1) a changeover delay is a period of time during which reinforcers are unavailable; and (2) a changeover delay is a period of time during which changeovers are not emitted. This latter requirement is sometimes explicitly arranged, but even if it is not so arranged, the subjects simply do not emit changeovers during the changeover delay (Baum, 1974c; Menlove, 1975). The first requirement constrains reinforcer delivery; the second constrains the frequency of changing over. Tustin and Davison varied the second type of requirement by arranging VI (and also FI) schedules on the changeover key. Only when these schedules had completed timing could a changeover response alternate the food schedule, which ran continuously in the usual fashion. The first aspect of a changeover delay was kept constant in that every response on the changeover key, effective or not, eliminated the possibility of a main-key response being reinforced for 1.5 s. Tustin and Davison varied the changeover schedules (always equal between the keys) in the range 15 s to 360 s. We present here a reanalysis of their published data, which were not analyzed directly by Tustin and Davison to show choice-sensitivity changes. It is worth noting, from a design point of view, that their VI changeover schedules were arithmetic and comprised 13 intervals, so that the same minimum interchange-over time was not always associated with the same main-key alternative.

The measures taken by Tustin and Davison (1979) were: (1) main-key responses on each schedule; (2) changeover-key responses in the presence of each schedule; and (3) the time-allocation measures defined between schedules by each effective switch. These times were further divided to obtain the time allocated to the main key and to the changeover keys in the presence of each of the two main-key schedules. These measures were defined by the first response on the main key after responding on the switching key, and the first response on the switching key after responding on the main key. In the following analysis, the VI 60-s changeover-schedule data comprised seven conditions, the VI 360-s changeover-schedule data comprised five conditions, and the VI 15-s and VI 180-s changeover-schedule data comprised two conditions each. Figure 8.4 shows estimates of both response and time sensitivity to reinforcer frequency, and we have taken the liberty of adding estimates of 0.8 (response) and 1.0 (time) sensitivities for a VI 0-s (or FR 1) changeover-schedule requirement—the standard concurrent arithmetic VI schedule result (Taylor & Davison, 1983). We have also assumed a changeover-key sensitivity of 0 for the VI 0-s changeover-schedule requirement as the number of changeover responses to and from an alternative is always the same (± 1) for that procedure.

Three sets of data are shown for both response and time allocation. First, the main- and changeover-key behaviors are pooled. (Note that changeover behavior is normally allocated to food-key measures in a two-key concurrent schedule, but it is not on a switching-key procedure. The likely difference in using these two procedures is small, but may be significant, and may result in the two-key

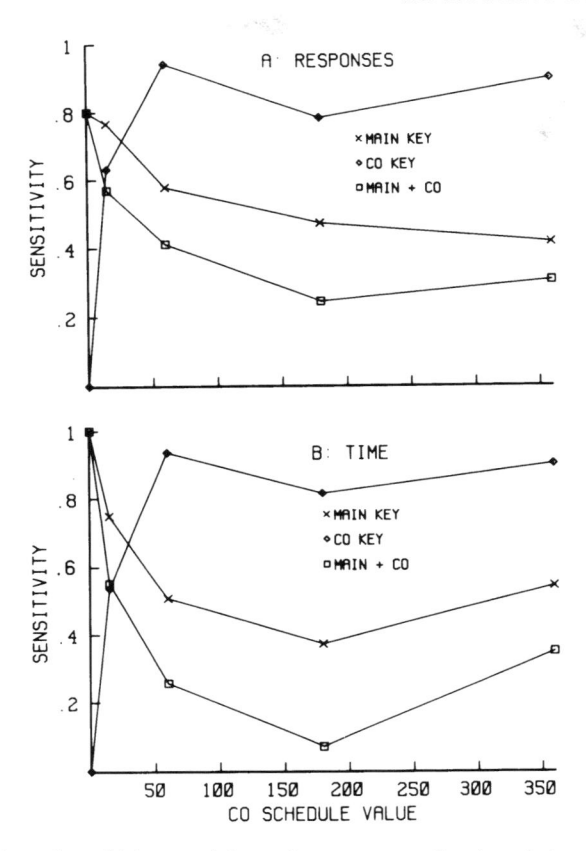

FIG. 8.4. Estimated sensitivity to reinforcer frequency as a function of the minimum mean interchangeover time arranged. Reinforcers were obtained on concurrent VI VI schedules, and the changeover schedules were also VI schedules. The data were reanalyzed from Tustin and Davison (1979).

procedure producing on the average a little more undermatching than the changeover-key procedure.) For both response and time measures, sensitivity fell as the changeover schedule was increased. Second, the sensitivity of the main-key performance only was plotted, and these measures also decreased with increasing changeover schedules for both responses and time measures. Indeed, as the changeover-schedule value was increased, the procedure became more like a multiple schedule in that the subjects were forced to remain in the presence of the alternatives for considerable periods. Thus, the main-key response sensitivity fell to between 0.4 and 0.5, a value typical of multiple-schedule performance (Charman & Davison, 1982).

Figure 8.4 also shows changeover-key performance sensitivity as the changeover schedules were increased. These sensitivity values are to the inverse reinforcer ratios in comparison with those for the main-key analyses because changing over to an alternative schedule is presumably increased by a higher reinforcer rate on the alternative schedule. As we assumed, changeover-response and changeover-time sensitivities commenced at zero for FR 1 changeover schedules because in those conditions frequencies of changeovers between the keys are always equal. Hence, the number of changeovers per session to each alternative (overall changeover rates) are equal. Sensitivity must therefore be zero. Changeover-performance sensitivities became greater as the change-over schedules were lengthened, apparently reaching an asymptote at around 0.9 for both changeover responses and changeover time. This sensitivity value is approximately that normally found for food-key performance. It is evident, therefore, that increasing the changeover-schedule requirements pro-gressively constrained the concurrent-schedule performance. When these changeover schedules were long, considerable undermatching of the total-time ratio spent on the schedules to the overall reinforcer ratio was found, suggesting that effective changeovers were emitted soon after the changeover schedules allowed a changeover. This resulted in more equal times spent on the two schedules than would occur if the changeover schedules were short.

What aspect of the procedure could have produced the high sensitivity of changeover performance ratios to inverse reinforcer ratios? Let us commence with the standard equation for time allocation on concurrent VI VI schedules:

$$\frac{T_i}{T_j} = c \left(\frac{R_i}{R_j} \right)^a .$$
(8.14)

Note that the number of effective changeovers from Schedule i to Schedule j, N_{ij}, equals the number of effective changeovers from Schedule j to Schedule i, N_{ji} (plus or minus 1). Since time allocation results from changing over, we could expand Equation 8.14 to include these necessarily equal changeover numbers:

$$\frac{T_i \cdot N_{ji}}{T_j \cdot N_{ij}} = c \left(\frac{R_i}{R_j} \right)^a = \frac{N_{ji}}{T_j} \cdot \frac{T_i}{N_{ij}} ,$$
(8.15)

where N_{ji}/T_j is the local rate of changing over in Alternative j. Equation 8.14 states that the ratio of local rates of effective changeovers is a power function of the overall reinforcer ratio.

As we introduce, and lengthen, changeover schedules, we progressively constrain T_i and T_j, making them more and more equal. We also remove the constraint that N_{ij} must equal N_{ji}, because some changeover responses are now ineffective in changing between the alternatives. In the limit, we may suppose that $T_i = T_j$, and if Equation 8.14 remains true—and we have no reason other than induction to believe this—then:

$$\frac{N_{ji}}{N_{ij}} = c \left(\frac{R_i}{R_j}\right)^a ,$$

with the same value of a as in Equation 8.14. This is indeed what Tustin and Davison (1979) found (Fig. 8.4). It suggests that time-allocation matching is due to changeover performance—a suggestion that is a tautology only when time allocation is unconstrained and changeover-response numbers are constrained. As an adjunct to such a theory, we could suppose that local response rates on similar schedules are equal (Baum & Rachlin, 1969) and that obtained response-allocation matching follows from a basic time-allocation matching process, which in turn follows from an inverse matching of local changeover rates.

For Tustin and Davison's (1979) data, Equation 8.15 should fit every experimental condition. The results of such an analysis of 17 conditions (averaged over subjects) gave $c = 0.9$, $a = 1.2$, with 96 percent of the total variance accounted for. Whereas the sensitivity is a little higher than usual time-allocation sensitivity values, the fit is good. Further, it suggests that a changeover theory of matching (see also Dreyfus et al., 1982) is worth further investigation.

8.6b. Changeover Contingencies and Main-Key Performance

We have already dealt with some of the effects of changeover-delay duration on main-key behavior allocation in Section 6.1. Recall that the evidence did not clearly indicate *any* change in sensitivity to reinforcer frequency with increasing changeover delay. There was some evidence, however, that sensitivity was lower than normal when there was *no* changeover delay.

A number of changeover variables other than delay have been investigated, and we later return to some of the effects that have been described. First, however, we look at some research reported by Baum (1982). He trained pigeons on concurrent VI VI schedules in special experimental chambers in which he could vary the length of a partition separating the two response keys. He also arranged a hurdle, situated at the end of the partition, and varied its height. The pigeons had to travel around the partition, and over the hurdle, in order to alternate between the keys. The arithmetic VI schedules were arranged dependently in most conditions. Initially, as travel time between the two keys was progressively increased with a reinforcer ratio of 1:4, response ratios tended to fall, and sensitivity to reinforcer frequency moved from undermatching to overmatching. Time ratios also showed some slight evidence of a decrease.

After the travel time had been increased, reinforcer ratios were varied. The travel requirement for Group 1 was an 8″ partition with a 3.25″ hurdle, and these subjects had an overall reinforcer rate of 1.5 per minute. Group 2 had a 4″

partition only and a reinforcer rate of 3 per minute. The reinforcer ratios were then varied. Under these conditions, the three Group 1 birds all showed substantial overmatching for both response (pooled $a = 1.93$) and time ($a = 1.48$) and time-after-changeover ($a = 2.29$) measures. On the other hand, the three Group 2 birds showed undermatching for response ($a = 0.53$) and time ($a = 0.63$) measures, but some overmatching for time-after-changeover measures ($a = 1.49$, two of the three sensitivities greater than 1). As Baum (1982) said, introducing a substantial travel requirement (Group 1) produced substantial overmatching. The only potential design flaw in this experiment is the confound between travel time and overall reinforcer rate. Baum argues that since the performance with the 4″ partition was the same for both groups, overall reinforcer rate probably had no effect. While we accept this probability, the result only weakly rules out a reinforcer-rate versus travel-time interaction.

Baum (1982) related his results to similar reports of overmatching. Pliskoff, Cicerone, and Nelson (1978) required FR 5 and FR 10 performances to produce changeovers. They found sensitivities to reinforcer frequencies of 1.27 (FR 5) and 1.78 (FR 10). Todorov (1971) punished changeovers using both electric shock and timeout. With electric shock, he obtained a sensitivity of 1.64 as compared with 0.56 when shocks did not follow changeovers. In Todorov's data, time-allocation sensitivities were generally smaller than response-allocation sensitivities.

Naturally, Baum (1982) suggested that the effects of changeover requirements could be accounted for by assuming that such requirements punished behavior. Thus, he attempted to account for his results using the subtractive punishment model (Section 8.3):

$$\frac{B_1}{B_2} = c\left(\frac{R_1 - \alpha C_1}{R_2 - \alpha C_2}\right), \tag{8.16}$$

in which C_1 and C_2 are the rates of changing over—evidently the overall rates, since he states that they will be approximately equal. This being so, $\alpha C_1 = \alpha C_2$, and Equation 8.16 is simply the generalized matching law with a constant subtracted from both reinforcer rates. Thus, the theoretical reinforcer ratio is more extreme than the measured reinforcer ratio (R_1/R_2) and overmatching results. Note, however, that C_1 and C_2 are the same only within conditions and are different across conditions. The fits to Equation 8.16 were, however, poor. Notice that it is impossible for Equation 8.16 to account for *undermatching* data (Group 2) with α positive—undermatching would result only if a constant was added to both reinforcer rates. We are surprised that the fit of Baum's data to Equation 8.16 was not better. This failure must have resulted from the obtained changes in the levels of C_1 and C_2 across conditions, because Equation 8.16 simulates overmatching very precisely when the subtractive constant is indeed constant across conditions.

A slightly different theoretical approach may be taken with Baum's (1982) data. In his experiment, when a pigeon changed from Alternative 1 to Alternative 2, it produced a period of time out from reinforcement, in particular (because of the travel requirement) from Alternative 2. Perhaps this, rather than the difficulty per se of emitting the changeover response, punishes the changeover. The argument here might be that in the usual concurrent-schedule situation, there is no punishment for changing over *except* in the context of ongoing reinforcer rates. This consideration implies a model such as:

$$\frac{B_1}{B_2} = c \left(\frac{R_1 - \alpha R_2}{R_2 - \alpha R_1} \right). \qquad (8.17)$$

This model provides an excellent fit to Baum's 8″ partition plus 3.25″ hurdle data. For the three birds, the results of analysis by Equation 8.17 were:

Bird 46YP: $\log c = 0.03$, $\alpha = 0.15$, VAC = 76 percent

Bird 291YP: $\log c = -0.09$, $\alpha = 0.21$, VAC = 98 percent

Bird 492BP: $\log c = -0.39$, $\alpha = 0.22$, VAC = 97 percent.

Equation 8.17 has some generality. If the punishers are, say, instantaneous shocks, the subtractive component is a dimensional constant multiplied by the shock frequency, as in the de Villiers (1980), Farley (1980) and Farley and Fantino (1978) models (Section 8.3). If the punisher is time out from reinforcers following a changeover, the subtractive term is a constant multiplied by the reinforcer rate on the alternative key. We might expect, also, that if changeovers were directly reinforced, then the subtractive term would be replaced by an additive term in Equation 8.17. That equation would then predict undermatching. Finally, Equation 8.17 is also algebraically and conceptually similar to the model of concurrent-schedule performance suggested by Davison and Jenkins (1985, Section 8.7).

Baum (1982) concluded that maybe both behavior emitted and time allocated during a changeover delay or a changeover ratio should be excluded from matching analyses, and, hence, that perhaps *overmatching*, rather than undermatching, is the norm. Indeed, when the effects of changeover ratios are studied, changeover performance is not measured as part of the food-related matching performance, and overmatching is reliably obtained (Pliskoff, Cicerone, & Nelson, 1978). Todorov's (1971) finding of overmatching when changeovers were punished would be seen to result from an effect similar to that produced by an arduous travel requirement. Both Silberberg and Fantino (1970) and Baum (1974c) found, in relatively standard concurrent-schedule arrangements, that overmatching characterized post-changeover-delay performance.

A contrary opinion would point out that if such an approach is accepted, a, sensitivity to reinforcer frequency, becomes a variable, rather than a constant, under the control of the travel requirement. There seems more consistency in a

values when all (within-changeover and post-changeover) behavior is taken into account. Taylor and Davison (1983) noted that this consistency extends to the changeover-ratio studies also if the ratio performance is added to the main-key performance (equivalent to *adding* a constant to both R_1 and R_2). Baum (1982), of course, obtained time-allocation overmatching when changeover time was added to main-key performance (Group 1), whereas studies that have varied standard changeover delays have not obtained consistent overmatching even with delays of 20 s or more (Scown, 1983). Thus, the *relation* between the procedural changeover delay and travel time is unclear and inconsistent. Evidently, it requires more detailed work. For ourselves, the consistency still seems to lie in taking within- and post-changeover delay measures together. One further point: It cannot be suggested that taking only post-travel measures of behavior is somehow more "natural." We are not sure that "natural" should be a criterion at all, but the naturalness of a changeover delay or travel requirement depends on the subject. Some species forage for prey continuously as they move about in their environment, others clearly emit no foraging behavior between forays into patches.

The results of an experiment similar to that done by Baum (1982) were reported by Boelens and Kop (1983). They used dependent concurrent VI VI schedules in Experiment 1 and independent schedules in Experiment 2. In both experiments, they varied a partition between the keys from 0 through 10 to 20 cm. It appears that they also varied the schedules (either VI 20 s VI 60 s or VI 60 s VI 20 s) for each partition length, but they do not state this clearly in their Procedure. The only data they report are response, time, and reinforcer data according to the schedule, rather than the key. Hence, key bias cannot be eliminated, and it is possible that both experiments have serious flaws. In estimating *a* values, all we can do, for each condition, is to assume zero key bias, calculate a point estimate of *a*, and then average *a* values across apparent VI-schedule reversals. This provides us with the data shown in Fig. 8.5. In our reanalysis of Experiment 1, it became evident that point estimates of *a* for apparent reversal conditions were frequently smaller than point estimates for the original conditions at each partition length (11 of 12 for response data, 9 of 12 for time data). This could mean either: (1) nearly all birds had a strong key bias in the same direction; or (2) a variation of reinforcer rates systematically decreased sensitivity values (cf Section 9.3, the analysis of Charman & Davison, 1982). Confusingly, in Experiment 2 this effect was reversed—2 of 10 replications of response-based *a* values were smaller, and 3 of 10 time-based *a* values were smaller. This *could* indicate that Experiment 2 commenced with the VI 20-s schedule on the key other than that on which it was arranged at the start of Experiment 1, assuming that the schedules were reversed between keys after each condition. Whatever the meaning of these data, they lead us to make two comments: (1) data and procedural details should be presented clearly in published papers; and (2) if they are not, a reader may be excused for taking little

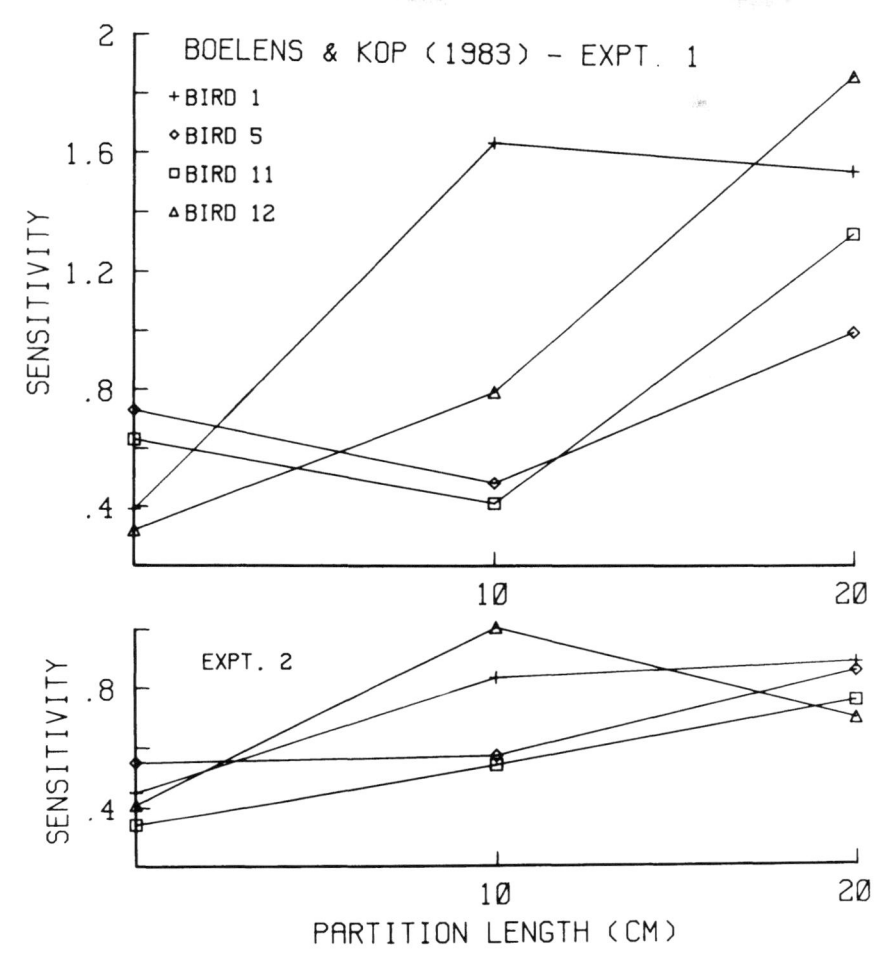

FIG. 8.5. Estimated sensitivity to reinforcer frequency (response data only) when the partition between two response keys was lengthened. The data are from Boelens and Kop (1983).

notice of the results. Our understanding of Boelens and Kop's data is not enhanced by our finding it difficult to determine whether Baum (1982), who did not report his data, found any initial decrease in sensitivity when he first varied the VI schedules. Still more confusion is produced by Boelens and Kop's noting that changeover rates were higher in even-numbered conditions (that is, the apparent reversals) than in odd-numbered conditions. They state that there was no apparent reason for this as it was "not the case that even-numbered conditions differed consistently from the preceding odd ones in the assignment of a schedule to a response key" (p. 37). In other words, key reversals were not done between successive conditions.

Any conclusions made on the basis of Boelens and Kop's (1983) research must be tentative in the extreme. However, the data (Fig. 8.5) suggest the following conclusion: There was *no* significant trend in the estimates of *a* in Experiment 1 for either response or time measures (Kendall trend test, Section 5.10, $N = 4$, $k = 3$, $\Sigma S = 6$). This conclusion conflicts with that of the authors, who reported that overmatching was observed with a partition length of 20 cm. In fact, three of the four birds showed response overmatching, and one showed time overmatching, with a 20 cm partition. According to a trend test, the results were clearer in Experiment 2. For response measures, *a* significantly increased with partition length ($N = 4$, $k = 3$, $\Sigma S = 10$), but *none* of the birds showed overmatching at the longest partition length. The trend in *a* was not significant for time measures ($\Sigma S = 6$), and time overmatching did not occur at any partition length. Evidently, more careful experimentation is required here.

One final, naive, point. It is, perhaps, not surprising that the relation between main-key performance and reinforcer ratios varies with the difficulty of changing over simply because changeover performance will, in a sense, "take up" some of the value of being on the main key. The reinforcers that are obtained by an organism can only be divided among the aspects of performance (responding, changing over, and emitting other behaviors). Presumably, no more than the reinforcer-number input can affect behavior, and presumably all those inputs must affect behavior. Perhaps we are saying that reinforcers can neither be created nor destroyed by the organism.

8.7. STIMULUS EFFECTS

In the usual arrangement of concurrent schedules, the response alternatives are clearly discriminable to the subject. For instance, on a two-key concurrent schedule, the two responses are pecking the left key and pecking the right key, which are not easy to confuse for most subjects. Equally, in the changeover-key procedure, the two responses (for example, peck the main key when it is red, or when it is green) are easily distinguished. What happens to generalized matching when the responses are difficult to distinguish? Obviously, this question is easier to answer empirically using the changeover-key procedure than using the two-key procedure. Miller, Saunders, and Bourland (1980) used a switching-key concurrent exponential VI VI schedule and signaled each component by line orientations. We presume that the schedules were arranged independently. For one group, the orientation difference was 0°, for a second group it was 15°, and for a third it was 45°. For each group, reinforcer-rate ratios were varied over six or seven conditions. Generalized matching analyses of the response-allocation data gave sensitivities (averaged over the two birds in each group) of 0.17 (0° separation), 0.33 (15° separation) and 0.99 (45° separation). These results are as expected, in the sense that if the two schedules are signaled by the same stimulus, the schedules essentially comprise a one-key concurrent schedule, and behavior cannot be differentially allocated to the keys. Thus, sensitivity must be expected to be zero. The fact that it was greater than zero when the stimuli were identical suggests that, to some extent, the subjects were discriminating the schedules in another way—perhaps on the basis of reinforcer frequencies. This minor procedural difficulty can easily be overcome by arranging that the schedules in operation change randomly after the delivery of reinforcers (see Davison, McCarthy, & Jensen, 1985; McCarthy, Davison, & Jenkins, 1982; Sections 11.9 and 11.10).

Miller, Saunders, and Bourland (1980) provided no model of the effects of stimulus disparity on concurrent-schedule performance, and chose simply to measure the disparity effect using the generalized matching sensitivity value. No other research directly on this effect has been reported. Davison and Jenkins (1985) offered a quantitative model for the effect (see also Section 6.1). This model assumes that the subjects allocate each delivered reinforcer to the response that produced it, according to their ability to discriminate the contingencies. This ability is measured by d_r, called contingency discriminability. The model is:

$$\frac{B_1}{B_2} = c\left(\frac{d_r R_1 + R_2}{d_r R_2 + R_1}\right). \tag{8.18}$$

When the contingencies are indiscriminable, that is, the stimuli signaling the components are identical and there is no other source of discriminability, $d_r = 1$. Under these conditions, Equation 8.18 predicts that the behavior ratio will be unaffected by the distribution of reinforcer rates between the schedules. On the other hand, when the stimuli are highly discriminable, d_r becomes very large, and the behavior ratio tends toward the reinforcer ratio, R_1/R_2. This latter relation is, of course, strict matching. Equation 8.18 fitted Miller, Saunders, and Bourland's data well, and Davison and Jenkins extended the model into a number of other areas.

Notice that the basic model (Equation 8.18) is not able to accommodate overmatching. However, with the addition of, say, punishing contingencies for changing over, negative terms may also occur in the numerator and denominator of the right-hand side of the equation (as in the punishment models, Section 8.3, and in Equation 8.17), and overmatching can be accommodated.

9

MULTIPLE-SCHEDULE RESEARCH

In Chapter 3 we dealt at some length with Herrnstein's (1970) description of absolute response rates and response-rate distribution in the components (that is, the successive periods during which different schedules are signaled by different stimuli) of multiple VI VI schedules. In the present chapter, we deal mainly with empirical research on matching in multiple schedules.

9.1. EFFECTS OF COMPONENT REINFORCER RATES

Reynolds (1961) was the first to notice that parametrically varying the reinforcer rates in multiple schedule components produced a relation between relative component response rates and relative component reinforcer rates. Reynolds used two procedures, both employing multiple VI FR schedules. In the first, he kept one component constant at VI 180 s and varied the FR schedule in the other component. In the second procedure, he maintained FR 150 in one component and varied the VI schedule in the other. Note that this latter procedure does not guarantee a constant FR component reinforcer rate. The component duration was 180 s. Reynolds reported a straight-line relation between relative response rate in the *constant* component and the obtained relative reinforcer rate in that component. The relation was the same for both series of conditions. Note that a straight-line relation between such relative measures with a slope less than one and a positive bias (as Reynolds found) implies that response rates would not be zero in a component in which Extinction was arranged. This *could*, of course, occur if the stimuli signaling the components were difficult to discriminate. Reynolds' data do indicate that response rates were not absolutely zero in

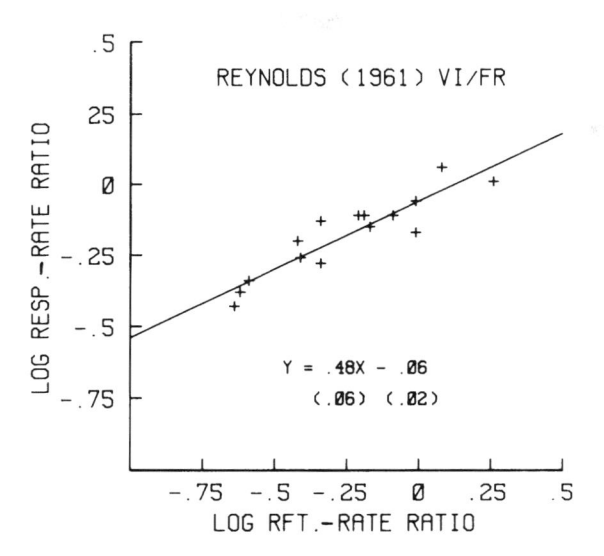

FIG. 9.1.   Data reported by Reynolds (1961) reanalyzed using the generalized matching law. The X axis is the log of the VI divided by the FR component reinforcer rates, and the Y axis is the log of the VI/FR component response rates.

Extinction components. The component stimuli (red and green keylights) would, however, be expected to be highly discriminable (see Charman & Davison, 1983b; Section 9.6).

To reanalyze Reynolds' (1961) data (estimated from his Fig. 4) using the generalized matching law, we convert his data to VI/FR component response- and reinforcer-rate ratios. This will allow us to determine whether there was any effect of different schedule type. The results of the reanalysis are displayed in Fig. 9.1, which shows that the data were quite well fit by a generalized matching relation with a sensitivity of 0.48 and no bias. The absence of bias suggests that different schedule types might not affect generalized matching in multiple-schedule performance.

Reynolds (1963b) collected a considerable amount of parametric data on multiple VI VI schedule performance. In three experiments, he first kept VI 180 s in one component and varied the VI schedule in the other. Then, he varied the schedules in both components. Last, he kept one component constant at VI 95 s and again varied the VI schedule in the other. The component duration was 180 s throughout. Reynolds noted that the response rate on the VI 95-s schedule was unaffected by variations in the other component schedule, but that the response rate in the VI 180-s component was affected by the reinforcer rate in the other component. This finding is important to any model that purports to describe absolute multiple-schedule response rates. So far as we know, only the model of McLean and White (1983) can explain this difference (see Section 9.9). Despite this absolute component response-rate effect, Reynolds again noted a relation

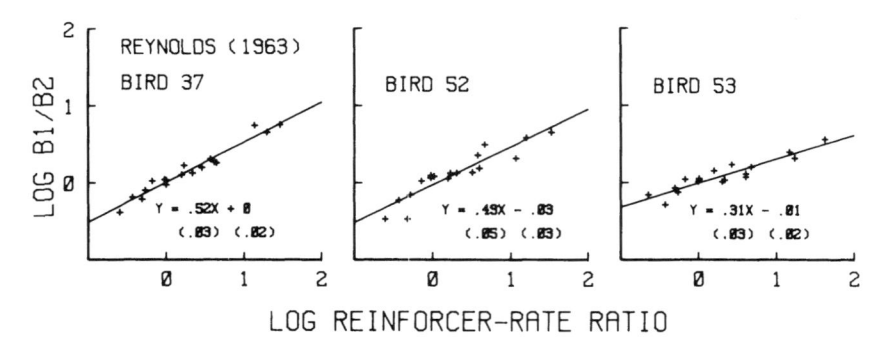

FIG. 9.2.   Log component response-rate ratios as a function of log component reinforcer-rate ratios for multiple VI VI schedules reported by Reynolds (1963b).

between relative component response rates and relative component reinforcer rates. Figure 9.2 provides a reanalysis of Reynolds' data read from his Figs. 3A and 5. The generalized matching relation again summarized the data well, and showed sensitivities to reinforcer rates in the range 0.31 to 0.52 (mean 0.44) with no bias. Again, the somewhat weak between-experiment comparison of Reynolds (1961) and Reynolds (1963b) suggests that multiple VI VI performance is distributed between the components in the same way as multiple VI FR performance.

As Reynolds (1963b) mentioned, the relation between component response rates and component reinforcer rates in multiple schedules is quite different from the relation found for concurrent-schedule performance. This difference, in a quantitative sense, was displayed by Lander and Irwin (1968) in the first paper to report a generalized matching analysis of behavior in general, and of multiple-schedule performance in particular. It goes without saying that the relation was not, then, termed generalized matching. We gain the impression that the reason Lander and Irwin took this type of quantitative approach owed a considerable amount to Psychophysics in general, and Stevens' law in particular. Indeed, they termed the power that related response ratios to reinforcer ratios ''sensitivity''. It is difficult to recreate Lander and Irwin's data from their paper. However, without fitting their data to the generalized matching law, Lander and Irwin reported that a power (a value) of 0.33 provided a good description of the relation, and that this value might also fit Reynolds' (1963b) data. They further suggested that $a = 1$ was characteristic of concurrent VI VI performance, and that $a = \infty$ might characterize concurrent FR FR performance (Herrnstein, 1958) in which subjects respond exclusively on one alternative. In the latter suggestion, they were of course wrong if the independent variable is the obtained (rather than arranged) reinforcer ratio. It is unclear whether Lander and Irwin plotted their data as a function of obtained or arranged reinforcer frequencies, but the manner in which the data from replications and from the two subjects precisely line up on the X axis tends to suggest that arranged rates were used. Interestingly, Lander and Irwin also mentioned that the data on reinforcer delays obtained by Chung & Herrnstein

(1967) might be described by an *a* value of 3, rather than 1. As we discuss in Section 6.5, it was not until 1978 that Williams and Fantino demonstrated that Chung and Herrnstein's data did not conform to strict matching ($a = 1$).

In the same year as Lander and Irwin's (1968) paper, Pliskoff, Shull, and Gollub (1968) reported data from an experiment using a multiple-concurrent schedule. Such a schedule is best conceptualized as a multiple schedule arranged normally, with other schedules arranged as concurrent alternatives during each component. In Pliskoff et al.'s experiment, the multiple schedule was signaled by red and green key colors, and the components were 15 min in duration. We call the reinforcer rates in these components R_{m1} and R_{m2} respectively. When the red multiple schedule was presented, the other key was blue. When the green multiple schedule was presented, the other key was yellow. In Pliskoff et al.'s experiment, blue and yellow both signaled the same reinforcer schedule, which we call the *common* schedule, with reinforcer rates R_{c1} and R_{c2}. The red and blue keys were available concurrently, as were the green and yellow keys. Within these successively available concurrent schedules, a 4-s changeover delay was arranged in six conditions (the seventh used a 2-s changeover delay). Table 9.1 shows the sequence of experimental conditions.

TABLE 9.1

Arranged VI Reinforcer Schedules in the Multiple-Schedule Components (Subscripted *m1* and *m2*) and in the Common Schedule (Subscripted *c*) Arranged by Pliskoff, Shull, and Gollub (1968)

Condition	VI_{m1}	VI_{m2}	VI_c
1	180	180	180
2	180	180	Ext[1]
3	180	180	60
4	90	360	180
5	90	360	Ext[1]
6	90	360	60
7[2]	90	313	60

[1]Extinction.
[2]2-s changeover delay in this condition.

Multiple-concurrent schedules allow a variety of analyses. First, each of the two concurrent-schedule performances may be analyzed separately. When this was done, Pliskoff et al. (1968) reported that an approximation to strict matching prevailed. However, their Figs. 2 and 3, which display this, show systematic deviations from matching to the eye tutored by the generalized matching law. Figure 9.3 shows a generalized matching analysis of Pliskoff et al.'s concurrent-schedule data for three birds. As we suspected, undermatching rather than strict

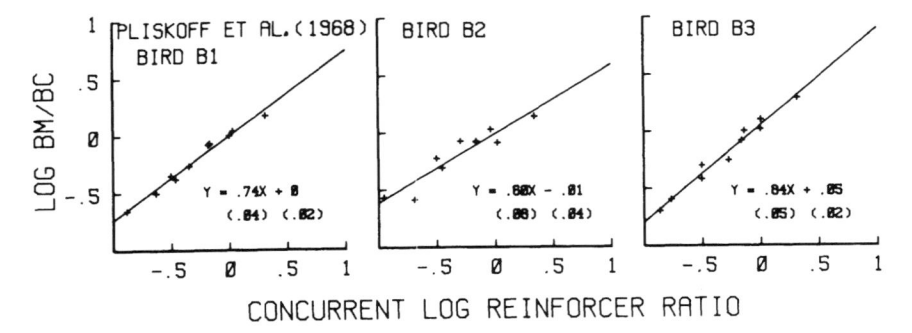

FIG. 9.3.   A generalized matching analysis of the concurrent-schedule data (log B_m/B_c) from both multiple-concurrent schedule components reported by Pliskoff, Shull, and Gollub (1968).

matching characterized the performance of all three birds (mean a = 0.73). Further, the values are within the normal range for concurrent VI VI schedules (Baum, 1979; Taylor & Davison, 1983).

Rather few data are available from Pliskoff et al. (1968) for a generalized matching analysis of multiple VI VI schedule performance. Neglecting Condition 7, there are six data points in total. But the possibility is pointed out by Pliskoff et al. that multiple-schedule performance might be affected by the reinforcer rate from the common schedule. If this is so, only two data points are available for each of the three common-schedule reinforcer rates (e.g., for the VI 60-s common schedule, multiple VI 180 s VI 180 s and multiple VI 90 s VI 360 s). From these pairs of data points, we calculated estimates of a, and Fig. 9.4 shows these estimates plotted as a function of the arranged number of reinforcers per hour on the common schedule.

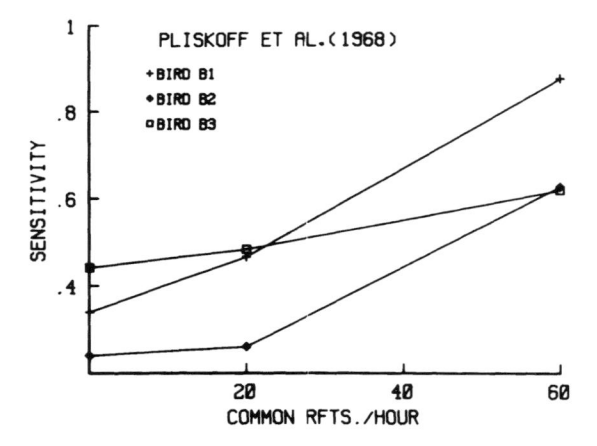

FIG. 9.4.   Multiple-schedule sensitivity to component reinforcer-rate ratios as a function of the rate of reinforcers arranged on an alternative, common-schedule, key. The data are from Pliskoff, Shull, and Gollub (1968).

For each bird, the value of a increased monotonically as the frequency of common-schedule reinforcers increased, and there is no need to test this trend statistically. Pliskoff et al. (1968) came to the same conclusion by plotting the multiple-schedule response ratios as a function of the common-schedule reinforcer rate. The present analysis is preferable as it takes into account any variation in the obtained reinforcer rates. We note here that this result was *not* replicated by Lobb and Davison (1977), but was found by McLean and White (1983). This difference is discussed later in this section.

Pliskoff, Shull, and Gollub (1968) suggested the following theoretical analysis of their results. Assuming strict matching on the concurrently available schedules:

$$\frac{B_{m1}}{B_{c1}} = \frac{R_{m1}}{R_{c1}} , \quad \text{and} \quad \frac{B_{m2}}{B_{c2}} = \frac{R_{m2}}{R_{c2}} ,$$

thus,

$$R_{c1} = \frac{B_{c1} \cdot R_{m1}}{B_{m1}} , \quad \text{and} \quad R_{c2} = \frac{B_{c2} \cdot R_{m2}}{B_{m2}} .$$

In Pliskoff et al.'s experiment, arranged R_{c1} = arranged R_{c2}. Assuming that the obtained rates of common reinforcers were the same (R_c), then:

$$\frac{B_{c1} \cdot R_{m1}}{B_{m1}} = \frac{B_{c2} \cdot R_{m2}}{B_{m2}} ,$$

or:

$$\frac{B_{m1}}{B_{m2}} = \frac{B_{c1} \cdot R_{m1}}{B_{c2} \cdot R_{m2}} . \tag{9.1}$$

Pliskoff et al. now take an expression, suggested by Catania (1963a) for absolute response rates on concurrent schedules:

$$B_i = \frac{kR_i}{(R_i + R_j)^{0.8}} \tag{9.2}$$

(but note the dimensional difficulties in this equation if k is measured as a response rate). Equation 9.2 is now substituted into Equation 9.1 to give:

$$\frac{B_{m1}}{B_{m2}} = \frac{R_{m1}}{R_{m2}} \cdot \left(\frac{R_{m2} + R_c}{R_{m1} + R_c}\right)^{0.8} . \tag{9.3}$$

An equation similar to 9.2, but making different initial assumptions, has been suggested by McLean and White (1983, see Section 9.9). Pliskoff et al. (1968) found that Equation 9.3 fitted their data, in relative terms, very well with no obvious systematic deviations. Note, however, that Equation 9.3 can be used only if R_c is known. The common-schedule reinforcer rate in a multiple-concurrent schedule, R_c, is equivalent to the rate of extraneous reinforcers, R_e, in a standard multiple schedule (see Chapter 3). This latter quantity is not directly measurable. Further, it may not remain constant as multiple-schedule reinforcer rates are varied, and it may not be equal between components (see, for example, Hinson and Staddon, 1978). The simplification that $R_{c1} = R_{c2}$ hinges rather strongly on the feedback function for R_c (and R_e). For instance, if R_c was provided by a ratio schedule, R_{c1} would most probably not equal R_{c2} when R_{m1} does not equal R_{m2}.

Lobb and Davison (1977) reported a systematic replication of Lander and Irwin's (1968) and Pliskoff et al.'s (1968) experiments. The procedure used by Lobb and Davison was similar to that used by Pliskoff et al., with a single common schedule arranged during both multiple-schedule components, and with a 3-s changeover delay operating between common-schedule and multiple-schedule reinforcers. The procedure of arranging the components was, however, different as the multiple-schedule components alternated after each multiple-schedule reinforcer was delivered, rather than after a fixed time. The component durations were thus inversely related to the component reinforcer rates. A changeover procedure was also used in which all multiple- and common-schedule reinforcers were obtained on the left key. A blue left key signaled the first multiple-schedule component, and a green left key the second multiple-schedule component. The common schedule was always signaled by a red left key, and a single response on the right, white, key produced alternations between the multiple and common schedules and started the changeover delay.

The 21 experimental conditions allowed a number of questions to be asked. First, did response allocation between the multiple VI 45-s VI 15-s components change when the common-schedule reinforcer rates were varied from 20 to about 110 per hour? Unlike Pliskoff et al.'s (1968) result, there was no trend over this considerably wider range of common-schedule reinforcer rates. This part of the experiment also provided a concurrent-schedule sensitivity estimate of $a = 0.78$, averaged over the six birds and over the two successive concurrent schedules. In the second and third parts of the experiment, the multiple-schedule component reinforcer-rate ratio was varied with VI 60 s as the common schedule, and then with Extinction as the common schedule. The VI 60-s common-schedule data gave a mean concurrent-schedule sensitivity of 0.82 and a mean multiple-schedule sensitivity of 0.35. No concurrent-schedule sensitivity can be calculated when the common schedule was Extinction, but the mean multiple-schedule sensitivity was 0.45. According to a Sign test, there was no difference between the multiple-schedule sensitivity estimates obtained when zero and 60 reinforcers per hour were arranged on the common schedule. This finding strongly supports the conclusion from the first part of the experiment that the rate of common-schedule reinforcers did not affect behavior allocation in the multiple schedule.

In the last part of Lobb and Davison's (1977) experiment, only the reinforcer rate in one of the multiple-schedule components was varied. This resulted in a concurrent-schedule sensitivity of 0.80 (mean across five birds) and a multiple-schedule sensitivity of 0.46 (five birds). Lobb and Davison's conclusions were that the concurrent-schedule sensitivity values were similar to those for concurrent schedules arranged in isolation. Therefore, concurrent-schedule performance (simultaneous choice) was independent of reinforcement conditions arranged successively in time—that is, of successive context. Multiple-schedule sensitivity (successive choice) was also similar to that for multiple schedules arranged in isolation, and was independent of the common-schedule reinforcer rate. Hence, successive behavior allocation is independent of the simultaneous context in which it occurs. This last finding, which conflicts with that of Pliskoff et al. (1968), must be accepted on the basis of Lobb and Davison providing a much more extensive data set, with an internal replication. However, the hindsight provided by McLean and White's (1983) data, which was consistent with Pliskoff et al.'s data, suggests that we look again at the procedural differences between Pliskoff et al. and Lobb and Davison. The notable difference is between the fixed, 15 min. component durations used by Pliskoff et al. and the inverse relation between component duration and component reinforcer rates arranged by Lobb and Davison. There is one reason that it is doubtful that such a procedural difference could produce the difference in results—this is Charman and Davison's (1982) failure to find *any* effect of arranging unequal component durations (see Section 9.3). More research is required here.

In summary, this research that we have discussed suggests that component response-rate ratios in multiple schedules undermatch component reinforcer-rate ratios with a sensitivity value of 0.3 to 0.5. These values lie well below those for concurrent VI VI schedules (Baum, 1979; Taylor & Davison, 1983). Much of the subsequent research on the effects of other independent variables supports the conclusion that sensitivity to reinforcer rate is less for multiple than for concurrent schedules. However, the value of the sensitivity may, under some circumstances, be a direct function of the reinforcer rate available at the same time (concurrently with) the multiple schedule. In terms of Herrnstein's (1970) approach, this means that a would be correlated with R_e, the extraneous, unmeasured, rate of reinforcers from alternate sources.

9.2. A NOTE ON MEASUREMENT

We have, with no argument, used component response-rate ratios and component reinforcer-rate ratios in the generalized matching analyses of multiple-schedule performances we have been discussing. The reason for this is given by

Herrnstein (1970). He pointed out that response and reinforcer rates should be measured according to the time available for those responses or reinforcers. Thus, for concurrent schedules, it is natural to use overall response and reinforcer rates given by $N_{B1}/(T_1 + T_2)$ and $N_{R1}/(T_1 + T_2)$, where N_{B1} and N_{R1} are the numbers of responses emitted and reinforcers obtained respectively, and T_1 and T_2 are the times spent in the presence of the two schedules. Since a changeover can always be made, at least in principle, the total session time is available for both schedules' responses and reinforcers. Thus, for concurrent schedules, the generalized matching law is:

$$\frac{N_{B1}}{T_1 + T_2} \cdot \frac{T_1 + T_2}{N_{B2}} = c\left(\frac{N_{R1}}{T_1 + T_2} \cdot \frac{T_1 + T_2}{N_{R2}}\right)^a ,$$

which simplifies to:

$$\frac{N_{B1}}{N_{B2}} = c\left(\frac{N_{R1}}{N_{R2}}\right)^a .$$

Thus, for concurrent schedules, the generalized matching relation between response- and reinforcer-rate ratios (per session) is the same as the relation between ratios of response and reinforcer *numbers* per session.

In multiple schedules, the total session time is *not* available for both schedules' responses and reinforcers, so the appropriate generalized matching relation is:

$$\frac{N_{B1}}{T_1} \cdot \frac{T_2}{N_{B2}} = c\left(\frac{N_{R1}}{T_1} \cdot \frac{T_2}{N_{R2}}\right)^a , \quad \text{which is}$$

$$\frac{N_{B1}}{N_{B2}} \cdot \frac{T_2}{T_1} = c\left(\frac{N_{R1}}{N_{R2}} \cdot \frac{T_2}{T_1}\right)^a .$$

Rearranging this equation shows that the relation between the ratios of component response *numbers* and component reinforcer *numbers* is not independent of component durations:

$$\frac{N_{B1}}{N_{B2}} = \left(\frac{N_{R1}}{N_{R2}}\right)^a \cdot \left(\frac{T_1}{T_2}\right)^{1-a} .$$

Only if $T_1 = T_2$, that is, the component durations are equal, can the relation be fit as ratios of response numbers versus ratios of reinforcer numbers because 1 to any power is 1. In all the studies dealt with so far, save that of Lobb and Davison (1977), the component durations were equal.

9.3. EFFECTS OF ABSOLUTE COMPONENT DURATION

Given the evident difference in sensitivity to reinforcer frequency between multiple and concurrent VI VI schedules, Shimp and Wheatley (1971) asked whether the difference could be a function of component duration. On a concurrent schedule, they reasoned, subjects usually spend only a few seconds at each alternative before switching, rather than the two or three minutes regularly used in multiple-schedule research. Shimp and Wheatley thus investigated performance on multiple RI RI schedules using component durations ranging from 2 to 180 s. Additionally, a changeover delay prevented reinforcers being produced within 1 s of a change in component. In their Conditions 3 to 6, a higher reinforcer rate was arranged in green than in red. In Conditions 7 to 11, the higher reinforcer rate was in green. In Conditions 12 to 15, the higher reinforcer rate was again in red. (This information is important in view of subsequent findings by Charman & Davison, 1982.) Shimp and Wheatley found that the relative rate of responding in a component approached the strict matching value (on 4:1 component reinforcer-rate ratios) more closely as the component durations were decreased. At component durations of 2 s and 5 s there was an approximate equality of relative component response rates and relative component reinforcer rates. Shimp and Wheatley also showed the relation between relative component response and reinforcer rates when 5-s component durations were arranged in a series of multiple RI RI conditions. These data fell close to the strict matching relation for all three subjects. We note here that *none* of these latter conditions were carried out immediately following a schedule reversal.

Todorov (1972) replicated the findings of Shimp and Wheatley (1971) in all major respects. He used multiple VI 30-s VI 90-s schedules throughout, no changeover delay, and variable component durations arranged according to a semi-random sequence from an arithmetic progression. The mean component duration was varied from 5 to 300 s. Again, relative response rates increased toward strict matching values as the components were shortened. The closest approach to strict matching was at 10-s mean component duration. Figure 9.5 shows point estimates of a values (assuming zero bias) for Todorov's three birds. The change in sensitivity with component duration is clear.

Seldom have two such consistent reports been published so closely together as those of Shimp and Wheatley (1971) and of Todorov (1972). It is not surprising, therefore, that these findings have been very generally accepted. The interpretation has been that strict matching occurs on multiple schedules with short components because short components make multiple schedules procedurally more like concurrent schedules. In terms of Herrnstein's (1970) theory, we would naturally expect more interaction between components as their durations decreased (de Villiers, 1977). Thus m would increase toward 1, its value on a concurrent schedule, as component duration was decreased (see Section 3.6). Indeed, Killeen (1972b) reported an experiment in which birds on multiple VI VI

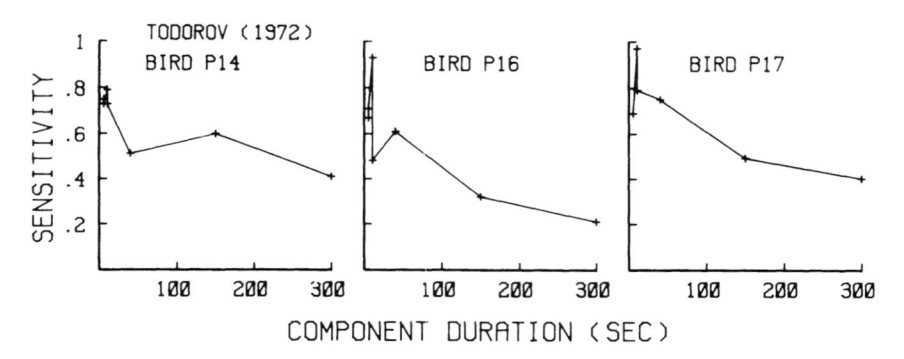

FIG. 9.5. Point estimates of multiple-schedule sensitivity to reinforcer rate as a function of component duration for three birds. The data are from Todorov (1972).

schedules were exposed to component durations, and component reinforcer rates, produced by yoked birds working on concurrent VI VI schedules. He reported that the distribution of behavior between the multiple-schedule components was the same as the distribution for the concurrent-schedule birds. This result has been taken by many researchers (see Charman & Davison, 1982) to support the short-component matching effect reported by Shimp and Wheatley (1971) and by Todorov (1972). The reason that Killeen's data do not do so was discussed by Charman and Davison: It is that matching in Killeen's experiment occurred as an equality between relative response numbers and relative reinforcer numbers, and the component durations were unequal. When component response *rates* and component reinforcer *rates* are analyzed, support for the short-component multiple-schedule effect is very much weaker (Charman & Davison, 1982). Still more support for the short-component matching effect was provided by Silberberg and Schrot (1974). Again, however, the data are equivocal because the yoking procedure used resulted in equal component reinforcer rates on the multiple schedule in many of the conditions. Obviously, the procedure of yoking will tend to do this because, if concurrent-schedule time-allocation matching occurs, concurrent-schedule local reinforcer rates *are* equal.

Despite the apparent support for Herrnstein's (1970) multiple-schedule response-allocation equation provided by the short-component effect, Edmon (1978) questioned the consistency between Shimp and Wheatley's (1971) and Todorov's (1972) data and Herrnstein's equation for absolute response rate in multiple-schedule components. This equation (Section 3.1) is:

$$B_i = \frac{kR_i}{R_i + mR_j + R_e} .$$

As m increases, so B_i, and similarly B_j, will fall. Thus, if component duration affects the value of m, absolute response rates should fall as component duration is decreased. Edmon reanalyzed Shimp and Wheatley's, and Todorov's, data and showed that response rates in the lower reinforcer-rate component decreased as

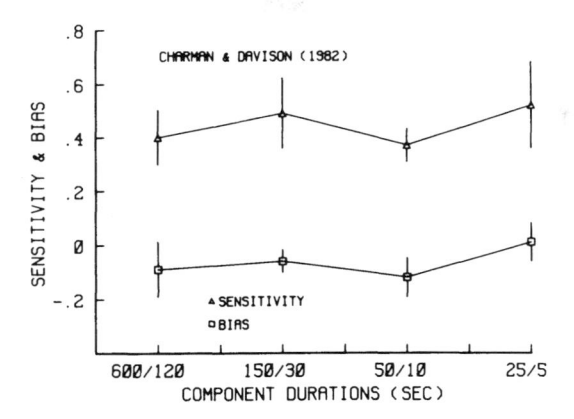

FIG. 9.6.   Group data reported by Charman and Davison (1982, Experiment 1). Estimates of the values of sensitivity (*a*) and bias (*log c*) in the generalized matching law for each of a set of absolute component durations. The vertical bars indicate ± one standard deviation unit.

component duration *increased* and that response rates in the higher reinforcer-rate components stayed essentially constant. As Edmon says, since Herrnstein's equation for the distribution of response rates is derived from his equation for absolute component response rates, neither Shimp and Wheatley's, nor Todorov's, data support Herrnstein's approach.

Charman and Davison (1982) undertook an experiment to investigate the effects of unequal component durations on the distribution of behavior between multiple-schedule components. In their first experiment they varied component reinforcer rates when the component durations were: 600 s and 120 s, 150 s and 30 s, 50 s and 10 s, and 25 s and 5 s. As Fig. 9.6 shows, there were no significant trends in either bias or sensitivity across absolute component duration, and the *a* values ranged from 0.37 to 0.52. Since these *a* values are similar to those obtained for multiple schedules with equal component durations, we can conclude that relative component duration has no effect on the sensitivity of multiple-schedule performances. But the data also seemed to be incompatible with the findings of Shimp and Wheatley (1971) and Todorov (1972). Some increase in sensitivity would be expected at least at 25-s and 5-s component durations. To check this, Charman and Davison varied component reinforcer rates with equal 5-s component durations using both a single-key and a two-key procedure (see Merigan, Miller & Gollub, 1975; Section 9.5). Figure 9.7 shows the group data reported by Charman and Davison (1982, Figs. 2 and 3), plotted according to the generalized matching law for both the single-key and two-key procedures. As Fig. 9.7 shows, sensitivities to component reinforcer rates were not different for the one- and two-key data, nor were they different from the sensitivities obtained in the first part of the experiment (Fig. 9.6). This was, therefore, a major failure to replicate the short-component multiple-schedule matching effect.

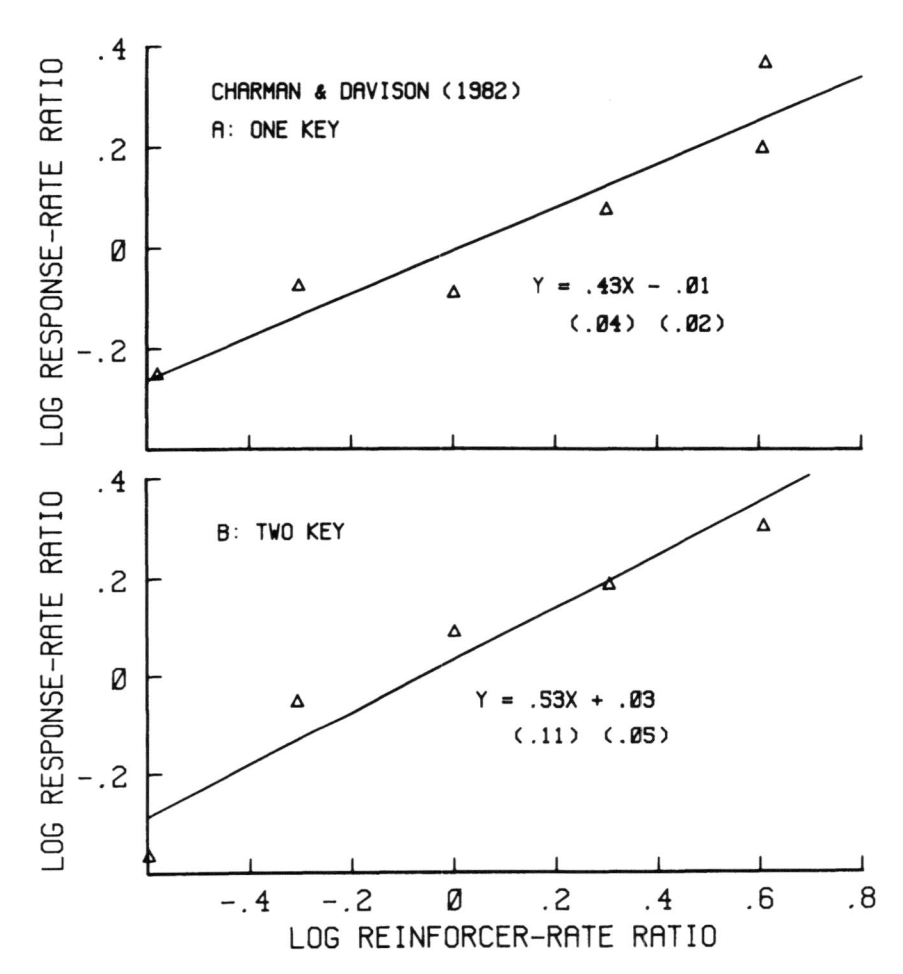

FIG. 9.7.   Group data reported by Charman and Davison (1982, Experiment 2) for one-key and two-key multiple VI VI schedules. The logarithm of the ratio of the red/green component response rates are plotted as a function of the logarithm of the obtained red/green component reinforcer rates.

This failure led Charman and Davison (1982) to search for any variable in their experiment that was different from that used in previous research. None was found. Charman and Davison's results described so far had been obtained by keeping component durations at set values and varying the component reinforcer rates in a sequence of conditions. This procedure was rather different from that of Shimp and Wheatley (1971), who seldom reversed the VI schedules between components, and from that of Todorov (1972), who arranged no schedule reversals. Thus, in their final experiment, Charman and Davison kept the component schedules at VI 30 s and VI 90 s and systematically decreased the component duration from 180 s to 6 s. They then reversed the schedules with a

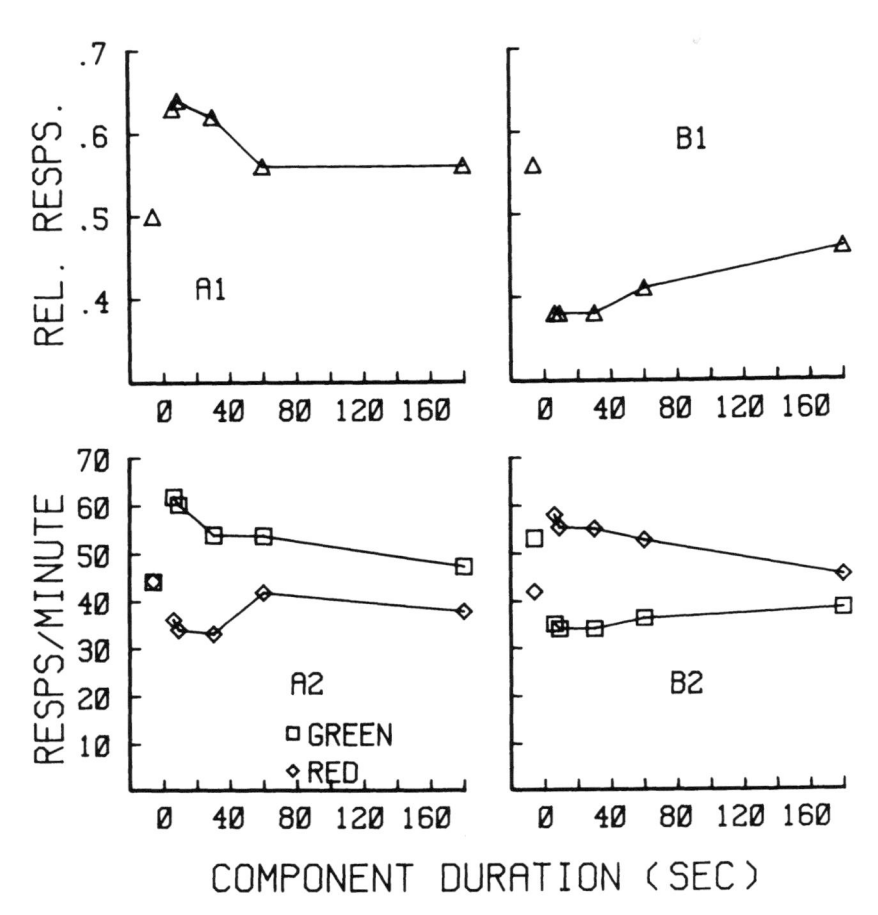

FIG. 9.8.   Group data reported by Charman and Davison (1982, Experiment 4). Panels A1 and B1 show the relative rates of responding in the red component as a function of component duration in seconds. Panels A2 and B2 show the number of responses emitted per minute in the red and green components as a function of component duration. In Panels A1 and A2, the multiple VI 30-s VI 90-s schedule reversal data at 6-s component durations are shown prior to the zero point on the X axis. The multiple VI 90-s VI 30-s schedule reversal data at 6-s component durations are similarly shown in Panels B1 and B2.

6-s component duration (see Panels A1 and A2 in Fig. 9.8). The procedure was then repeated with multiple VI 90-s VI 30-s schedules (see Panels B1 and B2 in Fig. 9.8). When component durations were decreased, relative response rates became more extreme, though they did not closely approximate strict matching at 6-s component durations. But when the schedules were reversed at 6-s component durations, the response-rate differential that had been produced by shortening the component durations was eliminated. These results are displayed in Fig. 9.8, in which Panels A2 and B2 show changes in absolute response rates as a function of component duration. Consistent with the findings of Edmon (1978), absolute response rates in the higher reinforcer-rate components increased with decreasing component durations. Response rates in the lower reinforcer-rate components, however, remained constant. Thus, the short-component multiple-schedule effect requires constant schedule differences and varied component durations for its production. A reversal in reinforcer schedules eliminates the effect. It is, therefore, a fragile effect of component-duration changes, and it has nothing to do with matching versus undermatching.

In summary, component duration affects multiple-schedule response allocation only under some particular experimental manipulations. We have no explanation for this. It is clearly a pitfall in experimental design, and more particularly in data interpretation, that had best be avoided. A local equality of dependent and independent variables may be interpreted as matching (the process) only after further research has been conducted to discover whether the assumed effect is indeed robust in the face of an explicit manipulation of the variable to which matching is assumed.

9.4. DEPRIVATION EFFECTS

Herrnstein and Loveland (1974) pointed out that changes in food deprivation would change the value of food reinforcers relative to the value of other reinforcers available in the experimental situation (R_e). Herrnstein's (1970) equation for response-rate ratios on multiple schedules (see Section 3.1) is:

$$\frac{B_1}{B_2} = \frac{R_1}{R_2} \cdot \left(\frac{R_2 + mR_1 + R_e}{R_1 + mR_2 + R_e} \right).$$

When deprivation for the experimentally delivered reinforcers is increased, say, the reinforcing value of R_1 and R_2 increases relative to the value of R_e. Assuming a constant value of 10 for R_e (which by definition is not concerned with the delivered reinforcers), and of 0.1 for m, Herrnstein and Loveland showed that undermatching results if $R_1 + R_2 = 10,000$, while an approximation to strict matching occurs if $R_1 + R_2 = 0.1$. Herrnstein and Loveland tested these implications by training birds on multiple VI 60-s VI 240-s schedules, and varying their body weights from 80 percent to 100 percent of their ad-lib weights. They found that component response-rate ratios moved toward component reinforcer-rate ratios for all five birds. At maximum body weight response-rate ratios equaled reinforcer-rate ratios.

Herrnstein and Loveland's (1974) experiment was similar in design to that of Shimp and Wheatley's (1971) and Todorov's (1972) investigation of the effect of component duration in this way: The component reinforcer rates were kept constant while another variable was manipulated. Charman and Davison (1983a) carried out an experiment to investigate whether Herrnstein and Loveland's results really implied matching (as a relation) when birds were not deprived, or whether the deprivation effect was as fragile as the component-duration effect. They were able to replicate Herrnstein and Loveland's finding in two ways: First, systematically, by varying component reinforcer rates when their subjects were at their maximum body weights. In this part of the experiment, estimates of a varied between 0.64 and 1.28, and the group data were plotted in Fig. 3.2 in Section 3.7. Second, directly, by increasing and decreasing deprivation with constant pairs of schedules. The results of this part of the experiment are shown in Figs. 9.9 and 9.10. Figure 9.9 shows absolute response rates as a function of percentage free-feeding body weight when the schedules were either multiple VI 90 s VI 30 s or multiple VI 27 s VI 135 s. In both sets of conditions, absolute response rates decreased as deprivation was reduced (i.e., as body weight increased). Figure 9.10 shows the relative rate of responding in the red component as a function of percentage ad-lib body weight for both sets of conditions. Clearly, relative response rates tended toward equality with relative reinforcer rates as deprivation was reduced (multiple VI 90 s VI 30 s), and moved away from strict matching as deprivation was once more increased (multiple VI 27 s VI 135 s).

The effect of deprivation on multiple-schedule performance is thus robust, and accords with Herrnstein's (1970) theory of multiple-schedule performance in that respect. However, Charman and Davison (1983a) were able to calculate values of m and R_e (by simultaneous equations). As Fig. 3.3 in Section 3.7 illustrated, the median value of m was 0.95 and showed no trend with deprivation. R_e also showed no trend with deprivation, and the median value of this parameter was -2.54 reinforcers per minute. Both the negative value of R_e and its lack of trend are inconsistent with Herrnstein's theory as used by Herrnstein and Loveland (1974). (Notice that in using Herrnstein and Loveland's theory, it is necessary to measure R_e in terms of R_1 and R_2 because only the latter are directly measurable. The development of the theory in Herrnstein and Loveland's paper assumed that R_e was constant and that the values of R_1 and R_2 changed with deprivation. Empirically measuring R_e in terms of R_1 and R_2 obviously comes to the same thing, as these measures are simply relative to one another.)

Charman and Davison (1983a) also analyzed their data in an alternative way, as suggested by McLean and White's (1983) model (see Section 9.9). McLean and White assumed *no* direct interaction between components of multiple schedules—that is, no equivalent of Herrnstein's (1970) component-interaction parameter, m—and generalized, rather than strict, matching. Thus, for each component,

$$B_i = \frac{kR_i^a}{R_i^a + bR_{ei}^a},\qquad (9.4)$$

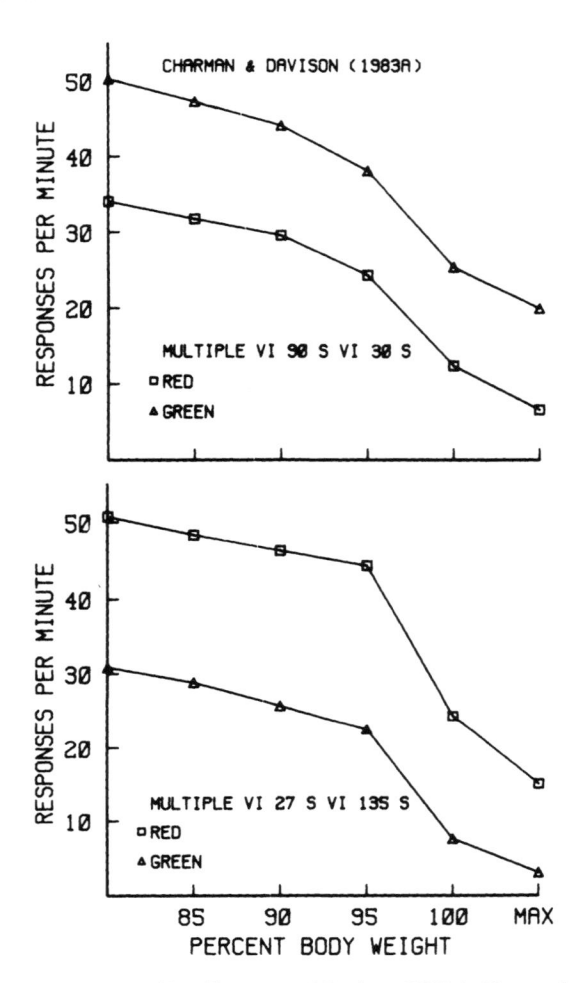

FIG. 9.9.   Group data reported by Charman and Davison (1983a). The number of responses per minute in the red and green components is shown as a function of the percentage free-feeding body weight.

where a and b are sensitivity and bias, respectively, and R_{ei} is the rate of extraneous reinforcers in Component i. That is, McLean and White did not assume that the rate of extraneous reinforcers was the same in both components. Because Charman and Davison arranged both an increasing body-weight series of conditions with one pair of schedules, and a decreasing series with another pair of schedules, they had four component response-and reinforcer-rate data points at each body weight. In order to investigate the effects of deprivation on k and R_{ei}, they fitted Equation 9.4 at each body weight under the simplifying assumption that $a = b = 1$. The results showed that k was constant, but R_{ei} increased, as body weight increased. This result is, of course, quite consistent

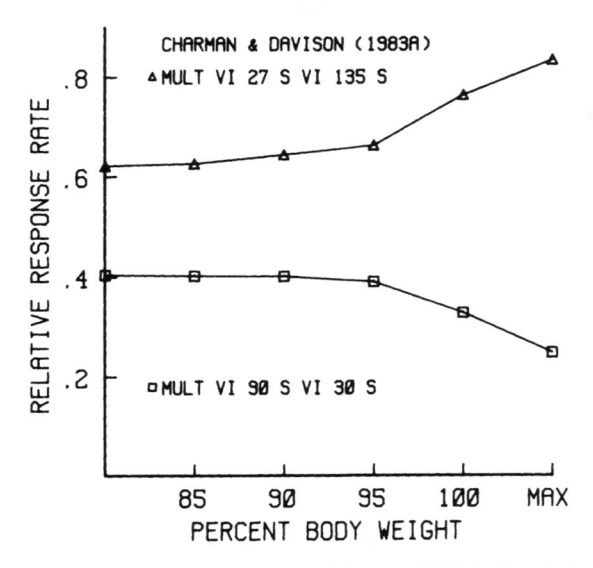

FIG. 9.10.   Group data reported by Charman and Davison (1983a). The relative rates of responding in the red component are shown as a function of the percentage free-feeding body weight for two different multiple schedules.

with Herrnstein and Loveland's (1974) explanation of the deprivation effect. As a result, Charman and Davison concluded that Herrnstein and Loveland's *qualitative* explanation of the effects of deprivation on multiple-schedule performance in terms of the changing relative values of experimental and extraneous reinforcers was correct. But the model that they used to describe the effect quantitatively was incorrect.

9.5. REINFORCER AMOUNT

Two researchers have presented data on the effects of varying reinforcer amounts on multiple VI VI schedule performance. First, Shettleworth and Nevin (1965) trained pigeons on multiple VI 120-s VI 120-s schedules using 180-s component durations (120 s in one condition). They varied the reinforcer-duration ratios from 0.5 to 9. A reanalysis of the data from their two birds is shown in Fig. 9.11. The sensitivities to reinforcer-duration ratios were 0.30 and 0.34.

Further data on the same question can be obtained from Merigan, Miller and Gollub (1975). In one part of their experiment they used VI 120-s schedules in both 120-s long components arranged on two keys. Merigan et al. fitted straight lines to the relation between *relative* response rates and *relative* reinforcer rates, which is not informative. A reanalysis of their data is shown in Fig. 9.12. The sensitivities for the four birds averaged 0.40.

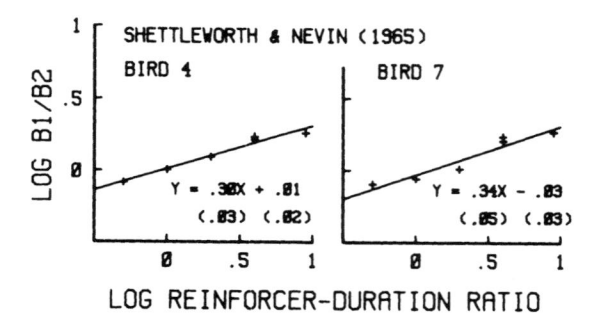

FIG. 9.11.   Log component response-rate ratios as a function of log reinforcer-duration ratios from Shettleworth and Nevin (1965).

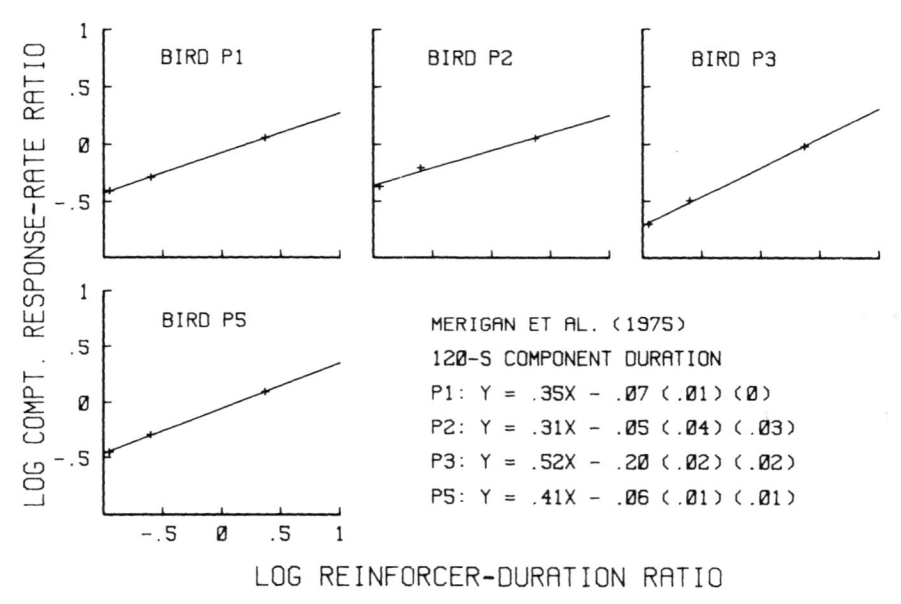

FIG. 9.12.   Log component response-rate ratios as a function of log reinforcer-duration ratios from Merigan, Miller, and Gollub (1975). The multiple schedule was arranged on two keys, and the components were 120 s long.

Our tentative conclusion from the above data might be that both component response rates and reinforcer durations produce the same effect (i.e., the same a value) on multiple VI VI schedule performance. In this respect, multiple-schedule performances may be unlike concurrent-schedule performances, as the latter give different sensitivity values for reinforcer rate and reinforcer duration. However, Merigan et al. (1975) found another problem that concerns the effects of reinforcer duration in short-component multiple schedules. When the multiple schedule was arranged on a single key and the component durations were decreased to 5 s, undermatching still occurred (mean sensitivity 0.41, Fig. 9.13).

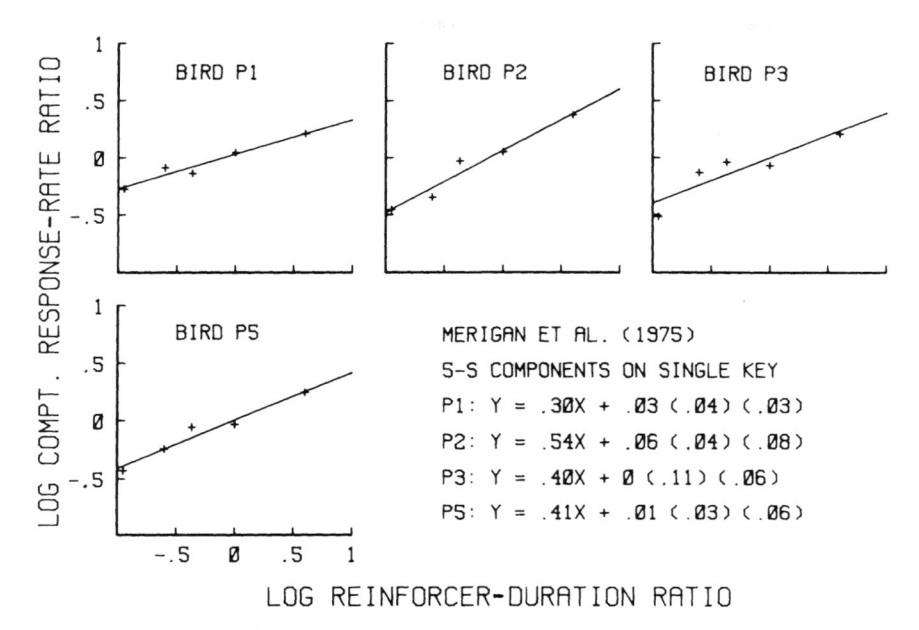

FIG. 9.13. Log component response-rate ratios as a function of log reinforcer-duration ratios from Merigan, Miller, and Gollub (1975). The multiple schedule was arranged on a single key, and the components were 5 s long.

This result was seen as contrary to the findings of Shimp and Wheatley (1971) and of Todorov (1972). But, because the component reinforcer rates were varied within a constant component duration, the result is consistent with the findings of Charman and Davison (1983a). However, when the 5-s components were arranged on two different keys, sensitivity to reinforcer rate averaged 0.72 (Fig. 9.14), and was higher than the single-key 5-s component-duration data for all four birds. As we have noted, Merigan et al. (1975) used a two-key procedure to obtain their 120-s component-duration data, and they did not investigate the effects of this component duration using a single-key procedure. But there is no reason to believe that one-key versus two-key procedures would affect long-component multiple-schedule performance differently. The explanation of Merigan et al.'s results remains a mystery, and clearly deserves further research.

9.6. STIMULUS EFFECTS IN MULTIPLE SCHEDULES

Since the multiple VI VI schedule is the traditional tool for stimulus control research, it might be expected that the parametric effects of variations in discriminative stimuli in multiple schedules would have been well researched. It is not so. We have found only two studies in the literature. The first was an investigation of the ability of pigeons to discriminate the typical red/green

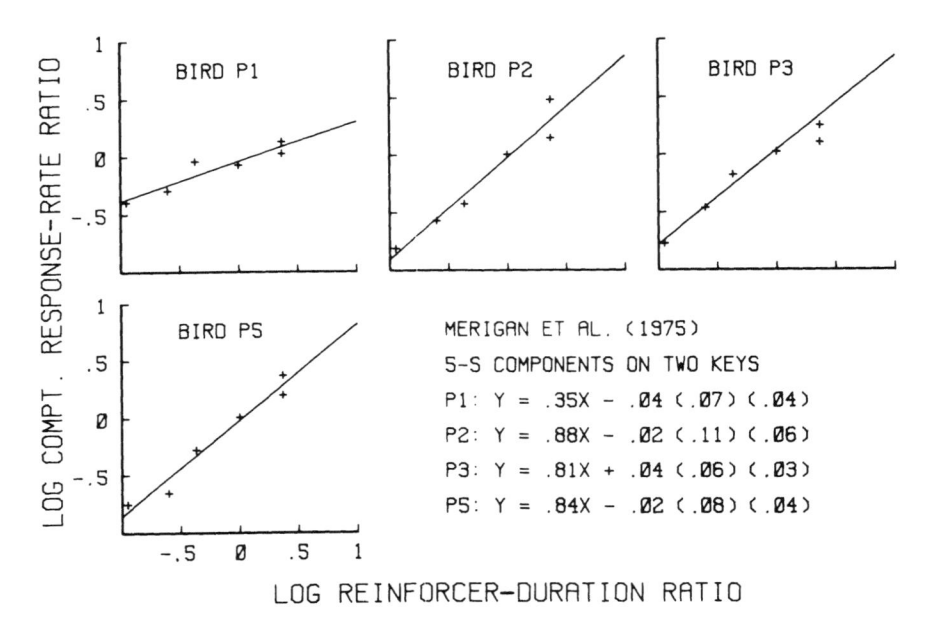

FIG. 9.14.   Log component response-rate ratios as a function of log reinforcer-duration ratios from Merigan, Miller, and Gollub (1975). The multiple schedule was arranged on two keys, and the components were 5 s long.

component stimuli in a multiple schedule as a function of component reinforcer rates. This was reported by Charman and Davison (1983b) using 180-s components. They varied the component reinforcer rates over five conditions using a special procedure in which the discriminative stimuli were displayed on both side keys of a pigeon chamber in both components. When the two keys were red, the left key provided reinforcers on a VI schedule, and when they were green the VI schedule was arranged on the right key. This procedure allowed Charman and Davison to measure the percentage of responses emitted on the VI key in each component, and hence to estimate the discriminability of the component stimuli (see Chapter 11). In all but one condition for one of the six birds, at least 99 percent of the total responses were emitted on the VI-schedule keys.

This result has a number of interesting implications. It shows that the degree of undermatching commonly shown in multiple VI VI schedule performance is *not* due to a failure of the subject to discriminate the stimuli signaling the components (compare the results of Miller, Saunders, and Bourland, 1980, Section 8.7). To put this finding another way, it has commonly been suggested (e.g., Mackintosh, 1974) that successive discriminations (multiple schedules) are poorer than simultaneous discriminations (concurrent schedules). In terms of the response differential obtained, this is clearly true. But the difference does not seem to be anything to do with stimulus control; that is, with the discriminability

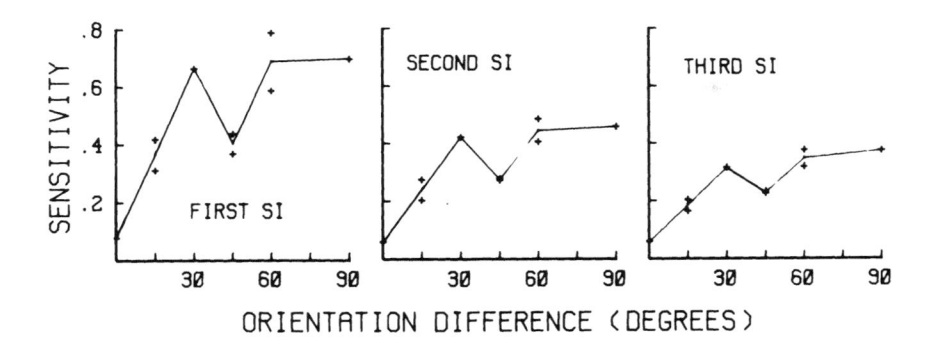

FIG. 9.15. Group data reported by White, Pipe, and McLean (1984). Sensitivity to component reinforcer-rate ratios is shown as a function of the line-orientation difference for performance within successive 16-s subintervals (SI) of 48-s multiple-schedule components.

of the stimuli (Chapter 11). Rather, it appears that the smaller differential in multiple-schedule performance is concerned with the process of reinforcement. Notice here that when researchers speak of "discrimination" or of a "discrimination index" they are not measuring stimulus effects in isolation. The reinforcer-rate differential also strongly affects such measures. For example, a "discrimination" failure after head injury may result from either a failure of discriminative stimulus input, or an inability of the subject to behave in a way appropriate to the contingencies of reinforcement. We reserve the term "discriminability" for stimulus measures that are independent of reinforcer effects (Chapter 11).

The second study on the effects of variations in multiple-schedule discriminative stimuli was reported by White, Pipe, and McLean (1984). They investigated pigeons' performances on multiple schedules in which line orientations of 0°, 30°, or 45° in Component 1 alternated with orientations of 45°, 60°, or 90° in Component 2. Their major results are summarized in Fig. 9.15. First, the sensitivity of response ratios to variations in relative component-reinforcer frequency increased with increasing line-orientation difference. Second, the sensitivity values decreased over successive subintervals of components, that is, with increasing time since component alternation.

9.7. EFFECTS OF COMPONENT RESPONSE REQUIREMENTS

The term "behavioral contrast" (Section 3.5) describes an increase in the rate of responding in an unchanged multiple-schedule component when the conditions of reinforcement (usually the reinforcer rate) are worsened in the alternative component (e.g., McSweeney, 1983; Williams, 1983). As McSweeney (1983) has noted, contrast may be reliably obtained in multiple schedules when pigeons peck keys, but it has been much more difficult to obtain when pigeons press levers (but McSweeney did obtain contrast). While the presence of behavioral contrast in a set of data neither implies matching nor any particular sensitivity value, the difficulty of finding contrast when pigeons press levers could be symptomatic of a failure of generalized matching, or perhaps of a low sensitivity to component reinforcer rates, under such procedures.

A generalized matching relation between component response rates and component reinforcer rates was, however, found by Davison and Ferguson (1978) when pigeons pressed levers. In their first set of conditions, they required lever presses in one component and keypecks in the other, and varied both component reinforcer rates. Obtained sensitivities to reinforcer-rate ratios ranged from 0.04 to 0.64 (mean 0.41) for their six birds. There was also a strong bias, averaging 0.61, toward the key component. This implied that the keypeck response was about four times more preferable than the lever-press response. In the second part of their experiment, lever presses were required in *both* components, and the schedules were varied. Sensitivities ranged from 0.09 to 0.57 (mean 0.35), and bias was negligible. Davison and Ferguson then arranged a series of varying component reinforcer rates with keypecks required in both components. In this procedure, the range of sensitivities was 0.3 to 0.78, and averaged 0.53. A Friedman analysis of variance carried out on the sensitivities for the individual birds showed a significant difference was present, with the lever-lever sensitivities lowest and the key-key sensitivities highest. If the change in response requirement is interpreted as a "force" change, this result is incompatible with concurrent-schedule results (because force variation does not affect concurrent-schedule sensitivity to reinforcer frequency; Section 7.11a). But if the type of requirement change is interpreted as a duration-of-operant change, Davison and Ferguson's result is compatible with concurrent-schedule research (again, see Section 7.11a).

Finally, Davison and Ferguson (1978) investigated performance on concurrent key-lever schedules. Bias, measured by response allocation, ranged from 0.17 to 1.2 (mean 0.65 over five birds) to the key response. This was not significantly different from the bias estimated from the multiple key-lever conditions. Mean time-allocation bias was 0.32 toward the *lever* response, perhaps confirming that the change in operant requirement was equivalent to a change in operant duration.

9.8. CONTINUOUS MULTIPLE-SCHEDULE PERFORMANCE

In Section 8.2 we showed that, when concurrent schedules were continuously available to subjects, performance was similar to that produced in conventional 45- to 60-min sessions. This degree of generality does not, unfortunately, extend to multiple-schedule performance. Elliffe and Davison (1985) reported an experiment in which pigeons worked, in their home cages, on multiple VI VI schedules that were available 24 hours per day. The components were 150 s long, and the pigeons' weights remained quite close to their free-feeding weights throughout the experiment. The subjects received all their food from the multiple schedules. Two series of conditions were arranged. First, two birds (251 and 252) worked on these schedules for five to seven conditions. Then a third bird (250) was added to the experiment and five component reinforcer-rate variations were arranged for all three birds. These data, then, constituted a direct replication for Birds 251 and 252. In both sequences, the arranged overall reinforcer rate was 1/min. The data from the latter sequence of conditions are shown in Fig. 9.16.

Mean sensitivity to component reinforcer-rate ratios was 1.58, and the bias values were not significantly different from zero. As Fig. 9.16 shows, the fits were excellent. These results should be compared with those of Herrnstein and Loveland (1974) and of Charman and Davison (1983a), who reported data from pigeons working on short-session multiple VI VI schedules when the subjects were at their normal body weights. Both experiments reported an approximation to strict matching ($a = 1$; Section 9.4). It is evident that Elliffe and Davison's (1985) data cannot be explained on the basis of zero deprivation alone, which would suggest a sensitivity of 1.0. Also, these data cannot be described by Herrnstein's (1970) multiple-schedule equation (Equation 3.8), which is unable to predict a sensitivity value greater than unity. It could be argued, however, that if the assumption that R_e was the same in both components was relaxed, then Herrnstein's equation could accommodate these results. Because, however, there are other problems with Herrnstein's approach (Section 3.8), it may not be worth pursuing this possibility. McLean and White's (1983) model (Section 9.9) does not assume equal R_e reinforcer rates in both components, and therefore can, in principle, accommodate Elliffe and Davison's results.

As we mention in Section 8.2, there are a number of differences between conventional short-session performances and continuous performances. One of these is the frequent use of a closed economy in continuous-schedule research. This term describes the fact that no food, other than that worked for, was available. Whereas this could be the source of overmatching in Elliffe and Davison's (1985) data, it seems doubtful whether overmatching would occur in short-session multiple-schedule performances where no post-sessional feeding was delivered. Thus, Elliffe and Davison (in preparation) examined two other possible controlling variables—the session duration and the overall reinforcer rate. One problem with continuous performances is that these two variables and body weight are interdependent. For instance, sessions cannot be shortened and body weight maintained without the experimenter being forced to increase the overall reinforcer rate. Thus, in two series of conditions, Elliffe and Davison (in preparation) manipulated body weight either by varying the session duration while keeping the component schedules constant (Part 1) or by decreasing the

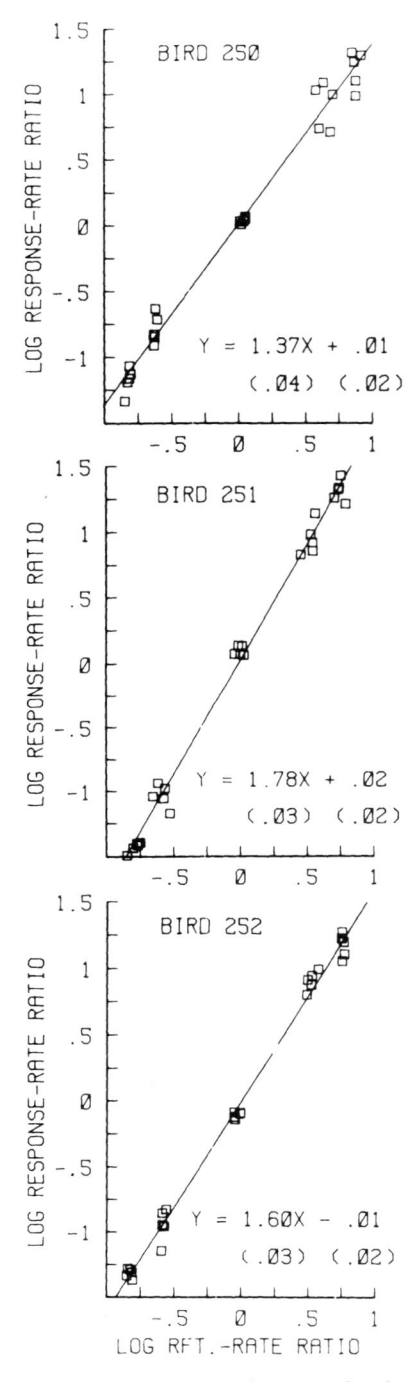

FIG. 9.16. Log component response-rate ratios as a function of log obtained component reinforcer-rate ratios on continuously available multiple VI VI schedules. The data are from Elliffe

overall reinforcer rate while keeping the sessions continuous (Part 2). For the component-schedule manipulations, the overall reinforcer rates were varied from 1 per minute to 1 per 10 minutes, and sensitivity values were obtained from, at minimum, one condition and its reversal at each overall reinforcer rate. The session-duration manipulations were from 100 minutes to 24 hours, and sensitivity values were obtained as single-condition point estimates. This latter procedure gave accurate values of sensitivity because the bias between the components was negligible (Fig. 9.16).

The results obtained by Elliffe and Davison (in preparation) are shown in Fig. 9.17. From this figure, it is clear that decreasing body weights by shortening the sessions reliably decreased sensitivity to reinforcer frequency. However, sensitivity showed no signs of decreasing when body weight was decreased by decreasing the overall reinforcer rate. This result rather clearly shows that deprivation, per se, does not control sensitivity to reinforcement on multiple schedules. Rather, the controlling variable in this experiment seems to be session duration. Notice, though, that this cannot be the whole story because sensitivity increases (to about 1.0) in short sessions as deprivation is decreased (Herrnstein & Loveland, 1974). There are, evidently, other interactions between the effects of session duration, overall reinforcer rate, and body weight that still require investigation.

Overall, the conclusions from Elliffe and Davison's (1985, in preparation) research must be that, whereas concurrent-schedule performances are probably the same in short-session laboratory research and in the natural environment (Section 8.2), that is not the case for multiple-schedule performances. This problem of generality needs further investigation.

9.9. THEORY OF MULTIPLE-SCHEDULE PERFORMANCE

McLean and White (1983) criticized Herrnstein's (1970) theory of multiple-schedule performance (Section 3.1) on three grounds: (1) it fails to account for increased component response-rate differentials when extraneous reinforcer rates are increased (Hinson & Staddon, 1978; Pliskoff, Shull, & Gollub, 1968; but see Lobb & Davison, 1977); (2) it fails to predict correctly the direction of component response-rate changes when component durations are decreased (Edmon, 1978; Section 9.3); and (3) it predicts that single-schedule response rates are higher than response rates when the same schedule is arranged in *both* components of a multiple schedule (McSweeney, 1980; see also Williams, 1983).

As an alternative to Herrnstein's (1970) assumption of successive-schedule interactions (via the parameter m), McLean and White (1983) offered an analysis using concurrent-schedule interactions only. There is no interaction constant m, but the extraneous reinforcer rates (R_{e1}, R_{e2}) in the components are not assumed

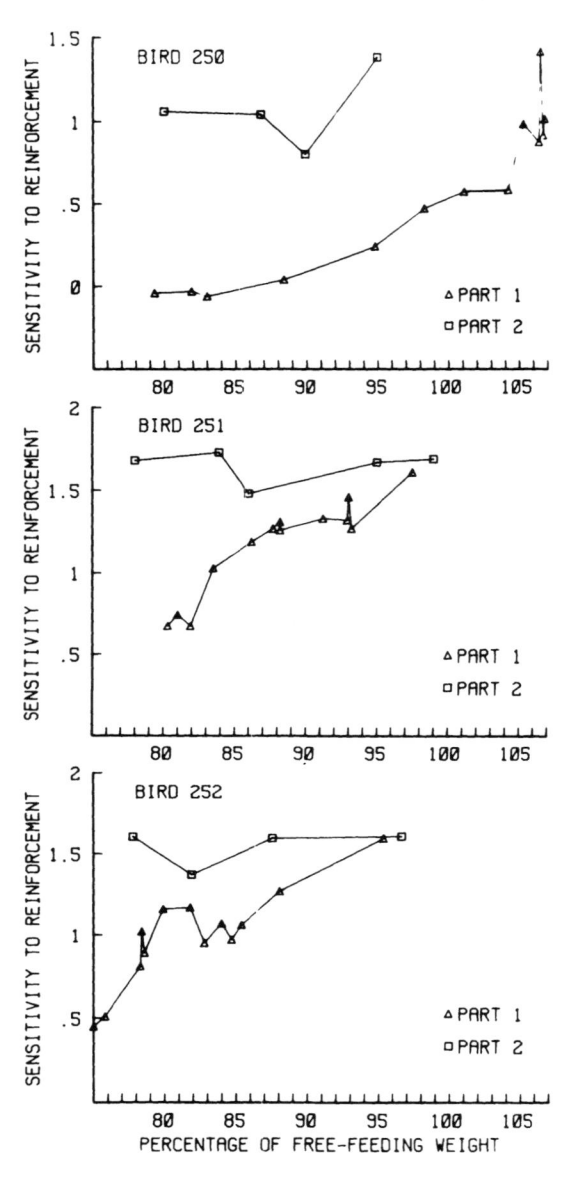

FIG. 9.17. Sensitivity to component reinforcer rates on multiple VI VI schedules as a function of the percentage of normal body weight. In Part 1, the session durations were varied, and in Part 2, the overall reinforcer rates were varied. The data are from Elliffe and Davison (in preparation).

equal. The McLean and White model is based on the generalized matching law for concurrent schedules written in relative terms. For the first multiple-schedule component, R_{m1} reinforcers are obtained on the multiple schedule, and R_{e1} reinforcers are concurrently obtained (either explicitly, as on a multiple-concurrent schedule, or implicitly, as on a standard multiple schedule):

$$\frac{B_{m1}}{B_{m1} + B_{e1}} = \frac{R_{m1}{}^a}{R_{m1}{}^a + cR_{e1}{}^a} .$$

The variable a is concurrent-schedule sensitivity to reinforcer frequency, and c is the reciprocal of the usual bias measure. Assuming that the asymptotic rate of responding in a component is constant ($B_{m1} + B_{e1} = k$), then:

$$B_{m1} = \frac{kR_{m1}{}^a}{R_{m1}{}^a + cR_{e1}{}^a} . \tag{9.5}$$

Equation 9.5 is similar to equations suggested by Davison and Hunter (1976), Hunter and Davison (1978), and Wearden (1981). Equation 9.5 implies:

$$B_{e1} = \frac{kcR_{e1}{}^a}{R_{m1}{}^a + cR_{e1}{}^a} .$$

and that, as assumed:

$$B_{m1} + B_{e1} = \frac{kR_{m1}{}^a + kcR_{e1}{}^a}{R_{m1}{}^a + cR_{e1}{}^a} = k . \tag{9.6}$$

An equation identical in form to Equation 9.5 can be written for performance in the second multiple-schedule component:

$$B_{m2} = \frac{k'R_{m2}{}^a}{R_{m2}{}^a + cR_{e2}{}^a} .$$

Making the assumptions that the asymptotic response rates in both components are the same ($k = k'$), and of course that the sensitivities (a) are the same, we can now write an equation for the response-rate ratio in the multiple-schedule components:

$$\frac{B_{m1}}{B_{m2}} = \left(\frac{R_{m1}}{R_{m2}}\right)^a \cdot \frac{R_{m2}{}^a + cR_{e2}{}^a}{R_{m1}{}^a + cR_{e1}{}^a} . \tag{9.7}$$

Equation 9.7 is similar to equations proposed by Bouzas and Baum (1976) and by Pliskoff, Shull, and Gollub (1968). McLean and White (1983) derived two implications from Equation 9.7. First, if R_{e1} and R_{e2} are kept equal and made large relative to R_{m1} and R_{m2}, then Equation 9.7 tends toward:

$$\frac{B_{m1}}{B_{m2}} = \left(\frac{R_{m1}}{R_{m2}}\right)^a .$$

Since a is the concurrent-schedule sensitivity, multiple-schedule sensitivity will increase toward concurrent-schedule sensitivity as $R_{e1} = R_{e2}$ increases. (Notice here that if R_{e1} does not equal R_{e2}, Equation 9.7 can predict *overmatching*—especially in conditions in which an increase in R_m leads to a decrease in the associated R_e.) This increase in sensitivity was reported by Pliskoff et al., but not by Lobb and Davison (1977). The second implication of Equation 9.7 is that constant and unequal R_{e1} and R_{e2} reinforcer rates will simply bias the generalized matching relation between component response-rate ratios and component reinforcer-rate ratios. If $R_{e1} > R_{e2}$, the bias will be toward the second component, and vice versa. McLean and White tested both of these implications by arranging an experimental analogue of R_e—VI schedules of food reinforcement arranged concurrently with each multiple-schedule component, or a multiple-concurrent schedule. "Real" R_e is still present, of course, but support for the theory hinges on the finding of directional changes in sensitivity and bias.

In their first experiment, McLean and White (1983) varied the multiple-schedule component reinforcer rates with first a VI 360-s schedule (10 reinforcers per hour) arranged concurrently with both components, and, second, with a VI 51-s schedule (70 reinforcers per hour) arranged concurrently. With 10 reinforcers per hour as the extraneous reinforcer rate, multiple-schedule sensitivities ranged from 0.24 to 0.54 (mean 0.37). With 70 reinforcers per hour, the range was 0.35 to 0.97 (mean 0.64), with all four birds showing an increase. There was effectively no bias. McLean and White also measured the time allocated to each component of the multiple-concurrent schedules. Multiple-schedule time-allocation sensitivity was, on average, 0.26 (10 reinforcers per hour) and 0.54 (70 reinforcers per hour), with all birds again showing the increase. Qualitative support for the theory was therefore good.

McLean and White (1983) also attempted to provide quantitative support for their theory. They first measured the combined concurrent-schedule response-allocation sensitivities in both multiple-schedule components (B_{m1}/B_{e1} and B_{m2}/B_{e2}). The mean response- and time-allocation sensitivities were 0.59 and 0.68 when the concurrent alternative arranged 10 reinforcers per hour. When 70 concurrent reinforcers per hour were arranged, the equivalent sensitivities were 0.68 and 0.70. Not all subjects showed higher sensitivities when the concurrently available reinforcer rate was higher. McLean and White then used the obtained values of concurrent-schedule response sensitivity to predict the obtained multiple-schedule response ratios. They used Equation 9.7 *without making the assumption that k was the same in both components*—that is, without cancelling k:

$$\frac{B_{m1}}{B_{m2}} = \left(\frac{R_{m1}}{R_{m2}}\right)^a \cdot \frac{R_{m2}{}^a + cR_{e2}{}^a}{R_{m1}{}^a + cR_{e1}{}^a} \cdot \frac{B_{m1} + B_{e1}}{B_{m2} + B_{e2}} \qquad (9.8)$$

Equation 9.8 does *not* provide independent predictions of B_{m1}/B_{m2} as these measures occur on both sides of the equation. In fact, the relation is tautologous if the values of sensitivity and bias from concurrent-schedule fits are used. This can be shown in the following way. We commence with the ratio forms of the concurrent-schedule fits:

$$\frac{B_{m1}}{B_{e1}} = \frac{1}{c}\left(\frac{R_{m1}}{R_{e1}}\right)^a , \quad \text{and} \quad \frac{B_{m2}}{B_{e2}} = \frac{1}{c}\left(\frac{R_{m2}}{R_{e2}}\right)^a .$$

Hence, dividing the second equation into the first, we obtain:

$$\frac{B_{m1}}{B_{m2}} \cdot \frac{B_{e2}}{B_{e1}} = \left(\frac{R_{m1}}{R_{m2}}\right)^a \cdot \left(\frac{R_{e2}}{R_{e1}}\right)^a . \qquad (9.9)$$

Equation 9.9 at least has all the dependent variables to the left of the equality. But the algebraic equivalent to the equation used to ''predict'' the data was:

$$\frac{B_{m1}}{B_{m2}} = \left(\frac{R_{m1}}{R_{m2}}\right)^a \cdot \left(\frac{R_{e2}}{R_{e1}}\right)^a \cdot \frac{B_{e1}}{B_{e2}} . \qquad (9.10)$$

Evidently, Equation 9.10, which is algebraically equivalent to Equation 9.8, must fit better than the worst concurrent-schedule curve fit, and somewhat worse than the best concurrent-schedule curve fit. This section shows some of the major pitfalls of tautology into which experimenters can sometimes fall. The way out, for McLean and White, is to fit Equation 9.7 to their data iteratively, and to compare the a values obtained in that way with those obtained from the concurrent-schedule curve fits.

This cavil, however, is in no way meant to detract from the fact that the *changes* in multiple-schedule sensitivity values with variations in the extraneous reinforcer rates provide strong support for McLean and White's (1983) model.

In the second part of their experiment, McLean and White (1983) first kept R_{e1} at VI 360 s and R_{e2} at VI 51 s for a series of variations of the multiple-schedule component reinforcer rates. They then reversed R_{e1} and R_{e2} and again varied the component reinforcer rates. In a generalized matching analysis of the multiple-schedule performance, using two birds, they demonstrated biases toward the first component when $R_{e1} < R_{e2}$, and toward the second component when $R_{e1} > R_{e2}$, for both time and response measures. Again, the directional prediction of their quantitative approach was confirmed.

In their discussion, McLean and White (1983) illustrate how their theory may describe the well documented fact that changing the reinforcer rate in one component of a multiple schedule changes the response rate in the other. On the face of it, this fact is evidence for the sort of successive interaction described by Herrnstein's (1970) parameter m. McLean and White assumed that total response rate in a component ($B_{mi} + B_{ei}$) is a constant, k. As a result, any reallocation of *behavior* from one multiple-schedule component (B_{m1}) to the other (B_{m2}) must be "matched" by an equal reallocation of behavior from B_{e2} to B_{e1}. This directly implies that if, say, R_{m2} was increased, then the ratio B_{m1}/B_{e1} would fall. Thus, concurrent-schedule performance in the first multiple-schedule component would be a function of both the reinforcer ratio in that component *and* the reinforcer ratio in the second multiple-schedule component. Descriptively (and this equation is *not* any part of the current theory, rather a tool for analysis) n should not be zero in the following equation:

$$\frac{B_{m1}}{B_{e1}} = \left(\frac{R_{m1}}{R_{e1}}\right)^a \cdot \left(\frac{R_{m2}}{R_{e2}}\right)^n . \qquad (9.11)$$

McLean and White fitted Equation 9.11 to their data, and to those of Pliskoff et al. (1968) and Lobb and Davison (1977), and showed that n was not reliably different from zero. Response allocation in each concurrent schedule thus shows what McLean and White call "successive independence," or what Lobb and Davison termed "independence from successive schedule context."

How can component interactions (e.g., contrast) in standard multiple-schedule performances be explained? Given that the above analysis showed reallocation of behavior between components did not occur, McLean and White (1983) suggest an alternative explanation. It is that R_e is reallocated between components. This effect could not occur in their study simply because analogues to R_{ei} were arranged on VI schedules, and by definition a reinforcer on one of these schedules cannot be reallocated to the other component. (Interestingly, such reallocation *could* have happened in Lobb and Davison's (1977) study because the *same* common VI schedule ran during both components.) In a standard multiple schedule, B_e may consist of behaviors like preening, scratching, and so on, which can possibly be held over until the next component. Real R_e schedules do not act at all like component-VI schedule "analogues." Another way of putting the same argument is that natural R_e schedules are more ratio-like than interval-like, and are not confined to particular components. In unpublished research using FR schedules arranged concurrently with multiple schedules, we have indeed found that FR reinforcers are reallocated between components when component reinforcer rates are changed. Hinson and Staddon (1978) also showed this effect with rats using multiple VI VI schedules of lever pressing with, and without, a running wheel concurrently available. As McLean and White's model would predict, contrast was greater with the running wheel available (R_e higher) than without it (R_e lower). Running was greater in the lower reinforcer-rate component, also as expected. All this argues against the generality of Lobb and Davison's finding that multiple-schedule response allocation was unaffected by the rate of concurrently available reinforcers. This difference in results still requires some explanation.

Overall, it seems that McLean and White's (1983) model warrants further research as it is a clear step ahead of Herrnstein's (1970) model. There are, of course, a number of variables with which it does not deal directly, such as the duration of components (as noted by McLean and White), and the finding that contrast was more controlled by the component reinforcer rate that *follows* a constant component rather than the component reinforcer rate that precedes it (see Williams, 1983). Williams and Wixted (1986) have provided an extension of Herrnstein's (1970) multiple-schedule model to describe this "following-component effect." Since this model effectively divides Herrnstein's m into two parts, one for the preceding and one for the following component, it has many of the same problems as Herrnstein's original formulation. The following-component effect may, however, be understandable through the notion that R_e may be carried over from one component to another. Some experimentation using three-component multiple schedules with, say, an FR requirement common to each, is required here.

9.10. CHAIN-SCHEDULE PERFORMANCE

There has been one attempt to use the generalized matching law to describe performance on two-link chain FI FI schedules. The idea is that if T_a and T_b are the times spent in the two links, and B_a and B_b are the rates of responding in each link, then:

$$\frac{B_a}{B_b} = c\left(\frac{T_b}{T_a}\right)^a,$$

because the reinforcer rate in Component B is proportional to $1/T_b$ and the "conditioned" reinforcer rate in Component A is proportional to $1/T_a$. We would expect there to be a strong bias toward responding in the terminal link, as presumably the greater reinforcer (food rather than terminal-link production) occurs there. This logic is similar to that used by Hollard and Davison (1971) to measure the relative reinforcing effectiveness of food versus brain stimulation. Davison (1974), who carried out the chain FI FI experiment, did indeed find such a bias. He reported an a value of about 0.2—a value similar to that for multiple FI FI performance reported by Barron and Davison (1972). However, the fits of the chain-schedule data to the generalized matching relation left a lot to be desired. In retrospect, the demonstration was not very convincing. Similar experiments, using chain VI VI schedules with another VI schedule concurrently available during both links, are now being carried out. Again, the data are not well fitted by the generalized matching law. We will keep the generalized matching analysis of chain-schedule performance in abeyance until further data are forthcoming.

9.11. SUMMARY OF MULTIPLE-SCHEDULE RESEARCH

This section could well consist of a rather extensive list of investigations that have not yet been carried out using multiple schedules (compare the range of variables that have been used with concurrent schedules). Rather, we will say that, for the somewhat limited research that has been reported, the generalized matching relation provides a good description of response allocation with a values of 0.3 to 0.5 (see the review by McSweeney, Farmer, Dougan, and Whipple, 1986). But we must admit that the different values of a obtained from multiple and concurrent schedules are not intuitively understandable, except as *given* constants. McLean and White's (1983) model looks promising, and this is based on a generalized matching analysis of concurrently emitted responses. McLean and White's theory explains why a appears lower in multiple-schedule than in concurrent-schedule performance. But, because we still seem not to have fully explained why a is 0.8 to 1.0 in concurrent-schedule performances, this may not be a great leap forward.

10 CONCURRENT-CHAIN PERFORMANCE

10.1. BASIC PROCEDURE

In concurrent schedules, subjects emit two or more responses that are intermittently followed by reinforcers. In contrast, a concurrent-chain schedule (sometimes called a concurrent-chains schedule) is a schedule in which subjects choose, on concurrent schedules, between *periods of access to schedules of reinforcement*. The concurrent-schedule parts of the procedure are called the *initial links* (or *choice phase*), and the periods of access to the schedules are called the *terminal links* (or *outcome phase*). The initial links and each of the terminal links are usually signaled by different discriminative stimuli, and sometimes they are arranged on different manipulanda. It is important to note, before discussing concurrent-chain schedules further, that such schedules differ from concurrent schedules quantitatively, not qualitatively. A concurrent-chain schedule with 0-s delays in both terminal links *is* a concurrent schedule, so any attempt at a quantitative description of concurrent-chain performance *must* reduce to a reasonable concurrent-schedule account when the terminal links are asymptotically short.

Figure 10.1 shows a diagram of a typical concurrent-chain schedule procedure, though, as we shall see, many variants of this basic procedure have been used. The key colors are, of course, arbitrary within the restriction that the stimuli signaling initial and each of the terminal links are highly discriminable from each other. Taking pigeons as subjects, the concurrent chain commences with two keys illuminated white with two schedules, I_1 and I_2. Concurrent, typically VI, schedules are in operation. When either schedule has completed timing the current interval, a response on that key has two effects: (1) it causes

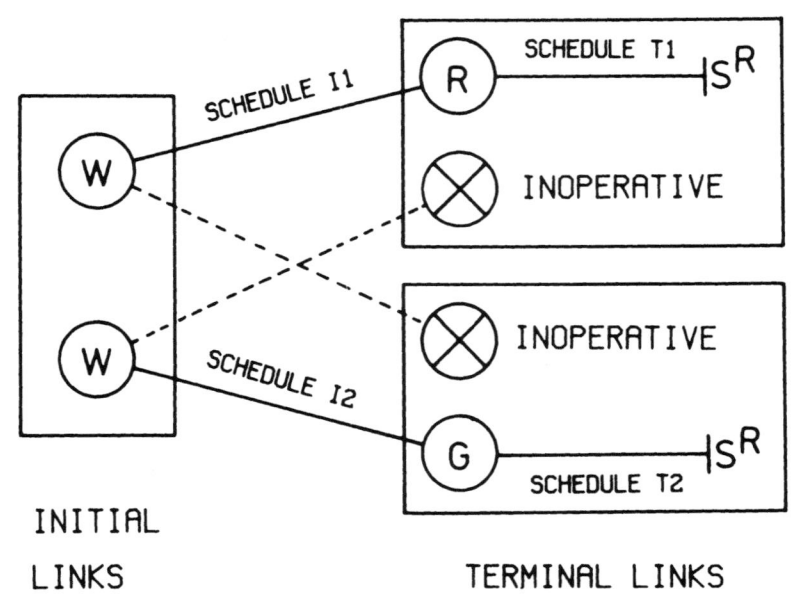

FIG. 10.1. A schematic diagram of the basic concurrent-chain procedure. Responding on concurrent initial links (schedules I_1 and I_2) on two keys produces one of two independent terminal-link schedules (schedules T_1 and T_2), each signaled by a distinctive stimulus. At the end of the terminal links, the initial links are reinstated. S^R indicates a reinforcer delivery, and W, G, and R signify (by way of example) white, green, and red keys.

the other key light to turn off (black out) and become inoperative, and the initial-link schedules to cease timing; and (2) it causes the key just pecked to change color and the terminal-link schedule on that key to commence. The terminal links on the two keys are signaled by different key colors, and they will often consist of different schedules. When the terminal-link schedule has been completed (this may be a ratio, interval, or response-independent schedule), a reinforcer is delivered, and following the reinforcer, the two initial-link keys are reinstated. At this point, the initial-link schedule associated with the terminal link just entered is restarted, and that associated with the other terminal link simply continues timing the same interval that was stopped when the alternative terminal link was entered.

10.2. MEASUREMENT IN CONCURRENT-CHAIN PERFORMANCES

The most common measure of concurrent-chain performance is the distribution of responses between the two manipulanda in the initial links. This measure was, as in concurrent-schedule research, originally reported most often as a relative response rate, but log-ratio measures are now becoming more frequent. This preference measure is naturally assumed to reflect the reinforcing effects, or values, of entering each terminal link or, sometimes, the conditioned reinforcement associated with the two terminal-link stimuli. The properties of this measure are different from those obtained from concurrent-schedule performances. In formal terms, the difference is this: In concurrent schedules, preference measures are taken while the subject is in the presence of the contingencies between which it is choosing, whereas in concurrent-chain schedules, it is taken at a time when the to-be-chosen contingencies are absent. An example may make this clearer. If we were to arrange concurrent FI 10-s DRL 10-s schedules, we would expect to find the subject responded a great deal more on the FI schedule than on the DRL schedule. Although this is an important fact about behavior, it does not tell us that, given a choice, a subject prefers an FI schedule to a DRL schedule of the same mean interval. Were we, however, to arrange a concurrent-chain schedule with equal initial links, and with FI 10-s and DRL 10-s terminal links, we might well find there to be very little response differential in the initial links. For instance, Rider (1983) experimentally demonstrated that FR response rates were higher than mixed ratio (MR) response rates in a concurrent FR MR schedule, but he found a preference for the MR schedule when these schedules were arranged as the terminal links of a concurrent chain. It is evident, therefore, that the concurrent-chain schedule may provide us with a measure of behavior allocation different from that provided by concurrent schedules (except, in the limit, when the terminal links are both zero seconds in duration, in which case the schedule is a concurrent schedule). In a sense, the concurrent-chain measure, being taken in the absence of the preference-controlling contingencies, should be simpler than the concurrent-schedule measure. But, in practice, the measure has been found to be more complex, and it continues to defy a quantification of the sort provided by the generalized matching law for concurrent- and multiple-schedule performances.

In the above example of concurrent FI DRL performance, we would also be likely to find that the obtained DRL reinforcer rate was less than the obtained FI reinforcer rate, although the maximum reinforcer rates on both schedules are identical. The same difference in reinforcer rates is likely to occur when these schedules are arranged as the terminal links of concurrent chains. A question often raised is whether, in modeling behavior, we should use arranged-schedule values (and thus be able to predict independently of the behavior which might occur), or whether an animal's behavior should be seen as a function of the environment to which the animal is exposed, rather than to the environment that is arranged. Both types of models have been proposed. The model suggested by Squires and Fantino (1971; Section 10.6) is an example of the former, whereas the generalized-matching approach is an example of the latter. Because the subject's own behavior can, via relative feedback functions, change (and usually amplify) some preference-controlling independent variables (such as the relative frequencies of terminal-link entries), we favor the latter approach.

There are a number of less commonly reported measures of concurrent-chain performance. Time allocation in the concurrent initial links has been reported on occasion, but it is often a less than satisfactory measure. The reason is that response rates in the concurrent initial links are generally lower than in concurrent schedules, especially if the terminal links provide low reinforcer rates or long delays to reinforcers, and hence long pauses between responses can occur. If time allocation is measured in the usual concurrent-schedule manner (Section 1.1a), it may be distorted by such pauses. Davison (1983) tried to overcome such problems by ceasing to collect time-allocation data when 5 s had elapsed since a response, but such a procedure is arbitrary and may have rather unpredictable effects on time-allocation measures. Response rates in the terminal links are often reported, though less often analyzed. Finally, the obtained number of times that each terminal link was entered has been reported only occasionally even though frequency of terminal-link entry has been shown to be a potent controller of behavior in the initial links.

10.3. HISTORY AND DEVELOPMENT OF
CONCURRENT-CHAIN RESEARCH

The concurrent-chain schedule as a research tool was introduced by Autor (1960; reprinted 1969). Autor arranged equal independent concurrent VI 60-s VI 60-s initial links. In one series of conditions, one terminal link was VI 15 s, whereas the other comprised VI schedules that, across conditions, had mean intervals of between 3.75 and 60 s. In a second series, he arranged variable-duration DRO terminal links, such that terminal-link reinforcers were delivered if no response had been emitted for a variable time after terminal-link entry. The terminal links were in effect for, generally, twice the mean terminal-link schedule value. Autor reported that the relative numbers of initial-link responses were similar whether the terminal links were VI or variable-DRO schedules, and that the relative frequency of initial-link responses was close to the relative frequency of arranged terminal-link reinforcer rates. In Experiment 2, Autor arranged a VR 40 schedule in one terminal link and varied the other from VR 16 to VR 100. The terminal links ended after two reinforcers had been obtained. Data analyses showed that, for both VI and VR terminal links, relative initial-link responses were close to both relative terminal-link reinforcer rates and reinforcer probabilities per response. Autor concluded that there was no real difference between frequency and probability of reinforcers in the presence of the terminal-link stimuli in determining the strength of these stimuli as conditioned reinforcers.

Herrnstein (1964a) reported a replication of parts of Autor's (1960, 1969) work. Herrnstein arranged two reinforcers for each terminal-link entry, obtainable in succession on the same schedule. The initial links were independent concurrent VI 60-s VI 60-s schedules, and though Herrnstein did not report the number of entries into each terminal link, he did state that virtually equal

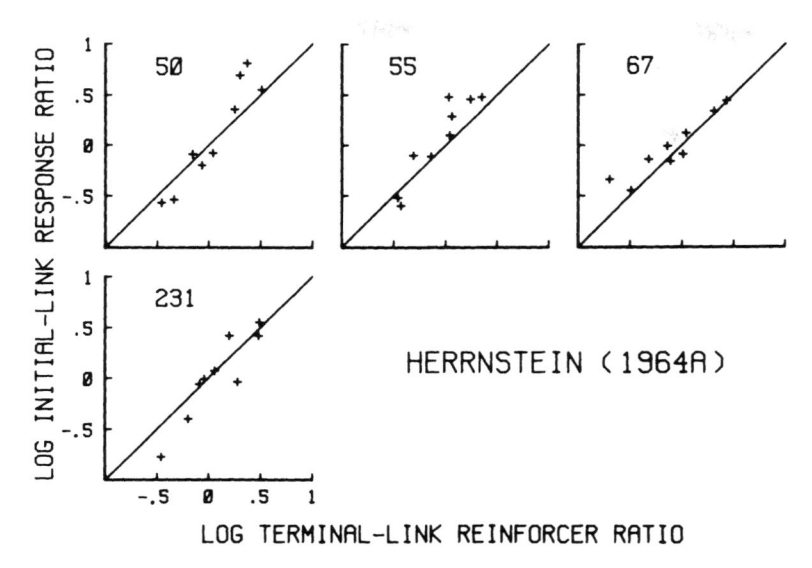

FIG. 10.2.   Log initial-link response ratios as a function of log terminal-link reinforcer-rate ratios when each terminal link comprised two successive reinforcers on VI or VR schedules (Herrnstein, 1964a).

numbers of reinforcers were obtained in the two terminal links. On one key, the terminal-link schedule was always a VR schedule (range VR 16 to VR 80), whereas the other terminal link was either a VI schedule (VI 15 s to VI 45 s) or a VR schedule (VR 16 to VR 40). Using the data from both terminal-link schedule combinations (VR versus VR, and VI versus VR), Herrnstein plotted the relative rate of initial-link responding against two derived variables, relative terminal-link reinforcer rate (replotted in Fig. 10.2 on log-ratio coordinates), and relative probability of a reinforcer given a response in the terminal links. Herrnstein concluded that relative initial-link response allocation was controlled by relative terminal-link reinforcer rates because this relation approximated the strict-matching function (then the accepted description of concurrent-schedule performance) better than did the relative probability relation—and the latter also showed considerably more variance. Comparing the data with concurrent-schedule data, he concluded that ". . . variations in either the frequency of primary reinforcement or in the frequency with which a secondary reinforcer is paired with a primary, have essentially identical effects" (p. 35).

As we mention in Section 1.3, Autor's (1960) and Herrnstein's (1964a) results provided mutual support for the elegantly simple suggestion that relative response rates strictly matched or equaled relative reinforcer frequencies. But this simplicity was maintained for only a very short time. Herrnstein (1964b) reported a further concurrent-chain experiment, again using independent concurrent VI 60-s VI 60-s initial links with two successive reinforcers in both terminal links. In three conditions, he arranged VI 15-s schedules in one terminal

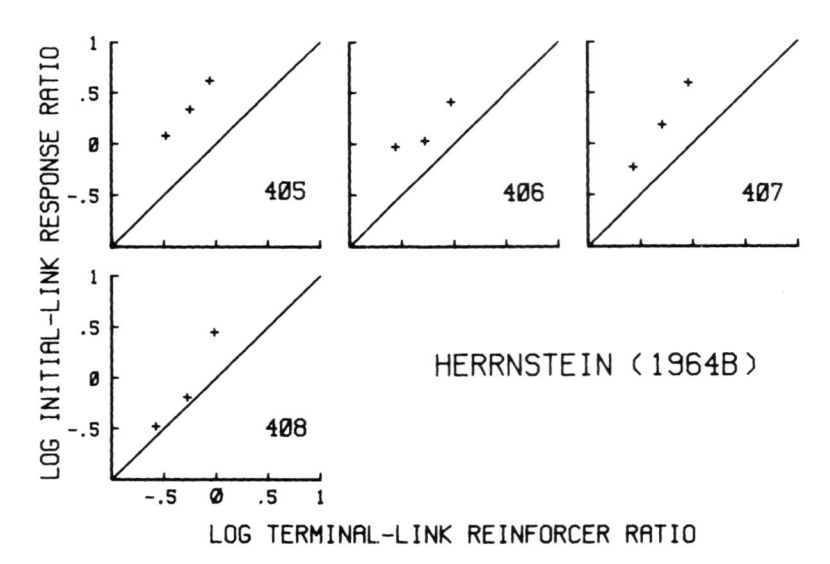

FIG. 10.3.   Log preference ratios for VI versus FI terminal-link schedules as a function of log terminal-link reinforcer ratios (Herrnstein, 1964b).

link, and FI schedules (4, 8, and 15 s) in the other terminal link. As shown in Fig. 10.3, the strict-matching relation did not prevail. Rather, strong preferences for the VI terminal link were found in the sense that the data fell well away from strict-matching predictions. (In a fourth condition, with FI 15-s and FI 4-s terminal links, the four subjects all preferred the FI 4-s terminal link more than predicted by strict matching.) On the basis of these results, Herrnstein suggested that the subjects were averaging the terminal-link intervals to reinforcers in some nonlinear fashion—that is, molar control of choice was not by the arithmetic mean of the intervals comprising the terminal-link VI schedule, but by some other averaging process. He briefly discussed the possibility of logarithmic timing, but reported that the implied geometric mean of the terminal-link VI intervals did not predict the preference data successfully.

At a data level, Herrnstein's (1964b) results showed a general preference for aperiodic, unpredictable, times to reinforcers over periodic, predictable, times. Similar results have been reported in concurrent-schedule performance (Section 7.5). From Herrnstein's (1964a, 1964b) results there arose an encapsulated research area concerned with trying to ascertain how subjects might be averaging intervals of time to reinforcers. We describe some of this research in Section 10.5 (generalized-mean analysis).

The following year, McDiarmid and Rilling (1965) used a concurrent FR 1 FR 1 initial-link procedure to demonstrate that lower reinforcer-rate schedules incorporating short delays to reinforcers were sometimes preferred to higher reinforcer-rate schedules that did not have short delays. Similarly, Davison (1968), using independent concurrent VI 60-s VI 60-s initial links with a 0.5-s

COD, arranged two successive reinforcers spaced 30-s apart in one terminal link, and varied the temporal distribution of two reinforcers in the other 60-s long terminal link. Preference appeared to be largely under the control of the time to the first reinforcer from terminal-link entry. Taken together, McDiarmid and Rilling's, and Davison's, results support Herrnstein's (1964b) conclusion that the control of preference in concurrent chains does not arise from the reinforcer rate calculated from the arithmetic mean of the terminal-link interreinforcement intervals. Any molar averaging of the terminal-link interreinforcement intervals must take delays to individual reinforcers, and the sequence of multiple reinforcers, into account in order to describe concurrent-chain preference. The strong implication is that control of preference results from the delays to each successive terminal-link reinforcer *from the point of terminal-link entry*, which in turn implies a somewhat more local analysis of the control of preference. But the majority of research reports in the following 10 years avoided the problem of the temporal sequence of reinforcers following each terminal-link entry by arranging only a single reinforcer in each terminal link. Such research thus needed to average, in one way or another, only the first delay. Even this enforced reduction in generality did not result in a full understanding of the more limited procedure. It might be argued that, had the original findings been followed up more closely, a number of subsequent pitfalls might have been avoided.

10.4. VARIANTS OF CONCURRENT-CHAIN PROCEDURES

It is useful, at this point, briefly to overview procedural variations of concurrent-chain schedules before looking more closely at subsequent research. Many procedural variations have been used, most often as inter-experiment differences associated with other independent-variable differences. Thus, because there have been few within-experiment controls, there is often little indication of the effects of such procedural differences on quantitative measures of preference. Possibly as a result of this, models of concurrent-chain performance often account well for the data from a single experiment, and poorly for the data from apparently closely related experiments. There is therefore a strong need for rather mundane experimental work on the effects of concurrent-chain procedural variations.

The first variation in procedure is the use of dependent, rather than independent, concurrent VI VI schedules in the initial links. Initial research typically used independent scheduling, but since Stubbs and Pliskoff (1969) introduced the dependent-scheduling procedure it has occasionally been used to equalize, or more generally control, the relative numbers of entries into each terminal link. As we have noted, response rates in the initial links of concurrent-chain schedules are often quite low, and with independent scheduling this can result in the ratio of terminal-link entries being quite different from the ratio arranged. Because the terminal-link entry frequency affects preference

(Section 10.6), it is a useful and simplifying procedure directly to control the entry ratios using dependent initial links (see particularly Snyderman, 1983). The result of using dependent initial-link scheduling is to make preference less extreme because the feedback function between the entry ratio and the preference ratio is flattened by such a procedure. But dependent scheduling may amplify a different problem. Again, because initial-link response rates are low, that procedure can decrease the overall frequency of terminal-link entries, and indeed produce a relation between degree of preference and initial-link duration. As we see in Section 10.6, lengthening the initial links itself decreases preference between different terminal links. In the only systematic comparison between dependent and independent initial-link scheduling, Davison (1983) found no difference in the *relation* between log initial-link response (or time) ratios and log terminal-link entry ratios in the two procedures, though as expected, entry ratios and preferences were more extreme for independent scheduling.

But Davison (1983) used only response-independent delays to reinforcers in the terminal links, and a 3-s changeover delay in the initial links. While changeover delays are common in concurrent-schedule research, they are uncommon in concurrent-chain research. The feeling has been, perhaps, that because reinforcers do not immediately follow initial-link responses in concurrent-chain schedules, a changeover-delay to eliminate concurrent superstitions (Section 1.2) is not necessary. Davison used a changeover delay because his experiment was designed directly to compare concurrent-schedule and concurrent-chain schedule data. Thus, while concurrent schedules are, in theory, concurrent-chain schedules with 0-s terminal links, the dimension of comparison has been upset by the qualitative difference of the COD presence versus absence. The general effects of the presence versus absence of, and of the duration of, changeover delays are unknown.

As we have seen, experiments differ as to the number of terminal-link reinforcers delivered per entry, and this independent variable has become the focus of a series of experiments. Care must be taken, though, in assuming that the data obtained from multiple terminal-link reinforcer procedures (e.g., Herrnstein, 1964a, 1964b) are similar to those with single reinforcer deliveries. Experiments can also differ according to whether the terminal-link schedules are synchronous with the terminal-link durations. In the general procedure that we define in Fig. 10.1, the terminal links ended in reinforcers. Thus, when that terminal link starts on the next entry, another whole interval or ratio will be presented. The alternative procedure is to arrange terminal links that end after fixed (not necessarily equal) durations independently of the terminal-link schedule. In such a procedure, upon terminal-link entry, the timing of the current interval or counting of the current ratio of the terminal-link schedules is simply continued. As a result, the schedules are asynchronous with the terminal-link durations, and reinforcers may have a constant probability of occurrence within the terminal links. Two recent experiments (Alsop & Davison, 1986; Davison &

Smith, 1986) have suggested that asynchronous terminal-link schedules might provide data quite different from the more usual synchronous procedure. A related concern has been the durations of the terminal links themselves (Poniewaz, 1984; Snyderman, 1983). In the standard procedure in which the terminal links end after a fixed number of reinforcers (usually one), the terminal-link durations are directly related to the terminal-link schedules. Thus, after a higher reinforcer-rate terminal link, the initial links are reinstated more quickly, which could perhaps change the relative value of the terminal links. To overcome such a problem, some researchers (e.g., Gentry & Marr, 1980) have arranged blackouts after terminal-link reinforcers to equalize the times before the initial links recommence.

Mazur (1984) recently introduced a new procedure for investigating preferences between terminal-link schedules. He used concurrent FR 1 FR 1 initial-link schedules (each initial-link response produces the terminal link). One terminal link provided a constant-value schedule, whereas the other provided a schedule with a value that changed as a function of preference. Such a procedure is known as a *titration* procedure (see also Lea, 1976). Mazur arranged that each choice of the constant schedule changed the titrating schedule toward a higher reinforcer rate, and each choice of the titrating schedule changed it toward a lower reinforcer rate. In this way, the subject's behavior titrates towards equal preference, or *indifference*, between the terminal links. This procedure has already provided some exciting data, but the question of whether Mazur's results will help in the analysis of concurrent-chain performances with longer initial links is still open (Davison & Smith, 1986).

10.5. TERMINAL-LINK EFFECTS AND GENERALIZED-MEAN ANALYSES

The initial interest in concurrent-chain research stemmed from Herrnstein's (1964b) finding that pigeons preferred a VI-schedule terminal link over an FI-schedule terminal link when the mean times to reinforcement were the same. This research, then, focussed on terminal-link effects and largely ignored the effects of initial-link schedules that were soon reported and that would need to modify predictions from generalized-mean analyses.

Killeen (1968a) directly confronted the VI versus FI terminal-link problem and collected a set of data using independent concurrent VI 56-s VI 56-s initial-link schedules. One terminal link was an FI schedule (range 5 to 25 s), whereas the other was geometric VI 23 s, arithmetic VI 31 s, or geometric VI 54 s. The difference between arithmetic and geometric schedules is that arithmetic intervals increase progressively by a fixed time difference, whereas geometric intervals increase by an increasing time difference (but both were, of course, arranged in an irregular order). From his stable-state data, Killeen was able to estimate *indifference* points, points at which the subjects judged the FI schedules as equal in value to the VI schedules. His results replicated Herrnstein's (1964b) results in that the subjects always preferred the VI terminal link over the FI terminal link more than predicted by strict matching to the mean terminal-link reinforcer ratios.

In order to discover how preference was controlled by terminal-link events, Killeen (1968a) analyzed his data on indifference points according to the generalized mean. The commonly-used *arithmetic* mean is only one of a possible infinity of measures of central tendency that can be used to describe a distribution. Some are named, such as the root-mean square, the harmonic mean, and the geometric mean. All of these, and many others (but not, we presume, the median and mode), can be described by a formula for the generalized mean (Hardy, Littlewood, and Polya, 1959):

$$M_r = \left[\frac{1}{N} \sum_{i=1}^{N} (y_i^r) \right]^{1/r}, \qquad (10.1)$$

where M_r is the value of the mean, N is the number of intervals in the set, and y_i is the value of the ith interval. r can take any whole-number or fractional value. When $r = 1$, M_r is the arithmetic mean; when $r = 2$, it is the root-mean square; and when $r = -1$, it is the harmonic mean.
Killeen (1968a) defined the "generalized reinforcer rate" as:

$$R_g = \frac{1}{N} \sum_{i=1}^{N} y_i^r, \qquad (10.2)$$

in which the variables are the same as in Equation 10.1, and R_g is the generalized reinforcer rate. Logarithmic preference ratios could thus be predicted from the log ratio of two such transformed reinforcer rates, with an appropriate value of r. Killeen's analysis showed that the indifference points were very well predicted when $r = -1$ in Equation 10.2, which gives harmonic reinforcer rates. (McDiarmid & Rilling, 1965, made a similar suggestion.) Both Killeen's and Herrnstein's (1964b) FI versus VI data are shown as a function of harmonic reinforcer-rate predictions in Fig. 10.4. This result means that the subjects appeared to be averaging not the times to reinforcers in the VI schedules (arithmetic averaging), but how soon the reinforcers were delivered—the immediacies of reinforcers (see Section 6.5). (Note that the harmonic averaging of a set of intervals is the same as the arithmetic average of the reciprocals of the intervals.) Such averaging has a strong effect on a set of intervals. For example, the arithmetic average of a VI schedule comprising 10 s, 20 s, and 30 s is 20 s, but the harmonic average is 16.4 s. Thus Killeen's result predicts that an FI 16.4 s terminal-link schedule should be judged equal to this VI schedule. To support his result, Killeen arranged an arithmetic VI 40-s schedule in one terminal link,

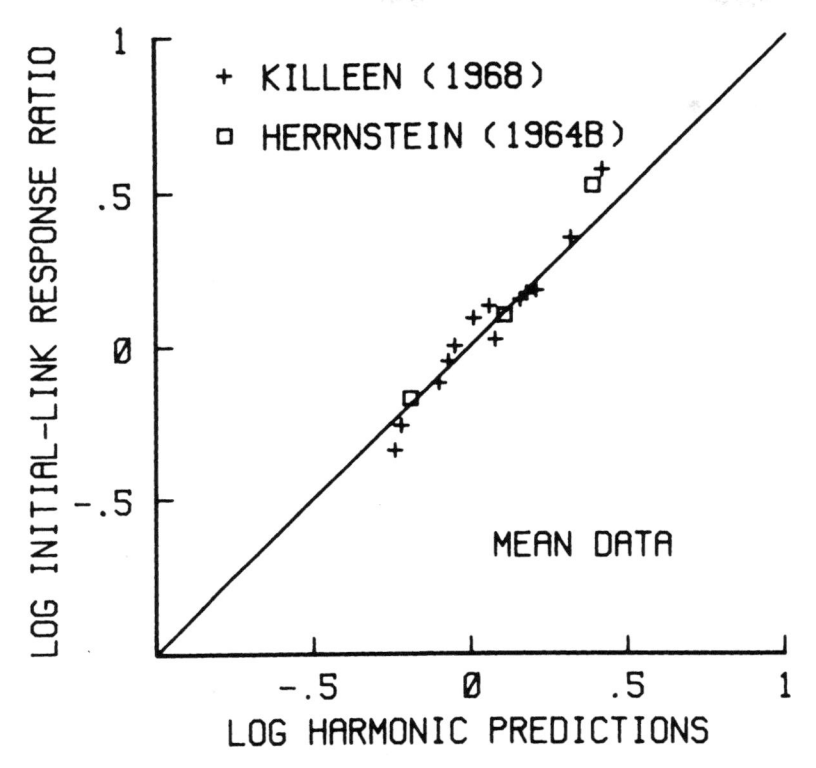

FIG. 10.4. Log initial-link response ratios as a function of the predictions of Killeen's (1968a) harmonic averaging model (Equation 10.2) for VI versus FI terminal links. The straight line shows the locus of perfect prediction.

and a geometric VI 80-s schedule in the other. Arithmetic averaging predicts a 2 to 1 preference for the former schedule, but since the harmonic means of the two schedules were, respectively, 24.4 s and 11.5 s, harmonic averaging predicts a 2 to 1 preference for the latter terminal link. The mean preference ratio was 2.22 toward the latter schedule, providing very strong support for harmonic averaging.

The effect of harmonic averaging is to weight more heavily, as compared with arithmetic averaging, smaller intervals to terminal-link reinforcers. Indeed, this weighting effect of shorter intervals becomes progressively greater as r becomes more negative. r then is a measure of the relative weighting of short, as compared to long, intervals to reinforcers.

Killeen's (1968a) result was clear cut, and consistent with Chung and Herrnstein's (1967) analysis of delay of reinforcement effects as relative immediacy of reinforcement. But these results were inconsistent with research reported by Fantino (1967), who arranged an FR schedule in one terminal link and a two-valued mixed-ratio schedule in the other. Using concurrent VI 180-s

VI 180-s, and concurrent VI 90-s VI 90-s, initial-link schedules, Fantino varied the schedule values in both terminal links. He found that initial-link preferences could be predicted from the geometric reinforcer rates of the mixed-schedule terminal-link times to reinforcers, rather than from the harmonic reinforcer rates. Research continued to chart the generality of harmonic averaging, but the results continued to be disappointing. Davison (1969) investigated preference between fixed-interval and mixed-interval 15-s 45-s terminal links with concurrent VI 60-s VI 60-s initial links. Varying the fixed interval over the range 10 to 30 s, he found that arithmetic, geometric, and harmonic averaging all predicted preference values closer to indifference than his data, but that a value of $r = -3$ (very strong weighting of the shorter mixed-interval duration) described preference well. However, Davison's experiment used a changeover delay of 0.5 s in the initial links—unlike Killeen (1968a). Thus, the difference in results might have been due to Davison's use of a changeover delay. But, equally possibly, the number of intervals comprising the mixed-interval (2) and the variable-interval (10 or 12) schedules could have affected the type of reinforcer-rate averaging.

Davison (1972) repeated part of Davison's (1969) experiment as closely as possible using no initial-link changeover delay. He found that $r = -2$ described these data, and hence that Davison's (1969) use of a changeover delay had made preferences more sensitive to terminal-link differences. He also investigated preference between FI terminal links and 3- and 7-valued mixed-interval terminal links, expecting, on the basis of Killeen's (1968a) results, that r would fall with increased number of intervals making up the variable schedule. However, $r = -2$ characterized the obtained preferences independently of the number of intervals. These results were quantitatively replicated by Hursh and Fantino (1973).

The situation was complicated at this time by the results of two experiments that investigated preference between FI terminal links. Killeen (1970), using independent VI 60-s VI 60-s initial links, arranged an FI 20-s schedule in one terminal link and varied the other from FI 5 s to FI 60 s over conditions. The subjects preferred the shorter FI more than predicted by strict matching (Herrnstein, 1964b), and the quantitative preference could be described by raising both terminal-link interreinforcement intervals to the power -2.5. Killeen saw this result as consistent with that of Davison (1969), given that Killeen did not use a changeover delay. Duncan and Fantino (1970) used a concurrent-chain schedule with concurrent VI 60-s VI 60-s initial links to measure preference between two FR terminal links and between two FI terminal links. The FR requirements ranged from 10 to 90 responses, and the FI intervals from 4 to 60 s. Duncan and Fantino found no constant value of r that was satisfactory for their data. Rather, they showed that the required negative value of r appeared to be related to the duration of the smaller interval to reinforcement in the terminal links (Fig. 10.5). The data obtained by Davison (1969), Fantino (1967), Herrnstein (1964b), and Killeen (1968a) appeared to be consistent with

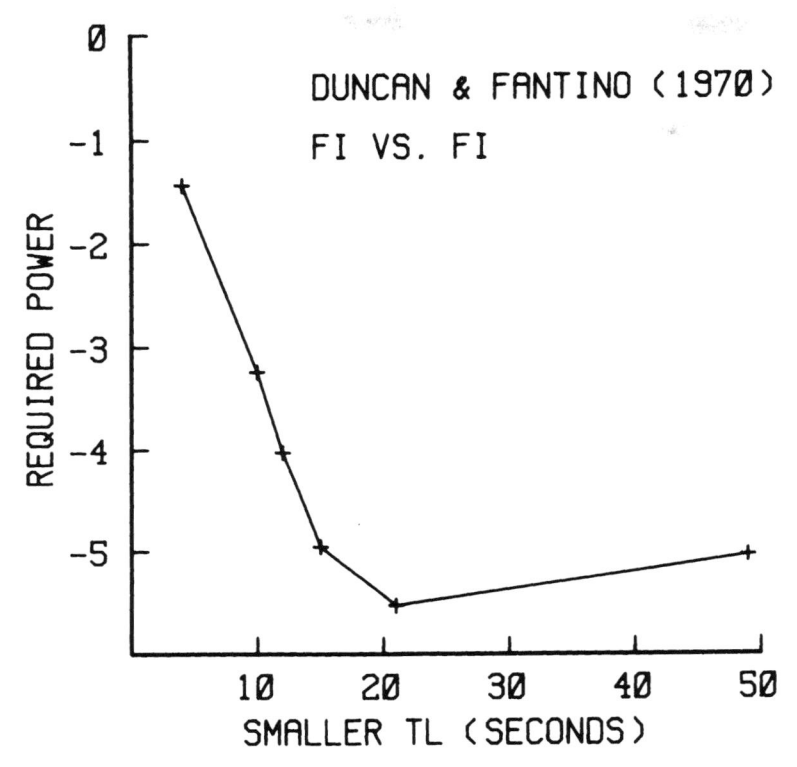

FIG. 10.5.   The best-fitting value of r in Equation 2 in FI versus FI choice as a function of the smaller terminal-link FI value (Duncan & Fantino, 1970). Note that the larger FI-schedule value was *not* monotonically related to the smaller FI-schedule value.

the relation obtained by Duncan and Fantino. But Davison's (1972) data, for which an r value of -2 was obtained, did not fit neatly on Duncan and Fantino's function, an r value of closer to -5 being predicted.

Duncan and Fantino's (1970) results were supported by MacEwen (1972), who used dependent concurrent VI 60-s VI 60-s initial links with two FI or two VI terminal links. The terminal-link schedules were always arranged in a 2 to 1 ratio of values, while the values were varied. MacEwen's results are shown in Fig. 10.6. As the terminal links were lengthened, preference increased in a negatively-accelerated fashion, with only a small change between smaller terminal links of 20 and 40 s (compare Fig. 10.5).

The value of r had, following Duncan and Fantino's (1970) research, become a free parameter rather than a description of how subjects average intervals to reinforcers. Had it been possible unequivocally to relate the value of r to the value of some independent variable (such as the smaller terminal-link interval), a continuation of generalized-mean research might have been profitable. However, the variable value of r (highlighted by subsequent, more extensive, results

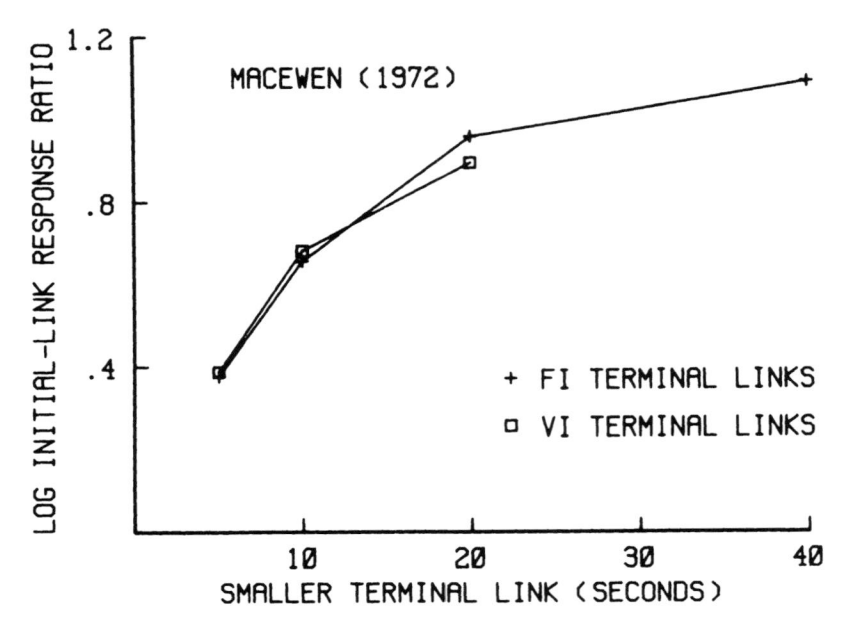

FIG. 10.6.   Log preference between two FI or between two VI terminal links as a function of the
value of the smaller interval or mean interval (MacEwen, 1972). The longer terminal link always had
twice the (mean) interval of the smaller terminal link.

on preference between FI terminal links), and the effects on preference of the
length of equal initial-link schedules, combined to force researchers to seek
elsewhere for a consistent account of concurrent-chain performance.

10.6. INITIAL-LINK EFFECTS

Fantino (1969) rightly noted that the amount of time that subjects spend choosing
in the initial links might affect preference between terminal-link schedules, and
that there had been a widespread use of concurrent VI 60-s VI 60-s initial-link
schedules in concurrent-chain research. Thus, one aspect of the generality of the
strict-matching to relative terminal-link reinforcer-rate model (Herrnstein,
1964a) for VI terminal-link schedules had not been tested. Fantino arranged four
conditions. In all, the terminal links were VI 30 s and VI 90 s. The initial links
were either independent concurrent VI 40 s VI 40 s, concurrent VI 120 s VI
120 s, or VI 600 s VI 600 s. The fourth condition used unequal initial-link
schedules for the first time, concurrent VI 90 s VI 30 s. Fantino's data are shown
in Fig. 10.7. There was a very clear reduction in preference with increasing
initial-link schedules. In the unequal-initial-link condition, the log preference

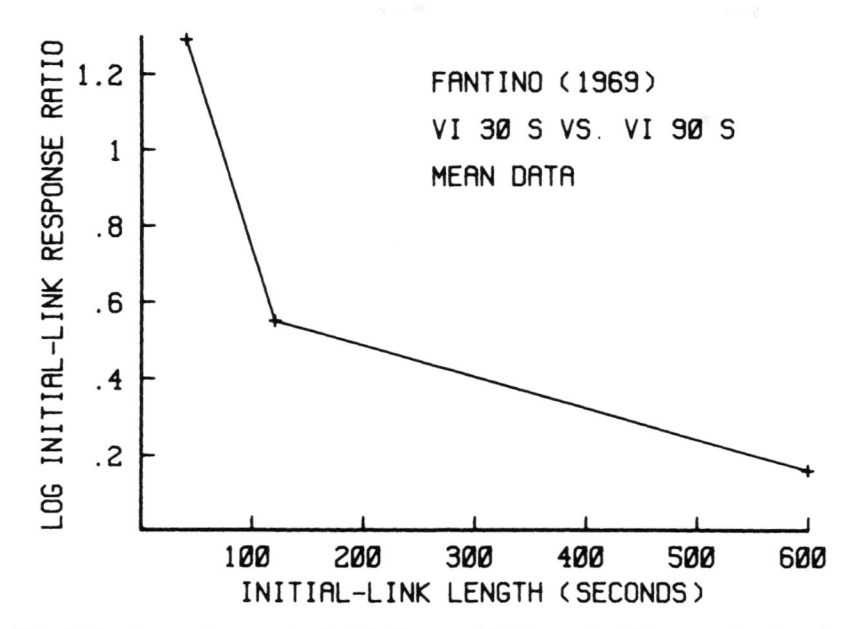

FIG. 10.7. Log preference ratio for VI 30-s over VI 90-s terminal links as a function of the initial-link VI-schedule value, which was always the same on both keys. The data were reported by Fantino (1969).

ratio was 1.19 toward the VI 30-s terminal link even though the subjects obtained this terminal link, in theory, on only 25 percent of terminal-link entries.

To account for these data, Fantino (1969) proposed a model that he called "the delay-reduction hypothesis." In this model, initial-link preference is controlled by the reduction in the expected time to reinforcement signaled by terminal-link entry. In ratio form it can be written:

$$\frac{B_{11}}{B_{12}} = \frac{T - t_{t1}}{T - t_{t2}},$$ (10.3)

$$= 0 \text{ if } t_{t1} > T$$

$$= \infty \text{ if } t_{t2} > T,$$

where B_{11} and B_{12} are the numbers of initial-link responses on the two keys, and t_{t1} and t_{t2} are the arithmetic mean terminal-link times to reinforcement on the two keys. T measures the average expected time to reinforcement calculated from the onset of the initial links. Thus, for instance, with concurrent VI 120-s VI 40-s initial links leading, respectively, to VI 30-s and VI 90-s terminal links, $T = 1/(1/40 + 1/120) + 0.75(90) + 0.25(30) = 105$ s. (The values 0.75 and 0.25 are the arranged probabilities of entering each terminal link.) The predicted ratio value of preference is thus $(105-30)/(105-90) = 5$, or a logarithmic value of 0.70.

Notice that Equation 10.3 predicts exclusive preference when the expected time to reinforcement *increases* on terminal-link entry—that is, when either t_{t1} or t_{t2} is greater than T. Because concurrent chains that use dependent initial links cannot produce exclusive preference without behavior ceasing altogether, Fantino has suggested that the delay-reduction hypothesis (Equation 10.3, and subsequent modifications) was not relevant to such procedures.

Squires and Fantino (1971) provided a much more extensive test of Equation 10.3. Using eight pigeons, they arranged both equal and unequal independent initial-link VI schedules (range 30 to 600 s), with equal schedules (either both VI 15 s or both VI 60 s) in the terminal links. They also arranged a number of conditions in which, with unequal initial-link schedules, they equalized the numbers of terminal-link reinforcers obtained by arranging more than one scheduled reinforcer before the terminal link ended. Thus, when the initial links were concurrent VI 60 s VI 600 s, both leading to VI 15-s schedules, 10 reinforcers on VI 15 s were arranged on each terminal-link entry from the VI 600-s schedule, but only one per terminal link entered from the VI 60-s schedule.

Equation 10.3 makes the unlikely prediction that subjects will be indifferent between equal terminal links even if the initial links are unequal. Thus, a modification of Equation 10.3 designed to overcome this problem was proposed and tested by Squires and Fantino (1971). This variant takes into account the total arranged overall reinforcer rate on each key during the initial and terminal links combined. Again in ratio form, the model became:

$$\frac{B_{11}}{B_{12}} = \frac{R_1}{R_2} \cdot \frac{T - t_{t1}}{T - t_{t2}} ,\tag{10.4}$$

with the same limits as Equation 10.3. R_1 and R_2 are the overall reinforcer rates on the two keys. Figure 10.8 shows the obtained log-ratio data as a function of the predictions from Equation 10.4 for the data averaged over the subjects. Equation 10.4 does a reasonable job of describing Squires and Fantino's data, but, as shown in Fig. 10.8, it does overpredict preferences quite consistently.

Notice that the Squires and Fantino (1971) model (but not the Fantino [1969] model) reduces to strict matching when the terminal-link schedules are asymptotically short. The ability to predict concurrent-schedule performance correctly is obviously important in modeling a procedure that is a quantitative extension of concurrent scheduling, but because concurrent-schedule research moved toward an acceptance of undermatching rather than strict matching (Chapter 4), this aspect of the Squires-Fantino model became a drawback, rather than a benefit. One of the strongest points of the Squires-Fantino model is that it does not rely on *any* free parameters. This, though, is also a drawback in that a bias parameter is probably necessary—it would certainly be necessary in some situations, such as the use of unequal pressures between the keys. Recognizing the problem of undermatching, and also that of consistent overestimation of preference values

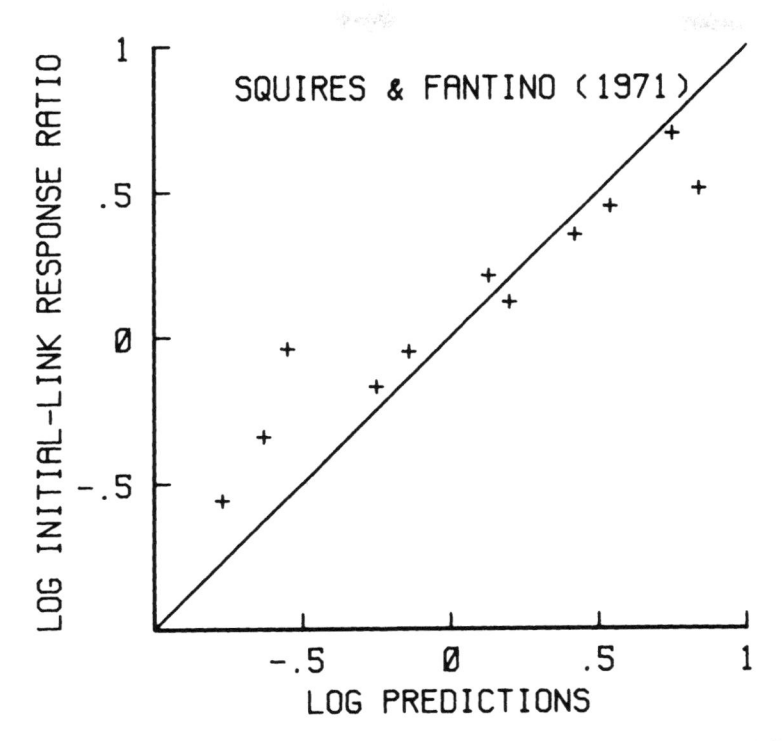

FIG. 10.8.   Log preference between various terminal-link VI schedules, with various different initial-link schedules arranged, as a function of the predictions of the model proposed by Squires and Fantino (1971). The data are from Squires and Fantino. The straight line shows the locus of perfect prediction.

(Fig. 10.8), Fantino and Davison (1983) introduced a modification of Equation 10.4 in which the overall reinforcer rates were raised to the power of 0.5. This has the effect of making predictions more consistent with the data, but it leaves concurrent-schedule performance with a fixed sensitivity of 0.5.

A second point to note about the Fantino (1969), Squires and Fantino (1971), and Fantino and Davison (1983) models is that the models use arranged, rather than obtained, independent variables. While such an approach is useful in that it allows predictions to be made before data collection, it can be argued that it is what subjects obtain, rather than what the experimenter arranges, that controls preference.

It may be helpful here to describe some of the obvious differences between concurrent and concurrent-chain performances. Figure 10.9 shows some data conditions selected from Fantino and Davison (1983). The left panels show preference between two VI 20-s terminal links when the initial-link schedules were varied, providing a series of differing frequencies of terminal-link entries. In the upper panel, one initial link was VI 15 s (which might be arranged on

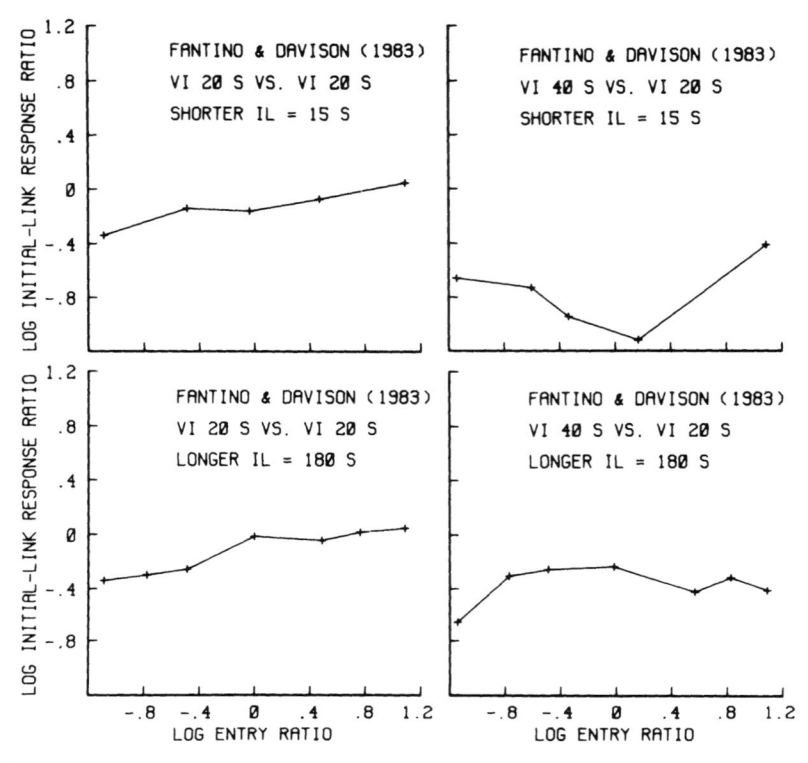

FIG. 10.9.   Log preference ratios between VI terminal-link schedules according to the log ratio of terminal-link entry frequencies. The data in the left panels were obtained when both terminal links were VI 20 s, and those in the right panels when the terminal links were VI 20 s and VI 40 s. In the upper panels, one initial link was VI 15 s and the other was equal or longer. In the lower panels, one initial link was VI 180 s and the other was equal or shorter.

either key), whereas the other was the same value or longer. In the lower panel, one initial-link schedule was VI 180 s, whereas the other was equal or shorter. The results from these two manipulations were essentially identical, and this identity is consistent with concurrent-schedule research in which preference seems to be independent of overall reinforcer rate (Section 6.2). The right panels of Fig. 10.9 show a similar pair of initial-link manipulations, but with VI 40-s versus VI 20-s terminal links. Unlike concurrent-schedule results (e.g., preference between differing response forces), the functions are nonlinear, but the explanation is reasonably straightforward. In the upper figure, the more unequal were the initial-link schedules, the longer was the time spent in the initial links. As we know, and as the Squires-Fantino (1971) model predicts, preference becomes less extreme as the initial links become longer. In the lower panel, as the initial links are made more unequal, the shorter the time spent in the initial links, and hence the more extreme was the preference. Such results are quite contrary to notions that subjects attempt to maximize rates of reinforcers. To take a particular condition, not represented in Fig. 10.9, when the initial links were FR 1 versus VI 180 s, and the respective terminal links were VI 40 s and VI 20 s, log preference was -1.15 though the log entry ratio was $+1.08$. Thus, the subjects strongly preferred the shorter terminal link over the longer terminal link, even though the overall times to reinforcers were 200 s on the preferred choice, and 40 s on the nonpreferred choice!

It is worthwhile here to summarize the main empirical findings that have been made, independently of models of choice. These findings were termed the "lores" of concurrent-chain performance by Davison (1987). It seems quite clear that lengthening initial links (relative to terminal links) leads to decreased control by terminal-link differences and increased control by initial-link differences. Thus, it follows that lengthening terminal links (relative to initial links) leads to decreased control by initial-link differences and increased control by terminal-link differences. In summary, control of initial-link preference is directly related to the relative durations of the initial and terminal links. Notice that this "lore" embodies the concurrent-schedule case (tautologously, all control from the initial-link schedules) and the multiple-schedule case (no initial links, complete control by the "terminal-link" schedules). The "lore" is also embodied in the delay-reduction hypothesis, and in other models that have been proposed for concurrent-chain performance (e.g., Killeen, 1982; Davison & Temple, 1973). We seem to have a number of good models that correctly describe ordinal aspects of choice, but, as Davison (1987) suggested, none of these models does a particularly good quantitative job.

10.7. TRANSITIVITY AND FUNCTIONAL EQUIVALENCE

Transitivity is a property of a set of choices. For instance, assume that, in a binary choice, an animal prefers Event A over Event B, and also that it prefers Event B over Event C. If Events A and C are now presented to the animal in a choice, a preference for Event A over Event C is called *transitive*, whereas a preference for Event C over Event A is called *intransitive*. Different degrees of transitivity have been defined (Coombs, 1964; Navarick & Fantino, 1972, 1974, 1975): If the preference for A over C is simply greater than, or equal to, indifference, choice is characterized by *weak transitivity*; if the choice is greater than, or equal to, the smaller of the A/B and B/C choices, choice is *moderately transitive*; if it is greater than, or equal to, the larger of the A/B and B/C choices, choice is *strongly transitive*. Navarick and Fantino also define a further degree of transitivity called "functional equivalence," which is particularly apposite to this area of research. If an animal is indifferent between A and B, then functional equivalence would be shown by the subject showing, quantitatively, the *same* degree of preference for A over C and B over C.

The models that have been suggested for various types of choices (for instance, VI versus FI terminal links; Killeen, 1968a) are attempts to define how measures of independent variables should be taken so that functional equivalence in choice obtains. A VI 20-s schedule may be functionally equivalent to an FI 10-s schedule on Killeen's model. That is, it should be the case that a VI 20-s terminal link versus some other terminal link (for example, VR 45) gives an equal preference value to an FI 10-s terminal link versus VR 45. (Notice, by the way, that such procedures do not test any particular model; rather, they are model-free.) From a large number of tests of this sort, Navarick and Fantino (1972) concluded that functional equivalence did not often occur, and occurred less frequently when the terminal links were longer. This, Navarick and Fantino pointed out, was consistent with the finding that a single transform of terminal-link reinforcer rates failed to predict preferences between varying terminal links (Section 10.5), and with Duncan and Fantino's (1970) finding that the exponent to which the terminal-link reinforcer-rate ratio had to be raised to predict preference was an increasing function of the smaller interval to reinforcement.

Navarick and Fantino (1972, 1974, 1975) and Fantino and Navarick (1974) concluded appropriately that the control of concurrent-chain choice is not *unidimensional*—there is no single variable, such as reinforcer rate or reinforcer delay, that determines initial-link preference. Rather, as is evident from so much of the research that has been reported, the control is *multidimensional*—with such variables as reinforcer rates, required terminal-link rates, segmentations, smaller terminal-link intervals, and the successive arrangement of reinforcers on each terminal-link entry contributing, at least under some circumstances. Concurrent-chain schedules are not, as Rachlin and Herrnstein suggested in an early, but unpublished, paper, a "complicated method for extracting the simple laws of behavior"!

10.8. EFFECTS OF RESPONDING IN THE TERMINAL LINKS

Two early results (Neuringer, 1969; Shimp, 1969b) suggested that pigeons were indifferent between fixed intervals to reinforcers and fixed delays to reinforcers in the terminal links (see Section 6.5). Neuringer arranged concurrent VI 90-s VI 90-s initial links with a 1.5-s changeover delay. In Experiment 1, in one terminal link both keys blacked out, and a reinforcer was delivered, independently of responding, after a fixed time. In the other terminal link, an FI schedule was arranged. The FI schedule and blackout were always of equal duration and ranged from 2 to 60 s. The data generally fell close to indifference with no trend across absolute terminal-link duration, but deviated a small but consistent amount toward the FI terminal link. In Experiment 2, unequal delays and FI schedules were arranged. The pigeons used in Experiment 1 were exposed to FI 10 s versus FT (fixed time) 2 s, then FI 10 s versus FT 20 s. For a second group of subjects Neuringer arranged FI 2 s versus FT 10 s, then FI 20 s versus FT 10

s. Relative response rates changed by about 0.42 for both groups, and the results suggested a (relative) preference for the interval over the delay schedule of only 0.05 to 0.06. In a third experiment, Neuringer investigated the effects of leaving the houselight on during the delay period, and of a pure delay in blackout versus a delay in blackout to which was added a single-response requirement at the end of the period. The pigeons were indifferent between the terminal links in both these conditions, indicating that the very small effect of FI versus FT scheduling was due to the presence of the blackout.

Shimp (1969b), as part of an experiment on the concurrent reinforcement of IRTs, arranged a concurrent-chain schedule with independent VI 60-s VI 60-s initial links, and terminal-link delays of 2 versus 2 s, 2 versus 8 s, and 20 versus 8 s. Single responses were required at the end of the blackout periods to produce reinforcers, hence the schedules were chain FT FR 1 schedules. Shimp reported that relative initial-link response rates were similar to relative terminal-link reinforcer rates, as was reported by Chung and Herrnstein (1967) (but see Section 6.5). From this experiment, according to the *zeitgeist*, we were able to conclude that the effects of (differing) delays with no response contingencies (Chung & Herrnstein) produced similar effects to delays terminating in single-response contingencies. Thus, the feeling arising from Neuringer's (1969) and Shimp's (1969b) experiments was that terminal-link response contingencies played no real role in the control of initial-link preference in concurrent-chain schedules. With the benefit of hindsight, the problem with this conclusion is that the arranged initial-link schedules were quite long (90 s or 60 s), and preference measured in longer initial links is less sensitive to terminal-link contingencies than is preference measured in shorter initial links (Section 10.4). Thus, in an unpublished experiment, Davison, Denison and Alsop maintained an FI 30-s schedule in one terminal link, and an FT 30-s schedule (with no response required) in the other, and varied the initial links from concurrent VI 5 s VI 5 s to concurrent VI 90 s VI 90 s over a number of conditions. They also carried out condition reversals (in which the FT versus FI contingencies were reversed between the keys) to control for key bias. While some subjects showed large preferences for one or other terminal link, these were concerned largely with which key was being pecked, rather than which type of terminal-link was being produced. There was no discernible preference for either type of terminal link.

The indifference in preference between FI and FT terminal links of the same duration also applies to VI and VT terminal links, as was demonstrated by Killeen (1968b) using independent concurrent VI 60-s VI 60-s initial links. Killeen's result was replicated and extended by Moore and Fantino (1975). They used concurrent VI 60-s VI 60-s initial links. In one experimental condition, one terminal link was VT 65 s while the other was tandem VT 60 s FR 5 LH 5 s. In the second condition, the subject chose between VT 125 s and tandem VT 120 s FR 5 LH 5 s. The pigeons were indifferent between these terminal links. Similarly, Brinker and Treadway (1975) using concurrent VI 30-s VI 30-s initial links showed that only one of four Japanese quail showed a consistent preference for VI schedules over VT schedules. However, they also found large biases toward terminal-link key colors.

Other available data, however, suggest that the simple control of initial-link preference by time to reinforcers (be they fixed or variable) is not the whole story. Fantino (1968) reported that pigeons preferred a simple FI terminal link to one that required that a substantial number of responses were emitted in the same time period (which might be called an FI schedule with a DRH requirement). Moore and Fantino (1975) suggested that a preference was found in Fantino's experiment because a particular rate was required in one terminal link, and the schedules were fixed intervals. Moore and Fantino's first experiment, described previously, indicated that even requiring a particular rate within a variable-schedule terminal link (via the LH contingency) did not produce a preference. Moore and Fantino's second experiment clarified the difference between the results of their first experiment and that of Fantino (1968). They instituted high-rate (FR) contingencies at the beginning of FI terminal links, when pigeons would not normally respond (Schneider, 1969), and found a preference for FT schedules over such schedules. They concluded that freely occurring terminal-link response-rate differences, or rate differences forced during parts of schedules in which subjects would normally be working, do not affect preference. But forced rate differences during parts of schedules during which animals do not work (such as discriminable periods of extinction; Schneider, 1969) decrease preference for that terminal link. However, Nevin (1979) reported a consistent preference for tandem VI DRL over tandem VI DRH terminal links, calling Moore and Fantino's conclusions into question.

10.9. CHOICE BETWEEN CHAINED AND TANDEM SCHEDULES

Schneider (1972) raised the question of whether choice in the initial links of concurrent-chain schedules was controlled by the conditioned reinforcing effect of the production of the stimulus signaling terminal-link entry, or whether it was controlled directly by the delays of reinforcers from terminal-link entry. He investigated this question by arranging a chained schedule in one terminal link, in which terminal-link entry was followed by the production of a stimulus signaling the first link of a two-component chain—hence, a stimulus not directly associated with food delivery. The other terminal link was a tandem schedule, in which terminal-link entry produced the stimulus present at food delivery. He used concurrent VI 60-s VI 60-s initial links. In Experiment 1, Schneider found a very small preference, which he demonstrated was a key preference, rather than a preference for one type of terminal link over the other. His results, averaged over four subjects, are shown in Table 10.1.

Conditions 5 and 6 demonstrated a strong preference only when the

TABLE 10.1
Experimental Conditions and Results from Schneider (1972)
Experiment 1

										Mean Log Preference Ratio
Terminal Links (Seconds)										*for Key 1*
1.	Tandem	VI	30	VI	30	Tandem	VI	30	VI	30	0.03
2.	Chain	VI	30	VI	30	Tandem	VI	30	VI	30	0.10
3a.	Chain	VI	45	VI	15	Tandem	VI	45	VI	15	0.10
3b.	Tandem	VI	45	VI	15	Chain	VI	45	VI	15	0.07
4.	Tandem	VI	15	VI	45	Chain	VI	15	VI	45	0.07
5.	Chain	VI	30	VI	30	Tandem	VI	15	VI	15	-0.21
6.	Tandem	VI	30	VI	30	Chain	VI	15	VI	15	-0.25

TABLE 10.2
Experimental Conditions and Results from Schneider (1972)
Experiment 2

										Mean Log Preference Ratio
Terminal Links (Seconds)										*for Key 1*
1.	Chain	VI	30	VI	30	Chain	VI	30	VI	30	0.02
2.	Chain	VI	15	VI	45	Chain	VI	30	VI	30	0.07
3.	Chain	VI	45	VI	15	Chain	VI	30	VI	30	0.03
4.	Chain	VI	45	VI	15	Chain	VI	15	VI	45	0.00
5.	Chain	VI	30	VI	30	Chain	VI	15	VI	15	-0.27
6.	Tandem	VI	30	VI	30	Chain	VI	15	VI	15	-0.29

terminal-link overall reinforcer rates were different, and also that when they were different, the stimuli presented in the terminal links were irrelevant. Most importantly, his data also showed lower response rates in the first link of the chain than in the second link, and hence that the subjects were discriminating the stimuli signaling the links of the chain.

In Experiment 2 (Table 10.2), Schneider (1972) arranged mainly chain schedules in both terminal links.

Again, there was no effect of the temporal location of stimuli, and hence of the temporal location of the contingencies between responding and stimulus changes, in the terminal links. Initial-link preference was controlled only by the reinforcer rates in the terminal links (Conditions 5 and 6). However, the meaning of these results is less clear because terminal-link response rates were *not* consistently lower in the first (nonreinforced) than in the second (reinforced) link of the terminal-link chains. Rather, terminal-link rates were greater in shorter than in longer links of the chains. Despite Schneider's claim that this latter finding indicated that appropriate discriminations were being made between the terminal-link chain stimuli, the indications are that the subjects might have been discriminating between schedule values, rather than between the links of the chains. This problem was, however, overcome in Experiment 3, in which Schneider investigated preference between chain FI FI (rather than chain VI VI) schedules in a series of conditions similar to those arranged in Experiment 2. He found very large response-rate differences between the first and second links of the terminal-link chains, and indifference in preference with equal overall times to reinforcers.

In Experiment 4, Schneider (1972) investigated chain VI FT schedules in both terminal links because a pilot study had indicated a strong deviation from equality between relative initial-link preference and relative terminal-link reinforcer rates (Herrnstein, 1964a) using such schedules. The inequality was replicated (sensitivity to the terminal-link reinforcer ratio was greatly in excess of 1.0), but control conditions with simple VI terminal links demonstrated that this result was not due to the chaining operation. With the benefit of hindsight, such results do not cause any surprise (and indeed can be handled by models such as that given by Squires & Fantino, 1971) and, as Schneider noted, whatever transformation of terminal-link reinforcer rates (Section 10.5) is appropriate for unsegmented terminal links may also be appropriate for segmented terminal links.

Duncan and Fantino (1972) reported an apparently similar experiment, but the results appeared to be directly opposite to Schneider's (1972) results. Also using concurrent VI 60-s VI 60-s initial links, they arranged a simple FI schedule in one terminal link and a chain FI FI schedule in the other. When the overall times to reinforcers were the same in both terminal links, there was very strong preference for the simple (unsegmented) terminal link. When preference was between 2- and 3-link chain schedules in the terminal links, preference was generally toward the two-link chain, but the preference was neither great nor consistent. But, as Duncan and Fantino note, their experiment and Schneider's (1972) are only comparable on the basis of number of terminal-link stimuli—one in the simple or tandem terminal link, and two, with one temporally distant from the reinforcer, in the chain terminal link. They are not comparable in terms of the *contingencies* in the terminal links. A tandem schedule has two successive response contingencies, as does the chain schedule. A simple FI or VI schedule has only one. This indicates, as Duncan and Fantino noted, that simple FI schedules should be preferred to tandem FI FI schedules providing the same reinforcer rate. Therefore, Schneider arranged the appropriate controls for interpreting the effects of stimuli (and conditioned reinforcement) per se, while Duncan and Fantino did not. An interesting possibility is that similar effects might occur in concurrent schedules, with response allocation some function of the ratio of required contingencies. What would response allocation be in

TABLE 10.3
Experimental Conditions, and Mean Results, Reported by Leung and Winton (1985).[a]

Terminal Links (Seconds)										COD?	Mean Log Preference
1.	VI	60				Chain	VI	30	VI	30	Y	0.13
2.	Tandem	VI	30	VI	30	Chain	VI	30	VI	30	Y	0.12
3.	Tandem	VI	30	VI	30	Chain	VI	30	VI	30	N	0.03
4.	Tandem	FI	7.5	FI	7.5	Chain	FI	7.5	FI	7.5	Y	0.35
5.	FI	15				Chain	FI	7.5	FI	7.5	N	0.29
6.	FI	15				Chain	FI	7.5	FI	7.5	Y	0.36
7.	FI	60				Chain	FI	30	FI	30	Y	1.51
8.	FI	60				Chain	FI	30	FI	30	N	1.25

concurrent VI 60 s Tandem VI 15 s VI 15 s VI 15 s VI 15 s? The answer to this question may help us understand the results (on reinforcer duration) obtained by Davison and Hogsden (1984; Section 6.3). Notice, by the way, that this explanation is similar to that given for the preference for terminal links that do not require the subjects to respond during periods of explicit nonreinforcement (Section 10.7).

A different set of results, and hence a different explanation, were given by Leung and Winton (1985). They arranged independent concurrent VI 60-s VI 60-s schedules in the initial links with chain, tandem, or simple-schedule terminal links, reversing the schedules between the terminal links to control for key bias. They also compared performance with, and without, a 1.5-s COD in the initial links. A summary of their conditions is shown in Table 10.3.

It is evident that Schneider's (1972) results were replicated when both (1) no COD was arranged in the initial links, *and* (2) when the terminal-link reinforcer rates were 1 per minute (Procedure 3). When the COD was in operation at 1 reinforcer per minute, there was a small preference for the unsegmented terminal links whether or not the unsegmented chain had an additional contingency (Procedures 1 and 2). Preference for the unsegmented terminal link was greater again *either* when the terminal-link reinforcer rates were 4 per minute *or* when the terminal-link schedules were FI schedules. Some important control conditions are missing, and because preference between unsegmented and segmented FI terminal links increased when reinforcer rates were lowered (Procedures 5 to 8), these data are difficult to interpret. However, the fact that some consistent preferences between tandem and chained schedules were obtained indicates that we still have a lot to learn in this area. The most convincing part of Leung and Winton's results is the effect of adding a COD which, in every comparison in Table 10.3, resulted in a more extreme preference.

10.10. COMBINATIONS OF INDEPENDENT VARIABLES

We have already dealt at some length with the combination of two independent variables—terminal-link reinforcer distributions and the relative frequency of terminal-link presentation—on initial-link preference. The concatenated generalized matching law with constant parameters (Section 10.6; see Fig. 10.9) failed to account for preference.

A second combination of independent variables has been quite extensively investigated under the heading of "*self-control.*" Self-control concerns choice between differing reinforcer amounts which also differ in delay (Ainslie, 1974, 1975; Rachlin & Green, 1972). If a subject chooses a larger, but more delayed, reinforcer over a smaller, but more immediate, reinforcer it is said to show self-control. There is some implication here that in self-control the subject should be gaining a greater total amount of reinforcement per time than if it shows the alternative, *impulsive*, choice, but this is seldom made explicit. Empirical work (Ainslie, 1974; Rachlin & Green, 1972) shows that preference for the larger, more delayed, reinforcer increases when the overall delays to the reinforcers are increased, and that in some conditions a preference reversal from impulsiveness to self-control can be seen as delays are increased. Such results are predicted by the concatenated strict matching law (Navarick & Fantino, 1976; Rachlin & Green, 1972; Section 4.2):

$$\frac{B_1}{B_2} = \frac{D_2}{D_1} \cdot \frac{M_1}{M_2} \, , \qquad (10.5)$$

where D is the delay and M is the magnitude of the reinforcers. If $M_1 = 1$ s and $M_2 = 4$ s, and if $D_1 = 1$ s and $D_2 = 10$ s, the predicted log preference is 0.4, toward the smaller, more immediate, reinforcer. If both delays are now increased by 10 s, the predicted preference is -0.34, toward the larger, less immediate, reinforcer. Preference reversal thus occurred.

There is nothing special, except in terms of nomenclature, about this effect. For instance, the combination of reinforcer rates of 1 per minute and 4 per minute and magnitudes of 4 s and 2 s, respectively, on the keys is predicted by Equation 10.5 to give a preference of -0.3, but if we *add* 5 reinforcers per minute to both choices, the prediction becomes 0.12. Preference reversal again occurs, but there is no name for this effect. Such effects occur simply because adding constant amounts to both the numerator and denominator of ratios makes the value of that ratio closer to 1.0.

While the above discussion has shown that the concatenated strict matching law can predict the direction of preference changes in self-control and similar procedures, we have already shown that the generalized matching law better describes independent-variable effects than does the strict matching law. Generalizing Equation 10.5 does not change the direction in which predicted preferences change with variations in times to reinforcers, but it will change the quantitative value of predicted preferences and hence the point of preference reversal. But we have also shown that the generalized matching law (with constant parameters) does not adequately describe either reinforcer-magnitude effects (Section 6.3) or reinforcer-delay effects (Sections 6.5 and 10.5). Green and Snyderman (1980) found that the generalized version of Equation 10.5 described their data better than did either the strict version or Fantino's (1969) model modified to deal with reinforcer magnitudes as well as rates (but note that generalized Equation 10.5 has two free parameters, whereas the strict version, and Fantino's model, have none). However, the obtained-predicted fits using the best power transformations were not entirely satisfactory, and Green and Snyderman mentioned the possibility that neither the powers required for delays nor magnitudes were constant. Snyderman (1983) provided a careful replication of the Green and Snyderman experiment, and found that the generalization of Equation 10.5 (with constant powers) was fundamentally inaccurate in describing his data. No other model of self-control (Fantino, 1969; Ito & Asaki, 1982; Killeen, 1982) was satisfactory either.

A further problem was specified by Mazur and Logue (1978). Their subjects chose between an immediate 2-s reinforcer and a 6-s reinforcer delayed 6 s. Control subjects under this procedure almost never chose the larger, delayed, reinforcer. Experimental subjects were first exposed to equal 6-s delays, and they chose the larger reinforcer. Then the delay to the smaller reinforcer was decreased to 0 s over 342 sessions. Preference for the larger reinforcer was maintained in most experimental subjects under this fading procedure, and this preference was maintained for two subjects when the contingencies were reversed between the keys. If such fading procedures can affect choice, then concurrent-chain models that do not take history into account may be doomed. However, Mazur and Logue used an independent concurrent FR 1 FR 1 initial-link procedure, and thus the relative frequency of outcomes (in all but the three forced 2-s reinforcer duration choices per session) would have equaled the relative frequency of preference.

Mazur and Logue's (1978) results were replicated in the first experiment reported by Logue, Rodriguez, Pena-Correal, and Mauro (1984), with the same problems concerning uncontrolled frequencies of terminal-link entries. However, in Experiment 2, Logue et al. used a concurrent-chain procedure with concurrent linear VI 30-s VI 30-s initial links. In a linear VI, when the timing of an interval is completed, the availability of that reinforcer is stored, and the timing of the next interval continues. Any number of reinforcers may be stored in this way for each choice. This procedure keeps the ratio of terminal-link entries constant as set by the initial-link schedules, as in the dependent-scheduling procedure (Section 1.1c). Unlike the dependent-scheduling procedure, concurrent linear VI schedules also tend to keep the overall frequency of terminal-link entry close to the set value. By varying both reinforcer delays and reinforcer durations, Logue et al. showed that mean sensitivity to reinforcer-delay ratios (in the generalized version of Equation 10.5) was less for fading-exposed subjects (0.7) than for nonfading-exposed subjects (1.5). For fading-exposed subjects, sensitivity to reinforcer delay was always less than sensitivity to reinforcer duration, but the reverse was true for three of the four nonfading-exposed subjects. Experience does affect at least sensitivity to delay ratios when terminal-link frequency ratios are controlled—a result that may make concurrent-chain schedule analyses even more intractable.

10.11. GENERALIZED MATCHING AND CONCURRENT-CHAIN PERFORMANCE

We have shown throughout this book that the generalized matching law can act as a good descriptor and organizer of many of the data on choice. But we have not seen this relation applied with much vigor to concurrent-chain performances. The reason is that the generalized matching law obviously cannot *explain* many of the effects that researchers have found so interesting—segmentation effects and conditioned reinforcement, the method of averaging terminal-link reinforcer rates, or the effects of the absolute durations of initial-link schedules. The concatenated generalized matching law nicely described preference for combined rates of reinforcers and key-force requirements, with constant parameters (Section 7.11a). But as Williams and Fantino (1978) showed, the sensitivity of initial-link preference to terminal-link delay ratios was a function of the smaller delay, as Duncan and Fantino (1970) had shown for terminal-link FI schedules. Where does the generalized matching law stand without parameter invariance? The argument could be made that it has withstood a modicum of unexplained parameter variation for some time (for instance, multiple versus concurrent schedules [Chapter 9], and concurrent arithmetic versus exponential schedules [Section 6.1]). Therefore, if it could be shown that generalized-matching parameter values were a function of the values of particular independent variables, it would represent a gain in support for that relation, rather than denial of the relation. Duncan and Fantino's results, for example, trace out the function relating sensitivity to terminal-link reinforcer ratios to the smaller terminal-link interval to reinforcement.

Wardlaw and Davison (1974) were the first researchers explicitly to use a generalized-matching analysis of concurrent-chain data. They arranged equal independent concurrent VI initial links (27, 38, 49, or 115 s), with no COD. One terminal link was always FI 5 s, whereas the other was varied over conditions from FI 5 s to FI 30 s. They found that preference between constant pairs of terminal links increased as the initial-link schedules were decreased, as Fantino (1969) had found for VI terminal links. In analyzing their data, Wardlaw and Davison first fitted the generalized matching law to performance in each chain separately, as Davison (1974; Section 9.10) had done for single-chain schedules. The general form of the relation was:

$$\frac{B_i}{B_t} = c\left(\frac{R_i}{R_t}\right)^a , \qquad (10.6)$$

where the subscripts i and t indicate the initial and terminal links. R_i is the rate of entry into the terminal link of the chain. c and a were not constants, but were linear functions of the overall initial-link reinforcer rates (by which is meant, here, the overall rate of production of the terminal links):

$$a = -1.31 R_i + 0.46, \quad c = -0.76 R_i - 0.83 . \qquad (10.7a, 10.7b)$$

Wardlaw and Davison also applied a generalized-matching analysis to performance in the terminal links alone (see Barron & Davison, 1972, for a multiple FI FI generalized-matching analysis). The terminal-link relation was independent of the initial-link schedules:

$$\frac{B_{t1}}{B_{t2}} = 1.14\left(\frac{R_{t1}}{R_{t2}}\right)^{0.41} . \qquad (10.8)$$

Since Equation 10.6 applied to both chains, and since $R_{i1} = R_{i2}$, Wardlaw and Davison took the ratio of the equations for the two chains, giving:

$$\frac{B_{i1}}{B_{i2}} = \frac{B_{t1}}{B_{t2}} \cdot \left(\frac{R_{t1}}{R_{t2}}\right)^{1.31R_i - .46} . \qquad (10.9)$$

Since the terminal-link response ratio is given by Equation 10.8, the equation to describe initial-link preferences in terms of initial- and terminal-link reinforcer rates is:

$$\frac{B_{i1}}{B_{i2}} = 1.14\left(\frac{R_{t1}}{R_{t2}}\right)^{1.31R_i - 0.05} . \qquad (10.10)$$

(Note that c in Equation 10.6 divides out of Equation 10.10.) Equation 10.10 accounted for 92 percent of the variance from 20 experimental conditions. Our interest in this work is twofold: First, the method of analysis in terms of chains and multiple-schedule terminal links may be of use in the future; second, it indicates how the generalized matching law can be extended to describe the effects of initial-link length on the sensitivity of initial-link choice to terminal-link schedules.

In a further report, Davison (1976) carried out an experiment similar to that of Wardlaw and Davison (1974) using FI terminal links, no initial-link changeover delay, but unequal, rather than equal, independent concurrent VI VI initial links. One initial link was always VI 27 s, while the other was varied from VI 27 s to VI 115 s. One terminal link was always FI 5 s, while the other was either 5 or 15 s. These data lend themselves more directly to a standard concatenated generalized-matching analysis. First, when both terminal links were FI 5 s, the sensitivity of the initial-link preference ratio to the ratio of terminal-link entries was 0.51 (range 0.36 to 1.09), with a consistent (key) bias that averaged 0.24. Between 90 and 98 percent of the individual-subject variance was accounted for. When the terminal links were FI 5 s versus FI 15 s, and the shorter initial link led to the longer terminal link, we would expect a bias toward the shorter terminal link. A mean bias of 1.15 (range 0.84 to 1.27) was obtained, but the sensitivity to the terminal-link entry ratio was 0.89 (range 0.79 to 1.19), consistently higher than that for FI 5 s versus FI 5 s terminal links. Finally, when the terminal links were FI 15 s versus FI 5 s, and the shorter initial-link schedule led to the shorter terminal link, bias was -0.50 (range -0.15 to -1.44) to the shorter terminal link, and sensitivity to terminal-link entries was 0.20 (range 0.14 to 0.73), lower than the FI 5 s FI 5 s choice for 4 of the 5 birds. Evidently, while the generalized matching law can be used to describe concurrent-chain performance, sensitivity to the terminal-link entry ratio is not simply a function of the length of the initial links. Rather, it is affected by whether the shorter initial link leads to the shorter or longer terminal link. (It is worthwhile noting that, while the Squires & Fantino [1971] model is not supposed to apply to FI terminal links, it does ordinally predict different preference ratios under such conditions.)

To formalize this type of development, Davison (1986) made explicit the way in which the generalized matching law might be applied to explain at least some concurrent-chain performances. First, in the initial links, preference should be controlled by the frequency ratio of obtaining the terminal links. The relation between the preference ratio and the terminal-link entry ratio might be a generalized-matching relation with a particular key bias (c_i). The sensitivity of this relation might be a direct function of the overall rate of obtaining terminal links, and possibly an inverse function of the overall rate of terminal-link reinforcers. Second, initial-link preference might have a generalized-matching relation to the terminal-link reinforcer ratio, with a particular key or color bias. This relation might have a sensitivity value that is a direct function of the duration of the terminal links and an inverse function of the length of the initial links:

$$\frac{B_{i1}}{B_{i2}} = c_i \left(\frac{R_{i1}}{R_{i2}}\right)^{f(R_{t1}/R_{t1})} \cdot c_t \left(\frac{R_{t1}}{R_{t2}}\right)^{f(R_{t1}/R_{t1})} \tag{10.11}$$

Notice how Equation 10.11 embodies the "lore" of concurrent-chain preference (Section 10.6), and how it is a direct application of the concatenated generalized matching law—but with variable, rather than constant, sensitivities. The terminal-link schedules are treated as if they were two reinforcer amounts. Davison (1986) showed that Equation 10.11 accounted for quantitative concurrent-chain data as well as did the Squires-Fantino (1971) and the Killeen (1982) models. But none of these models (Equation 10.11 included), according to criteria used by Davison, made a particularly good job of describing concurrent-chain performance. Also, in another approach to the same problems, Davison (1983) showed that when a changeover delay of 3 s operated in the concurrent VI VI initial links, the function relating log preference and log terminal-link entry ratios was independent of the length of the terminal-link delays (c.f., Duncan & Fantino, 1970) and possibly also of the duration of the terminal-link schedules (c.f., MacEwen, 1972). Such a constancy in the sensitivity to the terminal-link schedule values would simplify Equation 10.11 considerably. Thus, a second approach to the unravelling of concurrent-chain performance may be procedural—the use of a COD (see also Leung & Winton, 1985).

10.12. CONCLUSION

Initial research on concurrent-chain schedule performance provided a face-valid technique for the investigation of preference between independent reinforcing situations, and some quantitatively simple and understandable results. But, as is so common in research, successive experiments, although occasionally making some local advances, have generally complicated the picture, and have made quantification more difficult. In this chapter, we mention some of the current difficulties, but still others await resolution: Whether choice is preferred over a nonchoice situation (Catania, 1975, 1980, Catania & Sagvolden, 1980; Hayes, Kapust, Leonard, & Rosenfarb, 1981); whether preference between two concurrent chains is affected by the presence of, or the value of, a third concurrent chain (Davison & Temple, 1974; Fantino & Dunn, 1983); whether multiple-schedule terminal links are always preferred over mixed-schedule terminal links (Alsop & Davison, 1986; Fantino & Moore, 1980); how may effects of terminal-link reinforcers subsequent to the first after initial-link entry be described (Mazur, 1984; Mazur, Snyderman, & Coe, 1985; Moore, 1979; Poniewaz, 1984); and so on. The benefits of obtaining an adequate concurrent-chain performance description (which must also subsume concurrent-schedule performance) would be immense, and would allow the concurrent-chain procedure to be used as a properly calibrated measurement technique in other areas of research. Although such a description seems at least as distant as ever, the motivation to work toward this seems entirely undiminished.

11 MATCHING MODELS OF SIGNAL DETECTION

11.1. INTRODUCTION

The law of effect has been largely concerned with the effects of reinforcer contingencies on behavior under highly discriminable conditions. There has been little regard paid to the role of controlling stimuli in matching research (but see Logue, 1983; Miller, Saunders, & Bourland, 1980, Section 8.7; White, Pipe, & McLean, 1984; Section 9.6). Yet, failures to obtain the expected response-reinforcer relation have often been ascribed to failures of the stimulus-response relation (e.g., Baum, 1974a). In an attempt to measure stimulus effects in schedule-control experiments, one common research practice has been to apply, cookbook fashion, detection-theory statistics to data obtained from operant-conditioning experiments (Wright, 1982). Such approaches (e.g., Logue, 1983; Stubbs, 1980) are not of concern here. Rather, our interest lies solely with attempts to integrate *quantitatively* the matching law with the theory of signal detection (see Davison & McCarthy, 1980; Davison & Tustin, 1978; Nevin, 1981; Nevin, Jenkins, Whittaker, & Yarensky, 1977, 1982). It is the goal of behavioral detection theory to include the effects of discriminative stimuli in the law of effect and thus to provide a unitary model of stimulus and reinforcer control in a variety of discrete-trials detection paradigms and free-operant conditioning procedures. (Usually, in a trials procedure, a subject is allowed to emit only one response at some point in a series of environmental events—this series constituting the trial. In a free-operant procedure, many responses may be emitted in the presence of one or more environmental events.)

216

11.2. THE STANDARD YES-NO DETECTION EXPERIMENT

With minor variations, the signal-detection task is a discrete-trials procedure in which stimuli are presented to a subject trained to report which of two or more stimuli were presented. With human subjects, typically two stimulus classes (signal superimposed on noise, and noise alone), and two response classes ("Yes, there was a signal" and "No, there was no signal") are arranged. Thus, there are four stimulus-response events: Hits (correctly reporting the signal as present), correct rejections (correctly reporting the stimulus as absent), false alarms (reporting the signal as present when it was absent), and misses (reporting the signal as absent when it was present). Hits and correct rejections typically lead to reinforcers, and false alarms and misses lead to penalties. It is the explicit use of these reinforcement and punishment contingencies that provides direct contact with analyses of choice behavior (Nevin, 1969).

According to signal-detection theory (SDT), two independent parameters (d' and β) suffice to allow detailed predictions of behavior in any detection experiment. The parameter d' measures the discriminability of the stimuli. It is identified with the distance, in standard-deviation units, between the means of two hypothesized Gaussian density functions representing the subjective effects of signal-plus-noise and noise alone. (Other assumptions about the subjective distributions of signal and noise require different definitions of the discriminability parameter; Green & Swets, 1974; Treisman, 1977). The parameter β, termed response criterion or bias, quantifies the subject's preexperimental history, his or her expectations based on the instructions and the a priori probability of signal presentation, and the consequences of responding. In its normative version, SDT assumes that the subject's decision as to whether signal plus noise or noise alone was presented is based on a likelihood ratio, $l(x)$. The likelihood ratio is the ratio of the probability density of an observation if a signal is present to the probability density of that observation if a signal is absent. The subject is assumed further to partition the likelihood-ratio continuum so that one response occurs if $l(x) > \beta$, and the other if $l(x) < \beta$.

The animal analogue of the human task outlined above simply involves training pigeons, say, to peck the left key when one stimulus (S_1) was presented, and to peck the right key when another stimulus (S_2) was presented. With two stimuli and two responses, four possible outcomes are again defined. Figure 11.1 shows the typical stimulus-response matrix for this detection procedure. In this figure, for convenience, W, X, Y, and Z refer to the cells of the matrix. Thus, with B denoting responses and R denoting reinforcers, B_w is the number of correct left-key pecks following S_1 presentations (hits), B_x is the number of incorrect right-key pecks following S_1 presentations (misses), B_y is the number of incorrect left-key pecks following S_2 presentations (false alarms), and B_z is the number of correct right-key pecks following S_2 presentations (correct rejections). Correct responses (B_w and B_z) may be reinforced with food or brain stimulation,

STIMULI	RESPONSES: LEFT	RESPONSES: RIGHT
S_1	W HIT	X MISS
S_2	Y FA	Z CR

FIG. 11.1. The matrix of stimulus and response events in an animal analogue of the human Yes-No signal-detection task. S_1 and S_2 denote the two discriminative stimuli, and Left and Right the two response alternatives. W, X, Y, and Z denote the number of events (responses and reinforcers) occurring in each cell.

say, each time a correct response is emitted (e.g., Hume, 1974a, b; Hume & Irwin, 1974). Alternatively, food reinforcers for correct responses may be presented intermittently on VI schedules (e.g., McCarthy & Davison, 1979; 1984) or on probabilistic VR schedules (e.g., Elsmore, 1972; McCarthy & Davison, 1979, 1980a, b; Stubbs, 1976). The numbers of reinforcers obtained in the cells of the matrix are designated R_w, R_x, R_y and R_z. Usually, incorrect responses have no consequence ($R_x = R_y = 0$) or they are punished in some way (e.g., by timeout, Hume, 1974b; but see Section 11.6).

In both human and animal research, discriminability (d') is a function of the physical difference between the stimuli (e.g., Blough & Blough, 1977; Clopton, 1972; Green & Swets, 1974; Hobson, 1975; Hodos & Bonbright, 1972; Hume, 1974a, b; Hume & Irwin, 1974; Rilling & McDiarmid, 1965; Terman, 1970; Terman & Terman, 1972; Wright, 1972). Changes in criterion (β), independent of discriminability, have been shown to result from variations in two major independent variables. The first is the relative frequency with which the two discriminative stimuli (S_1 and S_2) are presented (e.g., Clopton, 1972; Elsmore, 1972; Galanter & Holman, 1967; Hume & Irwin, 1974; Markowitz & Swets, 1967; Schulman & Greenberg, 1970; Terman & Terman, 1972). The second common biasing variable is the relative magnitude of the consequences of each detection response (e.g., Dusoir, 1983; Green & Swets, 1974; Hume, 1974a, b; Hume & Irwin, 1974; Swets, Tanner, & Birdsall, 1961; Tanner & Swets, 1954; Wright, 1972; Wright & Nevin, 1974).

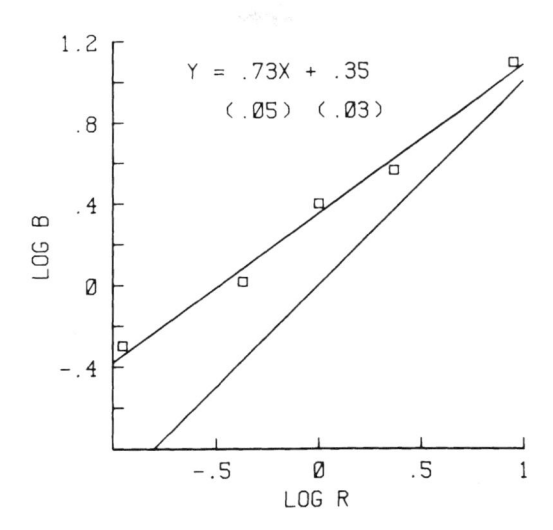

FIG. 11.2.   Data reported by Green and Swets (1974) reanalyzed according to the generalized matching law (Equation 4.2). The logarithm of the Yes-No response ratio (log B) is plotted as a function of the logarithm of the arranged reinforcer-frequency ratio (log R). For comparison purposes, a line of strict matching ($Y = sX$) is also shown.

11.3. SIGNAL DETECTION AS MATCHING

The Yes-No detection task described in Fig. 11.1 can be viewed as two concurrent reinforcement Extinction schedules, each operating under a distinctive stimulus (Davison & Tustin, 1978; Nevin, 1969). That is, in the presence of each discriminative stimulus (S_1 and S_2), two response alternatives (left and right keys) are concurrently available to the animal. In the presence of S_1, left-key pecks (hits) are reinforced, whereas right-key pecks (misses) are not. In the presence of S_2, right-key pecks (correct rejections) are reinforced, whereas left-key pecks (false alarms) are not. It was this observation that allowed the laws governing choice behavior on complex schedules of reinforcement to be applied to the detection paradigm.

The pioneering work on this approach was carried out by Nevin (1969). He reanalyzed some human detection data reported by Green and Swets (1974, pp. 88-90) and showed that the probability of responding "Yes" approximately matched the relative frequency of reinforcers scheduled for responding "Yes." We have replotted these data in log-ratio form in Fig. 11.2. A least-squares linear regression analysis was used to obtain the best-fitting generalized matching law equation (Equation 4.2). As Fig. 11.2 shows, detection performance undermatched the arranged reinforcer-frequency ratio ($a = 0.73$). In addition, there was a significant bias (log $c = 0.35$) toward responding "Yes, a signal was presented."

11.4. MATCHING MODELS FOR THE STANDARD DISCRETE-TRIALS SIGNAL-DETECTION PROCEDURE

11.4a. Generalized Matching

Davison and Tustin (1978) proposed a behavioral detection model based on the generalized matching law (Equation 4.3). In the signal-detection paradigm (Fig. 11.1), the generalized matching law suggests that if the two stimuli, S_1 and S_2, are indiscriminable, the distribution of total left- and right-key responses will be sensitive only to the ratio of reinforcers obtained for left and right responses, that is, to R_w/R_z. Under these conditions, the arrangement is simply a concurrent VI VI schedule. Davison and Tustin suggested that, as the stimuli became more discriminable, the subjects' behavior would become progressively more biased toward emitting a left-key peck when S_1 was presented and toward emitting a right-key peck when S_2 was presented (Fig. 11.1). As biases are constant additive quantities in the logarithmic form of the generalized matching law (Equation 4.2), Davison and Tustin proposed separate generalized matching equations to describe behavior in the presence of *each* of the two stimuli in the detection task. When only correct responses are reinforced ($R_x = R_y = 0$), the two equations are: On S_1 trials:

$$\log\left(\frac{B_w}{B_x}\right) = a_{r1} \log\left(\frac{R_w}{R_z}\right) + \log c + \log d , \qquad (11.1)$$

and, on S_2 trials,

$$\log\left(\frac{B_y}{B_z}\right) = a_{r2} \log\left(\frac{R_w}{R_z}\right) + \log c - \log d , \qquad (11.2)$$

where B and R denote the number of responses emitted and the number of reinforcers obtained, respectively, and the subscripts refer to the cells of the matrix in Fig. 11.1. Note that Equations 11.1 and 11.2 describe behavior when the biasing effect of stimulus differences is constant, that is, when the difference between S_1 and S_2 is not varied. When stimulus difference is varied, $\log d$ is a *variable*.

The parameter $\log d$ measures the discriminability of the two stimuli. As stimulus separation increases, more responses will be emitted on the left than on the right key when S_1 is presented, and more responses will be emitted on the right than on the left key when S_2 is presented. Since the numerators in both Equations 11.1 and 11.2 are left-key responses, $\log d$ is positive in Equation 11.1 and negative in Equation 11.2. As in the generalized matching law, the parameters a_{r1} and a_{r2} measure the sensitivity of choice to changes in the reinforcer distribution between the choices. The ratio of obtained reinforcers quantifies a reinforcer-frequency bias (McCarthy & Davison, 1980b, 1981a) arising from different numbers of reinforcers obtained for correct left- and right-key responses. Equally, when reinforcer frequencies are held constant and reinforcer durations are varied, the ratio of reinforcer magnitudes will quantify a reinforcer-magnitude bias (McCarthy & Davison, 1979; Boldero, Davison, & McCarthy, 1985).

The obtained reinforcer-frequency ratio is a biaser in the sense that ratios of left to right choices are determined by the overall left-to-right obtained reinforcer ratio (R_w/R_z). But, as in the generalized matching law, changing the relative frequencies of reinforcers will change behavior with a certain sensitivity. The sensitivity parameter, a_r, measures the relation between changes in a biaser and changes in behavior. When one biaser (e.g., reinforcer frequency) is varied, and another (e.g., reinforcer duration) is kept constant, precise estimates of both the value of the constant biaser, and the sensitivity with which behavior changes with the varied biaser, can be obtained. The reinforcer-frequency ratio (or reinforcer-duration ratio, etc.) is thus a biaser in the same sense as in SDT where, for example, the payoff matrix (the distribution of reinforcers and punishers over the cells of Fig. 11.1) may be varied. The criterion changes resulting from the payoff-matrix manipulation generate a receiver-operating characteristic (see Section 11.5) from which an estimate of discriminability is obtained. Log c is, as in the generalized matching law, inherent bias, a constant preference that remains invariant across changes in the reinforcer-frequency bias. Inherent bias may arise from the experimental equipment. For example, different forces might be required to emit the two responses (Hunter & Davison, 1982), and this will bias behavior with a certain sensitivity. But if the environmental biaser is constant, the sensitivity to this biaser cannot be calculated without assuming that there are no other biases operative. Inherent bias may also arise from the subject itself, perhaps as a preference for responding "Yes, there was a signal" (Killeen, 1977, 1981; see also Fig. 11.2), or perhaps from a preference for responding on the left rather than on the right key over and above any obvious force or similar differences.

11.4b. Strict Matching

Nevin, Jenkins, Whittaker, and Yarensky (1977) suggested a behavioral detection model that is formally identical to Davison and Tustin's (1978) model except in one respect. Nevin et al. used the strict matching law (Herrnstein, 1970; Chapter 2) rather than the generalized matching law (Chapter 4), thus not allowing for undermatching or overmatching or for inherent bias.

The conceptual background of Nevin et al.'s (1977) model is, however, somewhat different from that of Davison and Tustin's (1978) model. As Nevin (1981) outlined, it assumes that the effect of a reinforcer for a response in the presence of one stimulus generalizes to strengthen the same response in the presence of the other stimulus. The magnitude of this generalization will depend on the discriminability of the two stimuli: If they are indiscriminable, the generalization is maximal; if they are perfectly discriminable, there is no generalization. The degree of generalization is measured by a similarity parameter, η (Luce, 1959, 1963) which takes values between 0 (perfect discriminability, no generalizability) and 1.0 (no discriminability, maximal generalizability). Thus, in terms of Fig. 11.1, the reinforcement for emitting a left-key peck in S_2 is ηR_w, and for emitting a right-key peck in S_1, ηR_z. Nevin et al. reasoned that the subject would distribute its responses so as to match the ratio of direct (R_w & R_z) and generalized (ηR_z & ηR_w) reinforcers. Formally, their model in logarithmic form is: On S_1 trials:

$$\log\left(\frac{B_w}{B_x}\right) = \log\left(\frac{R_w}{R_z}\right) - \log \eta \ ,$$

and, on S_2 trials:

$$\log\left(\frac{B_y}{B_z}\right) = \log\left(\frac{R_w}{R_z}\right) + \log \eta \ .$$

Since η falls between 0 and 1, -log η is positive, and + log η is negative, giving the same formal model as suggested by Davison and Tustin (Equations 11.1 and 11.2) but with unit reinforcer sensitivity and no inherent bias. However, the necessity for the inclusion of sensitivity and inherent-bias parameters will become clear in the following sections (see also McCarthy & Davison, 1981b).

11.4c. Some Data Supporting Generalized Matching in Signal Detection

Consider a discrete-trials task in which a pigeon was trained to peck the left-side key when the brighter of two white lights (S_1) was presented on the center key, and to peck the right-side key when the dimmer of two white lights (S_2) was presented on the center key. Suppose that the luminance of the two white lights was held constant, and the frequency with which correct left- and right-key choices produced food was varied.

Figure 11.3 shows the data that might be obtained, plotted according to Equations 11.1 and 11.2. Here, the logarithm of the ratio of the numbers of responses emitted on S_1 trials, log (B_w/B_x), and on S_2 trials, log (B_y/B_z), are plotted as a function of the logarithm of the ratio of the numbers of food reinforcers obtained for correct left- and right-key choices, log (R_w/R_z). Straight lines were fit to the data shown in Fig. 11.3 by the method of least squares. The equations of the fitted lines, and the standard deviations of the slopes and intercepts, are shown in the figure.

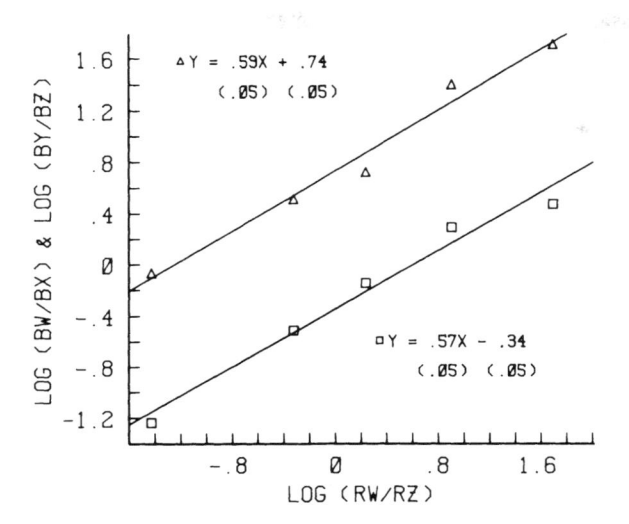

FIG. 11.3.   The logarithm of the ratio of the numbers of left-and right-key responses emitted on S_1 trials, log (B_w/B_x), and on S_2 trials, log (B_y/B_z), as a function of the logarithm of the ratio of the numbers of food reinforcers obtained for correct left- and right-key choices, log (R_w/R_z). These plots correspond to Equations 11.1 and 11.2, respectively. Also shown are the best-fitting straight lines by the method of least squares, their equations, and the standard deviations of their parameters.

The slopes of Equations 11.1 and 11.2, a_{r1} and a_{r2}, respectively, are measures of the sensitivity of choice in S_1 and S_2 to changes in the reinforcer-frequency bias. The slope for S_1 performance was 0.59 (SD 0.05), and the slope for S_2 performance was 0.57 (SD 0.05). There are three important points to note about these data. First, the slopes were both positive, implying that relative reinforcer-frequency variation did indeed bias choice. Second, choice ratios in the presence of each stimulus showed sensitivities significantly less than 1.0. Third, the subject's behavior allocation was equally sensitive to changes in relative reinforcer frequency in the presence of each stimulus (a_{r1} did not differ from a_{r2} in Equations 11.1 and 11.2).

The intercept of the equation fitted to S_1 performance (log c + log d, Equation 11.1) and the intercept of the equation fitted to S_2 performance (log c − log d) provide estimates of both the subject's ability to discriminate between the two white-light intensities (log d) and of inherent bias (log c). If the S_2 intercept is subtracted from the S_1 intercept, the result is 2 log d. Thus, log d is given by one-half the difference between the intercepts, which here is 0.54. Further, since the two lines were parallel, discriminability remained constant at this value across all changes in relative reinforcer frequency. Similarly, one-half the *sum* of the two intercepts gives an inherent bias (log c) value of 0.18, that is, a small inherent preference for responding on the left key. Of course, if the intercepts were equal in absolute value, there would be no inherent bias.

In the normative version of SDT, variations in stimulus parameters are

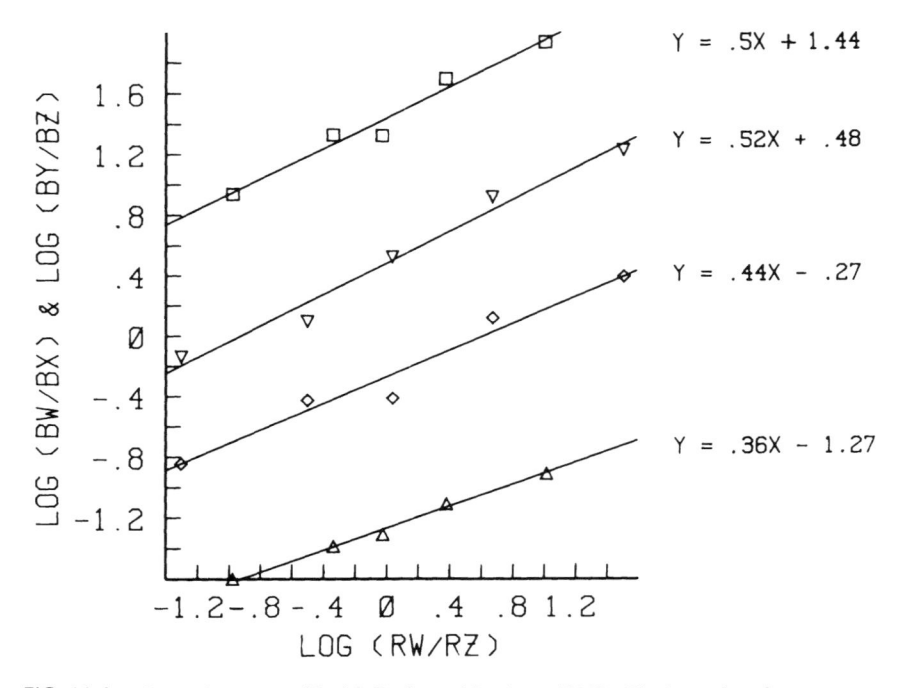

FIG. 11.4.   Group data reported by McCarthy and Davison (1980b). The log ratios of responses on S_1 trials, log (B_w/B_x), and on S_2 trials, log (B_y/B_z) are plotted as a function of the log obtained reinforcer-frequency ratio, log (R_w/R_z). The squares and upright triangles show performance in S_1 (Equation 11.1) and in S_2 (Equation 11.2), respectively, for the 5-s versus 30-s conditions. The inverted triangles and diamonds show performance in S_1 and in S_2, respectively, for the 20-s versus 30-s conditions. The best-fitting straight lines by the method of least squares are shown.

presumed to affect only discriminability, whereas variations in nonsensory parameters (e.g., the magnitude of payoff) are presumed only to affect the location of the criterion (or, the degree of response bias). The Davison-Tustin (1978) model embodies this separation between the effects of sensory and nonsensory variables by assuming that the behavioral effects of discriminability and reinforcer bias are additive in logarithmic terms (Equations 11.1 and 11.2). Hence, there is no interaction between these two variables in their effect on behavior.

McCarthy and Davison (1980b) empirically investigated this assumption of independence by examining the biasing effects of changes in the obtained reinforcer-frequency ratio on the detection performance of pigeons in both an easy and a difficult discrimination task. They trained six pigeons, using a standard discrete-trials detection procedure, to discriminate between two differ-ent durations of white light (S_1 and S_2) at two levels of discriminability. At one level, S_1 was a 5-s white-light duration and S_2 was a 30-s white-light duration. At the other, S_1 was 20 s and S_2 was 30 s. Relative reinforcer frequency was varied across five conditions at each discriminability level. Figure 11.4 shows the data obtained, averaged across the six birds and plotted according to Equations 11.1 and 11.2. These data show that discriminability was higher for the 5-s versus 30-s conditions than for the 20-s versus 30-s conditions. This result is seen by computing one-half the difference between the intercepts of the fitted lines (Equations 11.1 and 11.2) for each stimulus pair. For 5 s versus 30 s, log d was 1.36, and for 20 s versus 30 s, log d was 0.38. These data also show that, despite the different discriminability level, detection performance was equally sensitive to relative reinforcer-frequency variation. That is, there was no difference between the slope values for Equations 11.1 and 11.2 across the two stimulus pairs (McCarthy & Davison, 1980b). For 5 s versus 30 s, $a_{r1} = 0.50$ and $a_{r2} = 0.36$; for 20 s versus 30 s, $a_{r1} = 0.52$ and $a_{r2} = 0.44$. To summarize, the reinforcer-frequency sensitivities were not significantly different in the presence of each stimulus at each discriminability levels. Further, the value of reinforcer-frequency sensitivity was unaffected by the change in discriminability. Hence, as assumed by Davison and Tustin (1978), there was no interaction between discriminability and relative reinforcer frequency in their effects on choice. Equations 11.1 and 11.2 can therefore be used to specify how independent measures of stimulus discriminability and response bias can be obtained.

11.5. STIMULUS DISCRIMINABILITY

Given that $a_{r1} = a_{r2}$, Equation 11.2 can be subtracted from Equation 11.1 to eliminate the effects of reinforcer-frequency bias and inherent bias on detection performance:

$$\log\left(\frac{B_w}{B_x}\right) - \log\left(\frac{B_y}{B_z}\right) = 2 \log d . \tag{11.3}$$

Thus, rearranging Equation 11.3, a bias-free point estimate of discriminability is given by:

$$\log d = .5 \log\left(\frac{B_w \cdot B_z}{B_x \cdot B_y}\right) . \tag{11.4}$$

We call Equation 11.3 a *stimulus function* (McCarthy & Davison, 1980a) because it relates behavior to the discriminative stimuli independent of any biaser. Davison and Tustin (1978) noted that discriminability, as measured by Equation 11.4, was identical to discriminability indices used by some signal-detection theorists (e.g., η, Luce, 1963) and equivalent to those used by

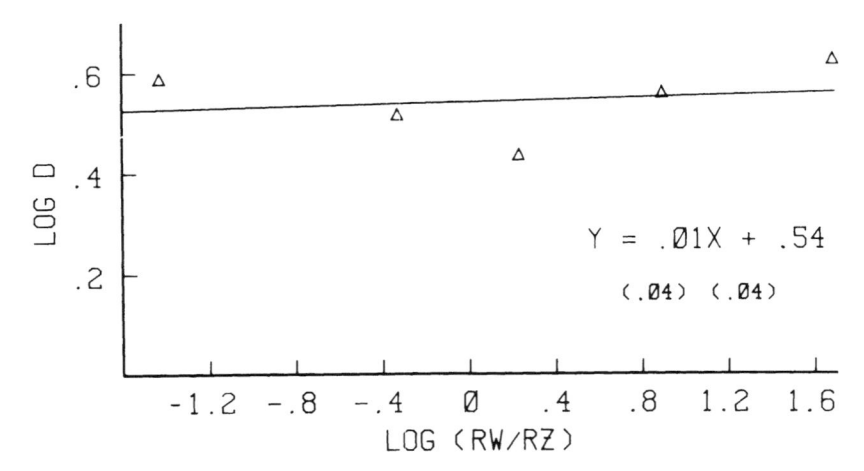

FIG. 11.5.   Point estimates of stimulus discriminability (log d; Equation 11.4) for the data shown in Fig. 11.3, plotted as a function of the logarithm of the obtained reinforcer-frequency ratio, log (R_w/R_z). The best-fitting straight line by the method of least squares is shown, together with its equation and the standard deviations of the parameter estimates.

others (e.g., d', Green & Swets, 1974). McCarthy and Davison (1979, 1980b, 1984) have measured the discriminability of different light intensities and different stimulus durations using Equation 11.4. They have shown discriminability to be independent of relative reinforcer frequency (McCarthy & Davison, 1979, 1980b, 1984), absolute reinforcer rate (McCarthy & Davison, 1982), and relative reinforcer duration (Boldero, Davison, & McCarthy, 1985). They have also shown (Davison & McCarthy, 1980) that discriminability *is* affected by reinforcing errors in a detection procedure (Section 11.6). On the other hand, discriminability is affected by local variations in reinforcer probability within sessions. For instance, both Nevin and MacWilliams (1983) and Stubbs (1968) showed that when detection performance was reinforced on FR schedules, discriminability systematically increased through the ratio.

Consider now the data shown in Fig. 11.3. As shown in Section 11.4c, the functions plotted in Fig. 11.3 allow an estimate of discriminability to be obtained from one-half the difference between the intercepts for Equations 11.1 and 11.2. Essentially, this computation gives the value of discriminability (log d) when there is no reinforcer-frequency bias; that is, when log $(R_w/R_z) = 0$. However, since the two lines are parallel ($a_{r1} = a_{r2}$), the difference between each data pair is constant for all values of the reinforcer ratio. Hence, discriminability is constant across changes in relative reinforcer frequency. A plot of point estimates of discriminability (Equation 11.4) for each condition as a function of the obtained reinforcer-frequency ratio should therefore have a slope of zero and an intercept equal to log d. Such is the state of affairs shown in Fig. 11.5. In Fig. 11.5, point estimates of log d, for each pair of data points shown in Fig. 11.3, are plotted as a function of the reinforcer-frequency bias, log (R_w/R_z). A least-squares linear-regression analysis was used to estimate the slope and intercept values. The slope (0.01, SD 0.04) was not significantly different from zero (i.e., was not more than two standard deviations from zero), implying that discriminability did not change with changes in relative reinforcer frequency. (We are aware that the data shown in Fig. 11.5 suggest that discriminability increases as the log reinforcer ratios become more different from 0. This result, however, is idiosyncratic to this particular data set.) The intercept gave a log d value of 0.54, identical to that obtained from the fits of Equations 11.1 and 11.2 (Fig. 11.3).

The stimulus function (Equation 11.3) is analogous to the isosensitivity function of SDT. In detection studies, a receiver-operating characteristic (ROC), or isosensitivity function, is typically obtained in Yes-No tasks by inducing the subject to alter his or her criterion either (1) by varying the probability of stimulus presentation (SPP), and hence allowing the obtained reinforcer-frequency ratio to covary (Section 11.7); or (2) by varying the symmetry of the payoff matrix for correct detections. Such functions show how a subject's distribution of choices depends upon the bias generated by varying either SPP or the payoff matrix when the physical characteristics of the stimuli are held constant. Thus, Equation 11.3 is equivalent to detection-theory isosensitivity functions when the stimuli are held constant and biasers, such as relative reinforcer frequency, are varied. It should be pointed out, however, that the only direct prediction of behavior in the two stimuli comes from Equations 11.1 and 11.2. The stimulus function (Equation 11.3) specifies only the *relation* between the dependent variables, log (B_w/B_x) and log (B_y/B_z).

Figure 11.6 shows the ROC function for the data shown in Fig. 11.3; that is, the choice ratio in S_1, B_w/B_x, is plotted as a function of the choice ratio in S_2, B_y/B_z, on probability coordinates (that is, probability of a hit versus probability of a false alarm, Fig. 11.1). Figure 11.6 shows the ROC function to be approximately symmetric about the minor diagonal, implying a slope of 1.0 on normal-deviate coordinates. When the data shown in Fig. 11.6 were converted to normal-deviate (z-score) measures, a linear regression gave a slope of 0.95 (SD 0.06).

One major concern in signal-detection research has been the shape (or, on normalized functions, the slope) of empirical isosensitivity functions, and the relation that this variable may have to the parameters of the stimuli. In the normative version of SDT (Green & Swets, 1974), when the hypothesized distributions stemming from the stimuli that underlie the isosensitivity function are Gaussian and of equal variance, ROC functions of unit slope result when plotted on normalized coordinates. Gaussian distributions of unequal variance, Rice and Rayleigh distributions, or exponential distributions, on the other hand, give rise to slopes that depart from unity when plotted on normalized coordinates. Nonunit-slope ROC functions have frequently been found in human

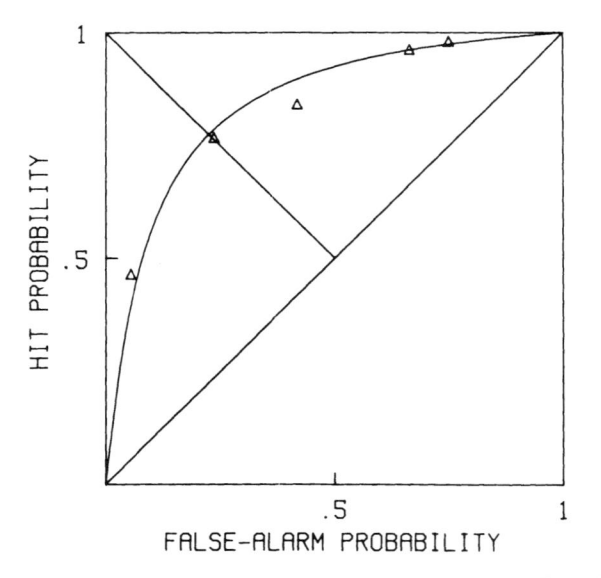

FIG. 11.6. The isosensitivity function for the data shown in Fig. 11.3. The probability of a hit is plotted as a function of the probability of a false alarm.

detection studies where they have been interpreted as providing information about the transducer function relating physical and sensory continua (Green & McGill, 1970; Green & Swets, 1974; Jeffress, 1964, 1967, 1968; McGill, 1967; Tanner & Birdsall, 1958; Thijssen & Vendrik, 1968), or attributed to the effects of nonsensory factors such as criterion variance (e.g., Treisman, 1977; Wickelgren, 1968). Detection studies with animals also have reported slopes that deviate from unity (e.g., Hack, 1963; Wright, 1972, 1974).

Within the present theoretical framework, an isosensitivity function with unit slope (on normalized coordinates) results when the subjects are equally sensitive to relative reinforcer-frequency variation in the presence of each stimulus; that is, a_{r1} (Equation 11.1) $= a_{r2}$ (Equation 11.2). This situation is illustrated in Figs. 11.3, 11.5, and 11.6. Figures 11.7 and 11.8 analogously describe the situation that results when a_{r1} does not equal a_{r2}. Differential sensitivities to reinforcer-frequency bias in the presence of the two stimuli could arise if, for example, different responses were required in S_1 and S_2. Davison and Ferguson (1978; Section 7.11c), for instance, found that keypecking in the pigeon was more sensitive to reinforcer-frequency variation than was lever pressing.

If a_{r1} does not equal a_{r2}, the stimulus function (Equation 11.3) of Davison and Tustin's (1978) model becomes:

$$\log\left(\frac{B_w}{B_x}\right) - \log\left(\frac{B_y}{B_z}\right) = (a_{r1} - a_{r2}) \log\left(\frac{R_w}{R_z}\right) + 2 \log d \ . \qquad (11.5)$$

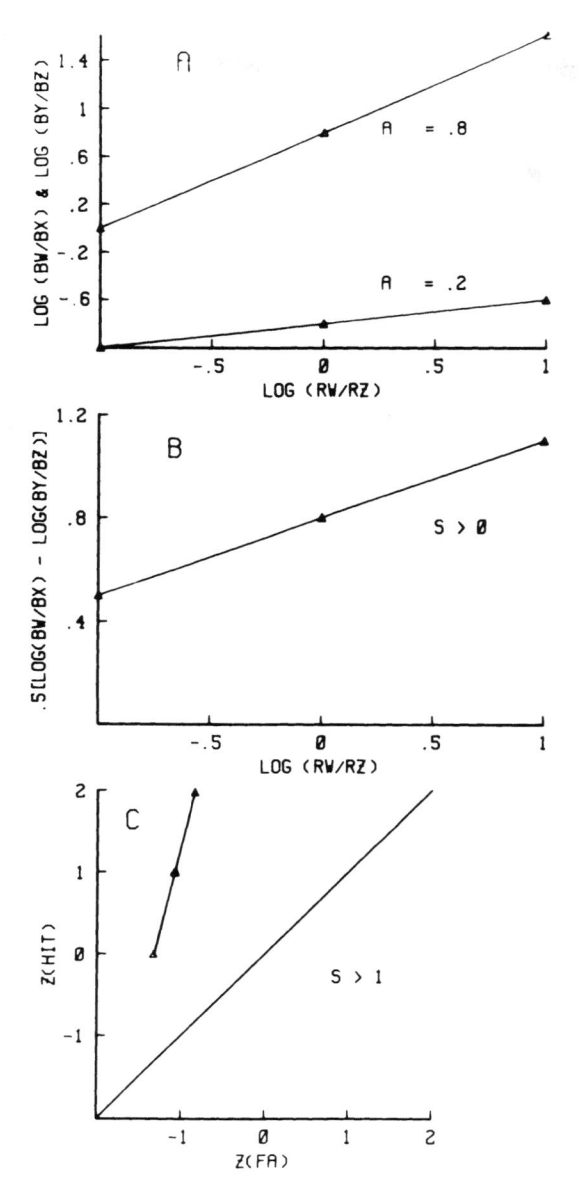

FIG. 11.7. The relation between Equations 11.1 and 11.2 (Panel A), the stimulus function (Equation 11.5, Panel B), and the normalized detection-theory isosensitivity function (Panel C) when a_{r1} (Equation 11.1) is greater than a_{r2} (Equation 11.2). The data are hypothetical. In Panel A, the slope of the functions (a_{r1} or a_{r2}) is designated "A". In Panels B and C, the slope of the function is designated "S."

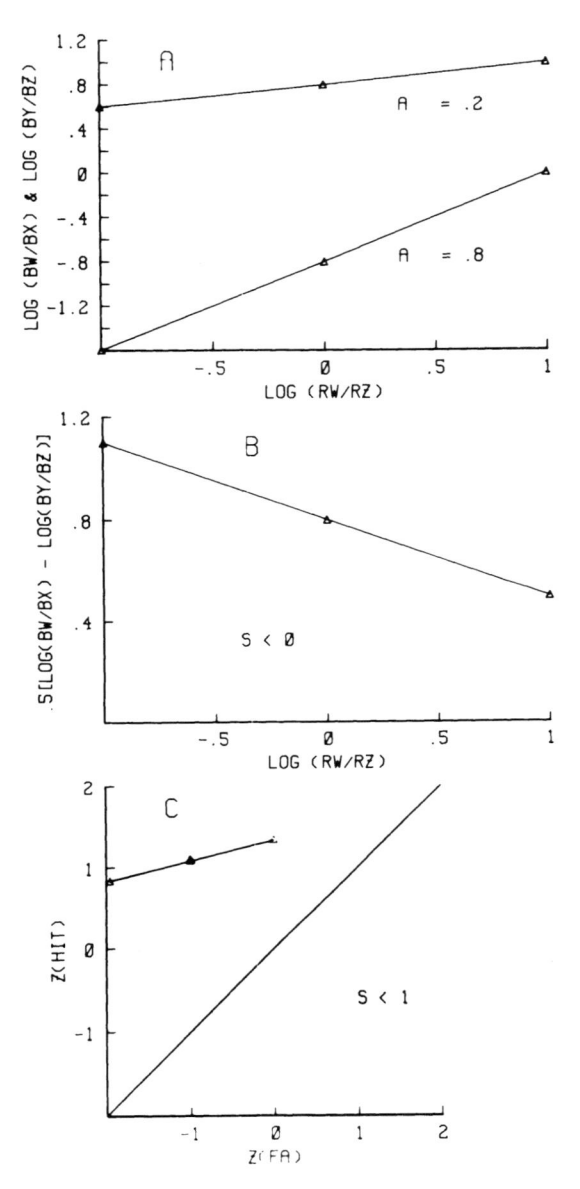

FIG. 11.8. The relation between Equations 11.1 and 11.2 (Panel A), the stimulus function (Equation 11.5, Panel B), and the normalized detection-theory isosensitivity function (Panel C) when a_{r1} (Equation 11.1) is less than a_{r2} (Equation 11.2). The data are hypothetical. In Panel A, the slope of the functions (a_{r1} or a_{r2}) is designated "A". In Panels B and C, the slope of the function is designated "S."

Figure 11.7A shows Equations 11.1 and 11.2 when a_{r1} (0.80) is greater than a_{r2} (0.20). Figure 11.7B shows the stimulus function (Equation 11.5) in which discriminability (log d) is positively and linearly related to the reinforcer-frequency bias. The resultant nonunit ROC function is shown on normalized coordinates in Fig. 11.7C. Figure 11.8A shows Equations 11.1 and 11.2 when a_{r1} (0.20) is less than a_{r2} (0.80). Figure 11.8B shows the corresponding stimulus function in which log d is negatively and linearly related to the reinforcer-frequency bias. The resultant nonunit ROC function is shown in Fig. 11.8C.

11.6. STIMULUS DISCRIMINABILITY AND REINFORCERS FOR ERRORS

Data obtained from standard SDT procedures have typically shown discriminability to be independent of reinforcer parameters. As noted in Section 11.5, McCarthy and Davison (1979, 1980b, 1984) have found the discriminability of differing light intensities or durations to be independent of variations in relative reinforcer frequency, absolute rate of reinforcers (McCarthy & Davison, 1982; but see also Nevin et al., 1982), and the relative duration of reinforcement (Boldero et al., 1985). However, Nevin, Olson, Mandell, and Yarensky (1975) showed that a conventional measure of stimulus discriminability (A'; Grier, 1971) was not invariant with respect to payoffs when reinforcers were obtained for incorrect responses and the discriminative stimuli were held constant. Rather, as illustrated in Fig. 11.9, measured discriminability decreased as the probability of error reinforcers increased. (It is usual, in this area of research, to call responses in cells X and Y of the matrix in Fig. 11.1 "errors", even when they are occasionally reinforced.) Figure 11.9 shows mean data reported by Davison and McCarthy (1980) for pigeons discriminating the duration of stimuli when errors were followed by food reinforcers with increasing probability (0 to 0.9) while the probability of reinforcement for correct responses was constant at 0.7.

As Fig. 11.9 clearly shows, discriminability (log d; Equation 11.4) fell as the arranged probability of a reinforcer for an error increased (see also Logue, 1983). The obtained frequencies of receiving reinforcers for correct responses relative to all obtained reinforcers also is shown in Fig. 11.9. This measure was highly correlated with the estimated value of discriminability. On the basis of these results and those of Nevin et al. (1975), Davison and McCarthy (1980) extended Davison and Tustin's (1978) model to account for the reinforcers-for-errors data. While Davison and McCarthy assumed that *discriminability* (log d; the maximal ability of the subject to tell the two stimuli apart) remained constant when errors were reinforced, they made the added assumption that the degree of *discrimination* that can be shown when errors are reinforced is a joint function of the discriminability of the stimuli (log d) and the degree of association between reinforcers and stimulus presentations. Davison and McCarthy suggested that the

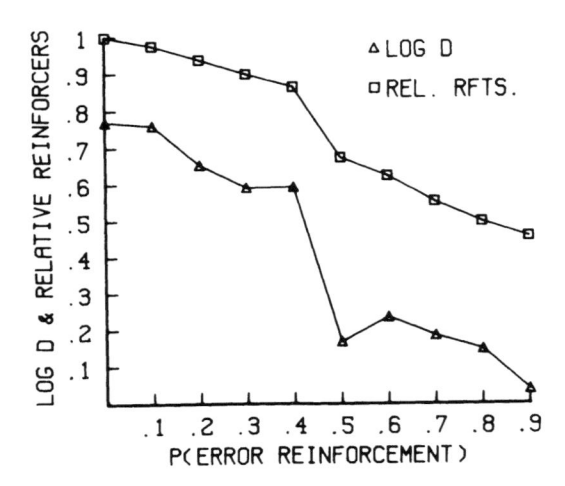

FIG. 11.9.   Group data reported by Davison and McCarthy (1980). Stimulus discriminability and the obtained relative number of reinforcers for correct responses are shown as a function of the arranged probability of reinforcers for errors.

degree of association (which is like a correlation coefficient) could be measured by dividing the difference between the obtained frequencies of correct and error reinforcers by the total obtained frequency of reinforcers. This measure takes the value of 1 when no error reinforcers are obtained, and 0 when errors and correct responses obtain equal frequencies of reinforcers. Thus:

$$\text{Discrimination} = \left(\frac{R_c - R_e}{R_c + R_e}\right) \cdot \log d \; ,$$

where R_c is the number of reinforcers obtained for correct responses ($R_w + R_z$) and R_e is the number of reinforcers obtained for errors ($R_x + R_y$). Thus, taking the decremental effect of imperfect stimulus-reinforcer association into account, the stimulus function may be rewritten as:

$$\log\left(\frac{B_w}{B_x}\right) - \log\left(\frac{B_y}{B_z}\right) = 2\left(\frac{R_c - R_e}{R_c + R_e}\right) \cdot \log d \; . \tag{11.6}$$

This equation illustrates how discriminability as conventionally measured (the left side of Equation 11.6) will be degraded by reinforcing errors. Indeed, when errors are reinforced, the behavioral measure is of *discrimination*, rather than of discriminability, because the measure is not independent of reinforcer effects. When no error reinforcers are obtained, Equation 11.6 reduces to the simpler stimulus function of the Davison and Tustin model (Equation 11.3).

We note here that Nevin (personal communication) has suggested that the stimulus-reinforcer association might better be measured as the phi coefficient, a nonparametric measure of association in 2 x 2 matrices, and that quantitatively the phi coefficient does provide more accurate data descriptions.

11.7. RESPONSE BIAS

We now return to the two basic equations of the Davison-Tustin (1978) model and discuss how they measure and interpret response bias. When Equations 11.1 and 11.2 are added, the discriminability parameter, log d, is removed and a bias function (McCarthy & Davison, 1980a) results:

$$\log\left(\frac{B_w}{B_x}\right) + \log\left(\frac{B_y}{B_z}\right) = 2\,a_r\,\log\left(\frac{R_w}{R_z}\right) + 2\log c \ . \tag{11.7}$$

This equation relates choice in the presence of the two stimuli to the combined effects of inherent bias (log c) and the bias caused by variations in the relative reinforcer frequency. Thus, rearranging:

$$.5\,\log\left(\frac{B_w \cdot B_y}{B_x \cdot B_z}\right) = a_r\,\log\left(\frac{R_w}{R_z}\right) + \log c \ . \tag{11.8}$$

We call the measure on the left side of Equation 11.8 *response bias* (McCarthy & Davison, 1979), and it provides the same behavioral estimate of bias (or, criterion) as that used in SDT (e.g., log β). The right side of Equation 11.8 specifies the environmental conditions that produce the response bias—in this case, relative reinforcer-frequency variation and inherent bias. Research has also suggested that other variables known to affect concurrent-schedule choice can also be used to bias detection performance. Relative reinforcer duration (Boldero et al., 1985; Dusoir, 1983) has been shown to act as a biaser. Among other independent variables that also might be expected to act in this way are reinforcer delays (Williams & Fantino, 1978), reinforcer qualities (Hollard & Davison, 1971), and response requirements (Davison & Ferguson, 1978; Hunter & Davison, 1982).

Response bias, as measured by the left side of Equation 11.8, is equivalent to the reciprocal of the measure given by Luce (1963). Unlike Luce's formulation, however, the present behavioral model distinguishes clearly between two types of bias—that arising from variations in relative reinforcer or response parameters (the variables as specified on the right of Equation 11.8, generically called reinforcer bias), and that arising from constant differences between relative response or reinforcer parameters (inherent bias, log c). These two sources of bias are subsumed under the single rubric of "criterion" in signal-detection research, whereas the present approach partitions criterion (response bias) into a constant and a variable component.

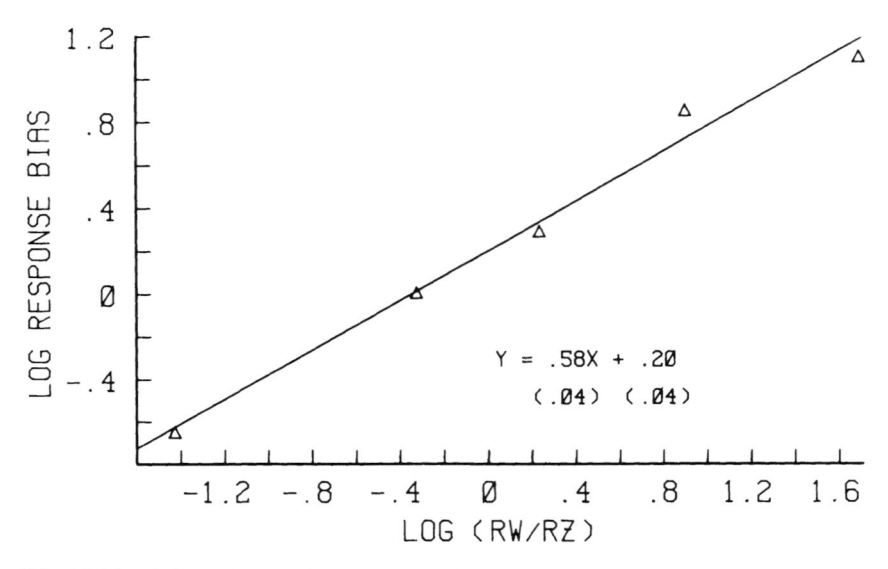

FIG. 11.10.   Point estimates of response bias (Equation 11.8) for the data shown in Fig. 11.3 plotted as a function of the logarithm of the obtained reinforcer-frequency ratio, log (R_w/R_z). The best-fitting straight line by the method of least squares is shown, together with its equation. The standard deviations of the parameter estimates are shown in parentheses.

11.7a. Biasers of Signal Detection

Consider now the data presented in Fig. 11.3. The positive slopes shown there for S_1 performance (Equation 11.1) and for S_2 performance (Equation 11.2) show that choice changed as a function of variations in the relative distribution of reinforcers between the left and right keys. Figure 11.10 shows these data replotted according to Equation 11.8—that is, response bias (one-half the sum of the log choice ratios in each stimulus) is plotted as a function of relative reinforcer-frequency bias. A least-squares linear regression analysis was used to estimate the slope (a_r, the sensitivity of response bias to changes in the reinforcer bias) and intercept (log c, inherent bias). As Fig. 11.10 shows, the value of log c was 0.20, indicating a constant preference for responding on the left key or, alternatively, for reporting the presence of S_1 (see Fig. 11.1). The value of a_r was 0.58. Within a discrete-trials procedure, values of a_r in the range 0.4 (McCarthy & Davison, 1980b) to 0.8 (McCarthy & Davison, 1979, 1984) have usually been obtained. Similarly, in concurrent VI VI schedule performance, although modal sensitivity for response measures is about 0.8 (Baum, 1979; Section 6.1), sensitivity to reinforcer frequency values in the range 0.6 to 0.8 are not uncommon (Baum, 1979; Taylor & Davison, 1983).

   Boldero et al. (1985) found that the detection performance of pigeons was less sensitive to the variation of relative reinforcer duration than to the variation of relative reinforcer frequency. The slopes were 0.24 when the independent variable in Equation 11.8 was reinforcer duration and 0.63 when it was reinforcer frequency. The same difference also has been obtained for concurrent VI VI schedule performance (Schneider, 1973; Todorov, 1973; Section 6.3). In the detection-theory literature, variations in the size of the payoff (reinforcer) for correct detections (e.g., points awarded for human subjects; Dusoir, 1983; number of brain stimulations for animals; Hume, 1974a, b) have often been reported to produce some degree of response bias. However, measures of the *sensitivity* of subjects to variations in payoff magnitude have not been reported in these studies. Boldero et al.'s results suggest that relative reinforcer frequency is a more effective biaser of detection performance than is relative reinforcer duration.

By far the most common biasing manipulation carried out in the detection literature has been varying the relative frequency of presenting the discriminative stimuli or the signal and noise. Stimulus presentation probability (SPP) has been reported to bias performance in a number of animal and human detection paradigms (e.g., Clopton, 1972; Elsmore, 1972; Galanter & Holman, 1967; Hume & Irwin, 1974; Markowitz & Swets, 1967; Schulman & Greenberg, 1970; Terman & Terman, 1972). However, Equations 11.1 and 11.2 of Davison and Tustin's (1978) detection model contain no term to accommodate this finding.

Variation in SPP is said to alter the criterion (response bias) of the subject. However, it is common in detection procedures either to reinforce every correct response (e.g., Dusoir, 1983; Hume, 1974a, b; Hume & Irwin, 1974), or to reinforce correct responses intermittently on probabilistic or VR schedules (e.g., Elsmore, 1972; Hobson, 1975, 1978). These procedures are called *uncontrolled reinforcer-ratio* procedures (McCarthy & Davison, 1980a, 1984) because the relative number of reinforcers obtained for correct detections can vary widely with the subject's behavior and with SPP. Suppose, for example, that S_1 is presented on 90 percent of trials and that left-key pecks are correct following S_1 presentations. If each correct response is reinforced, 90 percent of the sessional reinforcers may be obtained from the left key. Variations in SPP have, therefore, been confounded with variations in the obtained reinforcer-frequency ratio (McCarthy & Davison, 1979, 1984). When relative reinforcer frequency was held constant and equal between the two response alternatives (using dependent scheduling) and SPP alone was varied, McCarthy and Davison (1979) found no change in response bias. This finding is illustrated in Fig. 11.11, which shows group data reported by McCarthy and Davison (1979) for pigeons on a light-intensity detection task. Response bias is shown both as a function of the obtained log reinforcer ratio when SPP was varied and the reinforcer ratio covaried, and also as a function of the obtained log stimulus-frequency ratio when SPP was again varied but the reinforcer-frequency ratio was held constant at 1.0. Figure 11.11 clearly shows that variations in the reinforcer ratio did bias detection performance ($a_r = 0.90$), but that variation in the stimulus-frequency ratio did not (slope $= 0.02$).

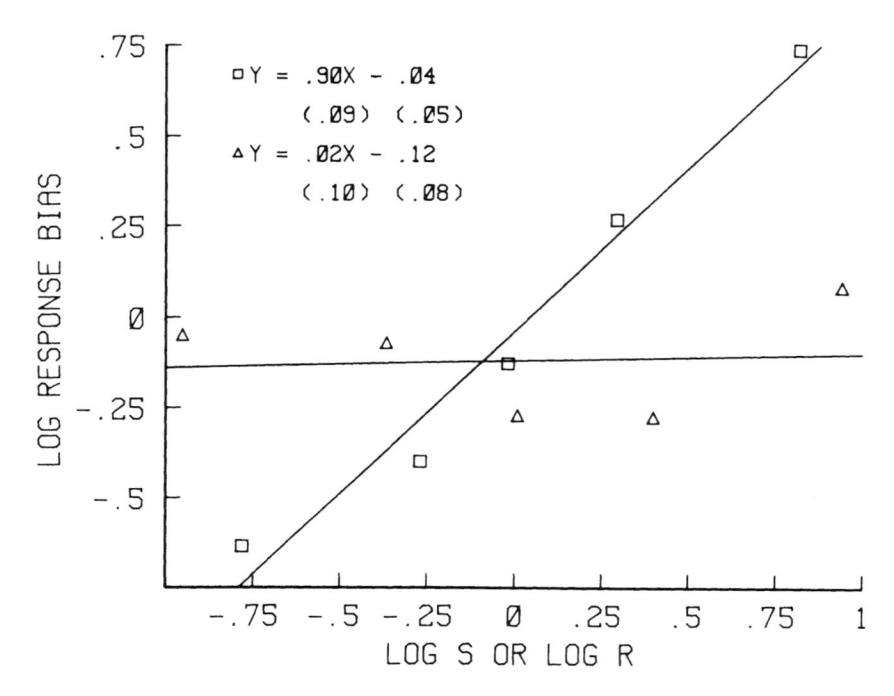

FIG. 11.11.   Group data reported by McCarthy and Davison (1979). Log response bias (Equation 11.8) is shown as a function either of the log obtained stimulus-frequency ratio (log S, triangles), or of the log obtained reinforcer-frequency ratio (log R, squares). The best-fitting straight lines by the method of least squares are shown, together with their equations and the standard deviations of the parameter estimates.

11.7b. Isobias and Alloiobias

Once relative reinforcer frequency, and not relative stimulus frequency, is identified as the effective biaser in detection experiments, it stands to reason that a constant measure of response bias (isobias) can be obtained only from a procedure that keeps fixed the obtained reinforcer-frequency ratio for correct detections. Such procedures were introduced into concurrent schedule research by Stubbs and Pliskoff (1969; Section 1.1c), and were subsequently used by Stubbs (1976) and McCarthy and Davison (1984) in detection experiments. In such a *controlled reinforcer-ratio* procedure (McCarthy & Davison, 1980a), changes in SPP or changes in the subject's preference cannot alter the relative distribution of reinforcers between the two choice alternatives. In other words, reinforcer-frequency bias is constant, and response bias (Equation 11.8) would be expected to be constant.

Figures 11.12 and 11.13 illustrate, in two different ways, the manner in which response bias may be affected by the controlled versus the uncontrolled scheduling of reinforcers for correct detections. The data are group means

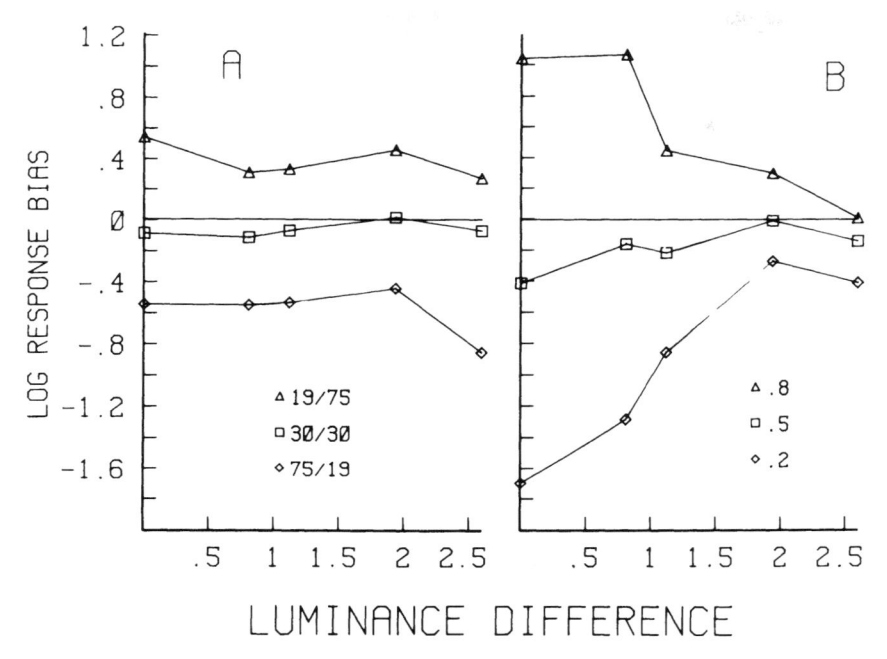

FIG. 11.12.   Group data reported by McCarthy and Davison (1984) for the controlled (Panel A) and the uncontrolled (Panel B) reinforcer-ratio procedures. Point estimates of response bias are plotted as a function of luminance difference (measured in cd/m²) for the three degrees of reinforcer-frequency bias. The parameters shown on the figures are the concurrent VI VI reinforcer-schedule values in A, and the probability of presenting the two stimuli in B. See text for further explanation.

reported by McCarthy and Davison (1984) from an experiment in which pigeons were trained to detect luminance differences. The luminance of S_1 was kept constant at 5.48 cd/m² and that of S_2 was varied from 2.88 to 5.48 cd/m². In order to investigate the relation between response bias, relative reinforcer frequency, and stimulus discriminability, McCarthy and Davison arranged three relative reinforcer frequencies (to produce three degrees of response bias) at each of five luminance differences. The biasing manipulations were carried out using two different reinforcer-scheduling procedures. In the first procedure, a controlled reinforcer-ratio procedure, correct side-key pecks were reinforced on concurrent VI VI schedules arranged dependently (Stubbs & Pliskoff, 1969), thus keeping the obtained relative reinforcer frequency constant at the three arranged levels across the luminance-difference changes. The second procedure was an uncontrolled reinforcer-ratio procedure, in which correct detections were reinforced on a single VI schedule, and bias was varied by arranging three different stimulus-presentation probabilities and hence, by covariation, differing reinforcer ratios for correct detections.

In both procedures, discriminability (log d; Equation 11.4) was monotonically related to luminance difference, and discriminability measures did not differ

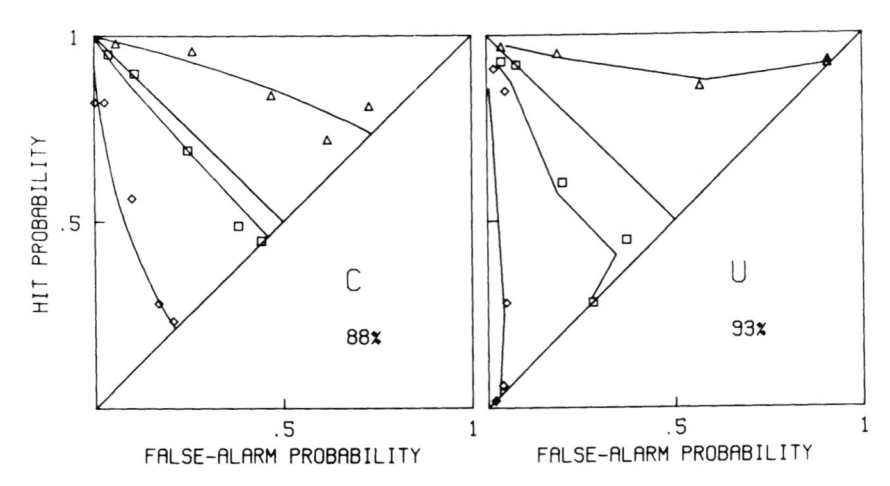

FIG. 11.13.   Group data reported by McCarthy and Davison (1984) showing the probability of a hit as a function of the probability of a false alarm for the data plotted in Fig. 11.12. The left-hand graph shows isobias functions predicted by Equation 11.8 for the controlled (C) reinforcer-ratio procedure. The right-hand graph shows alloiobias functions predicted by Equation 11.8 for the uncontrolled (U) reinforcer-ratio procedure. The percentage of data variance accounted for by Equation 11.8 is shown on each graph. Further explanation is given in the text.

significantly between the two reinforcer-scheduling procedures. Reinforcer-frequency bias remained constant in the controlled reinforcer-ratio procedure as discriminability decreased, as was arranged. However, in the uncontrolled reinforcer-ratio procedure, reinforcer bias became more extreme as discriminability decreased—that is, obtained reinforcer ratios were more extreme at lower than they were at higher discriminability levels.

Figure 11.12 shows the resultant changes in response bias. Panel A shows mean point estimates of response bias (Equation 11.8) for the controlled procedure across luminance differences. The horizontal line denotes zero response bias; points lying above this line denote a left-key bias, and points lying below denote a right-key bias.

It is clear from Fig. 11.12A that response bias remained constant at all luminance levels. The correlation between response bias and reinforcer bias was 0.94 (McCarthy & Davison, 1984). Thus, the controlled procedure generated isobias, or equal-bias, estimates across different discriminability levels. In the uncontrolled procedure (Panel B), response bias did not remain constant across discriminability levels. Irrespective of the (constant) SPP values, response bias was related to the obtained reinforcer-frequency ratio. That is, response bias was negligible at large luminance differences (high discriminability) and extreme at small or zero luminance differences (c.f., McCarthy, 1983). The mean correlation between response bias and reinforcer-frequency bias was 0.96. Thus, the uncontrolled procedure generated alloiobias, or changing-bias, estimates across different discriminability levels. These changes in response bias were due to the uncontrolled changes in the reinforcer-frequency ratio.

Figure 11.13 shows the same data as in Fig. 11.12 replotted on probability coordinates in the detection-theory unit square (ROC space). Here, the major diagonal represents zero discriminability and the minor diagonal represents zero bias. The plotted functions show the predictions of the Davison and Tustin (1978) model for both the controlled and uncontrolled procedures.

The functions shown in Fig. 11.13 were obtained by fitting Equation 11.8 to the data (in log-ratio form) using a structural-relations procedure (Isaac, 1970; see Section 5.2) that minimizes the error variance at $90°$ to the fitted line. This technique was used, as we explain in Section 5.2, because we must assume variance in both measures. Here, we make the additional assumption that, because the measures are similar in type, the variances are equal. In these fits, McCarthy and Davison (1984) reported mean a_r values of 0.85 and 0.71, and log c values of -0.08 and -0.17, for the controlled and uncontrolled procedures respectively. These parameter estimates were then used with the arranged reinforcer-frequency bias (controlled) or the obtained reinforcer-frequency bias (uncontrolled) to predict hit and false-alarm values in log-ratio form, and these were then converted to probabilities. Note that in the controlled procedure the reinforcer-frequency bias is treated as a constant, whereas in the uncontrolled procedure it is treated as a *variable*, in Equation 11.8.

Figure 11.13 shows that Equation 11.8 of the Davison and Tustin (1978) model described the resultant mean response-bias functions well (VAC = 88 percent and 93 percent, respectively, for the controlled and uncontrolled procedures). By contrast, the best-fitting SDT equal-β functions accounted for an average 58 percent and 69 percent of the data variance, respectively (McCarthy & Davison, 1984). In addition, Fig. 11.13 clearly shows how different response-bias functions were generated by different reinforcer-scheduling arrangements. In particular, the controlled reinforcer-ratio procedure gave *isobias* functions—that is, each data point on the function represents the same value of response bias for different levels of discriminability. By contrast, the uncontrolled reinforcer-ratio procedure generated *alloiobias* functions, with each data point on a function generating a different level of response bias for each level of discriminability.

11.8. THE FREE-OPERANT SIGNAL-DETECTION PROCEDURE

The standard discrete-trials detection paradigm outlined in Section 11.2 is a special case of a more general free-operant design, already mentioned in Section 8.7. In the free-operant design, two components of a multiple schedule, each associated with a discriminative stimulus, are arranged. Within each multiple-schedule component, a two-key concurrent schedule is in operation with, say, a VI schedule on one key and Extinction on the other. The key on which the VI schedule is arranged is, say, the left key in Component 1, and the right key in Component 2. This, of course, is a multiple concurrent VI Extinction concurrent Extinction VI schedule (see Section 9.1). The procedure just outlined is the free-operant analogue to the usual detection task with reinforcers available in the W and Z cells (Fig. 11.1). If the Extinction schedules are replaced with VI schedules, the task becomes an analogue of the signal-detection reinforcement-for-errors procedure (Davison & McCarthy, 1980; Logue, 1983; Section 11.6). The free-operant detection procedure allows many responses, rather than a single response, to be emitted on each stimulus presentation. Normally, by the way, we need to add a further contingency in the free-operant procedure that is absent in the discrete-trials procedure. It is that stimulus changes should occur after each reinforcer is delivered (the same stimulus might be re-presented) in order that subjects will not discriminate the components on the basis of reinforcer-rate differences rather than stimulus differences.

Since much of the work on the effects of reinforcers on behavior, and on the way in which environmental stimuli can control behavior, has been and is being done with free-operant, rather than discrete-trials, procedures, the ability to generalize behavioral detection theory to the free-operant case is highly important. If this can be done, then two benefits accrue: First, the area known as Stimulus Control will become amenable to quantitative analysis; and second, the functions of discriminative stimuli in both simple- and complex-schedule performance may also be quantified. In the next section we investigate how far this generalization has been advanced.

11.9. STIMULUS DISCRIMINABILITY IN FREE-OPERANT DETECTION

Discrimination, as usually measured in multiple schedules (e.g., the number or rate of responses emitted in one component divided by the total number or rate of responses) is a biased measure of stimulus control (McCarthy, Davison, & Jenkins, 1982). It is affected not only by stimulus differences, but also by other biasing factors such as reinforcer-rate, reinforcer-duration, and response-requirement differences between the components—that is, by all the nonsensory variables that affect behavior allocation on concurrent (Chapters 6 to 8) and on multiple (Chapter 9) schedules. In addition, the provision per se of reinforcers in one component, or a difference in the reinforcer rates in the two components, can sometimes provide unequivocal discriminative information to a subject. (Some of the most convincing data, showing how performance on mixed FR FR schedules can come under the discriminative control of reinforcer delivery, were reported by Ferster and Skinner, 1957).

The problems with the measurement of stimulus effects on multiple schedule performance can be seen most clearly by the application of the generalized matching law to multiple-schedule performance. Although there is no discriminative-stimulus term within the generalized matching law, a clear assumption exists that the alternative reinforcer sources are highly discriminable (Baum, 1979). Indeed, as we discuss in Section 8.7, Miller, Saunders, and Bourland (1980) demonstrated that the sensitivity of concurrent-schedule behavior allocation to reinforcer-frequency ratios decreased when the discriminability of the choice alternatives was decreased. They did not offer a model for this effect (but see Davison & Jenkins, 1985; Sections 6.1 & 8.7), though the value of a could be used as a measure of stimulus effect. However, this measure bears no clear relation to any of the more usual psychophysical measures.

McCarthy et al. (1982) suggested that the common ground between discrete-trials detection procedures and free-operant schedule-control experiments may be provided by the random-component multiple-concurrent schedule with components terminating in reinforcers, and subsequent components determined probabilistically (as described briefly earlier). The random sequence of components ending in reinforcers ensures that discrimination can be based only on the discriminative stimuli signaling the components. Further, the orthogonality of stimulus and reinforcer effects is provided by arranging the reinforcer schedule on one key in S_1, and on the other in S_2, with the alternate keys providing no reinforcers. McCarthy et al. used this procedure in an endeavor to provide the quantitative link between signal-detection, stimulus-control, and schedule-control research. They investigated whether absolute measures of discriminability obtained from free-operant multiple-concurrent schedule procedures were similar to those obtained from a typical discrete-trials procedure.

The random-component multiple-concurrent schedule used in Procedure A by McCarthy et al. (1982) arranged concurrent VI 60-s Extinction and concurrent Extinction VI 60-s schedules in the two multiple-schedule components. The components were signaled by two different luminances. The probability of presenting the stimuli, and hence the components, was varied from 0.1 to 0.9 in steps of 0.2. This procedure (McCarthy & Davison, 1979) varied the *number* of reinforcers obtained on the left and right keys during a session whereas the *rate* of reinforcers in the presence of the two stimuli (the component reinforcer rate) remained constant at about 1 per minute. Figure 11.14 shows point estimates of discriminability (obtained using Equation 11.4 with the group data) as a function of the obtained log reinforcer-frequency ratio. As expected, the discriminability of the component stimuli remained constant (mean log $d = 1.25$) as the log reinforcer-frequency ratio was varied.

McCarthy et al. (1982; Procedure C) then measured the discriminability of the same two light intensities using a standard discrete-trials detection procedure (Section 11.2). In this procedure, the discriminative stimuli were removed (following an observing response) before the choice keys were made available. The reinforcer-frequency ratio was again varied by changing the probability of stim-

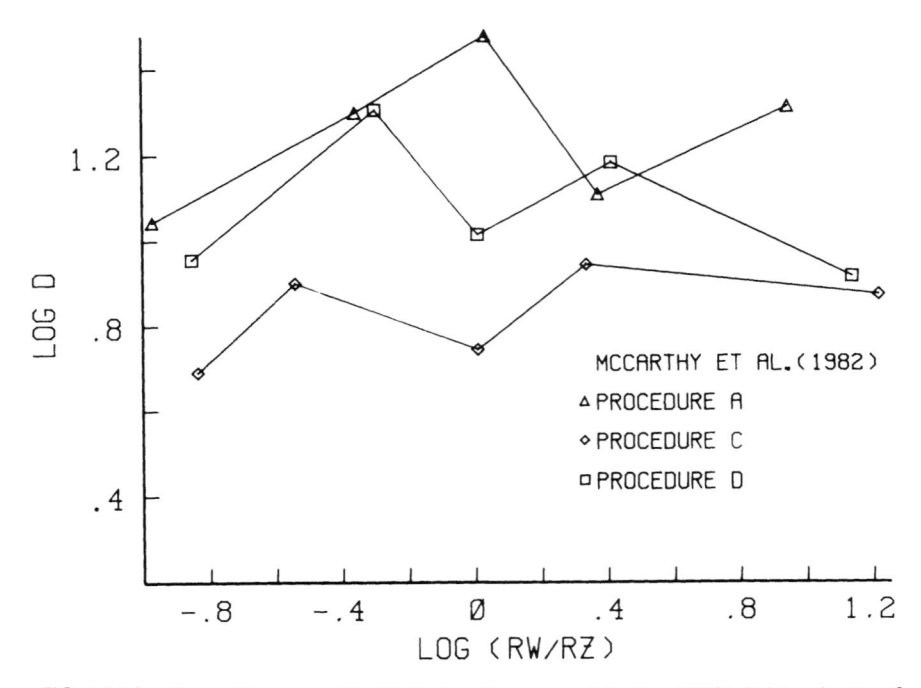

FIG. 11.14.   Group data reported by McCarthy, Davison, and Jenkins (1982). Point estimates of stimulus discriminability (log d, Equation 11.4) are plotted as a function of the logarithm of the obtained reinforcer-frequency ratio, log (R_w/R_z). For Procedure A, the schedules were multiple (concurrent VI 60 s Extinction) (concurrent Extinction VI 60 s). Procedure C used a discrete-trials signal-detection task in which the discriminative stimuli were removed prior to the presentation of the choice keys. Procedure D used a discrete-trials signal-detection task in which the choice was emitted in the presence of the discriminative stimuli.

ulus (hence, component) presentation. Discriminability estimates from this procedure are shown also in Fig. 11.14. Discriminability was significantly lower in the discrete-trials procedure than in the free-operant procedure (mean log $d = 0.83$ & 1.25 respectively). McCarthy et al. suggested that the decrement in discriminability in the discrete-trials task was caused by the small delay between stimulus offset and the choice-key response. To check on this explanation, they showed in Procedure D that when the discriminative stimuli remained on during the choice phase of the discrete-trials task, discriminability was not significantly different from that obtained in the free-operant procedure (Fig. 11.14). Thus, the free-operant and discrete-trials procedures gave the same measure of discriminability when the latter, like the former, provided stimulus information during the choice.

The results of McCarthy et al.'s (1982) experiment demonstrated that Davison and Tustin's (1978) behavioral detection model could usefully be applied to free-operant data. In particular, a measure of stimulus effects, independent of reinforcer effects, was now available for schedule-control research.

11.10   STIMULUS AND BIAS FUNCTIONS IN FREE-OPERANT DETECTION

The manipulation of component frequency is relatively unusual in the study of stimulus control on multiple-schedule performance. More common is the manipulation of the reinforcer rates in the presence of the discriminative stimuli (see, for example, Section 9.1). Thus, Davison, McCarthy, and Jensen (1985) attempted to extend McCarthy et al.'s (1982) findings to the effects of reinforcer-rate variations in multiple-concurrent free-operant detection procedures.

Davison et al. (1985) trained six pigeons on multiple (concurrent VI Extinction) (concurrent Extinction VI) schedules when the stimuli signalling the components were two different light intensities (Experiments 1a and 1b) and when the two intensities were identical (Experiments 2a and 2b). As in McCarthy et al.'s (1982) experiment, the components changed probabilistically after each reinforcer. In Experiments 1a and 2a, component-presentation probability was varied, and in Experiments 1b and 2b, component reinforcer rates were varied.

Figure 11.15 shows the group data analyzed according to the stimulus function (Equation 11.3) of Davison and Tustin's (1978) model. The measures used in the analysis were component response and reinforcer rates. In Fig. 11.15, discriminability (log d) is plotted either as a function of the logarithm of the component-presentation ratio (which equals the log ratio of the left-to-right reinforcer frequencies) in Experiments 1a and 2a, or as a function of the component reinforcer-rate ratio in Experiments 1b and 2b. Note here that Equation 11.3 shows the response measure only as a function of discriminability, not of reinforcer-number or -rate ratios. Hence, if log d is independent of the biasing effect of reinforcer-number or reinforcer-rate ratios, this measure should have a slope of zero when plotted as a function of the biaser. The intercept of such a function estimates discriminability.

Figure 11.15 shows that discriminability was high when the intensities signaling the components were different (log d was 0.92 and 1.09 for Experiments 1a and 1b respectively). When the luminances were equal, discriminability was very low (log d was -0.01 and 0.04, respectively, for Experiments 2a and 2b). In addition, discriminability measures did not change with changes in either biaser under either discriminabiilty level. This demonstrates the independence of the discriminability measure in free-operant procedures from reinforcer bias.

Figure 11.16 shows the group data plotted according to the bias function (Equation 11.8) of Davison and Tustin's (1978) model. As this figure shows, response bias, or the response allocation between the two choices, was more strongly affected by component reinforcer-rate variations than by component-probability variation when discriminability was high (a_r was 0.66 and 0.37, respectively, for Experiments 1b and 1a). However, the reverse situation was found when discriminability was low (a_r = 0.13 and 0.76, respectively, for

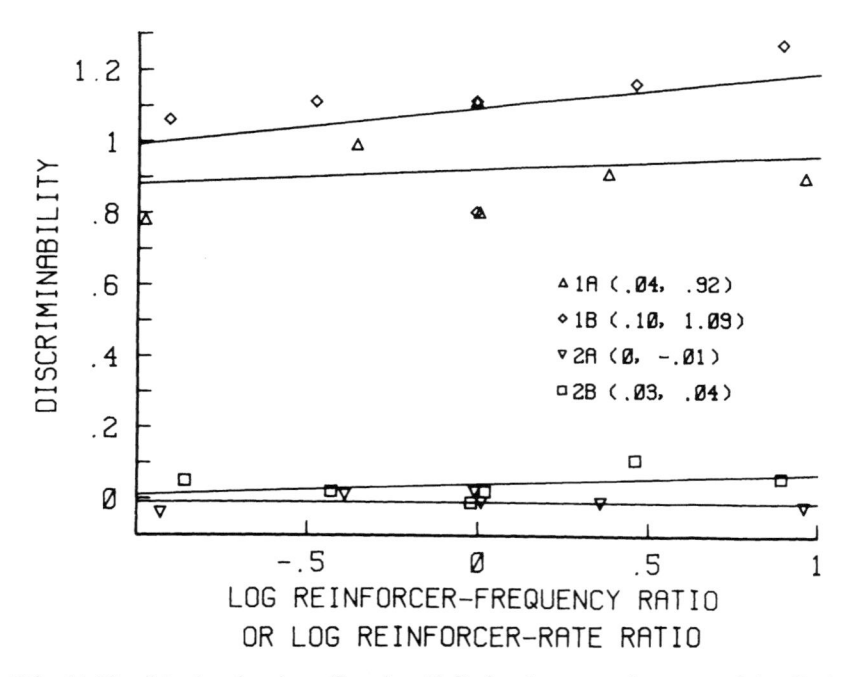

FIG. 11.15. Stimulus functions (Equation 11.3) for the group data reported by Davison, McCarthy, and Jensen (1985) when the component reinforcer-frequency ratio was varied at high (Experiment 1a) and low (Experiment 2a) discriminability, and also when the component reinforcer-rate ratio was varied at high (Experiment 1b) and low (Experiment 2b) discriminability. The best-fitting straight lines by the method of least squares are shown for each function, together with their slopes and intercepts (in parentheses).

Experiments 2b and 2a). As pointed out by Davison et al. (1985), the finding posed a difficulty for the generalization of the Davison and Tustin (1978) model to the free-operant paradigm. Any model of detection performance in free-operant multiple-concurrent schedules must describe the differences in reinforcer sensitivity with variations in discriminability seen in Fig. 11.16. In particular, as discriminability increases, a model of the left-right behavioral distribution must be progressively less affected by the sessional left-right reinforcer ratios, and progressively more affected by the left-right component reinforcer-rate ratios. The Davison-Tustin formulation (Equations 11.1 and 11.2) does not have these properties. Rather, their model assumes that reinforcer sensitivity, a_r, is constant across changes in discriminability, as has been shown to be the case in discrete-trial procedures (McCarthy & Davison, 1980b, 1984; Section 11.4). Collectively, the data presented in Figs. 11.15 and 11.16 suggest that, whereas the Davison-Tustin discriminability measure (log d) is accurate for free-operant detection procedures (McCarthy et al., 1982; Davison et al., 1985), the bias function of that model cannot be directly generalized to the free-operant paradigm.

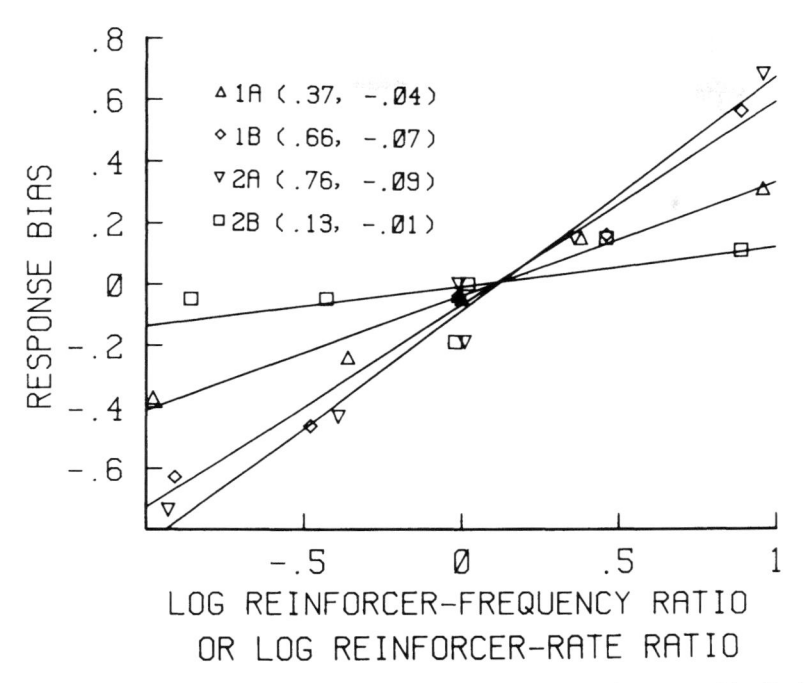

FIG. 11.16. Response-bias functions (Equation 11.8) for the group data reported by Davison, McCarthy, and Jensen (1985) when the component reinforcer-frequency ratio was varied at high (Experiment 1a) and low (Experiment 2a) discriminability, and when the component reinforcer-rate ratio was varied at high (Experiment 1b) and low (Experiment 2b) discriminability. The best-fitting straight lines by the method of least squares are shown for each function, together with their slopes and intercepts (in parentheses).

A model that does have the required properties, and that is a logical extension of Davison and Tustin's (1978) formulation, was proposed by Davison et al. (1985). This latter model explicitly uses reinforcer *rates* as the independent variable and differentiates between control by overall left-right reinforcer rates (at low discriminability) and control by component reinforcer rates (at high discriminability). The basic assumption of the model is that the apparent reinforcer rates in cells W and Z of the detection matrix (Fig. 11.1) can be expressed as:

$$R_w = \frac{dN_w}{dT_{s1} + T_{s2}},$$ (11.9)

and,

$$R_z = \frac{dN_z}{T_{s1} + dT_{s2}},$$ (11.10)

where d is the discriminability (in antilog form) of the stimuli. N_w and N_z are the numbers of reinforcers obtained in cells W and Z respectively, and T_{s1} and T_{s2} are the times spent in the presence of S_1 and S_2, respectively. Equation 11.9 tends toward N_w/T_{s1} (the component reinforcer rate) when discriminability is high, and it equals $N_w/T_{s1} + T_{s2})$ (the overall reinforcer rate) when discriminability is absent ($d = 1$). A similar logic can be applied to Equation 11.10. Thus, two equations may be written that are equivalent to Equations 11.1 and 11.2. In the presence of S_1:

$$\log\left(\frac{B_w}{B_x}\right) = a_r \log\left(\frac{N_w}{N_z} \cdot \frac{dT_{s2} + T_{s1}}{dT_{s1} + T_{s2}}\right) + \log d + \log c , \quad (11.11)$$

and in the presence of S_2:

$$\log\left(\frac{B_y}{B_z}\right) = a_r \log\left(\frac{N_w}{N_z} \cdot \frac{dT_{s2} + T_{s1}}{dT_{s1} + T_{s2}}\right) - \log d + \log c . \quad (11.12)$$

Subtracting Equation 11.12 from Equation 11.11 and assuming that the reinforcer sensitivities (a_r) are the same in S_1 and S_2 produces the stimulus function:

$$.5 \log\left(\frac{B_w \cdot B_z}{B_x \cdot B_y}\right) = \log d , \quad (11.13)$$

which is identical to the original Davison-Tustin expression (Equation 11.4). Equation 11.13 asserts that discriminability is independent of response bias in a free-operant detection procedure, as was found by McCarthy et al. (1982) and by Davison et al. (1985: Fig. 11.15).

The bias function is obtained by adding Equations 11.11 and 11.12, giving:

$$.5 \log\left(\frac{B_w \cdot B_y}{B_x \cdot B_z}\right) = a_r \log\left(\frac{N_w}{N_z} \cdot \frac{dT_{s2} + T_{s1}}{dT_{s1} + T_{s2}}\right) + \log c . \quad (11.14)$$

Equation 11.14 asserts that discriminability (d) will generally affect the measure of response bias. However, when the times spent in the presence of the discriminative stimuli are equal ($T_{s1} = T_{s2}$), Equation 11.15 reduces to the original Davison-Tustin expression (Equation 11.8), and asserts that variations in discriminability (d) will not affect reinforcer sensitivity (a_r).

When, as in Experiments 1b and 2b of Davison et al. (1985), the component reinforcer rates are varied with the overall left/right reinforcer frequencies equal, the model predicts that response bias will be sensitive to the times spent in the components, but to a degree that is dependent on the level of discriminability. When discriminability is high, the component-time ratio approaches the ratio T_{s2}/T_{s1}, which is proportional to N_w/N_z. When discriminability is low, the component-time ratio approaches unity. On the other hand, when the overall left/right reinforcer frequencies and times spent in the components are varied at high discriminability (Experiment 1a), the model predicts an attenuation of response bias. This is because the component-time measure will approach T_{s2}/T_{s1}, and increasing N_w will increase T_{s1}. When discriminability is low (Experiment 2a), however, the time ratio will tend to unity, and hence the sensitivity of choice to the ratio of the numbers of reinforcers will be high. Qualitatively, these are exactly the results found by Davison et al. as summarized in Fig. 11.16.

The model offered by Davison et al. (1985), Equations 11.11 and 11.12, for free-operant detection is a logical extension of Davison and Tustin's (1978) model for the situation in which reinforcers are distributed over time in the presence of discriminative stimuli. However, a major question still remains: Does the revised bias function (Equation 11.15) adequately describe behavior in discrete-trials detection procedures? As noted by Davison et al., the model may well be ambiguous when applied to the discrete-trials paradigm. In a multiple-concurrent schedule, the time spent in the presence of the discriminative stimuli, and the time spent choosing and obtaining reinforcers, are one and the same. Hence, T_{s1} and T_{s2} may be interpreted either as the times spent in the stimuli, or the times spent choosing. In discrete-trials detection studies, the time in the stimuli or the latencies of choices are not routinely measured (but see Terman & Terman, 1973). These measures are necessary for an adequate assessment of Equations 11.11 and 11.12 in the discrete-trials paradigm. It is possible, for example, that latencies of choice to a more frequently presented, or more frequently reinforced, stimulus will be shorter than those to the alternate stimulus (Terman, 1981). Such speculations will necessitate further research using the discrete-trials paradigm to test fully the generality of the free-operant detection model suggested by Davison et al.

11.11. IMPLICATIONS FOR STIMULUS-CONTROL RESEARCH

Stimulus-control research has generally not employed a procedure, such as the random-component multiple-concurrent schedule, in which stimulus and reinforcer effects are orthogonal. Rather, as noted in Section 11.9, procedures (such as multiple schedules) have been used in which stimulus differences and reinforcer differences may affect behavior in the same way. For multiple-schedule performance, the only measures that can be taken are measures of *discrimination* (not discriminability; see Section 11.6) to which both reinforcer and stimulus effects contribute. The interaction of stimuli and reinforcers in their effects on behavior is difficult to understand and to analyze if the behavioral measures computed are similarly affected by both independent variables. As Davison et al. (1985) suggested, the widespread use of procedures in which stimulus and reinforcer effects can be orthogonally measured would considerably clarify research into stimulus control.

12 FOR THE FUTURE

It seems probable that the empirical study of behavior allocation will continue, on the lines discussed here, for some time because many potential areas of research have as yet received only scant attention. The area, however, is due for reorganization. It was the major paradigm shift, formalized by Herrnstein (1970), that moved the study of behavior away from a consideration of absolute behavior toward the study of behavior in context. The new paradigm commenced with a series of empirical results (strict matching) that, when set in the context of prior learning theories, appeared simple and elegant. At that time, learning theories had become complex and diverse (see, for example, Volume 2 of Koch, 1959). Two factors ensured the acceptance of the new approach: at one level, the scientific reinforcer of parsimony; and at another level, the more prosaic reinforcers of simply being able to comprehend and teach the new approach. Strict matching ruled. But like any other new, clean, elegant paradigm, it has become complicated and diverse again. We are now faced with the generalized matching law. We are concerned about nonunit sensitivity and the environmental conditions that produce this, and we are troubled by the possibility that we might have to generalize to dual-sensitivity models (Davison, 1982; Prelec, 1984), and we have begun to wonder whether all log independent-variable ratios produce linear changes in log behavior ratios (e.g., delay of reinforcers and amount of reinforcers). The context of our research is now driving us toward another paradigm shift.

At present, it is unclear in which direction this shift might take us. Two major problems restrain us. The first is that any paradigm shift must take into account and organize a now extensive body of results—namely, those discussed in this book, and others that we have not touched. A new theory to describe nominal effects, and even ordinal changes, is perhaps not too difficult. But here is the second problem: It is the amount of *quantitative* data available. It is a joy to work in the experimental analysis of behavior allocation because of the tradition of researchers publishing their raw data for the perusal of others in the field. In no other area of Psychology could a book that contains extensive reanalyses of previously reported data be written. Any paradigm shift must, because of the nature of the area, be able to handle the available data at a quantitative level, rather than just a nominal or ordinal level. This will be no easy task. Although we have not discussed theories in any detail in this book, we believe that neither the molar maximizing nor the molecular maximizing, nor the melioration, approaches have been shown to describe adequately more than a small part of the available raw data. Other approaches, such as the contingency-discriminability approach, are too recent to be adequately assessed, although this approach, as demonstrated by Davison and Jenkins (1985), is in principle able to describe all results that had previously been described using the generalized matching law.

A paradigm shift will not affect the data that have been collected in this area, except possibly by asserting that the data are irrelevant. But it is hard to see how data on behavior allocation could be consigned to irrelevance, because the measures do capture an intuitively and practically relevant aspect of behavior. It is possible that a paradigm shift may view the data in a different way such that manipulations carried out in previous research are not manipulations of the relevant variables at all, or are manipulations over an insufficient range for the data to be useful. For instance, if local reinforcer rates are the important independent variable, then variations of relative reinforcer rates in concurrent schedules will simply provide little or no local reinforcer-rate variations.

In a more minor shift, part of the research area described here might remain intact. For instance, it might be shown (but it is doubtful) that multiple-schedule performances are qualitatively different from concurrent-schedule performances, and that each requires a radically different account. We would then, of course, await a further shift to reconcile the two accounts again. Another possibility might be that the generalized matching law power-function account is replaced by a contingency-discriminability account. In such a shift, the bias aspect of the signal-detection account (Chapter 11), which is based on generalized matching, would simply be replaced by the contingency-discriminability account (as suggested by Davison & Jenkins, 1985). The stimulus discriminability part of the detection account, which does not rest in any important way upon generalized matching, would remain unchanged. It is important in a minor shift that we reject no more of the original structure than is necessary.

It is equally possible that a shift may occur at a more procedural level. The findings that performance is sometimes different according to whether the experimental economy is open or closed (Hursh, 1980), or according to the length of the session (Chapter 9), may push us toward procedures that will help us gain such data and toward new theories that will account for those data. Also, the increasing use of customized feedback functions may lead us into areas of experimental space that could not be charted by conventional schedules. A particularly beautiful example of this is provided by Vaughan and Miller (1984), who designed an experiment using schedules in which reinforcer rates progressively decreased as response rates increased.

We make no predictions as to the nature of the next minor or major shift, and we even doubt that such a shift will be recognized when it occurs. But we do believe that shifts and paradigm modifications should be data driven, and hence we see the job of the laboratory researcher as gently and systematically testing the limits of generality of the current paradigm. An example here is the attempt to apply the generalized matching law to chain, and to concurrent-chain, schedule performances. The former application has yet to be adequately researched. The latter application has failed, but only in the sense that values of sensitivity and bias that we expected to be constant were found to be variable (Davison, 1983). These failures at the limits of generalization are extremely informative, and they provide precise pointers to parameter modifications—but *only* in the context of an already wide generality within the original boundaries. On its own, a knight's move in research away from an area of generality is of little interest if it fails. Such a result allows us to assert a point in an area at which generality does not apply, but it does not allow us to identify the boundary in multidimensional experimental space at which generality is lost. To do this, experimenters must backtrack in experimental space in order to complete the map. But if such a knight's move does find generality, we have gained a great deal at little cost. Whether an experimenter favors the quantum leap or the ambulatory perimeter excursion depends on the area under investigation and the sort of training the researcher has received, among many other variables. We rather favor the latter approach, but there can be no moral judgments here!

We do have a problem in nomenclature that needs resolution. A matching law seems to imply that a measure of a dependent variable equals—matches—a measure of the independent variable. Matching focuses on the equality. This state of affairs must surely be true for all quantitative approaches to any research area! Thus, the generalized matching law is a matching law, and so, for instance, is the contingency-discriminability approach. A maximizing approach, on the other hand, implies a dynamic process such that behavior changes until some dimension(s) of some environmental event(s), over some time window, is or are maximized or minimized. Maximization is descriptive of the assumed process. Matching, in one sense, is descriptive only of a mathematical relation, but in another sense it describes the process of a subject's behavior systematically changing until the equality between measures is achieved. The term "matching" has been used in both these, and other, senses, and this has led to some confusion. Timberlake (1982) reserved the term "matching theory" for Herrnstein's absolute response-rate equation (Equation 2.1). The same equation has also been variously termed the quantitative law of effect, the law of simple action, Herrnstein's equation, and Herrnstein's hyperbola. Further, anything that is a generalization of the matching law is a generalized matching law.

The problem really arises from the terms "matching" and "generalized" being rather too general and nonspecific, and as a result the meaning of the terms is woolly. Other problems occur with inconstant usage, across experimenters, of the term "undermatching." Again, a single experimental procedure may go by a number of different names (e.g., the Stubbs and Pliskoff procedure, dependent scheduling, forced-choice procedure, and interdependent scheduling). All this makes for difficulties in communication, but it does have one major benefit: It forces the reader to look not at the general description in a published report but at the Procedure section and the equations in detail. Perhaps, indeed, nominalism is quite out of place in a quantitative analysis of behavior—we should concentrate on algebraic models and procedural feedback functions. Names can be reserved to characterize general approaches, but even this would, we suspect, be an interim measure. On the other hand, in a developed and stable science, the nominal approach is unambiguous. For instance, we all know (or can find out) precisely what is meant by Hooke's Law, by Newton's First Law, and by the Laws of Motion.

This brings us to another problem. The use of the term "law," in the generalized matching law, evidently upsets a large number of people. The meaning of the word "law" has become considerably degraded from its original, absolute, meaning ("invariable sequence between certain conditions and phenomena"; *Pocket Oxford Dictionary*). Its use these days is consonant with the legal conception of "case law"—a body of empirical interpretations that have a certain consistency (or, "law as settled by precedent"; *Pocket Oxford Dictionary*). No one in his or her right mind would want to suggest that the matching law is an immutable law of nature. For a considerable period yet it will be subject to substantial revision, and even to outright rejection. So, whereas we might wish that the word "law" had not yet been used in this field of endeavor, it is probably too late to try to change current received usage.

A few words need to be said about styles of experimentation. We can, perhaps, define two end points of a dimension of research design and execution. One is exemplified by the *experimentum crucis*—the brief, elegant, experiment that makes or breaks (at least apparently) a theoretical position. These are not necessarily the same as the knights' moves discussed above. The difficulty here, as noted by Miller (1984), is in getting two or more theoretical positions to agree that a particular experiment is indeed crucial. A timely example is Vaughan and Miller's (1984) experiment, which appears to have crucially supported the response-strengthening (molar-matching) account over maximizing theories in which molar reinforcer rate is maximized, either alone or in a context of minimizing behavior output. We doubt whether maximization theorists will find the experiment crucial.

The other end of the dimension is the one- or two-dimensional parametric experiment that is a general test of an approach, or perhaps a test of the way in which a theory deals with the interaction of two independent variables, rather than a binary test of one approach versus another. While such an experiment is not crucial in the usual sense, it is an excellent vehicle for demonstrating either the adequacy or the inadequacy of a theoretical position. It frequently provides sufficient data to suggest an alternative approach. Such an experiment, if successful, can also considerably extend the generality of a theoretical account. It should be clear that we prefer the second, parametric, approach, though both types of experiment have their place. Indeed, it is noticeable that the crucial experiment has considerably more effect on the behavior of scientists than does the parametric experiment. The effect of such an experiment is sometimes so catastrophic that the behavior of scientists changes radically after its presentation, so much so that even aspects of a theory not assessed in that particular experiment are discarded. We find such wholesale rejection a little disquieting.

We also believe that we need to highlight some problems that occur at a more molecular level in parametric experimentation. In reviewing the literature on behavior allocation, we have frequently found incomplete independent-variable manipulations. For example, two subjects are taken through a complete independent-variable manipulation, and two or three other subjects are exposed, perhaps, to only two values of the independent variable. This kind of design makes it difficult to assess the consistency of the independent-dependent variable relation across subjects—for example, whether the relation is consistently linear or curvilinear. Such a design will provide two precise and two imprecise estimates of a parameter value. If the independent-dependent variable relation is known to be linear, then this set of estimates of the relation is perhaps satisfactory. But if the relation is not linear, or not known to be linear, then the data set is less useful, and progress will eventually demand a systematic, parametric, replication.

We know that carrying out complete parametric investigations is tedious. We also know that complete investigations are more difficult to publish than incomplete investigations, usually because the difficulties are made crystal-clear to reviewers by the extent of the data set. Davison's law operates here: ''The more data that are collected, the less will an experimenter understand those data''! We also believe that the crucial experimenter and the crucial experiment are more highly thought of than the parametric experimenter and the parametric experiment. The crucial experimenter is bright and incisive, the parametric experimenter dull and plodding. But in a quantitative science of behavior such as ours, which is data based and data driven, we belive that the contribution of the latter is, if anything, greater than that of the former. Where are the incisive experiments of the Learning Theorists of the 1940s now?

The study of behavior allocation has come a long way since psychologists first noted quantitative regularities in concurrent- and multiple-schedule data. We believe that there is a long and exciting path still to follow. The adventure is that we do not know where the path might lead.

REFERENCES

Ainslie, G.W. (1974). Impulse control in pigeons. *Journal of the Experimental Analysis of Behavior, 21*, 485-489.

Ainslie, G.W. (1975). Specious reward: A behavioral theory of impulsiveness and impulse control. *Psychological Bulletin, 82*, 463-496.

Akaike, H. (1969). Fitting autoregressive models for prediction. *Annals of the Institute of Statistical Mathematics, 21*, 243-247.

Akaike, H. (1974). A new look at statistical model identification. *IEEE Transactions on Automatic Control, 19*, 716-722.

Allen, C.M. (1981). On the exponent in the "generalized" matching equation. *Journal of the Experimental Analysis of Behavior, 35*, 125-127.

Alsop, B., & Davison, M. (1986). Preference for multiple versus mixed schedules of reinforcement. *Journal of the Experimental Analysis of Behavior, 45*, 33-45.

Anderson, N.H. (1978). Measurement of motivation and incentive. *Behavior Research Methods & Instrumentation, 10*, 360-375.

Autor, S.M. (1960). The strength of conditioned reinforcers as a function of frequency and probability of reinforcement. Unpublished Doctoral Dissertation, Harvard University, 1960. Reprinted in Hendry, D.P. (1969). *Conditioned reinforcement* (pp. 127-162). Homewood, IL: The Dorsey Press.

Bacotti, A.V. (1977). Matching under concurrent fixed-ratio variable-interval schedules of food presentation. *Journal of the Experimental Analysis of Behavior, 25*, 171-182.

Barron, B., & Davison, M.C. (1972). Performance on multiple fixed-interval schedules. *Journal of the Experimental Analysis of Behavior, 17*, 375-379.

Baum, W.M. (1972). Choice in a continuous procedure. *Psychonomic Science, 28*, 263-265.

Baum, W.M. (1973). Time allocation and negative reinforcement. *Journal of the Experimental Analysis of Behavior, 20*, 313-322.

Baum, W.M. (1974a). On two types of deviation from the matching law: Bias and undermatching. *Journal of the Experimental Analysis of Behavior, 22,* 231-242.

Baum, W.M. (1974b). Choice in free-ranging wild pigeons. *Science, 185,* 78-79.

Baum, W.M. (1974c). Chained concurrent schedules: Reinforcement as situation transition. *Journal of the Experimental Analysis of Behavior, 22,* 91-101.

Baum, W.M. (1976). Time-based and count-based measurement of preference. *Journal of the Experimental Analysis of Behavior, 26,* 27-35.

Baum, W.M. (1979). Matching, undermatching and overmatching in studies of choice. *Journal of the Experimental Analysis of Behavior, 32,* 269-281.

Baum, W.M. (1982). Choice, changeover, and travel. *Journal of the Experimental Analysis of Behavior, 38,* 35-49.

Baum, W.M. (1983). Matching, statistics, and common sense. *Journal of the Experimental Analysis of Behavior, 39,* 499-501.

Baum, W.M., & Rachlin, H.C. (1969). Choice as time allocation. *Journal of the Experimental Analysis of Behavior, 12,* 861-874.

Bauman, R.A., Shull, R.L., & Brownstein, A.J. (1975). Time allocation on concurrent schedules with asymmetrical response requirements. *Journal of the Experimental Analysis of Behavior, 24,* 53-57.

Beautrais, P.G., & Davison, M.C. (1977). Response and time allocation in concurrent second-order schedules. *Journal of the Experimental Analysis of Behavior, 25,* 61-69.

Blough, D., & Blough, P. (1977). Animal psychophysics. In W.K. Honig & J.E.R. Staddon (Eds.), *Handbook of Operant Behavior* (pp. 514-539). Englewood Cliffs, NJ: Prentice Hall.

Boelens, H., & Kop, P.F.M. (1983). Concurrent schedules: Spatial separation of response alternatives. *Journal of the Experimental Analysis of Behavior, 40,* 35-45.

Boldero, J., Davison, M., & McCarthy, D. (1985). Reinforcer frequency and reinforcer magnitude as biasers of signal detection. *Behavioural Processes, 10,* 131-143.

Bouzas, A., & Baum, W.M. (1976). Behavioral contrast of time allocation. *Journal of the Experimental Analysis of Behavior, 25,* 179-184.

Bradley, J.V. (1968). *Distribution-free statistical tests.* Englewood Cliffs, NJ: Prentice Hall.

Bradshaw, C.M., Szabadi, E., & Bevan, P. (1976). Behavior of humans in variable-interval schedules of reinforcement. *Journal of the Experimental Analysis of Behavior, 26,* 135-141.

Bradshaw, C.M., Szabadi, E., & Bevan, P. (1977). Effect of punishment on human variable-interval performance. *Journal of the Experimental Analysis of Behavior, 27,* 275-279.

Bradshaw, C.M., Szabadi, E., & Bevan, P. (1978). Effects of variable-interval punishment on the behavior of humans in variable-interval schedules of monetary reinforcement. *Journal of the Experimental Analysis of Behavior, 29,* 161-166.

Bradshaw, C.M., Szabadi, E., & Bevan, P. (1979). The effect of punishment on free-operant choice behavior in humans. *Journal of the Experimental Analysis of Behavior, 31,* 71-81.

Brethower, D.M., & Reynolds, G.S. (1962). A facilitative effect of punishment on unpunished behavior. *Journal of the Experimental Analysis of Behavior, 5,* 191-199.

Brinker, R.P., & Treadway, J.T. (1975). Preference and discrimination between response-dependent and response-independent schedules of reinforcement. *Journal of the Experimental Analysis of Behavior, 24*, 73-77.

Brownstein, A.J. (1971). Concurrent schedules of response-independent reinforcement: Duration of a reinforcing stimulus. *Journal of the Experimental Analysis of Behavior, 15*, 211-214.

Brownstein, A.J., & Pliskoff, S.S. (1968). Some effects of relative reinforcement rate and changeover delay in response-independent concurrent schedules of reinforcement. *Journal of the Experimental Analysis of Behavior, 11*, 683-688.

Catania, A.C. (1962). Independence of concurrent responding maintained by interval schedules of reinforcement. *Journal of the Experimental Analysis of Behavior, 5*, 175-184.

Catania, A.C. (1963a). Concurrent performances: Reinforcement interaction and response independence. *Journal of the Experimental Analysis of Behavior, 6*, 253-263.

Catania, A.C. (1963b). Concurrent performances: A baseline for the study of reinforcement magnitude. *Journal of the Experimental Analysis of Behavior, 6*, 299-300.

Catania, A.C. (1966). Concurrent operants. In W.K. Honig (Ed.), *Operant behavior: Areas of research and application* (pp. 213-270). NY: Appleton-Century-Crofts.

Catania, A.C. (1975). Freedom and knowledge: An experimental analysis of preference in pigeons. *Journal of the Experimental Analysis of Behavior, 24*, 89-106.

Catania, A.C. (1980). Freedom of choice: A behavioral analysis. In G.H. Bower (Ed.), *The psychology of learning and motivation* (Vol. 14). NY: Academic Press.

Catania, A.C. & Cutts, D. (1963). Experimental control of superstitious responding in humans. *Journal of the Experimental Analysis of Behavior, 6*, 203-208.

Catania, A.C., & Reynolds, G.S. (1968). A quantitative analysis of the responding maintained by interval schedules of reinforcement. *Journal of the Experimental Analysis of Behavior, 11*, 327-383.

Catania, A.C., & Sagvolden, T. (1980). Preference for free choice over forced choice in pigeons. *Journal of the Experimental Analysis of Behavior, 34*, 77-86.

Charman, L., & Davison, M. (1982). On the effects of component durations and component reinforcement rates in multiple schedules. *Journal of the Experimental Analysis of Behavior, 37*, 417-439.

Charman, L., & Davison, M. (1983a). On the effects of food deprivation and component reinforcer rates on multiple-schedule performance. *Journal of the Experimental Analysis of Behavior, 40*, 239-251.

Charman, L., & Davison, M. (1983b). Undermatching and stimulus discrimination in multiple schedules. *Behaviour Analysis Letters, 3*, 77-84.

Chung, S.-H. (1965a). Effects of delayed reinforcement in a concurrent situation. *Journal of the Experimental Analysis of Behavior, 8*, 439-444.

Chung, S.-H. (1965b). Effects of effort on response rate. *Journal of the Experimental Analysis of Behavior, 8*, 1-7.

Chung, S.-H., & Herrnstein, R.J. (1967). Choice and delay of reinforcement. *Journal of the Experimental Analysis of Behavior, 10*, 67-74.

Clopton, B.M. (1972). Detection of increments in noise by monkeys. *Journal of the Experimental Analysis of Behavior, 17*, 473-481.

Cohen, I.L. (1973). A note on Herrnstein's equation. *Journal of the Experimental Analysis of Behavior, 19*, 527-528.

Cohen, S.L. (1975). Concurrent second-order schedules of reinforcement. *Journal of the Experimental Analysis of Behavior, 24*, 333-341.

Commons, M.L., Herrnstein, R.J., & Rachlin, H. (1982) (Eds.). *Quantitative Analyses of Behavior, Vol. II: Matching and Maximizing Accounts*. Cambridge, MA: Ballinger.

Coombs, C.H. (1964). *A theory of data*. NY: Wiley.

Davison, M.C. (1968). Reinforcement rate and immediacy of reinforcement as factors in choice. *Psychonomic Science, 10*, 181-182.

Davison, M.C. (1969). Preference for mixed-interval versus fixed-interval schedules. *Journal of the Experimental Analysis of Behavior, 12*, 247-252.

Davison, M. (1972). Preference for mixed-interval versus fixed-interval schedules: Number of component intervals. *Journal of the Experimental Analysis of Behavior, 17*, 169-176.

Davison, M. (1974). A functional analysis of chained fixed-interval schedule performance. *Journal of the Experimental Analysis of Behavior, 21*, 323-330.

Davison, M.C. (1976). Preference for fixed-interval schedules: Effects of unequal initial-link length. *Journal of the Experimental Analysis of Behavior, 25*, 371-376.

Davison, M. (1982). Performance in concurrent variable-interval fixed-ratio schedules. *Journal of the Experimental Analysis of Behavior, 37*, 81-96.

Davison, M. (1983). Bias and sensitivity to reinforcement in a concurrent-chain schedule. *Journal of the Experimental Analysis of Behavior, 40*, 15-34.

Davison, M. (1987). The analysis of concurrent-chain performance. In M.L. Commons, J.E. Mazur, J.A. Nevin, & H. Rachlin (Eds.), *Quantitative analyses of behavior, Vol. V: Effects of delay and of intervening events on reinforcement value* (pp. 225-244). Hillsdale, NJ: Erlbaum.

Davison, M., & Ferguson, A. (1978). The effects of different component response requirements in multiple and concurrent schedules. *Journal of the Experimental Analysis of Behavior, 29*, 283-295.

Davison, M., & Hogsden, I. (1984). Concurrent variable-interval schedule performance: Fixed versus mixed reinforcer durations. *Journal of the Experimental Analysis of Behavior, 41*, 169-182.

Davison, M.C., & Hunter, I.W. (1976). Performance on variable-interval schedules arranged singly and concurrently. *Journal of the Experimental Analysis of Behavior, 25*, 335-345.

Davison, M.C., & Hunter, I.W. (1979). Concurrent schedules: Undermatching and control by previous experimental conditions. *Journal of the Experimental Analysis of Behavior, 32*, 233-244.

Davison, M., & Jenkins, P.E. (1985). Stimulus discriminability, contingency discriminability, and schedule performance. *Animal Learning and Behavior, 13*, 77-84.

Davison, M., & McCarthy, D. (1980). Reinforcement for errors in a signal-detection procedure. *Journal of the Experimental Analysis of Behavior, 34*, 35-47.

Davison, M., & McCarthy, D. (1981). Undermatching and structural relations. *Behaviour Analysis Letters, 1*, 67-72.

Davison, M., McCarthy, D., & Jensen, C. (1985). Component probability and component reinforcer rate as biasers of free-operant detection. *Journal of the Experimental Analysis of Behavior, 44,* 103-120.

Davison, M., & Smith, C. (1986). Some aspects of preference between immediate and delayed periods of reinforcement. *Journal of Experimental Psychology: Animal Behavior Processes, 12,* 291-300.

Davison, M.C., & Temple, W. (1973). Preference for fixed-interval schedules: An alternative model. *Journal of the Experimental Analysis of Behavior, 20,* 393-403.

Davison, M.C., & Temple, W. (1974). Preference for fixed-interval terminal links in a three-key concurrent-chain schedule. *Journal of the Experimental Analysis of Behavior, 22,* 11-19.

Davison, M.C., & Tustin, R.D. (1978). The relation between the generalized matching law and signal-detection theory. *Journal of the Experimental Analysis of Behavior, 29,* 331-336.

Deluty, M.Z. (1976). Choice and the rate of punishment in concurrent schedules. *Journal of the Experimental Analysis of Behavior, 25,* 75-80.

Deluty, M.Z., & Church, R.M. (1978). Time-allocation matching between punishing situations. *Journal of the Experimental Analysis of Behavior, 29,* 191-198.

de Villiers, P.A. (1972). Reinforcement and response-rate interaction in multiple random-interval avoidance schedules. *Journal of the Experimental Analysis of Behavior, 18,* 499-507.

de Villiers, P.A. (1974). The law of effect and avoidance: A quantitative relationship between response rate and shock-frequency reduction. *Journal of the Experimental Analysis of Behavior, 21,* 223-235.

de Villiers, P.A. (1977). Choice in concurrent schedules and a quantitative formulation of the law of effect. In W.K. Honig & J.E.R. Staddon (Eds.), *Handbook of operant behavior* (pp. 233-287). Englewood Cliffs, NJ: Prentice-Hall.

de Villiers, P.A. (1980). Toward a quantitative theory of punishment. *Journal of the Experimental Analysis of Behavior, 33,* 15-25.

de Villiers, P.A. (1982). Toward a quantitative theory of punishment. In M.L. Commons, R.J. Herrnstein, & H. Rachlin (Eds.), *Quantitative analyses of behavior. Vol. II: Matching and maximizing accounts.*(pp. 327-344). Cambridge, MA: Ballinger.

de Villiers, P.A., & Herrnstein, R.J. (1976). Toward a law of response strength. *Psychological Bulletin, 83,* 1131-1153.

Dowd, J.E., & Riggs, D.S. (1965). A comparison of estimates of Michaelis-Menten kinetic constants from various linear transformations. *The Journal of Biological Chemistry, 240,* 863-869.

Dreyfus, L.R., Dorman, L.G., Fetterman, J.G., & Stubbs, D.A. (1982). An invariant relation between changing over and reinforcement. *Journal of the Experimental Analysis of Behavior, 38,* 327-338.

Duncan, B., & Fantino, E. (1970). Choice for periodic schedules of reinforcement. *Journal of the Experimental Analysis of Behavior, 14,* 73-86.

Duncan, B., & Fantino, E. (1972). The Psychological distance to reward. *Journal of the Experimental Analysis of Behavior, 18,* 23-34.

Dusoir, T. (1983). Isobias curves in some detection tasks. *Perception and Psychophysics, 33,* 403-412.

Edmon, E.L. (1978). Multiple-schedule component duration: A reanalysis of Shimp and

Wheatley (1971) and Todorov (1972). *Journal of the Experimental Analysis of Behavior*, *30*, 239-241.

Elliffe, D., & Davison, M. (1985). Performance in continuously available multiple schedules. *Journal of the Experimental Analysis of Behavior 44*, 343-353.

Elsmore, T.F. (1972). Duration discrimination: Effects of probability of stimulus presentation. *Journal of the Experimental Analysis of Behavior*, *18*, 465-469.

Epstein, R. (1981). Amount consumed as a function of magazine-cycle duration. *Behaviour Analysis Letters*, *1*, 63-66.

Estes, W.K. (1969). Outline of a theory of punishment. In B. Campbell & R.M. Church (Eds.), *Punishment and aversive behavior*. (pp. 57-82). Englewood Cliffs, NJ: Prentice-Hall.

Fantino, E. (1967). Preference for mixed- versus fixed-ratio schedules. *Journal of the Experimental Analysis of Behavior*, *10*, 35-43.

Fantino, E. (1968). Effects of required rates of responding upon choice. *Journal of the Experimental Analysis of Behavior*, *11*, 15-22.

Fantino, E. (1969). Choice and rate of reinforcement. *Journal of the Experimental Analysis of Behavior*, *12*, 723-730.

Fantino, E., & Davison, M. (1983). Choice: Some quantitative relations. *Journal of the Experimental Analysis of Behavior*, *40*, 1-13.

Fantino, E., & Dunn, R. (1983). The delay-reduction hypothesis: Extension to three-alternative choice. *Journal of Experimental Psychology: Animal Behavior Processes*, *9*, 132-146.

Fantino, E., & Moore, J. (1980). Uncertainty reduction, conditioned reinforcement, and observing. *Journal of the Experimental Analysis of Behavior*, *33*, 3-13.

Fantino, E., & Navarick, D. (1974). Recent developments in choice. In G.H. Bower (Ed.), *The psychology of learning and motivation* (Vol. 8) (pp. 147-185). NY: Academic Press.

Fantino, E., Squires, N., Delbrück, N., & Peterson, C. (1972). Choice behavior and the accessibility of the reinforcer. *Journal of the Experimental Analysis of Behavior*, *18*, 35-43.

Farley, J. (1980). Reinforcement and punishment effects in concurrent schedules: A test of two models. *Journal of the Experimental Analysis of Behavior*, *33*, 311-326.

Farley, J., & Fantino, E. (1978). The symmetrical law of effect and the matching relation in choice behavior. *Journal of the Experimental Analysis of Behavior*, *29*, 37-60.

Felton, M., & Lyon, D.O. (1966). The post-reinforcement pause. *Journal of the Experimental Analysis of Behavior*, *9*, 131-134.

Ferguson, G.A. (1965). *Nonparametric trend analysis*. Montreal: McGill University Press.

Ferster, C.B., & Skinner, B.F. (1957). *Schedules of reinforcement*. NY: Appleton-Century-Crofts.

Findley, J.D. (1958). Preference and switching under concurrent scheduling. *Journal of the Experimental Analysis of Behavior*, *1*, 123-144.

Galanter, E., & Holman, G.L. (1967). Some invariances of the isosensitivity function and their implications for the utility function of money. *Journal of Experimental Psychology*, *73*, 333-339.

Gentry, G.D., & Marr, M.J. (1980). Choice and reinforcement delay. *Journal of the Experimental Analysis of Behavior*, *33*, 27-37.

Green, D.M. & McGill, W.J. (1970). On the equivalence of detection probabilities and well-known statistical quantities. *Psychological Review*, 77, 294-301.

Green, D.M. & Swets, J.A. (1974). *Signal detection theory and psychophysics*. NY: Wiley.

Green, L., & Snyderman, M. (1980). Choice between rewards differing in amount and delay: Toward a choice model of self control. *Journal of the Experimental Analysis of Behavior*, *34*, 135-147.

Grier, J.B. (1971). Nonparametric indices for sensitivity and bias: Computing formulas. *Psychological Bulletin*, *75*, 424-429.

Hack, M.H. (1963). Signal detection in the rat. *Science*, *139*, 758-759.

Hardy, G.A., Littlewood, J.E., & Polya, G. (1959). *Inequalities*. Cambridge, UK: Cambridge University Press.

Harnett, P., McCarthy, D., & Davison, M. (1984). Delayed signal detection, differential reinforcement, and short-term memory in the pigeon. *Journal of the Experimental Analysis of Behavior*, *42*, 87-111.

Hayes, S.C., Kapust, J., Leonard, S.R., & Rosenfarb, I. (1981). Escape from freedom: Choosing not to choose in pigeons. *Journal of the Experimental Analysis of Behavior*, *36*, 1-7.

Herrnstein, R.J. (1958). Some factors influencing behavior in a two-response situation. *Transactions of the New York Academy of Sciences*, *21*, 35-45.

Herrnstein, R.J. (1961). Relative and absolute strength of response as a function of frequency of reinforcement. *Journal of the Experimental Analysis of Behavior*, *4*, 267-272.

Herrnstein, R.J. (1964a). Secondary reinforcement and rate of primary reinforcement. *Journal of the Experimental Analysis of Behavior*, *7*, 27-36.

Herrnstein, R.J. (1964b). Aperiodicity as a factor in choice. *Journal of the Experimental Analysis of Behavior*, *7*, 179-182.

Herrnstein, R.J. (1966). Superstition: A corollary of the principles of operant conditioning. In W.K. Honig (Ed.), *Operant behavior: Areas of research and application* (pp. 33-51). NY: Appleton-Century-Crofts.

Herrnstein, R.J. (1970). On the law of effect. *Journal of the Experimental Analysis of Behavior*, *13*, 243-266.

Herrnstein, R.J. (1974). Formal properties of the matching law. *Journal of the Experimental Analysis of Behavior*, *21*, 159-164.

Herrnstein, R.J. (1979). Derivatives of matching. *Psychological Review*, *86*, 486-495.

Herrnstein, R.J. (1982). Melioration as behavioral dynamism. In M.L. Commons, R.J. Herrnstein, & H. Rachlin (Eds.), *Quantitative analyses of behavior, Vol. II: Matching and maximizing accounts* (pp. 433-458). Cambridge, MA: Ballinger.

Herrnstein, R.J., & Heyman, G.M. (1979). Is matching compatible with reinforcement maximization on concurrent variable interval, variable ratio? *Journal of the Experimental Analysis of Behavior*, *31*, 209-223.

Herrnstein, R.J., & Loveland, D.H. (1974). Hunger and contrast in multiple schedules. *Journal of the Experimental Analysis of Behavior*, *21*, 511-517.

Herrnstein, R.J., & Loveland, D.H. (1975). Maximizing and matching on concurrent ratio schedules. *Journal of the Experimental Analysis of Behavior, 24*, 107-116.

Herrnstein, R.J., & Vaughan, W., Jr. (1980). Melioration and behavioral allocation. In J.E.R. Staddon (Ed.), *Limits to action*. NY: Academic Press.

Heyman, G.M. (1979). A Markov model description of changeover probabilities on concurrent variable-interval schedules. *Journal of the Experimental Analysis of Behavior, 31*, 41-51.

Hineline, P.N. (1970). Negative reinforcement without shock reduction. *Journal of the Experimental Analysis of Behavior, 14*, 259-268.

Hinson, J.M., & Staddon, J.E.R. (1978). Behavioral competition: A mechanism for schedule interactions. *Science, 202*, 432-434.

Hobson, S.L. (1975). Discriminability of fixed-ratio schedules for pigeons: Effects of absolute ratio size. *Journal of the Experimental Analysis of Behavior, 23*, 25-35.

Hobson, S.L. (1978). Discriminability of fixed-ratio schedules for pigeons: Effects of payoff value. *Journal of the Experimental Analysis of Behavior, 30*, 69-81.

Hodos, W., & Bonbright, J.C., Jr. (1972). The detection of visual intensity differences by pigeons. *Journal of the Experimental Analysis of Behavior, 18*, 471-479.

Hollander, M., & Wolfe, D.A. (1973). *Nonparametric statistical methods*. NY: Wiley.

Hollard, V., & Davison, M.C. (1971). Preference for qualitatively different reinforcers. *Journal of the Experimental Analysis of Behavior, 16*, 375-380.

Hollard, V., & Davison, M.C. (1978). Histological data: Hollard and Davison (1971). *Journal of the Experimental Analysis of Behavior, 29*, 149.

Holz, W.C. (1968). Punishment and rate of positive reinforcement. *Journal of the Experimental Analysis of Behavior, 11*, 285-292.

Hume, A.L. (1974a). Auditory detection and optimal response biases. *Perception and Psychophysics, 15*, 425-433.

Hume, A.L. (1974b). Optimal response biases and the slope of ROC curves as a function of signal intensity, signal probability, and relative payoff. *Perception and Psychophysics, 16*, 377-384.

Hume, A.L., & Irwin, R.J. (1974). Bias functions and operating characteristics of rats discriminating auditory stimuli. *Journal of the Experimental Analysis of Behavior, 21*, 285-295.

Hunter, I.W., & Davison, M.C. (1978). Response rate and changeover performance on concurrent variable-interval schedules. *Journal of the Experimental Analysis of Behavior, 29*, 535-556.

Hunter, I., & Davison, M. (1982). Independence of response force and reinforcement rate on concurrent variable-interval schedule performance. *Journal of the Experimental Analysis of Behavior, 37*, 183-197.

Hunter, I.I., & Davison, M. (1985). Determination of a behavioral transfer function: White noise analysis of session-to-session response-ratio dynamics on concurrent VI VI schedules. *Journal of the Experimental Analysis of Behavior 43*, 43-59.

Hursh, S.R. (1980). Economic concepts for the analysis of behavior. *Journal of the Experimental Analysis of Behavior, 34*, 219-238.

Hursh, S.R., & Fantino, E. (1973). Relative delay of reinforcement and choice. *Journal of the Experimental Analysis of Behavior, 19*, 437-450.

Isaac, P.D. (1970). Linear regression, structural relations and measurement error. *Psychological Bulletin, 74*, 213-218.

Ito, M., & Asaki, K. (1982). Choice behavior of rats in a concurrent-chains schedule: Amount and delay of reinforcement. *Journal of the Experimental Analysis of Behavior, 37*, 383-392.

Jeffress, L.A. (1964). Stimulus-orientated approach to detection. *Journal of the Acoustical Society of America, 36*, 766-774.

Jeffress, L.A. (1967). Stimulus-orientated approach to detection reexamined. *Journal of the Acoustical Society of America, 41*, 480-488.

Jeffress, L.A. (1968). Mathematical and electrical models of auditory detection. *Journal of the Acoustical Society of America, 44*, 187-203.

Keller, J.V., & Gollub, L.R. (1977). Duration and rate of reinforcement as determinants of concurrent responding. *Journal of the Experimental Analysis of Behavior, 28*, 145-153.

Kendall, M.C. & Stuart, A. (1977). *The advanced theory of statistics* (4th ed.). London: Griffin.

Killeen, P. (1968a). On the measurement of reinforcement frequency in the study of preference. *Journal of the Experimental Analysis of Behavior, 11*, 263-269.

Killeen, P. (1968b). Response rate as a factor in choice. *Psychonomic Science, 12*, 34.

Killeen, P. (1970). Preference for fixed-interval schedules of reinforcement. *Journal of the Experimental Analysis of Behavior, 14*, 127-131.

Killeen, P. (1972a). The matching law. *Journal of the Experimental Analysis of Behavior, 17*, 489-495.

Killeen, P. (1972b). A yoked-chamber comparison of concurrent and multiple schedules. *Journal of the Experimental Analysis of Behavior, 18*, 13-22.

Killeen, P.R. (1977). Superstition: A matter of bias, not detectability. *Science, 199*, 88-89.

Killeen, P. (1978). Stability criteria. *Journal of the Experimental Analysis of Behavior, 29*, 17-25.

Killeen, P.R. (1981). Learning as causal inference. In M.L. Commons & J.A. Nevin (Eds.), *Quantitative analyses of behavior, Vol. I: Discriminative properties of reinforcement schedules* (pp. 89-112). Cambridge, MA: Ballinger.

Killeen, P.R. (1982). Incentive theory: II. Models for choice. *Journal of the Experimental Analysis of Behavior, 38*, 217-232.

Killeen, P.R., & Smith, J.P. (1984) Perception of contingency in conditioning: Scalar timing, response bias, and the erasure of memory by reinforcement. *Journal of Experimental Psychology: Animal Behavior Processes, 10*, 333-345.

Koch, S. (Ed.) (1959). *Psychology: A study of a science, Vol. 2*. NY: McGraw-Hill.

LaBounty, C.E., & Reynolds, G.S. (1973). An analysis of response and time matching to reinforcement in concurrent ratio-interval schedules. *Journal of the Experimental Analysis of Behavior, 19*, 155-166.

Lander, D.G., & Irwin, R.J. (1968). Multiple schedules: Effects of the distribution of reinforcements between components on the distribution of responses between components. *Journal of the Experimental Analysis of Behavior, 11*, 517-524.

Lea, S.E.G. (1976). Titration of schedule parameters by pigeons. *Journal of the Experimental Analysis of Behavior, 25*, 43-54.

Leung, J-P., & Winton, A.S.W. (1985). Preference for unsegmented interreinforcement intervals in concurrent chains. *Journal of the Experimental Analysis of Behavior*, *44*, 89-101.

Lewis, P., Gardner, E.T., & Hutton, L. (1976). Integrated delays to shock as negative reinforcement. *Journal of the Experimental Analysis of Behavior*, *26*, 379-386.

Lobb, B., & Davison, M.C. (1975). Preference in concurrent interval schedules: A systematic replication. *Journal of the Experimental Analysis of Behavior*, *24*, 191-197.

Lobb, B., & Davison, M.C. (1977). Multiple and concurrent schedule performance: Independence from concurrent and successive schedule contexts. *Journal of the Experimental Analysis of Behavior*, *28*, 27-39.

Logue, A.W. (1983). Signal detection and matching: Analyzing choice on concurrent variable-interval schedules. *Journal of the Experimental Analysis of Behavior*, *39*, 107-127.

Logue, A.W., & de Villiers, P.A. (1978). Matching in concurrent variable-interval avoidance schedules. *Journal of the Experimental Analysis of Behavior*, *29*, 61-66.

Logue, A.W., Rodriguez, M.L., Pena-Correal, T.E., & Mauro, B.C. (1984). Choice in a self-control paradigm: Quantification of experience-based differences. *Journal of the Experimental Analysis of Behavior*, *41*, 53-67.

Luce, R.D. (1959). *Individual choice behavior: A theoretical analysis*. NY: Wiley.

Luce, R.D. (1963). Detection and recognition. In R.D. Luce, R.R. Bush, & E. Galanter (Eds.), *Handbook of mathematical psychology* (pp. 105-189). NY: Wiley.

MacEwen, D. (1972). The effects of terminal-link fixed-interval and variable-interval schedules on responding under concurrent-chained schedules. *Journal of the Experimental Analysis of Behavior*, *18*, 253-261.

Mackintosh, N.J. (1974). *The psychology of animal learning*. NY: Academic Press.

Marascuilo, L.A., & McSweeney, M. (1977). *Nonparametric and distribution-free methods for the social sciences*. Monterey, CA: Brooks-Cole.

Markowitz, J., & Swets, J.A. (1967). Factors affecting the slope of empirical ROC curves: Comparison of binary and rating responses. *Perception and Psychophysics*, *2*, 91-100.

Matthews, L.R., & Temple, W. (1979). Concurrent-schedule assessment of food preferences in cows. *Journal of the Experimental Analysis of Behavior*, *32*, 245-254.

Mazur, J.E. (1984). Tests of an equivalence rule for fixed and variable reinforcer delays. *Journal of Experimental Psychology: Animal Behavior Processes*, *10*, 426-436.

Mazur, J.E. (1987). An adjusting procedure for studying delayed reinforcement. In M.L. Commons, J.E. Mazur, J.A. Nevin, & H. Rachlin (Eds.), *Quantitative analyses of behavior, Vol. V: Effects of delay and of intervening events on reinforcement value* (pp. 55-73). Hillsdale, NJ: Erlbaum.

Mazur, J.E., & Logue, A.W. (1978). Choice in a "self-control" paradigm: Effects of a fading procedure. *Journal of the Experimental Analysis of Behavior*, *30*, 11-17.

Mazur, J.E., Snyderman, M., & Coe, D. (1985). Influence of delay and rate of reinforcement on discrete-trial choice. *Journal of Experimental Psychology: Animal Behavior Processes*, *11*, 565-575.

McCarthy, D. (1983). Measures of response bias at minimum-detectable luminance levels in the pigeon. *Journal of the Experimental Analysis of Behavior*, *39*, 87-106.

McCarthy, D., & Davison, M. (1979). Signal probability, reinforcement, and signal detection. *Journal of the Experimental Analysis of Behavior*, *32*, 373-386.

McCarthy, D., & Davison, M. (1980a). On the discriminability of stimulus duration. *Journal of the Experimental Analysis of Behavior*, *33*, 187-211.

McCarthy, D., & Davison, M. (1980b). Independence of sensitivity to relative reinforcement rate and discriminability in signal detection. *Journal of the Experimental Analysis of Behavior*, *34*, 273-284.

McCarthy, D., & Davison, M. (1981a). Toward a behavioral theory of bias in signal detection. *Perception and Psychophysics*, *29*, 371-382.

McCarthy, D., & Davison, M. (1981b). Matching and signal detection. In M.L. Commons & J.A. Nevin (Eds.), *Quantitative analyses of behavior, Vol. I: Discriminative properties of reinforcement schedules* (pp. 393-417). Cambridge, MA: Ballinger.

McCarthy, D., & Davison, M. (1982). Independence of stimulus discriminability from absolute rate of reinforcement in a signal-detection procedure. *Journal of the Experimental Analysis of Behavior*, *37*, 371-382.

McCarthy, D., & Davison, M. (1984). Isobias and alloiobias functions in animal psychophysics. *Journal of Experimental Psychology: Animal Behavior Processes*, *10*, 390-409.

McCarthy, D., Davison, M., & Jenkins, P.E. (1982). Stimulus discriminability in discrete-trial and free-operant detection procedures. *Journal of the Experimental Analysis of Behavior*, *37*, 199-215.

McDiarmid, C., & Rilling, M. (1965). Reinforcement delay and reinforcement rate as determiners of schedule preference. *Psychonomic Science*, *2*, 195-196.

McDowell, J.J (1981). Wilkinson's method of estimating the parameters of Herrnstein's hyperbola. *Journal of the Experimental Analysis of Behavior*, *35*, 413-414.

McDowell, J.J (1986). On the falsifiability of matching theory. *Journal of the Experimental Analysis of Behavior*, *45*, 63-74.

McDowell, J.J, & Kessel, R. (1979). A multivariate rate equation for variable-interval performance. *Journal of the Experimental Analysis of Behavior*, *31*, 267-283.

McDowell, J.J, & Wood, H.M. (1984). Confirmation of linear system theory prediction: Changes in Herrnstein's *k* as a function of changes in reinforcer magnitude. *Journal of the Experimental Analysis of Behavior*, *41*, 183-192.

McDowell, J.J, & Wood, H.M. (1985). Confirmation of linear system theory prediction: Rate of change of Herrnstein's *k* as a function of response-force requirements. *Journal of the Experimental Analysis of Behavior*, *43*, 61-73.

McGill, W.J. (1967). Neural counting mechanisms and energy detection in audition. *Journal of Mathematical Psychology*, *4*, 351-376.

McLean, A.P., & White, K.G. (1983). Temporal constraints on choice: Sensitivity and bias in multiple schedules. *Journal of the Experimental Analysis of Behavior*, *39*, 405-426.

McSweeney, F.K. (1975a). Concurrent schedule responding as a function of body weight. *Animal Learning and Behavior*, *3*, 264-270.

McSweeney, F.K. (1975b). Matching and contrast on several concurrent treadle-press schedules. *Journal of the Experimental Analysis of Behavior*, *23*, 193-198.

McSweeney, F.K. (1980). Differences between rates of responding emitted during simple and multiple schedules. *Animal Learning and Behavior, 8*, 392-400.

McSweeney, F.K. (1982). Positive and negative contrast as a function of component duration for key-pecking and treadle pressing. *Journal of the Experimental Analysis of Behavior, 37*, 281-293.

McSweeney, F.K. (1983). Positive behavioral contrast when pigeons press treadles during multiple schedules. *Journal of the Experimental Analysis of Behavior, 39*, 149-156.

McSweeney, F.K., & DeRicco, D.A. (1976). Rates of responding in the pigeon generated by simple and complex schedules which provide the same rate of reinforcement. *Animal Learning and Behavior, 4*, 379-385.

McSweeney, F.K., Farmer, V.A., Dougan, J.D., & Whipple, J.E. (1986). The generalized matching law as a description of multiple-schedule responding. *Journal of the Experimental Analysis of Behavior, 45*, 83-101.

McSweeney, F.K., Melville, C.L., Buck, M.A. & Whipple, J.E. (1983). Local rates of responding and reinforcement during concurrent schedules. *Journal of the Experimental Analysis of Behavior, 40*, 79-98.

Menlove, R.L. (1975). Local patterns of responding maintained by concurrent and multiple schedules. *Journal of the Experimental Analysis of Behavior, 23*, 309-337.

Merigan, W.H., Miller, J.S., & Gollub, L.R. (1975). Short-component multiple schedules: Effects of relative reinforcement duration. *Journal of the Experimental Analysis of Behavior, 24*, 183-189.

Miller, H.L., Jr. (1976). Matching-based hedonic scaling in the pigeon. *Journal of the Experimental Analysis of Behavior, 26*, 335-347.

Miller, H.L., Jr. (1984). On the further maturing of behavior analysis: A review of Commons, Herrnstein and Rachlin's "Matching and Maximizing Accounts." *Journal of the Experimental Analysis of Behavior, 42*, 159-164.

Miller, H.L., & Loveland, D.H. (1974). Matching when the number of response alternatives is large. *Animal Learning and Behavior, 2*, 106-110.

Miller, J.T., Saunders, S.S., & Bourland, G. (1980). The role of stimulus disparity in concurrently available reinforcement schedules. *Animal Learning and Behavior, 8*, 635-641.

Mitchell, P., & White, K.G. (1977). Responding in the presence of free food: Differential exposure to the reinforcement source. *Bulletin of the Psychonomic Society, 10*, 121-124.

Moore, J. (1979). Choice and number of reinforcers. *Journal of the Experimental Analysis of Behavior, 32*, 51-63.

Moore, J., & Fantino, E. (1975). Choice and response contingencies. *Journal of the Experimental Analysis of Behavior, 23*, 339-347.

Mullins, E., Agunwamba, C.C., & Donahoe, A.J. (1982). On the analysis of studies of choice. *Journal of the Experimental Analysis of Behavior, 37*, 323-327.

Myers, D.L., & Myers, L.E. (1977). Undermatching: A reappraisal of performance on concurrent variable-interval schedules of reinforcement. *Journal of the Experimental Analysis of Behavior, 27*, 203-214.

Navarick, D.J., & Fantino, E. (1972). Transitivity as a property of choice. *Journal of the Experimental Analysis of Behavior, 18*, 389-401.

Navarick, D.J., & Fantino, E. (1974). Stochastic transitivity and unidimensional behavior theories. *Psychological Review, 81*, 426-441.

Navarick, D.J., & Fantino, E. (1975). Stochastic transitivity and the unidimensional control of choice. *Learning and Motivation, 6*, 179-201.

Navarick, D.J., & Fantino, E. (1976). Self control and general models of choice. *Journal of Experimental Psychology: Animal Behavior Processes, 2*, 75-87.

Neuringer, A.J. (1967). Effects of reinforcement magnitude on choice and rate of responding. *Journal of the Experimental Analysis of Behavior, 10*, 417-424.

Neuringer, A.J. (1969). Delayed reinforcement versus reinforcement after a fixed interval. *Journal of the Experimental Analysis of Behavior, 12*, 375-383.

Nevin, J.A. (1969). Signal-detection theory and operant behavior: A review of David M. Green and John A. Swets' "Signal-detection theory and psychophysics." *Journal of the Experimental Analysis of Behavior, 12*, 475-480.

Nevin, J.A. (1971). Rates and patterns of responding with concurrent fixed-interval and variable-interval reinforcement. *Journal of the Experimental Analysis of Behavior, 16*, 241-247.

Nevin, J.A. (1979). Reinforcement schedules and response strength. In M.D. Zeiler & P. Harzem (Eds.), *Advances in analysis of behavior: Vol. 1, Reinforcement and the organisation of behavior* (pp. 117-158). NY: Wiley.

Nevin, J.A. (1981). Psychophysics and reinforcement schedules. In M.L. Commons & J.A. Nevin (Eds.), *Quantitative analyses of behavior, Vol. 1: Discriminative properties of reinforcement schedules* (pp. 3-27). Cambridge, MA: Ballinger.

Nevin, J.A., & Baum, W.M. (1980). Feedback functions for variable-interval reinforcement. *Journal of the Experimental Analysis of Behavior, 34*, 207-217.

Nevin, J.A., Jenkins, P., Whittaker, S., & Yarensky, P. (1977). Signal detection and matching. Paper presented at the November meeting of the Psychonomic Society, Washington, D.C.

Nevin, J.A., Jenkins, P., Whittaker, S., & Yarensky, P. (1982). Reinforcement contingencies and signal detection. *Journal of the Experimental Analysis of Behavior, 37*, 65-79.

Nevin, J.A., & MacWilliams, S. (1983). Ratio reinforcement of signal detection. *Behaviour Analysis Letters, 3*, 317-324.

Nevin, J.A., Olson, K., Mandell, C., & Yarensky, P. (1975). Differential reinforcement and signal detection. *Journal of the Experimental Analysis of Behavior, 24*, 355-367.

Pliskoff, S.S. (1971). Effects of symmetrical and asymmetrical changeover delays on concurrent performances. *Journal of the Experimental Analysis of Behavior, 16*, 249-256.

Pliskoff, S.S., & Brown, T.G. (1976). Matching with a trio of concurrent variable-interval schedules of reinforcement. *Journal of the Experimental Analysis of Behavior, 25*, 69-73.

Pliskoff, S.S., Cicerone, R., & Nelson, T.D. (1978). Local response-rate constancy on concurrent variable-interval schedules of reinforcement. *Journal of the Experimental Analysis of Behavior, 29*, 431-446.

Pliskoff, S.S., Shull, R.L., & Gollub, L.R. (1968). The relation between response rates and reinforcer rates in multiple schedules. *Journal of the Experimental Analysis of Behavior, 11*, 271-284.

Poniewaz, W.R. (1984). Effects on preference of reinforcement delay, number of reinforcers, and terminal-link duration. *Journal of the Experimental Analysis of Behavior, 42*, 255-266.

Prelec, D. (1984). The assumptions underlying the generalized matching law. *Journal of the Experimental Analysis of Behavior, 41*, 101-107.

Prelec, D., & Herrnstein, R.J. (1978). Feedback functions for reinforcement: A paradigmatic experiment. *Animal Learning and Behavior, 6*, 181-186.

Premack, D. (1971). Catching up with commonsense, or two sides of a generalization: Reinforcement and punishment. In R. Glaser (Ed.), *The nature of reinforcement* (pp. 121-150). NY: Academic Press.

Rachlin, H. (1971). On the tautology of the matching law. *Journal of the Experimental Analysis of Behavior, 15*, 249-251.

Rachlin, H., & Green, L. (1972). Commitment, choice, and self control. *Journal of the Experimental Analysis of Behavior, 17*, 15-22.

Rachlin, H., Green, L., Kagel, J.H., & Battalio, R.C. (1976). Economic demand theory and psychological theories of choice. In G.H. Bower (Ed.), *The Psychology of Learning and Motivation* (Vol. 10) (pp. 129-154). NY: Academic Press.

Revusky, S.H. (1963). A relationship between responses per reinforcement and preference during concurrent VI VI. *Journal of the Experimental Analysis of Behavior, 6*, 518.

Reynolds, G.S. (1961). Relativity of response rate and reinforcement frequency in a multiple schedule. *Journal of the Experimental Analysis of Behavior, 4*, 179-184.

Reynolds, G.S. (1963a). On some determinants of choice in pigeons. *Journal of the Experimental Analysis of Behavior, 6*, 53-59.

Reynolds, G.S. (1963b). Some limitations on behavioral contrast and induction during successive discrimination. *Journal of the Experimental Analysis of Behavior, 6*, 131-139.

Rider, D.P. (1979). Concurrent ratio schedules: Fixed versus variable response requirements. *Journal of the Experimental Analysis of Behavior, 31*, 225-237.

Rider, D.P. (1983). Choice for aperiodic versus periodic ratio schedules: A comparison of concurrent and concurrent-chains procedures. *Journal of the Experimental Analysis of Behavior, 40*, 225-237.

Rilling, M.E., & McDiarmid, C.G. (1965). Signal detection in fixed-ratio schedules. *Science, 148*, 526-527.

Ruckdeschel, F.R. (1981). *Basic scientific subroutines, Vol. II*. Peterborough, NH: Byte/McGraw-Hill.

Schneider, B.A. (1969). A two-state analysis of fixed-interval responding in the pigeon. *Journal of the Experimental Analysis of Behavior, 12*, 677-687.

Schneider, J.W. (1972). Choice between two-component chained and tandem schedules. *Journal of the Experimental Analysis of Behavior, 18*, 45-60.

Schneider, J.W. (1973). Reinforcer effectiveness as a function of reinforcer rate and magnitude: A comparison of concurrent performances. *Journal of the Experimental Analysis of Behavior, 20*, 461-471.

Schroeder, S.R., & Holland, J.G. (1969). Reinforcement of eye movement with concurrent schedules. *Journal of the Experimental Analysis of Behavior, 12*, 897-903.

Schulman, A.I., & Greenberg, G.Z. (1970). Operating characteristics and a priori probability of the signal. *Perception and Psychophysics, 8,* 317-320.

Scown, J.M. (1983). Changeover delay and concurrent schedules. Unpublished doctoral dissertation. Waikato University, New Zealand.

Shettleworth, S., & Nevin, J.A. (1965). Relative rate of response and relative magnitude of reinforcement in multiple schedules. *Journal of the Experimental Analysis of Behavior, 8,* 199-202.

Shimp, C.P. (1968). Magnitude and frequency of reinforcement and frequencies of interresponse times. *Journal of the Experimental Analysis of Behavior, 11,* 525-535.

Shimp, C.P. (1969a). Optimum behavior in free-operant experiments. *Psychological Review, 76,* 97-112.

Shimp, C.P. (1969b). The concurrent reinforcement of two interresponse times: The relative frequency of an interresponse time equals its relative harmonic length. *Journal of the Experimental Analysis of Behavior, 12,* 403-411.

Shimp, C.P. (1971). Matching in a concurrent FI FI schedule. *Psychonomic Science, 22,* 27-28.

Shimp, C.P., & Wheatley, K.L. (1971). Matching to relative reinforcement frequency in multiple schedules with a short component duration. *Journal of the Experimental Analysis of Behavior, 15,* 205-210.

Shull, R.L., & Pliskoff, S.S. (1967). Changeover delay and concurrent schedules: Some effects on relative performance measures. *Journal of the Experimental Analysis of Behavior, 10,* 517-527.

Siegel, S. (1956). *Nonparametric statistics for the behavioral sciences.* NY: McGraw-Hill.

Silberberg, A., & Fantino, E. (1970). Choice, rate of reinforcement, and the changeover delay. *Journal of the Experimental Analysis of Behavior, 13,* 187-197.

Silberberg, A., & Schrot, J. (1974). A yoked-chamber comparison of concurrent and multiple schedules: The relation between component duration and responding. *Journal of the Experimental Analysis of Behavior, 22,* 21-30.

Skinner, B.F. (1950). Are theories of learning necessary? *Psychological Review, 57,* 193-216.

Skinner, B.F. (1956). A case history in scientific method. *American Psychologist, 11,* 221-233.

Snyderman, M. (1983). Delay and amount of reward in a concurrent chain. *Journal of the Experimental Analysis of Behavior, 39,* 437-447.

Snyderman, M. (1984). Body weight and response strength. *Behaviour Analysis Letters, 3,* 255-265.

Spealman, R.D., & Gollub, L.R. (1974). Behavioral interactions in multiple variable-interval schedules. *Journal of the Experimental Analysis of Behavior, 22,* 471-481.

Squires, N., & Fantino, E. (1971). A model for choice in simple concurrent and concurrent-chains schedules. *Journal of the Experimental Analysis of Behavior, 15,* 27-38.

Staddon, J.E.R. (1968). Spaced responding and choice: A preliminary analysis. *Journal of the Experimental Analysis of Behavior, 11,* 669-682.

Staddon, J.E.R. (1977). On Herrnstein's equation and related forms. *Journal of the Experimental Analysis of Behavior, 28,* 163-170.

Staddon, J.E.R., & Motheral, S. (1978). On matching and maximizing in operant choice. *Psychological Review, 85*, 436-444.

Stubbs, D.A. (1968). The discrimination of stimulus duration by pigeons. *Journal of the Experimental Analysis of Behavior, 11*, 223-238.

Stubbs, D.A. (1976). Response bias and the discrimination of stimulus duration. *Journal of the Experimental Analysis of Behavior, 25*, 243-250.

Stubbs, D.A. (1980). Temporal discrimination and a free-operant psychophysical procedure. *Journal of the Experimental Analysis of Behavior, 33*, 167-185.

Stubbs, D.A., & Pliskoff, S.S. (1969). Concurrent responding with fixed relative rate of reinforcement. *Journal of the Experimental Analysis of Behavior, 12*, 887-895.

Stubbs, D.A., Pliskoff, S.S., & Reid, H.M. (1977). Concurrent schedules: A quantitative relation between changeover behavior and its consequences. *Journal of the Experimental Analysis of Behavior, 27*, 85-96.

Swets, J.A., Tanner, W.P., Jr., & Birdsall, T.G. (1961). Decision processes in perception. *Psychological Review, 68*, 301-340.

Tanner, W.P., Jr., & Birdsall, T.G. (1958). Definitions of d' and n as psychophysical measures. *Journal of the Acoustical Society of America, 30*, 922-928.

Tanner, W.P., Jr., & Swets, J.A. (1954). A decision-making theory of visual detection. *Psychological Review, 61*, 401-409.

Taylor, R., & Davison, M. (1983). Sensitivity to reinforcement in concurrent arithmetic and exponential schedules. *Journal of the Experimental Analysis of Behavior, 39*, 191-198.

Terman, M. (1970). Discrimination of auditory intensities by rats. *Journal of the Experimental Analysis of Behavior, 13*, 145-160.

Terman, M. (1981). Behavioral dynamics of the psychometric function. In M.L. Commons & J.A. Nevin (Eds.), *Quantitative analyses of behavior, Vol. I: Discriminative properties of reinforcement schedules* (pp. 321-344). Cambridge, MA: Ballinger.

Terman, M., & Terman, J.S. (1972). Concurrent variation of response bias and sensitivity in an operant-psychophysical test. *Perception and Psychophysics, 11*, 428-432.

Terman, M., & Terman, J.S. (1973). Latency differentiation of hits and false alarms in an operant-psychophysical test. *Journal of the Experimental Analysis of Behavior, 20*, 439-445.

Thijssen, J.M., & Vendrick, A.J.H. (1968). Internal noise and transducer function in sensory detection experiments: Evaluation of psychometric curves and of ROC curves. *Perception and Psychophysics, 3*, 387-400.

Thorndike, E.L. (1913). *Educational psychology, Vol. II: The psychology of learning.* NY: Teachers College, Columbia University.

Timberlake, W. (1982). The emperor's clothes: Assumptions of the matching theory. In M.L. Commons, R.J. Herrnstein & H. Rachlin (Eds.), *Quantitative analyses of behavior, Vol. II: Matching and maximizing accounts* (pp. 549-569). Cambridge, MA: Ballinger.

Todorov, J.C. (1971). Concurrent performances: Effect of punishment contingent on the switching response. *Journal of the Experimental Analysis of Behavior, 16*, 51-62.

Todorov, J.C. (1972). Component duration and relative response rates in multiple schedules. *Journal of the Experimental Analysis of Behavior, 17*, 45-49.

Todorov, J.C. (1973). Interaction of frequency and magnitude of reinforcement on concurrent performances. *Journal of the Experimental Analysis of Behavior, 19*, 451-458.

Todorov, J.C., Castro, J.M. de O., Hanna, E.S., Bittencourt de Sa, M.C.N., & Barreto, M. de Q. (1983). Choice, experience, and the generalized matching law. *Journal of the Experimental Analysis of Behavior, 40*, 99-111.

Treisman, M. (1977). On the stability of d_s. *Psychological Bulletin, 84*, 235-243.

Trevett, A.J., Davison, M.C., & Williams, R.J. (1972). Performance in concurrent interval schedules. *Journal of the Experimental Analysis of Behavior, 17*, 369-374.

Tustin, R.D., & Davison, M.C. (1978). Distribution of response ratios in concurrent variable-interval performance. *Journal of the Experimental Analysis of Behavior, 29*, 561-564.

Tustin, R.D., & Davison, M. (1979). Choice: Effects of changeover schedules on concurrent performance. *Journal of the Experimental Analysis of Behavior, 32*, 75-91.

Vaughan, W., Jr. (1981). Melioration, matching, and maximization. *Journal of the Experimental Analysis of Behavior, 36*, 141-149.

Vaughan, W., Jr., & Miller, H.L., Jr. (1984). Optimization versus response-strength accounts of behavior. *Journal of the Experimental Analysis of Behavior, 42*, 337-348.

Wardlaw, G.R., & Davison, M.C. (1974). Preference for fixed-interval schedules: Effects of initial-link length. *Journal of the Experimental Analysis of Behavior, 21*, 331-340.

Wearden, J.H. (1980). Undermatching on concurrent variable-interval schedules and the power law. *Journal of the Experimental Analysis of Behavior, 33*, 149-152.

Wearden, J.H. (1981). Bias and undermatching: Implications for Herrnstein's equation. *Behaviour Analysis Letters, 1*, 177-185.

Wearden, J.H., & Burgess, I.S. (1982). Matching since Baum (1979). *Journal of the Experimental Analysis of Behavior, 38*, 339-348.

Wetherington, C.L., & Lucas, T.R. (1980). A note on fitting Herrnstein's equation. *Journal of the Experimental Analysis of Behavior, 34*, 199-206.

White, A.J., & Davison, M.C. (1973). Performance in concurrent fixed-interval schedules. *Journal of the Experimental Analysis of Behavior, 19*, 147-153.

White, K.G., & Mitchell, P. (1977). Preference for response-contingent versus free reinforcement. *Bulletin of the Psychonomic Society, 10*, 125-127.

White, K.G., Pipe, M.-E., & McLean, A. (1984). Stimulus and reinforcer relativity in multiple schedules: Local and dimensional effects on sensitivity to reinforcement. *Journal of the Experimental Analysis of Behavior, 41*, 69-81.

Wickelgren, W.A. (1968). Unidimensional strength theory and component analysis of noise in absolute and comparative judgements. *Journal of Mathematical Psychology, 5*, 102-122.

Wilkinson, G.N. (1961). Statistical estimation in enzyme kinetics. *Biochemical Journal, 80*, 324-332.

Williams, B.A. (1983). Another look at contrast in multiple schedules. *Journal of the Experimental Analysis of Behavior, 39*, 345-384.

Williams, B.A., & Fantino, E. (1978). Effects on choice of reinforcer delay and conditioned reinforcement. *Journal of the Experimental Analysis of Behavior, 29*, 77-86.

Williams, B.A., & Wixted, J.T. (1986). An equation for behavioral contrast. *Journal of the Experimental Analysis of Behavior, 45*, 47-62.

Wright, A.A. (1972). Psychometric and psychophysical hue discrimination functions for the pigeon. *Vision Research, 12*, 1447-1464.

Wright, A.A. (1974). Psychometric and psychophysical theory within a framework of response bias. *Psychological Review, 81*, 322-347.

Wright, A.A. (1982). Detection of learning and learning to detect. A review of M.L. Commons and J.A. Nevin (Eds.), Quantitative analyses of behavior, Vol. I: Discriminative properties of reinforcement schedules. *Contemporary Psychology, 27*, 566-567.

Wright, A.A., & Nevin, J.A. (1974). Signal detection methods for measurement of utility in animals. *Journal of the Experimental Analysis of Behavior, 21*, 373-380.

Ziriax, J.M., & Silberberg, A. (1984). Concurrent variable-interval variable-ratio schedules can provide only weak evidence for matching. *Journal of the Experimental Analysis of Behavior, 41*, 83-100.

Author Index

A

Agunwamba, C. C., 85, 266
Ainslie, G. W., 210, 255
Akaike, H., 113, 255
Allen, C. M., 48, 255
Alsop, B., 192, ,215, 255
Anderson, N. H., 23, 61, 87, 255
Asaki, K., 211, 263
Autor, S. M., 11, 188, 189, 255

B

Bacotti, A. V., 103, 255
Bareto, M. de Q., 82, 92, 271
Barron, B., 183, 213, 255
Battalio, R. C., 106, 268
Baum, W. M., 3, 13, 29, 30, 49, 51, 52, 53,
  54, 58, 80, 81, 82, 83, 84, 85, 87, 102,
  107, 113, 118, 119, 120, 128, 132, 133,
  139, 141, 142, 145, 146, 147, 148, 156,
  159, 179, 216, 234, 241, 255, 256, 267
Bauman, R. A., 108, 109, 126, 256
Beautrais, P. G., 70, 71, 101, 113, 116, 117,
  119, 256
Bevan, P., 23, 35, 131, 132, 256
Birdsall, T. G., 218, 228, 270
Bittencourt de Sa, M. C. N., 82, 92, 271
Blough, D., 218, 256
Blough, P., 218, 256

Boelens, H., 148, 149, 150, 256
Boldero, J., 221, 226, 231, 233, 234, 256
Bonbright, J. C., Jr., 218, 262
Bourland, G., 81, 150, 151, 172, 216, 241,
  266
Bouzas, A., 179, 256
Bradley, J. V., 71, 256
Bradshaw, C. M., 23, 35, 131, 132, 256
Brethower, D. M., 115, 130, 256
Brinker, R. P., 205, 257
Brown, T. G., 110, 111, 267
Brownstein, A. J., 12, 13, 88, 108, 109, 126,
  133, 256, 257
Buck, M. A., 38, 40, 266
Burgess, I. S., 85, 271

C

Castro, J. M. de O., 82, 92, 271
Catania, A. C., 7, 9, 10, 12, 13, 14, 60, 62,
  84, 88, 139, 157, 215, 257
Charman, L., 42, 44, 45, 75, 77, 78, 81, 83,
  143, 148, 153, 159, 161, 162, 163, 164,
  165, 167, 168, 169, 171, 172, 175, 257
Chung, S.-H., 14, 15, 60, 62, 96, 97, 113,
  114, 154, 195, 205, 257
Church, R. M., 133, 135, 259
Cicerone, R., 139, 146, 147, 267
Clopton, B. M., 218, 235, 257
Coe, D., 215, 264

Cohen, I. L., 22, 258
Cohen, S. L., 113, 116, 258
Commons, M. L., 57, 106, 135, 258
Coombs, C. H., 203, 258
Cutts, D., 9, 10, 257

D

Davison, M. (C.), 19, 25, 29, 35, 38, 42, 43,
44, 45, 47, 54, 55, 59, 65, 66, 68, 70, 71,
74, 75, 77, 78, 81, 82, 83, 84, 85, 89, 90,
92, 94, 95, 96, 97, 101, 103, 104, 105,
107, 111, 112, 113, 114, 116, 117, 119,
121, 122, 123, 124, 125, 126, 135, 140,
141, 142, 143, 145, 147, 148, 151, 153,
156, 157, 158, 159, 160, 161, 162, 163,
164, 165, 167, 168, 169, 171, 172, 174,
175, 176, 177, 178, 179, 180, 182, 183,
188, 190, 192, 193, 196, 197, 201, 202,
203, 209, 212, 214, 215, 216, 218, 219,
220, 221, 222, 224, 225, 226, 228, 231,
232, 233, 234, 235, 236, 237, 238, 239,
240, 241, 242, 243, 244, 245, 246, 247,
248, 249, 250, 251, 255, 256, 257, 258,
259, 260, 261, 262, 264, 265, 270, 271
de Villiers, P. A., 35, 36, 51, 54, 85, 115,
123, 130, 131, 132, 133, 134, 147, 161,
259, 264
Delbrück, N., 86, 87, 88, 89, 260
Deluty, M. Z., 130, 133, 135, 259
DeRicco, D. A., 42, 266
Donahoe, A. J., 85, 266
Dorman, L. G., 139, 145, 259
Dougan, J. D., 83, 184, 266
Dowd, J. E., 22, 259
Dreyfus, L. R., 139, 145, 259
Duncan, B., 97, 196, 197, 204, 208, 212, 215,
259
Dunn, R., 215, 260
Dusoir, T., 218, 233, 235, 259

E

Edmon, E. L., 42, 162, 166, 177, 259
Elliffe, D., 174, 175, 176, 177, 178, 260
Elsmore, T. F., 218, 235, 260
Epstein, R., 89, 91, 260
Estes, W. K., 130, 260

F

Fantino, E., 15, 86, 87, 88, 89, 97, 115, 131,
133, 147, 155, 187, 195, 196, 197, 198,
199, 200, 201, 202, 203, 204, 205, 206,
208, 210, 211, 212, 214, 215, 233, 259,
260, 262, 266, 267, 269, 272
Farley, J., 115, 131, 133, 147, 260
Farmer, V. A., 83, 184, 266
Felton, M., 2, 260
Ferguson, A., 19, 113, 119, 174, 228, 233,
258
Ferguson, G. A., 71, 78, 79, 260
Ferster, C. B., 1, 2, 3, 6, 99, 104, 240, 260
Fetterman, J. G., 139, 145, 259
Findley, J. D., 3, 5, 7, 8, 9, 260

G

Galanter, E., 218, 235, 260
Gardner, E. T., 135, 264
Gentry, G. D., 193, 261
Gollub, L. R., 41, 42, 91, 92, 155, 156, 157,
158, 159, 163, 169, 170, 171, 172, 177,
179, 182, 263, 266, 267, 269
Green, D. M., 217, 218, 219, 226, 227, 228,
261
Green, L., 106, 210, 211, 261, 268
Greenberg, G. Z., 218, 235, 269
Grier, J. B., 231, 261

H

Hack, M. H., 228, 261
Hanna, E. S., 82, 92, 271
Hardy, G. A., 194, 261
Harnett, P., 123, 261
Hayes, S. C., 215, 261
Herrnstein, R. J., 3, 5, 7, 8, 9, 11, 12, 14, 15,
16, 17, 19, 27, 31, 32, 33, 34, 35, 36, 37,
38, 40, 42, 43, 44, 45, 46, 47, 57, 60, 62,
64, 75, 83, 96, 97, 101, 106, 112, 114,
116, 126, 131, 134, 135, 136, 138, 139,
140, 152, 154, 159, 160, 161, 162, 166,
167, 169, 175, 177, 182, 183, 188, 189,
190, 191, 192, 193, 194, 195, 196, 198,
205, 221, 249, 257, 258, 259, 261, 262,
268
Heyman, G. M., 85, 106, 261, 262

Hineline, P. N., 135, 262
Hinson, J. M., 158, 177, 182, 262
Hobson, S. L., 218, 235, 262
Hodos, W., 218, 262
Hogsden, I., 89, 90, 209, 258
Holland, J. G., 119, 268
Hollander, M., 70, 71, 72, 262
Hollard, V., 54, 55, 94, 95, 96, 183, 233, 262
Holman, G. L., 218, 235, 260
Holz, W. C., 129, 130, 132, 262
Hume, A. L., 218, 235, 262
Hunter, I. (W.), 35, 47, 59, 111, 113, 114,
    119, 121, 122, 123, 124, 125, 126, 140,
    141, 179, 221, 233, 258, 262
Hursh, S. R., 127, 196, 250, 262
Hutton, L., 135, 264

I

Irwin, R. J., 52, 54, 154, 155, 158, 218, 235,
    262, 263
Isaac, P. D., 65, 74, 239, 263
Ito, M., 211, 263

J

Jeffress, L. A., 228, 263
Jenkins, P. (E.), 81, 82, 147, 151, 216, 221,
    231, 240, 241, 242, 243, 246, 250, 258,
    265, 267
Jensen, C., 151, 243, 244, 245, 246, 247, 248,
    258

K

Kagel, J. H., 106, 268
Kapust, J., 215, 261
Keller, J. V., 91, 92, 263
Kendall, M. C., 65, 73, 74, 263
Kessel, R., 47, 265
Killeen, P. (R.), 25, 56, 57, 81, 99, 135, 161,
    193, 194, 195, 196, 203, 205, 211, 215,
    221, 263
Koch, S., 249, 263
Kop, P. F. M., 148, 149, 150, 256

L

LaBounty, C. E., 106, 263
Lander, D. G., 52, 54, 154, 155, 158, 263
Lea, S. E. G., 193, 263
Leonard, S. R., 215, 261
Leung, J.-P., 209, 215, 264
Lewis, P., 135, 264
Littlewood, J. E., 194, 261
Lobb, B., 38, 43, 104, 105, 157, 158, 159,
    160, 177, 180, 182, 264
Logue, A. W., 134, 211, 216, 231, 240, 264
Loveland, D. H., 43, 45, 75, 83, 101, 109,
    110, 111, 140, 166, 169, 175, 177, 261,
    262, 266
Lucas, T. R., 22, 23, 36, 37, 271
Luce, R. D., 112, 222, 225, 233, 264
Lyon, D. O., 2, 260

M

MacEwen, D., 197, 198, 215, 264
Mackintosh, N. J., 172, 264
Mandell, C., 231, 267
Marascuilo, L. A., 72, 75, 78, 264
Markowitz, J., 218, 235, 264
Marr, M. J., 193, 261
Matthews, L. R., 96, 264
Mauro, B. C., 211, 264
Mazur, J. E., 123, 193, 211, 215, 264
McCarthy, D., 65, 74, 101, 123, 151, 216,
    218, 221, 222, 224, 225, 226, 231, 232,
    233, 234, 235, 236, 237, 238, 239, 240,
    241, 242, 243, 244, 245, 246, 247, 248,
    256, 258, 261, 264, 265
McDiarmid, C., 190, 194, 218, 265, 268
McDowell, J. J., 23, 37, 38, 47, 57, 116, 265
McGill, W. J., 228, 261, 265
McLean, A., 42, 45, 46, 47, 114, 153, 157,
    159, 167, 173, 175, 177, 179, 180, 181,
    182, 183, 184, 216, 265, 271
McSweeney, F. K., 36, 37, 38, 40, 42, 83,
    113, 119, 128, 173, 177, 184, 265, 266
McSweeney, M., 72, 75, 78, 264
McWilliams, S., 226, 267
Melville, C. L., 38, 40, 266
Menlove, R. L., 139, 142, 266
Merigan, W. H., 163, 169, 170, 171, 172, 266
Miller, H. L., Jr., 95, 109, 110, 111, 140,
    251, 252, 266, 271

Miller, J. S., 163, 169, 170, 171, 172, 266
Miller, J. T., 81, 150, 151, 172, 216, 241, 266
Mitchell, P., 126, 266, 271
Moore, J., 205, 206, 215, 260, 266
Motheral, S., 102, 270
Mullins, E., 85, 266
Myers, D. L., 38, 49, 80, 266
Myers, L. E., 38, 49, 80, 266

N

Navarick, D. (J.), 203, 204, 210, 260, 266, 267
Nelson, T. D., 139, 146, 147, 267
Neuringer, A. J., 14, 88, 96, 97, 98, 204, 205, 267
Nevin, J. A., 102, 105, 169, 170, 206, 216, 217, 218, 219, 221, 226, 231, 267, 269, 272

O

Olson, K., 231, 267

P

Pena-Correal, T. E., 211, 264
Peterson, C., 86, 87, 88, 89, 260
Pipe, M. -E., 173, 216, 271
Pliskoff, S. S., 11, 12, 13, 82, 110, 111, 123, 133, 139, 141, 146, 147, 155, 156, 157, 158, 159, 177, 179, 182, 191, 236, 237, 257, 267, 269, 270
Polya, G., 194, 261
Poniewaz, W. R., 193, 215, 268
Prelec, D., 48, 112, 249, 268
Premack, D., 129, 268

R

Rachlin, H. (C.), 13, 53, 54, 55, 56, 57, 58, 106, 113, 118, 119, 120, 133, 135, 141, 145, 210, 256, 258, 268
Reid, H. M., 139, 141, 270
Revusky, S. H., 40, 268
Reynolds, G. S., 11, 41, 84, 106, 115, 130, 152, 153, 154, 256, 257, 263, 268
Rider, D. P., 101, 103, 187, 268

Riggs, D. S., 22, 259
Rilling, M., 190, 194, 218, 265, 268
Rodriguez, M. L., 211, 264
Rosenfarb, I., 215, 261
Ruckdeschel, F. R., 24, 25, 268

S

Sagvolden, T., 215, 257
Saunders, S. S., 81, 150, 151, 172, 216, 241, 266
Schneider, B. A., 2, 84, 206, 268
Schneider, J. W., 89, 91, 206, 207, 208, 209, 235, 268
Schroeder, S. R., 119, 268
Schrot, J., 162, 269
Schulman, A. I., 218, 235, 269
Scown, J. M., 82, 148, 269
Shettleworth, S., 169, 170, 269
Shimp, C. P., 42, 43, 96, 97, 98, 104, 107, 108, 161, 162, 163, 164, 166, 171, 204, 205, 269
Shull, R. L., 11, 12, 82, 108, 109, 123, 126, 155, 156, 157, 158, 159, 177, 179, 182, 256, 267, 269
Siegel, S., 72, 74, 75, 78, 269
Silberberg, A., 106, 139, 147, 162, 269, 272
Skinner, B. F., 1, 2, 3, 6, 99, 104, 240, 260, 269
Smith, C., 193, 259
Smith, J. P., 81, 263
Snyderman, M., 36, 192, 193, 211, 215, 261, 264, 269
Spealman, R. D., 41, 42, 269
Squires, N., 86, 87, 88, 89, 187, 200, 201, 208, 214, 215, 260, 269
Staddon, J. E. R., 52, 54, 58, 102, 107, 158, 177, 182, 262, 269, 270
Stuart, A., 65, 73, 74, 263
Stubbs, D. A., 139, 141, 145, 191, 216, 218, 226, 236, 237, 259, 270
Swets, J. A., 217, 218, 219, 226, 227, 228, 235, 261, 264, 270
Szabadi, E., 23, 35, 131, 132, 256

T

Tanner, W. P., Jr., 218, 228, 270
Taylor, R., 47, 84, 85, 92, 112, 121, 142, 148, 156, 159, 234, 270

Temple, W., 96, 97, 203, 215, 259, 264
Terman, J. S., 218, 235, 247, 270
Terman, M., 218, 235, 247, 270
Thijssen, J. M., 228, 270
Thorndike, E. L., 132, 270
Timberlake, W., 251, 270
Todorov, J. C., 42, 43, 82, 88, 89, 91, 92,
    146, 147, 161, 162, 163, 164, 166, 235,
    270, 271
Treadway, J. T., 205, 257
Treisman, M., 217, 228, 271
Trevett, A. J., 25, 55, 104, 105, 271
Tustin, R. D., 65, 66, 82, 85, 142, 143, 145,
    216, 219, 220, 221, 225, 228, 231, 233,
    235, 239, 242, 243, 244, 245, 259, 271

V

Vaughan, W., Jr., 100, 136, 137, 138, 251,
    252, 262, 271
Vendrick, A. J. H., 228, 270

W

Wardlaw, G. R., 212, 213, 271
Wearden, J. H., 81, 85, 179, 271
Wetherington, C. L., 22, 23, 36, 37, 271

Wheatley, K. L., 42, 43, 161, 162, 163, 164,
    166, 171, 269
Whipple, J. E., 38, 40, 83, 184, 266
White, A. J., 104, 271
White, K. G., 42, 45, 46, 47, 114, 126, 153,
    157, 159, 167, 173, 175, 177, 179, 180,
    181, 182, 183, 184, 216, 265, 266, 271
Whittaker, S., 216, 221, 231, 267
Wickelgren, W. A., 228, 271
Wilkinson, G. N., 23, 24, 36, 37, 271
Williams, B. A., 15, 42, 97, 114, 155, 173,
    177, 183, 212, 233, 272
Williams, R. J., 25, 55, 104, 105, 271
Winton, A. S. W., 209, 215, 264
Wixted, J. T., 183, 272
Wolfe, D. A., 70, 71, 72, 262
Wood, H. M., 37, 38, 47, 116, 265
Wright, A. A., 216, 218, 228, 272

Y

Yarensky, P., 216, 221, 231, 267

Z

Ziriax, J. M., 106, 272

Subject Index

A

Akaike criterion, 113–114
Alloiobias, 236–239, *see also* Response bias
Avoidance, 132
    in concurrent schedules, 132–135
    in multiple schedules, 134–135

B

Behavioral contrast, *see* Contrast
Bias, 49–51, *see also* Generalized matching
    and Signal detection
Bias function, 233
    in signal detection, 233, 243–244, 246

C

Chain, or Chained, schedules, 183–184
    versus tandem schedules, in concurrent
    chains, 206–209
Changeover delay, or COD, 7, 10, 82–83,
    139, 142
Changeover-key procedure, 3, 5
Changeover ratio, 139
Changing over, 139–145, *see also* Concurrent
    schedules
    on concurrent schedules, 139–150

Choice phase, *see* Concurrent-chain schedules,
    initial links
Closed economy, 127, 175, *see also* Open
    economy
    in concurrent schedules, 127–128
    in multiple schedules, 175–177
Component rate, 39
Concatenated generalized matching law, 53,
    58–59, 120, *see also* Generalized match-
    ing
Concurrent schedules, 2
    avoidance, 132–135
    changeover delay, or COD, 7, 10, 82–83,
        139, 142
    changeover ratio, 139
    changing over, 139
        contingencies and changeover perfor-
        mance, 139–145
        contingencies and main-key performance,
        145–150
    continuous performance, 127–129
    deprivation, 127–128
    independent versus dependent (or nonin-
        dependent, or interdependent, or forced-
        choice) scheduling, 5–6
    interchangeover time, 139
    melioration, 135–138
    punishment, 129–132
    reinforcer parameters, 80–98
        amount and duration, 10, 14, 88–92

delay, 14, 96–98, 192, 210–212
frequency, or rate,
  overall, 86–87
  relative, 7, 80–87
quality, 92–96
response parameters, 113–119
  different operants, 119
  force, 113–116
  second-order schedules, 116–119
schedule types,
  arithmetic VI, 84
  DRL DRL, 52–53, 107
  exponential, or constant probability, VI, 84
  FI DRL, 187
  FI FI, 104
  FI FR, 106–107
  FI VI, 55, 105–106
  FR FI, 6
  FR FR, 100–103
  FR VI, 103–104
  FR VR, 100–103
  more-than-two keys, 109–112, 140–141
  VI VI, 6–12, 53–54, 80–92, 94–96, 113–115, 121–126, 128–134, 136–138, 141–150
  VI VR, 106
  VI VT, 108–109
VR VR, 100–103
  VT VT, 12, 53, 133
    avoidance, 133
  sensitivity to reinforcement, 51, 80–85
  session duration, 127–129
  species types,
    humans, 132
    cows, 96
  stable-state versus transition performance, 120–127
  stimulus effects, 150–151
  transitions and effects of previous conditions, 120–127
  travel time, 145–150
  type of economy, 127–128
Concurrent-chain schedules, 11, 97, 185–215
  choice between chained and tandem schedules, 206–209
  combinations of independent variables, 210–212
  and concurrent schedules, 201
  delay-reduction hypothesis, 199–200, 203
  generalized matching in, 212–215, 251
  generalized-mean analyses, 193–198

  history and development, 188–191
  initial-link effects, 198–203
  initial links, or choice phase, 11, 185–186, 191–193
  measurement in, 186–188
  procedure, 185–186
    variants, 191–193
  terminal-link effects, 193–198, 204–206
  terminal links, or outcome phase, 11, 185–186, 191–193
  transitivity and functional equivalence, 203–204
Contingency discriminability, 81, 151, 250–251
Constant-ratio rule, see Principle of indifference from irrelevant alternatives
Continuous performance,
  in concurrent schedules, 127–129
  in multiple schedules, 174–177
Contrafreeloading, 126
Contrast, 40, 42, see also Multiple schedules
  in multiple schedules, 173–174, 182
  and response force, 114–115
Controlled reinforcer-ratio procedure, 236–237, 239
Criterion, β, 217, 218, see also Signal detection

D

Delay of reinforcement, see Reinforcer Delay
Delay-reduction hypothesis, 199, see also Concurrent-chain schedules
Dependent schedules, see Concurrent schedules, independent versus dependent scheduling
Deprivation,
  in concurrent schedules, 83
  in multiple schedules, 166–169
Dimensions of equations, 63–64
Discriminability,
  in multiple schedules, 172–173
  in multiple-concurrent schedules, 240–244
  of reinforcer sources, 81, 151
  in signal detection, 217, 218, 220, 222–223, 240–242
  d', 217, 218
    in free-operant procedures, 240–244
    independence from reinforcer sensitivity, 224–225
  log d, 220, 223, 225

and reinforcers for errors, 231–233
Discrimination,
   in multiple schedules, 173, 240–241, 247
   in signal detection, 231–232

E

Economy, 127, 250
   closed, 127
   open, 127
Exponential, or constant probability,
   schedules, 84, *see also* Concurrent
   schedules

F

Feedback function, 100–103
   absolute, 100, 138
   for concurrent FR FR, 100–102
   for concurrent VI VI, 102
   relative, 100, 102, 138
Findley procedure, *see* Changeover-key
   procedure
Following-component effect, 183
Force requirement, 113, *see also* Concurrent
   schedules
   in concurrent schedules, 113–116
Forced-choice procedure, *see* Concurrent
   schedules, independent versus dependent
   scheduling
Freeloading, 126
Free-operant detection, 239–247
   bias function, 243–244
   discriminability, 241–242
   models, 245–247
   stimulus function, 243
Friedman analysis of variance, 77–78, *see also*
   Nonparametric tests

G

Generalized matching, 48–59, *see also* Generalized matching law
bias, 49–51
concatenation of independent variables, 53–
   55, 58–59, 120
in concurrent schedules, 52–55
   DRL DRL, 52–53, 107
   FI DRL, 187

FI FI, 104
FI FR, 6, 106–107
FI VI, 55, 105–106
FR FR, 100–103
FR VI, 103–104
VI VI, 53–54, 80–85, 121–126, 145–150
VI VR, 106
VI VT, 108–109
VR VR, 100–103
VT VT, 12, 53
in concurrent-chain schedules, 212–215
dimensions of experiments, 59–62
dual-sensitivity model, 104, 249
and effects of previous conditions, 120–127
generalized matching law, 48–52
in multiple-concurrent schedules, 155–159,
   179–183
in multiple schedules, 52
   and component duration, 161–166
   continuous performance, 174–177
   and reinforcer amount or duration, 169–
   171
   and response requirements, 173–174
   and stimulus effects, 171–173
   VI VI, 52, 153–183
   VI FR, 152–153
overmatching, 51
sensitivity to reinforcement, 51
and signal detection, 220–225
transitions and the effects of previous conditions, 120–127
and travel time, 140–150
undermatching, 51–52
Generalized matching law, 55–58, *see also*
   Generalized matching
Generalized mean, 194, *see also* Concurrent-
   chain schedules
   in concurrent-chain analysis, 193–198

H

Herrnstein's equations
   absolute response rates,
      in concurrent schedules, 18
      differing operants, 19–20
      differing responses, 20–22
   and contrast, 40–42
   in multiple schedules, 31–32
   in single schedules, 16–18
      fitting, 22–24, 25–27
      parameter estimation, 28–30

assumptions, 16–18, 31, 46–47
curve fitting, 22–24, 25–27
 and experimental design, 25–27
extraneous reinforcers, R_e, 17–18
 feedback function for, 32
and multiple schedules, 31–35, 40–45, 160, 177
 component duration, 42, 43, 162
 contrast, 40–42
 deprivation, 43–45, 166, 167
 interaction parameter, m, 31, 34, 46, 177
parameter estimates, 28–30
reinforcer amount or duration, 21
relative response rates,
 concurrent schedules, 18–21, 38–40
 multiple schedules, 31–38, 42–45
strict matching, 38
total output, k, 16, 17, 19–20, 28–30, 33, 38
Herrnstein's hyperbola, *see* Herrnstein's equations

I

"Impulsive choice", 210
Independent schedules, *see* Concurrent
 schedules, independent versus dependent
 scheduling
Initial links, *see* Concurrent-chain schedules
Interchangeover time, 139
Interval scale, 74, *see also* Nonparametric tests
Isobias, 236–239, *see also* Response bias
Isosensitivity function, 227

L

Law of effect, 3, 252, *see also* Negative law of
 effect
 in signal detection, 216
Law of least effort, 101
Learning, 123
Linear regression, 63–73
 nonparametric, 69–73
 assumptions, 69
 procedure, 70
 test for slope differences, 70–72
 testing the intercept, 72
 parametric, 63–69
 assumptions, 64–66
 interpretation, 68–69
 procedure, 66–68

 test for slope differences, 67
 testing the intercept, 67
structural relations, 73–74
 assumptions, 73
 procedure, 73–74
Local rate, 39
Local response rate, 12

M

Matching, 49, 51, 135–138, 251, 252
 generalized, 48–59
 dual sensitivity, 104–249
 falsifiability, 47, 56–57
 and signal detection, 219
 strict, 16–27, 31–47
Matching equation, 7, *see also* Matching
Matching law, *see* Matching *and* Generalized
 matching
Maximizing,
 Molar, 106, 135–138, 250
 Molecular, 106, 135, 250
Melioration, 135–138, 250
Multiple schedules, 31
 of avoidance, 134
 in closed economy, 175–177
 component duration, 42–43, 161–166
 component interactions, 31, 34, 36, 161–162, 167, 173, 177, 182–183
 component reinforcer rates, 152–160
 component response rates, 159–160
 component response requirements, 173–174
 continuous performance, 174–177
 contrast, 40–42, 173–174, 182
 deprivation, 43–45, 166–169
 following-component effect, 183
 and Herrnstein's equations, 31–35
 reinforcer amount and duration, 169–171
 response requirements, 173–174
 sensitivity to reinforcement, 83, 152–159, 174–177
 schedule types,
 RI RI, 161
 of avoidance, 134
 VI FR, 152–153
 VI VI, 52, 153, 156, 158, 161, 166, 169–172, 175–177, 182
 short-component effect, 42–43, 161–166
 stimulus effects, 171–173
 theories, 31–35, 167, 177–183
Multiple-concurrent schedules, 155–159, 179–183

random components, 241
in signal detection, 240–247
Multiple random-interval, or RI, schedules, 161
of avoidance, 134

N

Negative law of effect, 131–132
Nonindependent schedules, *see* Concurrent schedules, independent versus dependent scheduling
Nonparametric regression, *see* Linear aggression
Nonparametric tests, 69–79
for intercept, against a defined intercept, 72
many related samples, 77–78
Friedman analysis of variance, 77–78
Page test, 78
for parallel lines, 72–73
post-hoc tests, 78
two related samples, 74–77
interval measurement, 74
ordinal measurement, 74
randomization test, 76
sign test, 75
Wilcoxon matched-pairs signed-ranks test, 75–76
for slope, against a defined slope, 72
for trend, 78–79

O

Open economy, *see also* Closed economy
in concurrent schedules, 127
Ordinal scale, 74, *see also* Nonparametric tests
Outcome phase, *see* Concurrent-chain schedules, terminal links
Overall rate, 39
Overall reinforcer rate
in concurrent schedules, 86–87
in signal detection, 226, 245–247
Overmatching, 51, 147, *see also* Generalized matching

P

Page test, 78, *see also* Nonparametric tests
Parametric experimentation, 253

Parametric regression, *see* Linear regression
Premack's indifference principle, 129
Principle of indifference from irrelevant alternatives, 112
Product-sum rule, 54
Pseudorandum binary sequence, 124
Psychophysics, 57
Punishment, 129
in concurrent schedules, 129–132

R

Randomization test, 76–77, *see also* Nonparametric tests
Receiver-operating characteristic, 227
Reinforcer amount and duration,
in concurrent schedules, 10, 14, 88–92
in concurrent-chain schedules, 210–212
in multiple schedules, 169–171
in signal detection, 226
Reinforcer bias,
in signal detection, 233, 238
Reinforcer delay,
in concurrent schedules, 14, 96–98
in concurrent-chain schedules, 192, 210–212
Reinforcer duration, *see* Reinforcer amount and duration
Reinforcer frequency,
Overall,
in concurrent schedules, 86–87
in signal detection, 226, 245–247
in single schedules, 16–18, 22–24, 35–38
Relative
in concurrent schedules, 80–86
in multiple schedules, 152–159
in signal detection, 219–226, 228, 233–247
Reinforcer magnitude, *see* Reinforcer amount and duration
Reinforcer quality,
in concurrent schedules, 92–96
Replication, 27–28
Response bias
in signal detection, 234–239
alloiobias, 236–239
isobias, 236–239

S

Schedules of reinforcement, 1

concurrent, 2, *see also* Concurrent schedules
  independent versus dependent scheduling,
    5–6
  switching-key, changeover-key, or Find-
    ley, procedure, 3, 5
  two-key procedure, 3–5
concurrent-chain, 11, *see also* Concurrent-
    chain schedules
interval, 2
  fixed-interval, or FI, 2
  variable-interval, or VI, 2
multiple, 31, *see also* Multiple schedules
multiple-concurrent, 155, *see also* Multiple-
    concurrent schedules
naming of, 99
ratio, 2
  fixed-ratio, or FR, 2
  variable-ratio, or VR, 2
second-order, 116–119
tandem, 206
Second-order schedules, 116–119
"Self control", 210
Sensitivity to reinforcement,
  in concurrent schedules, 51, 80–85
  in multiple schedules, 83, 152–159, 174–177
  in signal detection, 220, 223–225, 228–231
Shock-frequency reduction, 131, *see also* Pun-
    ishment *and* Avoidance
Short-component effect, 42, 161–166, *see also*
    Multiple schedules
Sign test, 75, *see also* Nonparametric tests
Signal detection,
  alloiobias, 236–239
  bias function, 233, 243–247
    discrete trials, 233
    free-operant, 243–247
  biasers of, 234–235
  controlled reinforcer-ratio procedure, 236–
    239
  criterion, β, 217–218
  discrete trials, 216–218, 222, 224, 234, 239
  discriminability, 217–218, 220, 225–231,
    231–233
    d', 217–218
    log d, 220, 225–231
    and reinforcers for errors, 231–233
  free-operant procedure, 239–247
  inherent bias, 221, 223
  isobias, 236–239
  isosensitivity function, 227–231
  likelihood ratio, 217
  as matching,

generalized matching, 219–221, 222–225
  strict matching, 221–222
matrix, 217
models, 220, 222, 245–247
  in multiple-concurrent schedules, 239–242
receiver-operating characteristic, 227
and reinforcer bias, 221, 233, 238
response criterion, ∞, 217–218
response bias, 233–239
sensitivity to reinforcement, 220–221, 223–
    225, 228–231
stimulus function, 225, 243, 246
stimulus-presentation probability, 235
uncontrolled reinforcer-ratio procedure,
    235–239
Yes-No task, 217–219
Stability criteria, 25–26
Stable-state versus transition performance, in
    concurrent schedules, 120–127
Stimulus effects,
  in concurrent schedules, 150–151
  in multiple schedules, 171–173, 240–241,
    247
  in multiples-concurrent schedules, 241–243
  in signal detection, 217–218, 220, 223,
    225–233, 240–247
Stimulus function, 225
  in signal detection, 225, 227–231, 243, 246
Stimulus-presentation probability, 235
Strict matching, 8, 16–30, 49, 249
  and punishment, 130
  and signal detection, 221–222
Strict-matching law, *see* Strict matching
Structural relations, 73–74, *see also* Linear
    regression
Subtractive punishment model, 130–132, *see
    also* Punishment
  and travel time, 146–147
Switching-key procedure, *see* Changeover-key
    procedure
Systems identification, 124

T

Tandem schedules, 206–209
Theil test, 70–72, *see also* Linear regression
Terminal links, *see* Concurrent-chain schedules
Time allocation, 12
  in concurrent second-order schedules, 116–
    119
  in concurrent VI VI schedules, 12

in concurrent VT VT schedules, 12–13
Titration procedure,
  in concurrent chains, 193
Transitions and effects of previous conditions,
    120
  in concurrent schedules, 120–127
Transitivity and functional equivalence, 203–
    204
Travel time, 145–150
Two-key procedure, 3–5, *see also* Concurrent
    schedules

U

Uncontrolled reinforcer-ratio procedure, 235,
    237, 239
Undermatching, 51, 80–85, *see also* Con-

current schedules *and* Multiple schedules
  and Generalized matching
sources of,
  asymmetric pausing, 84
  changeover delay, 82–83
  deprivation, 83
  discrimination between alternatives, 80–
    82
  discrimination failure, 172
  inconstancy of preference, 84–85
  prolonged experimental exposure, 82,
    91–92

W

Wilcoxon matched-pairs signed-ranks test,
    75–76, *see also* Nonparametric tests